Inside Old E:

Mē þā treahteras   tala wīsedon
on þām micelan bēc …

(*Sol* 5–6)

Inside Old English

Essays in Honour of Bruce Mitchell

Edited by John Walmsley

WILEY Blackwell

Library of Congress Cataloging-in-Publication Data

Inside Old English : essays in honour of Bruce Mitchell / edited by John Walmsley.
   p. cm.
  Includes bibliographical references and indexes.
  ISBN-13: 978-1-4051-1483-7 (hardcover : alk. paper) ISBN-13: 978-1-119-12139-8 (papercover)
  ISBN-10: 1-4051-1483-5 (hardcover : alk. paper) ISBN-10: 1-119-12139-6 (papercover)
1. English philology—Old English, ca. 450–1100.   I. Mitchell, Bruce, 1920– .
II. Walmsley, John, 1937– .
  PE108.M58I57 2006
  429—dc22

                              2005015486
A catalogue record for this book is available from the British Library.

Cover image: Cotton Vitellius A. xv, fol. 173r

Set in 10/13pt Palatino by SPi Global, Pondicherry, India
Printed and bound in Malaysia by Vivar Printing Sdn Bhd.

1   2016

Bruce Mitchell
1920 – 2010

Contents

Notes on Contributors

Alfred Bammesberger studied English and French and Comparative Philology in the Universities of Munich and Oxford. He was a teacher in a secondary school, earned an MA at Yale University in 1964 and a doctorate in Munich in 1965. He finished his *Habilitation* in Freiburg in 1970. Since 1980 he has been a Professor of English Linguistics in The Catholic University of Eichstätt, Germany.

Daniel Donoghue is the John P. Marquand Professor of English at Harvard University. He is the author of *Old English Literature: a short introduction* (Blackwell 2004), *Lady Godiva: a literary history of the legend* (Blackwell 2003), and editor of *Beowulf: a verse translation, trans. Seamus Heaney* (Norton 2002). His publications also include an article co-authored with Bruce Mitchell: Parataxis and hypotaxis: a review of some terms used for Old English syntax, *Neuphilologische Mitteilungen*, 93 (1992): 163–83.

Roberta Frank, Douglas Tracy Smith Professor of English at Yale University, is the author of *Old Norse Court Poetry* (Cornell University Press 1978) and more than 50 articles on aspects of Old English and Old Norse language, literature and history. A former Director of the Centre for Medieval Studies in Toronto, she is a member of the International Advisory Board of the *Dictionary of Old English*. She co-edited (with Angus Cameron) *Computers and Old English Concordances* (University of Toronto Press 1970) and *A Plan for the Dictionary of Old English* (University of Toronto Press 1973).

Antonette diPaolo Healey is the Editor of the *Dictionary of Old English* and the Angus Cameron Professor of Old English Studies at the University of Toronto. She teaches in the Centre for Medieval Studies and the Department of English.

Risto Hiltunen is Professor of English at the University of Turku, Finland. His research interests include history of English, Old and Middle English, the English language in different legal settings, and discourse studies. His most recent work deals with the documents of the Salem witchcraft trials of 1692.

Susan Irvine is Senior Lecturer in English at University College London. She has published widely on Old English literature and language, including *Old English Homilies from MS Bodley 343* (Oxford University Press 1993), *The Anglo-Saxon Chronicle MS E* (in The Anglo-Saxon Chronicle: a collaborative series; D. S. Brewer 2004), and articles on the writings of Alfred and Ælfric, and on *The Dream of the Rood*. She has collaborated with Bruce Mitchell on a number of other publications: *Beowulf Repunctuated* (Medieval Institute, Western Michigan University and Richard Rawlinson Center for Anglo-Saxon Studies 2000), and a series of articles containing critical bibliographies of Old English syntax. She is currently working on the Alfredian *Boethius*.

Tadao Kubouchi graduated from Kochi University, Kochi, Japan in 1962 and studied English Philology at the Graduate School, University of Tokyo, 1963–1969. He taught at Hitotsubashi University (1969–1976), The University of Tokyo (1976–1999; Professor Emeritus 1999–) and Teikyo University (1999–2004), and he is currently Professor of English at Komazawa University, Tokyo. He was Director of the Centre for Medieval English Studies, Tokyo, 1988–1999. He is the author of *From Wulfstan to Richard Rolle: papers exploring the continuity of English prose* (D. S. Brewer 1999), and co-editor of *The Ancrene Wisse: a four-manuscript parallel text. Preface and parts 1–4* (Peter Lang 2003).

Michael Lapidge was Elrington and Bosworth Professor of Anglo-Saxon in the University of Cambridge (1991–1998), and Notre Dame Professor of English at the University of Notre Dame (1999–2004); he is now Emeritus Fellow of Clare College, Cambridge. He has published widely on the literature of Anglo-Saxon England (both Latin and Old English). His most recent book was *The Cult of St Swithun* (Oxford University Press 2004) and he is at present completing a study of *The Anglo-Saxon Library* (Oxford University Press). He is a Fellow of the British Academy.

Bernard Muir is Professor of Medieval Language and Literature at the University of Melbourne. His publications include *Edmer's Life of Saint Wilfrid* (with A. J. Turner, University of Exeter Press 1998), *The Exeter*

Anthology of Old English Poetry (2 vols, University of Exeter Press 2000; CD-ROM version, forthcoming), *Ductus: digital Latin paleography* (2002), *Edmer's Lives of Oda, Oswald and Dunstan* (with A. J. Turner, forthcoming) and *MS Junius 11* (Bodleian Digital Texts, 1, Bodleian Library 2004). He also edited *Reading Texts and Images: essays on medieval and renaissance art and patronage* (University of Exeter Press 2002).

Hiroshi Ogawa received his BA (1965) and MA (1967) from Kyushu University and DLitt (1985) from Tokyo Metropolitan University, and was also a visiting scholar at St Edmund Hall, Oxford, working with Bruce Mitchell in 1976–1977 and 1992–1993. He retired from the University of Tokyo in 2004 and is currently Professor of English at Showa Women's University (Tokyo). He is the author of *Old English Modal Verbs: a syntactical study* (*Anglistica* 26, Rosenkilde & Bagger 1989), *Studies in the History of Old English Prose* (Nan'un-do, 2000), and many articles on Old and Middle English, and is co-editor of *Old English Studies from Japan 1941–81* (*Old English Newsletter*, Subsidia 14, 1988).

Matti Rissanen is Emeritus Professor of English Philology at the University of Helsinki and a researcher in the Research Unit for Variation and Change in English at the same university. His special fields are the compilation of English historical corpora and the diachronic study of English syntax and vocabulary, with special reference to early grammaticalization. He contributed the chapter on syntax in *The Cambridge History of the English Language*, vol. III: 1476–1776 (Cambridge University Press 1992–2001).

Fred C. Robinson is Douglas Tracy Smith Professor Emeritus at Yale and the author of several books on Old English, including *The Tomb of Beowulf* (Blackwell 1993) and *The Editing of Old English* (Blackwell 1994) and of articles on English language and literature generally. He and Bruce Mitchell are co-authors of *A Guide to Old English* (Blackwell 1965) and *Beowulf: an edition with relevant shorter texts* (Blackwell 1998). He is Corresponding Fellow of the British Academy and Foreign Member of the Finnish Academy of Science and Letters.

John Walmsley studied English Language and Literature at St Edmund Hall, Oxford, and General Linguistics, and History of Education, at Edinburgh and Durham respectively. He held teaching posts at Hamburg University and St Mary's College, Newcastle-upon-Tyne, before being appointed Professor of English at the University of Bielefeld, Germany.

His publications cover topics in linguistics, applied linguistics and foreign language teaching, and the history of linguistics. Current interests include the role of linguistics in education. From 1993 to 1994 he was Visiting Fellow at the Research Centre for English and Applied Linguistics (RCEAL), Cambridge, UK.

Acknowledgements

The editor and publishers gratefully acknowledge permission from Dell Publishing, a division of Random House, Inc. to print ten lines from *Jorge Luis Borges: Selected Poems 1923–67* by Jorge Luis Borges, copyright © 1968, 1969, 1970, 1971, 1972 by Jorge Luis Borges, Emecé Editores, S.A. and Norman Thomas Di Giovanni.

It is also a pleasure to record one's debts to one's librarians. Without their courteous and patient expertise our academic endeavours would be much more arduous than they are. I am grateful in the first instance to the staff of my own university library in Bielefeld, Germany, and also to the staff of the British Library, London, the Bodleian Library, Oxford, and Cambridge University Library, for particular assistance.

On a more personal note, while preparing this volume I have received a great deal of assistance from my fellow contributors. I would like to thank all of them here for their support and forbearance over a sustained period, and also for responding quickly and effectively to my requests for their expert advice. I have learned a lot from them.

I would also like to take this opportunity to thank all those in the production team at Blackwells. From the inception of this project – some time ago now – to its successful completion they have been a model of flexibility and patience. Working with them has been a pleasure.

Finally, I would like to thank my wife Ursel, who has followed the progress of this project not only with interest but also with exemplary patience. At moments like these one begins to understand what Milton meant when he wrote: 'They also serve . . .'

Abbreviations

Short titles of Old English texts are, unless specified otherwise, given in accordance with Mitchell, Ball and Cameron (1975, 1979). Abbreviations of Middle English texts are as used in *MED*.

adj.	adjective
ASE	*Anglo-Saxon England*, Cambridge
ASPR	Anglo-Saxon Poetic Records, New York and London
BGDSL	*[Paul & Braunes] Beiträge zur Geschichte der deutschen Sprache und Literatur*, Halle
CME	Corpus of Middle English Prose and Verse, *HC*, Helsinki
CSASE	Cambridge Studies in Anglo-Saxon England, Cambridge
dat.	dative [case]
DOE	†Cameron, A., †Amos, A. C. & Healey A. diP. (eds) (2003) *The Dictionary of Old English: A to F*. Toronto: Pontifical Institute of Mediaeval Studies <http://www.chass.utoronto.co/oec>
EEMF	Early English Manuscripts in Facsimile, Copenhagen
EETS	Early English Text Society, London
ES	*English Studies*, Amsterdam
e.s.	Extra series (in the EETS references)
fem.	feminine [gender]
gen.	genitive [case]
Gmc.	Germanic

HC	*The Helsinki Corpus*, The University of Helsinki Department of English, Helsinki
JEGP	*Journal of English and Germanic Philology*, Bloomington, Indiana
LSE	Leeds Studies in English, Leeds
M*Ævum*	*Medium Ævum*, Oxford
MED	Kurath, H. & Kuhn, S. M. (eds) (1956–). *Middle English Dictionary*. Ann Arbor, MI: University of Michigan Press
MLN	*Modern Language Notes*, Baltimore
MPs	The Metrical Psalms of the Paris Psalter
Mitchell–Robinson	Mitchell, B. & Robinson, F. C. (1998). *Beowulf. An edition with relevant shorter texts*. Oxford: Blackwell
N&Q	*Notes and Queries*, London
NM	*Neuphilologische Mitteilungen*, Helsinki
nom.	nominative [case]
n.s.	New series
OE	Old English
OED	*A New English Dictionary on Historical Principles* (12 vols). Oxford: Clarendon Press. 2nd edn as *The Oxford English Dictionary* (20 vols), 1989
OES	Mitchell, B. (1985). *Old English Syntax* (2 vols). Oxford: Clarendon Press
OFr	Old Frisian
OHG	Old High German
ON	Old Norse
OS	Old Saxon
o.s.	Ordinary series (in the EETS references)
PMLA	*Publications of the Modern Language Association of America*, New York
pron.	pronoun
RES	*Review of English Studies*, Oxford
sg.	singular [number]
SOED	Onions, C. T. et al. (eds) (1933). *The Shorter Oxford English Dictionary on Historical Principles* (2 vols). Oxford: Oxford University Press. One-volume edn, 1964; 3rd edn, 1973
s.s.	Supplementary series (in the EETS references)
s.v.	see under

Foreword

This volume is not a *festschrift* of the usual kind. Though conceived from the beginning as a tribute to Bruce Mitchell from a select band of colleagues, friends and former students, it acquired from an early stage a dual character which has done much to shape its contents, style and presentation. The intention has been to produce not only a fitting tribute to a fine scholar but to reach at the same time as wide a readership as possible. Demanding topics are treated in a lively and accessible way; information usually contained in footnotes has been incorporated as far as possible in the body of the text. For ease of reference and for compactness, editions of Old English texts have been gathered in a single list. Other works frequently referred to have also been put into a single Select Bibliography at the end of the book. And any of Bruce Mitchell's publications referred to in this volume can be looked up in the Bibliography of Writings by Bruce Mitchell, also at the end.

To survive, all disciplines constantly have to redefine themselves, and philology is no exception. This volume appears at a time when Old English studies, in Europe at least, stand at something of a crossroads. About a century ago the new subject "English" was taking shape in British universities in the form of newly founded Honours Schools. The concerns reflected in this volume show how far the discipline has come since then. Progress is bound up with changes in values and, if one looks at the affiliations and associations English philology entered into when its study was being radically re-shaped at the beginning of the twentieth century and compares them with its associations today, at the dawn of the twenty-first, one can see how far the discipline has travelled. Bruce Mitchell, by argument and example, has throughout his long academic life been intimately associated with these changes.

At the same time, the volume opens up new territories for research. Without making any claim to be representative, the papers gathered here give some idea of the spectrum of issues currently being addressed by Anglo-Saxon scholars. In addition to highlighting themes currently of interest to the specialist, the papers also document innovative approaches to the literary, cultural and linguistic contexts of Old English. The reader is offered an accessible route into some of the salient problems of Old English scholarship, and at the same time authoritative insights into the approaches adopted to tackle them.

The contributors hope that, taken as a whole, the volume will be seen both as a fitting tribute to an outstanding scholar of Old English, and a modest marker – a straw in the wind, if you like – as to the directions in which Old English studies are currently moving.

J.W.

Bruce Mitchell

Bruce Mitchell's academic career, both his teaching and his scholarship, has been one of extraordinary accomplishment and distinction. Eminent scholars throughout the world are proud to acknowledge that they are former students of Bruce Mitchell, some as regularly enrolled Oxford students, others as postdoctoral scholars who enjoyed his mentorship while working at Oxford. In the realm of scholarship his impact on Old English studies has been extraordinary. His two-volume *Old English Syntax* stands as one of the half-dozen most important works of reference in the field. His *Guide to Old English*, now in its sixth edition, has served as the textbook in hundreds of Old English classes throughout the world, and his *Invitation to Old English and Anglo-Saxon England* has introduced large numbers of students and general readers to the study of Old English. For advanced students of the subject he has written sophisticated studies, critical as well as textual, of many Old English works, especially numerous and valuable contributions being made to the understanding of the poem *Beowulf*. A series of publications (both books and articles) have made scholars aware of the fundamental problem of punctuating Old English texts and have emphasized how modern punctuation imposed on Old English texts pervasively distorts our understanding of Old English. His *Critical Bibliography of Old English Syntax to the End of 1984* followed by a series of Supplements in *Neuphilologische Mitteilungen* have kept scholars abreast of ongoing developments in this important area of Old English studies. For half a century his essays and reviews have addressed subjects of comprehensive range both within and outside of Old English studies. Some of these are by necessity combative, but all are fair, good-humoured and courteous. Taken all together, his impact on the study of Old English as both teacher and scholar is literally incalculable: one has difficulty imagining how different the study of Old English would be today had Mitchell not become a scholar and teacher of the subject.

And yet, those who know him personally tend to agree that Bruce Mitchell is not like other academics. His practicality, his independence of mind, and his hearty, outgoing manner and instant popularity among people of all classes and callings make him something of a rarity in the groves of academe. And this is not surprising when one realizes that academics has been but one of his three careers. Born in Lismore, New South Wales in 1920, he came of age just in time for the Second World War. From 1941 to 1946 he served as lieutenant and then captain in the Australian Imperial Force, having an assignment as Intelligence Officer attached to an armoured unit. After his military career he became a businessman, managing a printing company in Melbourne. Before the War, however, he had for four years been a schoolteacher, and this, he decided, was the career to which he felt most drawn. He therefore left the business world and enrolled as a part-time student at the University of Melbourne, supporting himself by working as a gardener, builder's labourer, and railway porter. Taking a bachelor's degree with First Class Honours in English, he then proceeded to First Class Honours in Comparative Philology in the School of Classical Philology and to a Master's with First Class Honours in English Language and Literature in 1952. In the same year he entered Merton College, Oxford, and in 1959 was made a Doctor of Philosophy. Since 1955 he had been a Fellow and Tutor in English Language in St Edmund Hall. And it was from this point that his illustrious career as teacher and scholar began to unfold.

That he has received countless honours in recognition of his work is hardly surprising, but the international scope of this recognition is quite remarkable. He holds honorary doctorates from both Oxford and the University of Turku and has been voted an Honorary Member of the Finnish Academy of Science and Letters. He is an Honorary Fellow of the Australian Academy of the Humanities and an Honorary Member of the International Society of Anglo-Saxonists. He was a Visiting Fellow of the Japan Society for the Promotion of Science and holds the British Academy's Sir Israel Gollancz Memorial Prize for excellence in scholarship. A list of the countries to which he has been invited as a distinguished lecturer reads like a gazetteer of the world. To these and many other impressive honours the contributors to this volume wish to add their own tokens of esteem and appreciation.

Fred C. Robinson
Yale University

Eidtor's note: *Bruce Mitchell died on 30th January 2010*

Introduction

John Walmsley

The year 2000 marked not only the turn of a century, it was also the year in which the Oxford University English Faculty finally voted to abolish compulsory Old English from its undergraduate syllabus. The removal of this "quite gratuitous burden" from "quite the stodgiest and freakiest undergraduate English course in the country" (*Times Higher Education Supplement*, 12 May 2000) was greeted by those who had campaigned for it with undisguised glee. At first sight it looked like a new beginning for English, now freed to soar unfettered by gratuitous philological demands. In fact, the move represented the logical culmination of strained relations between English Literature and English Philology which had lasted for over a century.

"English" in the Nineteenth Century

The progressive institutionalization of the study of English at English universities during the latter half of the nineteenth century is intimately bound up with that of neighbouring disciplines – with classics, modern foreign languages, history, and – inside "English" – with the relations between literature and philology (in the form of Old and Middle English). The impulse to establish Honours Schools of English – or English Language and Literature – was associated with the rise of an educationally ambitious middle class which, however, did not have the requisite grounding in Latin and Greek to be able to study classics at university. A course in English was considered an acceptable alternative vehicle to classics, for transmitting the moral values of the Victorian middle class. On his appointment as the first Professor of English at the newly founded University College, London (UCL) in 1828, Dale (the Reverend Thomas

Dale) proclaimed, "I shall invariably aim . . . to impart moral as well as intellectual instruction . . . I shall esteem it my duty . . . to inculcate lessons of virtue" (Harte & North 1978: 39). Unlike Oxford and Cambridge, UCL was an institution which examined, but did not teach, undergraduate courses, at least until the twentieth century. Towards the end of the nineteenth century, English Literature was widely taught outside universities by extension lecturers such as John Churton Collins. Collins had studied classics (at Oxford), and in 1885 he was an unsuccessful applicant for the Merton Professorship of English Language and Literature. (Napier was appointed instead). For the next decade or so Collins participated in a vociferous campaign to secure recognition for English Literature and get an Honours School of English established at Oxford. There was pressure not only from outside the university, but also from within it to make moves in this direction – initially in the form of an Honours School in Modern Languages, of which English would be a part. When this motion was defeated by a tied vote in 1887, the proponents of a School specifically of "English" went ahead with a separate proposal, which went through. The arguments which Collins' contemporaries found so persuasive, and which have helped to colour the public view of philology and philologists – at least in Britain – ever since, have gone down in history. Philology, Collins said, is "of all the sciences . . . the most repugnant to men of artistic and literary tastes" (Collins 1891: 68); "as an instrument of culture it ranks . . . very low indeed. It certainly contributes nothing to the cultivation of the taste. It as certainly contributes nothing to the education of the emotions. The mind it neither enlarges, stimulates nor refines. On the contrary, it too often induces or confirms that peculiar woodenness and opacity, that singular coarseness of feeling and purblindness of moral and intellectual vision, which has in all ages been the characteristic of mere philologists" (p. 65), and "forcing philology into . . . a school of literature . . . will be to sacrifice the education of that large majority who . . . are not capable of benefiting from scientific studies, to the education of a small minority" (p. 68).

While these words provoke speculation about how philology was handled in the context of university studies, they also need to be understood in the context of Collins' own view of the matter. According to Collins, a School of English would prove an attractive alternative for "weaker" male students and for female students, neither of whom, it was presumed, were willing – or perhaps able – to pursue "scientific studies". In Collins' view, English Literature could not be properly understood without a satisfactory foundation in Latin. For others, such as Nettleship, history, was the proper discipline for it to be coupled with (Nettleship 1887: 7). And so Schools of English in various shapes and forms came into being in English universities.

The Twentieth Century

It took time for the new discipline to settle down with its neighbours, and different solutions were tried in different places. Oxford adopted the view that English literature constituted a continuous whole from its Anglo-Saxon beginnings down to the present (Gardner 1967: 30; Mitchell 1992: 15). To read the older literature it was obviously necessary to study Old and Middle English, just as German students have to learn Old High German and Middle High German in order to understand their own older literary monuments. But the yoking together of philological with purely literary studies perpetuated the dissonance which had initially been injected into the debate by Collins. Wyld spoke of "a natural hostility and jealousy between the representatives of these two great branches of study" . . . ("though certainly not in Oxford") (Wyld 1921: 42). The success of such a combination depends partly on how "philology" is interpreted and partly on how the teaching is done. Neither comes out particularly well, either in contemporary comment or retrospectively. Mitchell speaks of the tradition as one in which "the Anglo-Saxons were regarded as people who made interesting scribal errors rather than as individual members of society" (Mitchell 1992: 13). Cambridge was spared these frictions. In 1927 Old English was put into the Faculty of Archaeology and Anthropology, later becoming part of the Department of Anglo-Saxon, Norse and Celtic. One consequence of this was that Cambridge students, unlike those at most other universities, could study English with little or no requirement to occupy themselves with philological or linguistic studies.

English Language and the Schools

These constellations were to have widespread consequences in England and Wales in the second half of the twentieth century. The reason for this lies in the symbiotic relationship which exists between subjects in the school curriculum and disciplines in universities: school subjects such as maths, chemistry or history are heavily dependent on the theoretical underpinning provided by the universities. Universities in turn look to recruit their undergraduates from school leavers who have in many cases already begun to study the subject at school. The half-century from 1920 to 1970 in England and Wales illustrates what can happen when this relationship breaks down. Until the second half of the twentieth century most students at British universities were not able to study contemporary English (syntax, morphology, phonology) even if they had wanted to (Strang 1965: 20). It is not surprising, therefore, that the acquaintance with "English language" possessed by graduates going into teaching was more or less restricted to the kind of English needed to understand the most important monuments of Old and Middle English literature. Effectively, "English" came to mean "English Literature". When confronted with the requirements for Old English, freshmen would frequently ask, "Why must we do this?" For many students "language" came to be seen not as something living, interesting and – for want of a better word – relevant, but as "a dreary subject imposed by universities on students with aesthetic appreciation in order to discipline their minds . . . [or] . . . a form of English which ended in 1500 AD or at the latest 1600" (Daunt 1950–51: 235). The excitement and apprehension experienced by Borges when confronted by this foreign culture was, apparently, not widely shared: the sense of adventure and discovery were giving way to a narrower vision of literature increasingly concentrated on the self, the here and the now:

> At various times I have asked myself what reasons
> Moved me to study while my night came down,
> Without particular hope of satisfaction,
> The language of the blunt-tongued Anglo-Saxons.
>   . . . it must be that the soul
> Has some secret sufficient way of knowing
> That it is immortal, that its vast encompassing
> Circle can take in all, can accomplish all.
> Beyond my anxiety and beyond this writing
> The universe waits, inexhaustible, inviting.
>   (Borges 1989: II.280 quoted by
>   Mitchell-Robinson 1998: ix)

The swing to literature was given added impetus by the teaching of F. R. Leavis at Cambridge. Whereas "in the early 1920s it was desperately unclear why English was worth studying at all . . . by the early 1930s it had become a question of why it was worth wasting your time on anything else . . . [English had become] . . . *the* supremely civilizing pursuit" (Eagleton 1996: 27). This revolution in "English" and its teaching at the universities had its counterpart in schools. The approach pursued by Leavis renewed the moral impulse which had been at the root of the initial pressure to found Schools of English in the first place. Its flagship was the periodical *Scrutiny*: "*Scrutiny* was . . . the focus of a moral and cultural crusade: its adherents would go out to the schools and universities to do battle there, nurturing through the study of literature the kind of rich, complex, mature, discriminating, morally serious responses . . . which would equip individuals to survive in a mechanised society of trashy romances, alienated labour, banal advertisements and vulgarizing mass media" (Eagleton 1996: 29).

At the same time as philology became the target of attacks at university level, grammar was made a focus of attention in schools. There were a number of factors militating against the teaching of grammar in the early twentieth century, and the influential Fisher ("Newbolt") Report (Board of Education 1921) did little to impart a sense of direction. Traditional Latinate grammar was not accepted as a suitable model for English, but no one seemed to have anything satisfactory to put in its place: it was (the report said) "impossible at the present juncture to teach English grammar in the schools for the simple reason that no-one knows exactly what it is . . ." (Board of Education 1921: 289–90).

By the mid-1930s grammar had more or less disappeared from state schools, and this situation continued until the 1960s, when the consequences of this neglect of language became too obvious to be ignored. The teacher's aim in teaching English, it was maintained, was "to bring to life and develop his pupils' capacity for literature" [and] "developing the power of communication . . . cannot engage more than a small part of the interest and energy of the teacher and his pupils" (Thompson 1964: 288). The importance of literature in stemming the moral and intellectual threat meant that there was simply no time for work on language. The idea was that an extensive and intensive occupation with English literature was more than sufficient to develop literacy. The evidence from schools, though, was that the system was failing its pupils: complaints about standards of literacy multiplied in industry, in the universities and in public life generally. Even the pupils felt that they were being let down: "a large percentage of pupils can not write or understand the language properly" (student, quoted in Mitchell 1963: 183). To the charge that "developing the power of communication . . . cannot engage more than a small part of the interest and energy of the teacher and his pupils" Ing commented: "To read accurately can hardly be said to interfere with the 'capacity for literature'; and to read accurately is a large step towards writing clearly" (Ing 1963: 200).

By the mid-1960s, it was said, "Virtually no undergraduates come up to the university with English language as their primary and properly-nurtured interest; any who did so would be hard pressed to find a university that allowed them to study English language except as an ancillary to English literature" (Strang 1965: 20). All in all, it is as though the state school system had been subjected to a nationwide empirical experiment in which pupils were restricted largely to a diet of literature on the assumption that that was all that was needed, for literacy to develop. It was an experiment that failed, and since then, the pendulum has begun to swing the other way. Opponents of the English and Welsh National Curriculum need to ask themselves just how bad things had to become before government intervention was deemed to be necessary. At the same time, "English grammar" has had to re-invent itself. Now essentially non-prescriptive, it aims to provide pupils with alternative (sub-) languages for different situations – i.e. to increase their linguistic flexibility, and to provide a sophisticated vocabulary for discussing language with (Hudson & Walmsley in press).

Philology

In the English-speaking world "philologist" has long been a term of vague opprobrium (Palmer 1936: v). Many colleagues are not even sure what it is: students of the 1940s report enrolling for courses in "German philology" without ever being told what "philology" was. According to Frank, "it is not a good idea to describe yourself to a hiring committee as a philologist" (Frank 1997: 491).

The decline of philology is not infrequently linked to the rise of linguistics, or *Sprachwissenschaft* (Eto 2003). But readjustments between disciplines have as much to do with tensions inside the individual philology as with influences from outside it.

Philology's central concern is with texts and the understanding of texts. But "a text", as Frank reminds us, "is a human voice" (Frank 1997: 492).

Without a fundamental interest in what these voices have to say to us – over many generations – about the human condition and the individual responses to the alien, inscrutable universes which they inhabited, there is no point in pursuing philology further. Yet such questions are the stuff of literature. The essential difference between literature and philology is that whereas literature works on the assumption that the reader has unimpeded access to the work of art, the philologer accepts that the past is a different country: once the frontier has been crossed, the challenges begin. To make sense of these voices from the past, an understanding of the words and the way they are put together – their language – is only the first step. But hermeneutics (the art of understanding, one of the two major areas in the classical model of philology) requires more than mastery of the language. It means as far as humanly possible getting inside the author's mind: What was the text for? What were the author's intentions in writing the text, and how would the text have been understood in his or her own time? Borges knew this well. Nowhere is the hermeneutic programme better summed up than by Borges' arch-hermeneuticist P. Menard, whose ultimate goal was to become the author of *Don Quixote*: "The initial method he [P. Menard] conceived was relatively simple. Know Spanish well, recover the Catholic faith, take up arms against the Moors or the Turk, forget the history of Europe between . . . 1602 and 1918, *be* Miguel de Cervantes" (Borges 1983: 86 – my translation, J.W.). A programme of this nature makes demands on the philologer: it requires him or her to respect the text, its existence as a different sort of object from comparable objects from the present day; it requires historical empathy; and it requires extensive and detailed knowledge of the cultural, religious and political contexts in which the work was created. "If we would understand ancient literature, we must study ancient life and ancient society, and fling modern analogies to the winds" (Nettleship 1887: 11).

The philological enterprise works on the assumption that we know and agree exactly what "the text" is. Hence we need textual criticism, the second major area of philology. Even where texts have come down to us virtually unscathed, questions of authorship and authenticity frequently remain. Many of the texts deemed worthy of preservation in the cultures of the world, however, survive in poor condition – in the worst case, in unique copies. The philologer's job is, in the first instance, as far as possible to restore the text. Deciphering the scribe's handwriting is only the first problem of many. Where the text has been damaged, letters, syllables and even words may have to be conjecturally restored. And even where the text is complete and legible, the reader-editor may be confronted with readings which do not appear to make sense. Scribes in the past were as prone to error, even in apparently straightforward copying, as we are today.

To the reader-editor's job, then, also belongs the task of emending signs which are indisputably upon the page, to restore a meaning intended, but not expressed, by the author. To do this, the reader-editor must of course know the language of the text perfectly, or as nearly so as possible. For this task, grammar and lexicon (dictionary) are indispensable tools. Old English, wrote Sweet, was "a language, which, like all others, ought either to be studied properly with grammar and dictionary, or else let alone" (Sweet 1871: ix). Editing and interpreting texts, then, together with providing tools such as lexica and grammars, belong to the central tasks of philology. Translation, too, is part of the hermeneutic programme: without near mastery of the language, together with the ability to see the world as nearly as possible as the author saw it, satisfactory translation is not possible. The nineteenth-century view of philology as some kind of exercise in science is still present here, in that philology proceeds on the assumption that there *are* correct answers to many questions to which we can – by rational enquiry and objective procedures – provide satisfactory answers. We *can* of course make errors of translation; we may emend erratically. But these possibilities also imply the possibility of an attainable correct version, and much philological discourse is concerned with weighing up the pros and cons of individual solutions, together with the evidence for and against them.

English Literature

So, if Old English is no longer part of English literature, what is "English poetry" to mean? (I write English literature [small "l"] to mean "literature written in English." English Literature [capital "L"] I use to denote the academic discipline which takes English literature as its object of study). English poetry, Fenton tells us in his Oxford lectures, "begins whenever we decide to say the modern English language begins" (Fenton 2002: 1). This definition is original in two respects. First, it is essentially linguistic rather than literary: it appeals to a concept of "modern English" rather than to the continuity or otherwise of literary forms. Second, the definition is deictic, though it may not at first sight appear so. Fenton appeals to the ability to understand texts without the help of any scholarly apparatus: Old English is excluded from English poetry because "it is a different language, which has to be learnt like any foreign language" (Fenton 2002: 1). Middle English poetry is also excluded as it becomes "increasingly difficult to comprehend" (Fenton 2002: 4). But if "modern English:" were indeed to be defined by the speaker, then what "English poetry" was thought to be would differ according to where each individual speaker was standing in space and time. What is "English poetry" to us today would at some future point in time cease to be English poetry and have to become something else. This is where the problems start. Fenton's definition would exclude large swathes of what the wider speech community of English speakers think of as English poetry. Since it would be an illusion to think that the normal native speaker of English in the twenty-first century can understand Shakespeare simply by reading his words written on the page, Shakespeare, too, would have to be excluded. Here Fenton wobbles. Reluctant to push Shakespeare into some nameless limbo outside "English poetry", Fenton nevertheless has to acknowledge that "it has been true at certain times in the past that readers [*sic*] have found large parts of Shakespeare incomprehensible" (Fenton 2002: 5), and that to appreciate Shakespeare properly, one does indeed "need the help of notes" (p. 5). What is the solution? The matter is left unresolved.

The deictic definition of English poetry is illusory. Fenton writes as if his readers, like him, have no difficulty in understanding 400-year-old English poetry. But at what point does it stop being possible for our students to appreciate poetry without any specialized assistance? – with T. S. Eliot? Shelley? Blake? Pope? Donne?

Fenton's definition narrows the scope of English poetry enormously for most listeners; it also artificially reduces the distance between poet and audience, and in effect decontextualizes it. It is interesting to note that while Fenton assumes that students will have difficulties with earlier stages of their own language, space is not supposed to constitute a problem: "when a North American, an Australian, an Indian or a Jamaican writes a poem in English, that poem enters the corpus of English poetry" (Fenton 2002: 6) – a corpus from which Chaucer, Langland, Wyatt etc. have now been excluded. The perfectly reasonable view that North American English poetry "will be able to extend its charm only to those who genuinely know the American language" (Vendler 1986: 1) Fenton dismisses as "an absurd exaggeration" (Fenton 2002: 6).

Not only has the definition of English poetry been made a subjective one, the approach to this poetry is also to be essentially subjective – something else which militates against the study of Old English. As one Oxford student put it, "we revel in the freedom to construct original interpretations ... But when applying this same interpretative freedom to an Anglo-Saxon text, we are ... encouraged to take an objective historical approach, not a subjective one" (*Times Higher Education Supplement*, 26 May 2000).

This redefinition of the values of English Literature in the course of the twentieth century is striking. Conceived initially – in Oxford , at least – as a vehicle for moral values with strong ties to its classical origins and an essential philological component, English Literature has worked steadily to rid itself of these burdens one by one. The link to classics is no longer seen as compelling. English Literature now apparently shies away from any claim to objectivity, and the moral and intellectual imperatives which had fuelled it for so long, have fizzled out (Wells 2003: 125; Bergonzi 1986: 206; Eagleton 1996: 22).

By the year 2000 English Literature and philology had thus – in terms of the values they embody – become incompatible. If disciplines define themselves by common goals, methods and aspirations, a discipline which tries to force together such vastly different bedfellows is bound to fragment.

The State of the Art?

The papers presented here in honour of Bruce Mitchell cover a wide range of issues. One group of papers takes a genre as its starting point, a particular author or even an individual poem. Others are concerned with problems of the reception and transmission of texts; with varieties of language, and linguistic processes; with problems of meaning and its definition; and still others with the resources of Old English and the way these resources were exploited for stylistic effect.

Irvine's underlying theme is ambiguity. She starts from a notorious crux in *The Wanderer*, one of the most elusive of Old English poems. She teases out the syntax and semantics and shows how the syntactic and semantic resources are deployed to express the three-way relations between mind, self and memory. Tensions surface between speech and mind, voice and thought, introspection and communication, and between utterance and remembrance. According to Irvine, in choosing orality as one of its themes, the poem exploits its own condition of existence in a literary fiction of its own. Kubouchi takes as his material Wulfstan's homiletic texts and examines the use Wulfstan made of Scandinavian loanwords. Wulfstan was Bishop of London, outside the Danelaw, from AD996 to AD1002, and Archbishop of York, inside the Danelaw, from AD1002 to AD1023, which allows Kubouchi to set up correlations between variations in the language of the texts and the kind of audiences Wulfstan would be addressing. Kubouchi's paper also addresses the question of the role of written texts which were normally presented orally, and thus contributes to the more general theme of orality. He brings out well the sensitivity with which Wulfstan shaped his responses to the differing make-up of his audiences – varying his language according to whether his audience was educated or unlearned, large or small, and whether it was a general or a selected audience.

In a fluent and witty contribution, Ogawa considers how the authors of "composite homilies", which they were re-working from earlier sources, viewed earlier monuments in the tradition in which they found themselves. By comparing the methods and approach of different authors he is able to lay bare the structure and style of the homilies, including differences in the use of direct speech. The latter interestingly reveal how the author shifts perspective to make his point more effectively. Since Ogawa's theme covers different authors' treatment of their originals, his paper, too, sheds important light on one of the more important sub-themes of the volume – namely, on the relationship of Old English authors to Latin originals.

Bammesberger, like Irvine, starts from an individual poem – *Beowulf* – edited by Mitchell and Robinson in 1998. In his paper he offers interpretations for eight difficult half-lines of the *Beowulf* text. In a series of model studies Bammesberger deploys a wide spectrum of skills and knowledge to tease out plausible solutions. After defining the problem, he sets out a series of hypotheses which have been – or could be – entertained to solve it and eliminates them one by one until only the most plausible remains. As the case requires, etymological knowledge; knowledge of parallels in other texts, languages or dialects; syntactic, semantic, phonological or palaeographic considerations; dialect geography or metrics (rules of scansion) are drawn on to rule out the less plausible options. The conclusions Bammesberger draws have important implications not only for the *Beowulf* text itself, they also shed light on Anglo-Saxon scribal practice.

Muir looks at hundreds of alterations to medieval manuscripts for the light they shed on the transmission and reception of vernacular poetry by poets, anthologists (the editor-copier-adapter-poet) and scribes. The exact study of what scribes did with the material in front of them throws up important clues as to the competence of the scribes at different periods of history, while at the same time illustrating the dynamic nature of the reception and transmission of texts and the impact which the oral tradition had on written texts. In addition, Muir's contribution, too, has important consequences for editorial practice. Seen from this point of view, the conjectural emendation can itself be seen as an important tool in scholarly discourse, as the proposed emendation is attacked and defended along the slow journey towards the most likely reconstruction.

Punctuation constitutes a central problem in the editing of Old English texts (cf. Mitchell 1980). As Donoghue points out, the editing of Old English texts is usually done using punctuation systems which were developed long after the invention of printing. But an examination of Old English scribal practice throws up interesting discrepancies – between the punctuation of Old English and contemporary Latin, and between Old English prose and verse. To explain the punctuation of Old English manuscripts Donoghue examines three hypotheses, two of which he eliminates before presenting his own solution. A meticulous analysis of "clause dips" leads him to propose that the competent Anglo-Saxon reader was guided by a complex interaction of graphical cues with syntactic, metrical and formulaic information. He then shows how this solution explains why certain (functional) element orders are not attested in Old English poetry. The consequences of Donoghue's findings for the editing of Old English are manifest, but his paper also throws light on "the oral/literary matrix" and on the relation of Old English texts to Latin originals.

Grammars are conventionally treated as theoretical representations of the language of a completely homogeneous speech community. They present the fundamental categories and patterns – the resources, as it were, on which the varieties of the living language draw – either by omitting many of the options completely, or by selecting some options more frequently than others. Mitchell's *Old English Syntax* (*OES*) maps out these categories and patterns for Old English. Hiltunen and Rissanen in their different ways explore the theme of variation within these categories. Hiltunen makes an otherwise little explored word class – the interjection – the focus of interest by analysing the distribution and relative frequency of *eala, efne, hwæt, la* and *wa*. Embedding his analysis in a discourse-theoretical framework, he shows how the particular use made of interjections helps to distinguish oral from written discourse, and correlates with differences between prose and verse. At the same time Hiltunen's study pushes the study of grammar beyond the bounds of the sentence, where syntax conventionally ends, into the realm of pragmatics.

Both Hiltunen and Rissanen make use of computer-based corpora to extend the coverage and reliability of their data. Rissanen, however, concentrates on a single phrase – "to wit". The extent of the recorded data enables him to cover both synchronic and diachronic variation; in fact, Rissanen's study is a case study in grammaticalization, which by its very nature lays stress on the continuity of English. His methodological approach allows him to distinguish two uses of "to wit" – one as a discourse marker, the other as an appositive connective. At the same time, this study, too, takes into consideration the relationship of Old English structures to their Latin originals.

The relationship between English texts and Latin originals is one of the stronger sub-themes to emerge in this volume (cf. also in particular the papers by Lapidge and Ogawa). In a paper which links this theme – approached, though, from a quite different perspective – with the question of a distinct metalanguage for English, Walmsley concerns himself with the nature of the philologer's tools – the grammar. The robustness of the traditional grammatical categories over two thousand years has been the object of criticism, particularly in the structuralist literature. Walmsley shows how the treatment of English by early grammarians was less the result of ignorance or incompetence than the natural outcome of interaction between particular assumptions about how languages are best learned and taught, and the exigencies of a shifting language ecology.

Healey and Robinson both attack in their different ways problems of meaning. Healey throws up a question of fundamental importance for the hermeneutic programme: accepting grammar and lexicon as central tools of the philologists's work, how can the lexicographer know what the words of an unknown language meant? Here again the value of computer technology becomes apparent. But allied with the results of modern technology must be a sensitivity to the culture, an approach "which acknowledges difference between then and now, and accepts the difference sympathetically" (Healey, this volume). She exemplifies the application of lexicological techniques in a series of case studies in sense development. Healey also persuasively demonstrates how the precise shade of meaning of a given adjective is controlled by the noun with which it collocates.

Synchronically speaking, the meaning of a word is the product of its sense and reference, not its history. But Robinson shows (as does Bammesberger) how etymology can contribute to the solution of apparently intractable problems of meaning in Old English texts. He does this in a prose which entices the reader along his line of argumentation, until he springs on the reader the unlikely answer. In addition to allowing us to correct a hitherto erratic interpretation in this particular instance, Robinson in his article alerts scholars to a largely untapped source of evidence which could shed considerable light on hitherto unsolved problems of phonology and semantics.

The last two papers move beyond the narrower confines of syntax and semantics to examine the use which Anglo-Saxon authors made of the linguistic resources available to them. Frank picks up a feature characteristic of Old English poetry but little written about – understatement, or litotes – and shows how it was exploited for poetic effect. Understanding this phenomenon is not only part of the hermeneutic programme – the interpretation of texts – it also helps to provide some distance, while allowing us at the same time to appreciate the specific temper of the poetry. Frank skilfully shows how the proper appreciation of understatement can help with the analysis of otherwise puzzling passages in the texts, with the rendering of older texts in modern translations, and in clarifying poetic effects. She links litotes synchronically with resonances in contemporary Germanic cultures, but also brings out its diachronic aspects, as part of a continuity of expression which extends into contemporary English. Lapidge's topic is a sub-phenomenon of hyperbaton – namely, the removal of prepositions from their position preceding a noun phrase to some other position for artistic effect. "Postpositioning" implies some kind of neutral or unmarked structure from which the specific example deviates. As Lapidge shows, the topic throws up a wide spectrum of questions. On the basis of his corpus he explores the possible influence of Latin models on Old English poetry, and also the possibility that examples of postpositioning in the prose may be poeticisms adopted from earlier Old English poetry. He buttresses his arguments with evidence from the kind of Latin poetry Old English scribes might have studied.

To the informed reader, it will be apparent from the foregoing that the papers included in this volume are linked not only by a web of themes and sub-themes currently of interest to specialists in their field, but also by the closeness with which they overlap with concerns which crystallize in Mitchell's own *oeuvre*. One sees in this *oeuvre* the concern to reconstruct texts which will enable the reader to appreciate the literature; the mutually fructifying influence of syntax and semantics; but above all the impulse to close one of the major gaps in Old English scholarship – the lack of a comprehensive syntax of Old English. With his *Old English Syntax* Mitchell made available a major research tool, justly described as one of the "milestones marking out progress in the subject" (Lapidge, this volume). But, while constituting a landmark in the history of Old English studies which is unlikely to be surpassed for a very long time, if ever, the *OES* has itself proved to be a fertile source of ideas as to paths which the study of Old English might profitably explore. Among the more significant of these (some of which are taken up in this volume) are the description of individual genres, the language of poetry, stylistic variation, and the influence exercised by Latin on the formation of Old English, especially the literary language. In his Introduction to *OES* Mitchell expressed the hope that *OES* might serve as "a base from which a new generation of scholars, armed with new material, can produce definitive monographs on the various constructions and on the peculiarities of different periods and genres and of individual texts and authors" (*OES*: I.lxiv), adding with characteristic modesty, "I shall have failed in my primary purpose if it is not superseded" (p. lxiv).

Conclusion

The discipline of philology is centrally concerned with the reception and transmission of culture and its artefacts. It demands both a wide range of specialized skills, and effective tools, which themselves need updating as new facts are thrown up by research. Old English is of course not only of interest to students of literature. Old English texts offer invaluable information for the historian, too, as well as for the study of comparative Germanic syntax and for the diachronic treatment of English. But the literature of Old English is the prime embodiment of a complete culture – one from which we are separated by a long distance of time, but one which grew imperceptibly into the English-speaking world we know today. The philologist has to find the right balance between the requisite historical objectivity on the one hand (Brewer 1994: 43) and an awareness of continuity on the other. To the interpretation of texts the philologer needs to bring what Brewer calls the "historical empathy" currently out of fashion in the study of literature (p. 41). As I have tried to show, the values embodied in the pursuit of any given discipline change over time. Bruce Mitchell's work has over the past decades been not only bound up with a shift in the underlying values of philology, it has – notably through the *Guide to Old English* (1964) and his *Invitation to Old English and Anglo-Saxon England* (1995) – been instrumental in helping to bring about this shift. The focus of attention has moved away from phonology and comparative philology towards syntax, style and the lexicon – from the study of sound changes treated as "an abstract sound-system divorced from texts" (Mitchell 1992: 15) to the study of texts as testimonies of individual members of a particular society. It is ironic that the concepts of correctness (and error) and historical objectivity central to the philological enterprise are just those values of which English Literature has over the same period been struggling to divest itself.

And yet the importance of philological studies is greater today than it has ever been: "The state of editing of English literature is in a poor way" (Brewer 1994: 41). Many older texts need re-editing and annotating in the light of modern research simply to maintain scholarship at the level it has reached so far. Beyond that, "many areas of literary endeavour . . . still await scholarly attention" (Lapidge 1993: vii). In a fundamentally ahistorical age, society needs to be persuaded that the study of the past is not a luxury, but something central to its own identity. As Borges wryly put it (after seeing an Anglo-Saxon sword in York Minster): only the past is real – "sólo lo pasado es verdadero" (Borges 1989: II.283 – "A una espada en York Minster").

References and Further Reading

Bergonzi, B. (1986). *The Myth of Modernism and Twentieth Century Literature.* Brighton: Harvester.

Board of Education (1921). *The Teaching of English in England (The Fisher/Newbolt Report).* London: His Majesty's Stationery Office.

Borges, J. L. (1983). Pierre Menard, autor del Quijote. In J. L. Borges, *Narraciones,* 3rd edn (pp. 81–92). Madrid: Ediciones Cátedra (1st edn 1980).

Borges, J. L. (1989). *Obras completas* (4 vols). Barcelona: Emecé.

Brewer, D. (1994). Abuses of English studies. *The European English Messenger,* 3, 40–6.

Chadwick, H. M. (1941). *The Study of Anglo-Saxon.* Cambridge: Heffer (2nd edn rev. N. Chadwick, 1958).

Collins, J. C. (1891). *The Study of English Literature: a plea for its recognition and organization at the universities.* London: Macmillan.

Daunt, M. (1950–51). Literature is a branch of language. *Universities Quarterly,* V, 139–50.

Eagleton, T. (1996). *Literary Theory: an introduction,* 2nd edn. Oxford: Blackwell (1st edn 1983).

Eto, H. (2003). *Philologie vs. Sprachwissenschaft.* Münster: Nodus.

Fenton, J. (2002). *An Introduction to English Poetry.* London: Viking.

Frank, R. (1997). The unbearable lightness of being a philologist. *JEGP,* 96, 486–513.

Gardner, H. (1967). *Literary Studies: an inaugural lecture delivered before the University of Oxford on 1 June 1967.* Oxford: Clarendon Press.

Harte, N. & North, J. (1978). *The World of University College London, 1828–1978.* London: University College (rev. edn *The World of UCL, 1928–1990,* 1991).

Hudson, R. & Walmsley, J. (in press). The English Patient: English grammar and teaching in the twentieth century. *Journal of Linguistics.*

Ing, C. (1963). The Oxford Delegacy of Local Examinations and the 'Use of English' paper. *Oxford Magazine,* 21 Feb, 199–200.

Lapidge, M. (19–96). *Anglo-Latin Literature 900–1066* (2 vols). London: Hambledon Press.

Mitchell, B. (1963). The "Use of English" paper. *Oxford Magazine,* 14 Feb, 180–3.

Mitchell, B. (1992). *H. M. Chadwick, The Study of Anglo-Saxon: fifty years on* (H. M. Chadwick Memorial Lecture, 2). Cambridge: University of Cambridge, Department of Anglo-Saxon, Norse and Celtic.

Nettleship, H. (1887). *The Study of Modern European Languages and Literatures in the University of Oxford.* Oxford: Parker.

Palmer, L. R. (1936). *An Introduction to Modern Linguistics.* London: Macmillan.

Strang, B. M. H. (1965). *Metaphors and Models: an inaugural lecture delivered before the University of Newcastle-upon-Tyne on Monday, 12th October, 1964.* Newcastle: University of Newcastle-upon-Tyne.

Thompson, D. (1964). A reflection. In B. Jackson & D. Thompson (eds), *English in Education* (pp. 228–31). London: Chatto & Windus.

Times Higher Educational Supplement (12 May 2000). Goodbye to Beowulf, Valentine Cunningham (opinion). London: Times Newspapers.

Times Higher Education Supplement (26 May 2000). Bard, Beowulf and smart-arses, Rachel Hewitt (opinion). London: Times Newspapers.

Vendler, H. H. (ed.) (1986). *The Faber Book of Contemporary American Poetry.* London: Faber & Faber.

Wells, C. (2003). Die Linguistik und die Literaturwissenschaft an englischen Universitaeten in und seit den sechziger Jahren. In U. Hass-Zumkehr & C. Koenig (eds), *Literaturwissenschaft und Linguistik von 1960 bis heute* (pp. 121–30). Göttingen: Wallstein.

Wyld, H. C. (1921). *English Philology in English Universities: an inaugural lecture delivered in the Examination Schools in February, 1921.* Oxford: Clarendon Press.

Chapter 1

Eight Notes on the *Beowulf* Text

Alfred Bammesberger

In 1998 Bruce Mitchell and Fred C. Robinson published their landmark edition of *Beowulf* (Mitchell & Robinson 1998). The work can truly be considered as a *summa* of scholarship on this epic text. The following eight notes discuss individual passages in which some modifications of the traditional interpretations seem possible. In the individual cases the vocabulary does not present major problems, but difficulties arise in the syntactic analysis. All quotations are taken from Mitchell and Robinson (1998). Diacritics have been omitted unless required by the linguistic argument. The notes deal with eight half-lines of the *Beowulf* text: (1) *meodosetla ofteah* (5b), (2) *feond on helle* (101b), (3) *swylcum gifeþe bi∂* (299b), (4) *seon sibbegedriht* (387a), (5) *wiste þæm ahlæcan* (646b), (6) *word oþer fand* (870b), (7) *þa hine se broga angeat* (1291b) and (8) *on fæder stæle* (1479b).

1 *meodosetla ofteah* (5b)

The initial three lines of *Beowulf* refer to the glory of the Danish kings in former times. Then the mythical founder of the dynasty is introduced:

> Oft Scyld Scefing   sceaþena þreatum
> monegum mægþum   meodosetla ofteah
> *(Beo 4–5)*

Liuzza translates the two lines as follows: "Often Scyld Scefing seized the mead-benches from many tribes, troops of enemies" (Liuzza: 2000: 53). The at first sight almost obvious interpretation of *meodosetla ofteah* as 'he pulled away the mead-benches' is grammatically not acceptable, however:

meodosetla is certainly a genitive of the plural, but the verb *ofteon* 'pull away' governs the accusative.

The correct interpretation of *meodosetla ofteah* was suggested in an early paper by Holtzmann (1863) and repeated with further material by Sievers (1904): the form *ofteah* is not the preterite of *oftēon* 'pull away' (strong verb of class II going back to Gmc. **teuh-* and related to German *ziehen*), but must be interpreted as the preterite of *oftīon* 'refuse'. OE *of-tīon* is a strong verb of class I, points back to Gmc. **teih-* and is related to German *zeihen* (in *verzeihen* 'to pardon'). If we wanted to normalize the reading we could put in the form *oftāh*, which may have been the authorial version. But the two verbs OE *tion* (< Gmc. **teih-*) and *tēon* 'draw' (< Gmc. **teuh-*) were not consistently kept apart; on this development see Campbell (1959: 308).

Whether the two lines really mean that Scyld Scefing subjugated other tribes by taking away their mead-benches is anything but certain. Since the underlying verb is definitely *of-tīon* (< Gmc. **teih-*, class I of strong verbs) we should posit the verb's meaning as 'refuse'. The message would then be that Scyld Scefing did not allow other tribes to achieve independence; they had to remain under his rule. The half-line *sceapena þreatum* may be used in instrumental function and could refer to Scyld Scefing's own troops. The two quoted lines may thus be translated as follows: 'Often Scyld Scefing, together with his troops of warriors, refused mead-benches to many tribes' (i.e. he did not allow them independence).

2 *feond on helle* (101b)

Hrothgar decides to build a wonderful hall named *Heorot*. But only for a certain period of time can his Danish subjects enjoy the pleasure of Hrothgar's generosity, because the monster Grendel disturbs the peaceful proceedings and wreaks murderous havoc in the hall:

> Swa ða drihtguman   dreamum lifdon
> eadiglice   oð ðæt an ongan
> fyrene fremman   feond on helle
> (*Beo* 99–101)

These three lines have been translated as follows: "Thus these noble men lived blessedly in joy, until a certain fiend from hell began to wreak evil"

(Swanton 1978: 39). The translation is acceptable, and the vocabulary does not present notable difficulties. The half-line *feond on helle* is troublesome, however. Since *on* does not mean 'from', Swanton's translation 'a certain fiend from hell' cannot immediately be allowed to stand. Kemble had translated quite literally: "So the vassals lived in joy, happily; until that one began to practice crime, a fiend in hell" (Kemble 1837: 5). But this translation is also quite doubtful because Grendel was not in any sense 'in' hell at the time.

Many editors and commentators assume that *on helle* somehow functions as an adjective and means 'hellish', and indeed 'a hellish fiend' would be meaningful in the given context, since there is no doubt that Grendel was considered a devilish foe. No parallels for the assumed construction have been offered, however. It may therefore be doubted whether *feond on helle* can really mean 'a hellish fiend'.

Bugge (1887) had indeed earlier pointed out that *feond on helle* is problematic, and added the following observation: "Auch begann wol Grendel nicht erst jetzt *fyrene fremman* 'frevel zu üben'; das hatte er wol schon früher getan. Allein jetzt fing er an, frevel in der halle Heort zu üben, und dies war es, das dem freudigen leben in Heort ein ende machte." ["Furthermore it was not only then that Grendel started *fyrene fremman* 'to perpetrate evil deeds'; this he had done before. Only then did he start to perpetrate evil deeds in Heort, and it is this that brought an end to the joyful life in Heort."] This argumentation seems very plausible. Consequently Bugge suggested the following emendation of the text: *oð-ðæt ân ongan   fyrene fremman feónd on healle* (to mean 'until one fiend in the hall began to perpetrate evil deeds'; Bugge 1887: 80). Klaeber notes Bugge's suggestion in his apparatus, but does not admit Bugge's reading into his text. Palaeographically Bugge's suggestion can indeed hardly be defended: why should a scribe have changed the perfectly clear form <healle> to <helle>, above all if the word for 'hall' was meaningful in the given context?

Ultimately, however, Bugge's idea may be right. It would certainly be meaningful to say that Grendel, who is likely to have perpetrated various kinds of mischief before, began to wreak havoc "in the hall (Heorot)". In an Anglian version of the epic text the half-line may therefore have read (*feond on*) *halle* with retraction of *æ* before *l* + consonant. A West-Saxon scribe did not allow the sequence <-all-> to remain unchanged, but instead of the phonologically correct form *healle* he substituted *helle*.

Grendel is literally associated with "hell" a second time in the text of *Beowulf: ðy he þone feond overcwom, gehnægde helle gast* (*Beo* 1273b–4a). The sequence *helle gast*, frequently viewed as a compound, can certainly mean 'the creature of hell'. One could suggest, however, that the original version was <halle gast>: the form *halle* would then be a dative-instrumental in locatival function; we could translate the half-line as 'he subdued the creature [Grendel] in the hall'. But the reading *helle* in line 1274a cannot really be objected to, even if *halle* 'in the hall' would perhaps be slightly better from the semantic point of view. The half-line *feond on helle* (*Beo* 101b), on the other hand, is hardly acceptable. It is likely that the authorial version of the epic text read *on halle* 'in the hall', and the form <halle> was incorrectly transcribed into West-Saxon as <helle>.

3   *swylcum gifeþe bið* (299b)

Upon their arrival in Denmark, Hrothgar's coastguard intercepts Beowulf and his companions, but, on being informed of Beowulf's noble lineage and his intention to rid the king's hall Heorot of the monster Grendel the coastguard allows the foreigners to proceed: he shows them the way to Hrothgar's hall and promises to request that his attendants look after the vessel, so that Beowulf's party can safely return to their homeland after their mission is accomplished. The coastguard concludes his speech as follows:

>   Gewitaþ forð beran
> wæpen ond gewædu;   ic eow wisige;
> swylce ic maguþegnas   mine hate
> wið feonda gehwone   flotan eowerne,
> niwtyrwydne   nacan on sande
> arum healdan   oþ ðæt eft byreð
> ofer lagustreamas   leofne mannan
> wudu wundenhals   to Wedermearce;
> godfremmendra   swylcum gifeþe bið
> þæt þone hilderæs   hal gedigeð
>   (*Beo* 291b–300)

The vocabulary of this passage does not present notable problems, and the translation provided by Swanton would at first sight seem more or less acceptable: "Proceed, bearing weapons and armor; I will guide you.

Moreover, I will instruct my young thanes to guard your ship honorably against all enemies, the newly-tarred vessel on the sand, until the timbers with curved prow carry back the beloved man over the sea's currents to the Weders' coastline. May it be granted to one of such noble deeds that he survive the onslaught of the battle unharmed" (Swanton 1978: 49).

A major difficulty in interpreting the coastguard's speech, though, lies in the temporal subclause introduced by *oþ ðæt* 'until', because the referent of the grammatical object belonging to *byreð* 'carries' is not immediately clear: it could be assumed that *leofne mannan* (*Beo* 297b) should refer to Beowulf, but then it is doubtful who is meant by the genitive plural *godfremmendra* and the following relative construction introduced by *swylcum gifeþe bið*. Swanton's rendering seems ultimately unacceptable mainly for two reasons: since both *bið* and *gediged* are indicative forms there is no basis for assuming that any wish is expressed as would be indicated by the clause starting with "May it be granted. . . ."; furthermore, *godfremmendra* seems to be the genitive plural of either *godfremmend* or *godfremmende*, but in either case the word cannot mean 'noble deeds', because the form in *-end(e)* (belonging to the paradigm of the present participle) clearly functions as an agent noun meaning '(one) doing good', if *god-* is correctly transmitted. In any case, *godfremmendra* seems basically to mean 'warriors'. That *godfremmendra* should begin a separate main clause, as Swanton's translation indicates, seems quite unlikely. The traditional syntactic interpretation according to which the temporal subclause introduced by *oþ ðæt* ends with *gediged* seems indeed probable. But the construction of that temporal clause also poses problems. The following considerations may be of use in dealing with this difficulty.

If we assume that *leofne mannan* refers to Beowulf himself then it is conceivable that the genitive plural *godfremmendra* could refer to his companions. It is likely that *swylcum* introduces a relative clause: *godfremmendra swylcum gifeþe bið* probably means 'the one (= every one) of the warriors to whom it is given . . .'. We know that not all companions returned home: Hondscio was killed by Grendel. The issue will arise again in the note on *on fæder stæle* below. Liuzza's translation is correct: "Go forth, and bear weapons and armor – I shall guide your way; and I will command my young companions to guard honorably against all enemies your ship, newly-tarred, upon the sand, to watch it until the curved-necked wood bears hence across the ocean-streams a beloved man to the borders of the Weders – and such of these good men as will be granted

that they survive the storm of battle" (Liuzza 2000: 62). But the dash after
Weders is superfluous.

4   *seon sibbegedriht* (387a)

When Wulfgar announces to Hrothgar that the Geatish hero Beowulf has
come to Denmark in order to rid the hall Heorot of the monster Grendel,
the ageing Danish king praises Beowulf's noble descent and former heroic
achievements. Hrothgar urges Wulfgar to usher in the Geatish party:

> Beo ðu on ofeste,   hat in gan
> seon sibbegedriht   samod ætgædere,
> gesaga him eac wordum   þæt hie sint wilcuman
> Deniga leodum.
>
> > (*Beo* 386–9a)

This invitation to Beowulf and his companions to enter the hall, where
"they will be welcome to the Danes" does not present serious problems
with regard to its vocabulary. It should be mentioned, however, that
what has frequently been printed as a compound *sibbegedriht* may represent a syntagm consisting of the genitive of *sibb* 'relationship, friendship'
followed by its head *gedryht* 'troop, body of retainers'. The inherited
compound would be expected as *sibgedriht* (three syllables) and is attested
in *Exo* 214a, *Guth* 1372a (*sibgedryht*) and *Phoen* 618a (*sibgedryht*). The
sequence has been translated as 'band of kinsmen', which is acceptable,
although 'kinsmen' must not be taken literally.

What is not agreed upon is who precisely is meant at this point by
sibbegedriht. Theoretically, *sibbegedriht* could refer to the Danes, that is, to
Hrothgar's retainers, or to Beowulf's companions. Mitchell and Robinson
opt for the first alternative: "OE idiom and the element order combine to
suggest that *sibbegedriht* is the object, not the subject of *seon*: 'bid [them,
the Geats] come in to see the band of kinsmen [the Danes]'" (Mitchell &
Robinson 1998: 61). The translation offered by Swanton is quite similar:
"Make haste, bid them enter to see the noble company of kinsmen
assembled together" (1978: 53). Basically the same rendering is found in
the translation accompanying what has been called "the first real edition"
of *Beowulf* (Klaeber 1950: cxxvii): "Be thou in haste, bid them enter, *and*
see our friendly troop collected together" (Kemble 1837: 17).

Although this interpretation is certainly not to be rejected immediately, one wonders whether the object "them [the Geats]" could have been omitted in what is obviously assumed to be an accusative-and-infinitive construction. Apart from this minor objection, it must be asked what the objective of Hrothgar's invitation could be. There is hardly any reason why Hrothgar should invite Beowulf and his companions to "see" ('inspect'?) the Danish "band of kinsmen", since we know that the Danes were unable to cope with Grendel and had to bear up with the mischief wrought by the monster at night for twelve years: Hrothgar could not present his "band of kinsmen" with any satisfaction or pride. It would be pointless for him to invite Beowulf to come in and "have a look" at the Danes.

Since in line 729 the sequence *sibbegedriht* definitely refers to Beowulf's party, we may inquire whether *sibbegedriht* in Hrothgar's invitation may also refer to the Geats. It would definitely be meaningful for Hrothgar to say "let the [Geatish] band of kinsmen all of them together come in." Can the manuscript reading be grammatically analysed in this sense? Above all, what is then the function of *seon* in line 387a?

Since *hatan* 'bid' can be followed by an accusative-and-infinitive, it is reasonable to assume that *hat in gan (seon) sibbegedriht samod ætgædere* means 'bid the company of kinsmen all together come in'. This interpretation was offered by Grein (1974: 600), Bugge (1887: 86), and Klaeber (1950: 142). But it has by no means been accepted generally. Johannes Hoops preferred to identify the *sibbegedriht* with the Danes, but he also discussed the alternative and noted: "*seon* wäre dann eine Variation zu *in gan, sibbegedriht* wäre gleichfalls Subjekts-Akk. zu *hat*, und zu *seon* wäre als Objekt *me* zu ergänzen; also: 'heiß sie hereingehn, (heiß) die Sippenschar zusammen miteinander (mich) sehen'" (Hoops 1932a: 62).

It is doubtful, however, whether *me* as the object of *seon* can have been left out. Andrew found the ellipsis "harsh" no matter whether *sibbegedriht* referred to the Danes or to Beowulf's group (Andrew 1948: 71). It must also be pointed out that an invitation for the Geats to enter Heorot in order to "see" ('meet'?) Hrothgar does not seem entirely meaningful if uttered by the king: since Beowulf and his comrades have come to rid Heorot of Grendel, it would be logical for Hrothgar to ask them to appear before him, so that he could see (= find out, decide) whether they were fit for the job. Either "me" or "us" as assumed objects of *seon* would thus hardly make sense.

Grammatically, though, the manuscript text allows yet another interpretation, which seems to lead to an altogether preferable translation of the whole passage. In Old English the infinitive does not formally distinguish between active and passive functions. With regard to *Ne hyrde ic cymlicor ceol gegyrwan* (*Beo* 38), Wyatt notes expressly that for *gegyrwan* in Modern English the passive inf. would be used (Wyatt 1968: 4). The construction of *hatan* followed by an accusative with passive infinitive is found in lines 198b–9a: *het him yðlidan godne gegyrwan*, rendered by Andrew as "ordered a good ship to be prepared for him" (Andrew 1948: 134). The infinitive *seon* with passive meaning is attested in the following *Beowulf* passage: *þær mæg nihta gehwæm niðwundor seon* (*Beo* 1365) is usually assumed to mean 'there (one) can see every night a fearful wonder', which is possible. But it would also be conceivable that *seon* means 'can be seen' with *niðwundor* functioning as its subject: 'there every night a fearful wonder may be/is to be seen'.

We may therefore assume that *seon* in line 387a has a passive nuance and means (literally) 'to be seen'. Hrothgar's invitation becomes then quite clear: he is telling Wulfgar to 'bid [Beowulf's] band of kinsmen all together to come in in order to be seen (= in order to appear before the king and his entourage)'. The infinitive *seon* is to be classified as "final" after a verb of motion according to Callaway's categories (Callaway 1913: 132–48). Hrothgar's invitation is meant to convey the message that Beowulf and his companions are welcome to enter the hall and appear before the Danish king: all of them, not just a delegation, were to be received honourably and with full diplomatic protocol.

5   *wiste þæm ahlæcan* (646b)

Together with his companions Beowulf is honourably received by King Hrothgar in the hall Heorot. Beowulf promises to rid Heorot of the monster Grendel, who for twelve years has wrought havoc in the hall at night. But Unferth taunts Beowulf, whereupon the Geatish hero elaborates on his former exploits and emphasizes his prowess. The Danes then celebrate Beowulf's arrival until 'presently' (*semninga*, 644b) Hrothgar (*sunu Healfdenes*, 645a, 'Healfdene's son') 'wishes to retire' (*secean wolde   æfenræste*, 645b–6a):

wiste þæm ahlæcan

to þæm heahsele   hilde geþinged
siððan hie sunnan leoht   geseon meahton
oþðe nipende   niht ofer ealle
scaduhelma gesceapu   scriðan cwoman
wan under wolcnum.

(*Beo* 646b–51a)

From the immediate context it is clear that the subject of the predicate *wiste* (*Beo* 646b) '(he) knew' is Hrothgar (*sunu Healfdenes* 645a). Accordingly Mitchell and Robinson translate: "he [Hrothgar] had known an attack [to be] planned by the foe [Grendel] against the high hall from the time that they . . ." (Mitchell & Robinson 1998: 69). In the continuation of the text the insertion of a negative particle *ne* between *geseon* and *meahton* has repeatedly been proposed, but this seems quite futile. The text means that the battle had been assigned "from the time that they saw the light of sun until – at nightfall – when the shadowy creatures began to arrive wan under the clouds" (Mitchell 1992). With regard to *ahlæcan* in line 646b, however, some further thoughts may be of interest, since the function of this word is not agreed upon by *Beowulf* scholars.

In the Mitchell and Robinson translation just quoted *ahlæcan* is analysed as referring to Grendel. This was also Klaeber's view: "In other words, the king knew that fight had been in Grendel's mind all day long; Grendel had been waiting from morning till night to renew his attacks in the hall" (Klaeber 1950: 152). Nickel's translation is quite similar (Nickel 1976: 41). But in 1930 Kemp Malone pointed out that the general context of the poem did not allow this interpretation:

> Grendel haunted the hall nights, and hence the king might well infer that the monster would turn up that night as usual. But Hroðgar had every reason to think that Grendel would expect no fighting. The English poet tells us, indeed, that for twelve years the hall had stood empty at night (138ff.; cf. 411ff.). At most, Grendel might hope to catch another victim (712f.); *hild* was far from his thoughts. Beowulf it was, not Grendel, who all day long had it in mind to fight that night; immediately upon his arrival at the Danish court he told the king of his purpose in coming . . . (Malone 1930: 234ff.)

Three years later Malone discussed the quoted passage again. In the meantime Hoops had published two important monographs on *Beowulf* (Hoops 1932a, b). In these works Hoops argued in favour of *ahlæcan* referring to Grendel. One specific point made by Hoops is that *to þæm heahsele* implied 'movement to the hall', and since Beowulf was already inside the hall this would seem to indicate that the focus was on Grendel, who had to come to the hall (Hoops 1932a: 86ff). Malone accepted this point and published the following revised translation in 1933: "The son of Healfdene wished to seek his bed; he had known all day that a monster-fight (*lit.* a fight with the monster) was set to come to the high hall" (Malone 1933: 61f.). This rendering seems possible, although it remains somewhat doubtful whether the dative *ahlæcan* can really mean 'with (i.e. against) the monster'.

But before dealing any further with the construction of *ahlæcan* it is certainly also important to investigate the meaning of this word. Although the Old English noun *aglæca* has been discussed repeatedly from a variety of viewpoints, neither its meaning nor its etymology can in any sense be said to be agreed upon. In an extensive discussion Kuhn (1979) gave a list of meanings that can be assigned to *aglæca*. Kuhn himself rendered the meaning of *aglæca* as "a fighter, valiant warrior, dangerous opponent, one who struggles fiercely" (Kuhn 1979: 218; see also Stanley 1979: 75). Kuhn's account is based on 36 instances of *aglæca*, three compounds with a first element *aglac-* and three attestations of *aglac* as a separate noun. With regard to the attestations taken into account, he expressly noted that "All instances of these words occur in poetry, none in prose" (Kuhn 1979: 213).

A decade after the appearance of Kuhn's essay, Alex Nicholls published a paper on *aglæca* in *Byrhtferth's Manual*, which represents the only prose attestation of the word; Nicholls (1991) gives further references to secondary literature that will not be repeated here. Although the sequence *Beda, se æglæca lareow* (Crawford 1929: 74) has been emended (see Campbell 1972: 2), Nicholls argues convincingly that the manuscript reading should be accepted as correct. The syntax of *Beda, se æglæca lareow* is not immediately clear, but Nicholls' suggestion that *æglæca* is an adjective in the weak declension provides a plausible solution. What is absolutely clear, however, is that *æglæca* in *Beda, se æglæca lareow* cannot in any sense carry the meaning 'monstrous': only 'Bede, the formidable/awe-inspiring teacher' is meaningful in the given context. Nicholls' article will ultimately be of major importance in accounting for the origin and historical development of OE *aglæca*.

For the purposes of this note on *ahlæcan* in *Beowulf* (646b), it must be kept in mind that Old English *aglæca* had the connotation 'awe-inspiring'. For the *Beowulf* passage quoted above Kuhn offered the following skeleton for the translation: "he knew battle to be appointed at the high hall for the . . ." and rightly continued: "the referent can be either Beowulf or Grendel". This is true, and in this sense Kuhn's observation definitely represents an advance in *Beowulf* interpretation. But we may go even further. Grammatically, *þæm ahlæcan* can indeed be analyzed as a dative of the singular: this seems to be the usual assumption of *Beowulf* scholars, and Kuhn's interpretation is also based on this grammatical analysis. However, this is not the only possibility: there is no objection whatsoever to interpreting *þæm ahlæcan* morphologically as a dative of the plural. The weakening of *-um > -an* in *ahlæcan* (*<ahlæcum*) can be exemplified from our extant *Beowulf* text, as was shown by Klaeber (1950: lxxxi); on the phonology of this development, see, above all, Campbell (1959: 157). The development of *-um > -an* is a well-known feature of late Old English.

If we admit that *ahlæcan* can be analysed as a dative of the plural (dual), then this indirect object would mean that 'a battle was appointed for the (two) awe-inspiring ones' ['the terrible ones']. Although in the majority of its occurrences *aglæca* is used in the singular, in *Beowulf* (2592) *aglæcean* is again a non-singular form referring to Beowulf and the dragon. The preposition *to* does not cause trouble any longer: the battle was appointed *to* the hall, because Grendel still had to come to the hall, but Beowulf was already inside it.

6   *word oþer fand* (870b)

Beowulf is victorious in his fight against Grendel in the hall Heorot, and the monster, fatally wounded, just barely manages to flee. The following morning everybody rejoices that the twelve-year ordeal of nightly havoc wrought by Grendel has been brought to an end. King Hrothgar's men make their horses gallop. Then follows a passage about poetic recital:

> Hwilum cyninges þegn
> guma gilphlæden   gidda gemyndig
> se ðe ealfela   ealdgesegena
> worn gemunde,   word oþer fand
> soðe gebunden;   secg eft ongan
> sið Beowulfes   snyttrum styrian
> ond on sped wrecan   spel gerade,
> wordum wrixlan
>
> (*Beo* 867b–74a)

For the half-line *word oper fand* (870b) two completely different syntactic analyses may theoretically be proposed. The predicate in this half-line is certainly *fand*, 'found'. The subject of *fand* can be seen in *word* 'word'; in this case *oper* 'second' could function as its object. Grein translated: "ein Wort fand das andere, Wort reihte sich an Wort" (Grein 1974: 514). This interpretation is possible, although one would wish to be given parallels for this usage of *findan*. Whether *word oper fand* could have meant 'one word found another' in the sense of 'a poem was uttered' seems doubtful, however. Nowadays the more widespread interpretation of *word oper fand* is completely different: the subject of *fand* is assumed to be *cyninges pegn* (*Beo* 867b), the object of *fand* would then seem to be *word oper*. Syntactically this analysis is unobjectionable: 'The king's retainer found (devised) other words . . .'.

The problems of the whole passage were discussed by Stanley in his chapter "Beowulf", first published more than 35 years ago (Stanley 1966). Stanley gave the following translation of lines 867b–71a: "At times the king's retainer, a man filled with high rhetoric, with the memory of songs, who remembered a multitudinous wealth of ancient traditions, came upon other words (?) bound in truth (?)" (Stanley 1966: 118 fn.1). Structurally this translation is convincing. The second of the two question marks is perhaps not necessary: it would seem reasonable to say that the poet uttered words 'bound in truth', which is likely to mean that the contents of his poems were considered to be based on real happenings presented in a reliable way.

But Stanley's first question mark is fully justified: What, after all, should "other words" refer to? Although *word oper fand* has repeatedly been construed as a reference to poetic variation it is completely uncertain whether innovation was a poetic ideal in Old English times: "there is nothing that might lead one to the view that old traditions in new words represents an ideal among the Anglo-Saxons" (Stanley 1966: 125). It would make sense, however, to say that the minstrel 'came upon words bound in truth', because this would be likely to mean that he uttered a poem. Thus the problem lies in *oper*, and it seems that a new possibility of interpreting this word and consequently the whole passage can be suggested.

Beowulf offers a further example of *oðer* not functioning as the (adjectival) ordinal for 'second'. It seems best to render *ealodrincende oðer sædon* (*Beo* 1945) as 'men drinking ale said furthermore (moreover)'. We may therefore assume that *oper* can have an adverbial function and may be translated as 'furthermore, moreover'. In the quoted passage this yields good sense: we are told that *hwilum* ('at certain times') the king's men made their horses gallop, and *hwilum* ('at other times') the minstrel 'furthermore [~moreover] came upon words bound in truth'. The position of the stressed adverbial *oþer* in *word oþer fand* is identical with that of *stunde* in *word stunde ahof* (*El* 723b). Metrically *word oþer fand* is a D-verse comparable to *secg eft ongan* (*Beo* 871b) and *word stunde ahof* (*El* 723b). Further parallels include: *word æfter cwæð* (*Beo* 315b), *word æfter spræc* (*Beo* 341b) and *word inne abead* (*Beo* 390b). In all these instances *word* may be accusative plural of the neuter *a*-stem.

It is likely that a strong punctuation mark is required after *gebunden*, because *secg eft ongan* begins a new syntactic unit. It is noteworthy, however, that *ongan* does not necessarily mean 'began, started' here. Stanley translated the clause as follows: "The man did then tell with art the exploit of Beowulf, set forth with happy skill a well-told tale, weaving words" (Stanley 1966: 118, fn. 1). That *onginnan* need not exclusively mean 'start, begin' is perhaps most clearly seen in Beowulf's own words when he says *hæbbe ic mærða fela ongunnen on geogoþe* (*Beo* 408b–9a) 'I have undertaken [performed] many famous actions in my youth'. It is conceivable that the *scop* 'undertook to sing in honour of Beowulf's feat', but whether he explicitly dealt with Beowulf's exploits is not really stated in the text. Stanley's comment on this aspect of the text is worth quoting:

> The poet presents the *scop* to us as singing the hero's praise in the traditional manner in the traditional poetic medium. *Secg eft ongan / sið Beowulfes snyttrum styrian* (871–72), we are told; surely, we may expect something about Beowulf himself. Instead we get the ideal which is embodied in Beowulf expressed in terms of Sigemund and Heremod. The relevance of Sigemund, the dragon-slayer, is not made explicit, it is too obvious to need explanation; but how love fell to Beowulf whereas iniquity took possession of Heremod is clearly stated. (Stanley 1966: 132)

Ultimately the quoted *Beowulf* passage tells us nothing about whether poetic originality was valued in Anglo-Saxon times. Since *oþer* in *word oþer fand* (870b) can hardly mean 'new' but probably functions as an adverb meaning 'furthermore, moreover', it follows that *wordum wrixlan* 'exchange words' in line 874 is also unlikely to emphasize any innovatory aspect of Old English poetic diction.

7 *þa hine se broga angeat* (1291b)

Grendel's mother comes to Heorot in order to avenge her son's death. The events which lead to Æschere being killed by the ogress are described in eight lines:

> Ða wæs on healle   heardecg togen
> sweord ofer setlum,   sidrand manig
> hafen handa fæst;   helm ne gemunde
> byrnan side   þa hine se broga angeat.
> Heo wæs on ofste,   wolde ut þanon,
> feore beorgan,   þa heo onfunden wæs;
> hraðe heo æþelinga   anne hæfde
> fæste befangen,   þa heo to fenne gang.
> (*Beo* 1288–95)

This passage has recently been discussed by Elder (2002), and some of the points made in that paper seem plausible. That *broga* 'terror' in line 1291b could refer to Grendel's mother is conceivable, and the parallel for *broga* rendering Latin *monstrum* is convincing. Elder translated lines 1290b–91b "no one thought of helmet or roomy mail-coat when that monstrous thing perceived him" (Elder 2002: 316). That *broga* in line 1291b is personified and refers to Grendel's mother had already been suggested by Isaacs, but his translation is not convincing at all: "The helmet was not mindful of broad byrnie, when Grendel's dam (or terror, personified) seized him" (Isaacs 1963: 124).

But some lingering doubt remains whether this can be correct. In the immediately preceding lines we are told that the warriors drew their swords. It is therefore very surprising that it allegedly occurred to nobody to use helmet and mail-coat. The main problem certainly lies in the translation of *angeat*. That a warrior should have been frightened into inaction when Grendel's mother 'perceived' him is intrinsically unlikely. What semantic nuance 'perceived' could precisely convey here is unclear anyway: the meaning 'understand' would certainly not be suitable, but 'see, recognize' could hardly apply either, because it was of course dark. We clearly have to investigate the meaning of the verb *ongietan*.

With regard to the semantic range of *ongietan*, Elder comments as follows: ". . . 'perceive' is almost always a possible translation of this verb, whether or not alternatives like 'understand,' 'be sensible of,' or 'see' are preferred in a particular context" (Elder 2002: 316). This statement is perhaps acceptable, although there is no doubt that in Old English poetry and prose *ongietan* is very widely used in the sense of Latin *intelligere* ('understand'). The meaning 'understand' represents a semantic development of 'seize', and a comparable development is encountered in *grasp, comprehend, assume,* and other verbs in this semantic field (Buck 1949: 1207, 1020). *Beowulf* scholars widely assume that *angeat* in line 1291b should have the original meaning 'seized', but Elder maintains that a basic sense like 'seize' is nowhere else attested for Old English *ongietan*. It would then be very unlikely for *angeat* to mean 'seized' in the quoted *Beowulf* passage.

Although *ongietan* often occurs in the secondary senses of 'understand' or 'perceive', in at least one passage this kind of meaning will hardly do. In the Old English translation of Gregory's *Cura Pastoralis* the following clause refers to St Peter: *Ðæt rice & ðone anwald he na ne angeat wið Cornelius ða ða he hine sua suiðlice weorðian wolde.* Sweet translated: "He did not acknowledge his power and authority in the case of Cornelius, when he wished to honour him so excessively" (Sweet 1871: 114ff). The translation is acceptable: Gregory showed that Cornelius had behaved humbly towards Peter, and therefore Peter did not assume authority, whereas he definitely reprimanded sinners like Ananias and Sapphira. Neither 'understood' nor 'perceived' would be suitable as translations of *angeat*, whereas 'assumed' or 'took' seem quite possible. Perhaps the quoted clause may be rendered as 'He (Peter) did not assume power and authority against Cornelius since he wanted to honour him so greatly.' The corresponding passage in Gregory's original reads as follows: *quod honore sibi uehementer impenso coram bene agentibus fratribus non agnouit* (Judic 1992: 210); the Old English translation is not literal, and on the reception of Gregory's work in early Ireland and England Judic's informative chapter "Diffusion et Influence" (Judic 1992: 88–102) should be consulted.

A translation like 'took' or 'seized' for *angeat* in *Beowulf* line 1291b may therefore be taken into consideration after all. In at least one further *Beowulf* passage the preterite *ongeat* may mean 'attacked', although admittedly the usual translation as 'perceived' cannot be ruled out. In order to avenge Æschere Beowulf had swum down to the bottom of the mere, where the ogress was waiting for him. She seized him and carried him away. Beowulf recognized (*ongeat*, 1512b) that he was in a dry underwater cave. He saw light (1516b). *Ongeat þa se goda   grundwyrgenne, / merewif mihtig* (1518–19a) may mean 'the good one [Beowulf] then recognized (perceived, saw) the monster of the deep, the powerful water-woman', but in the given context 'attacked, seized' would certainly also make sense. Penttilä's remarks are fully relevant here: "With OE *ongietan* – perceptional in character – the visual impression is often preceded by an effort to see something. As pointed out by Rittershaus, the verb is often found in contexts in which it is doubtful whether the writer refers to grasping in the physical sense or grasping by means of the eyes" (Penttilä 1956: 173).

The clause *helm ne gemunde* / *byrnan side   þa hine se broga angeat* still requires a comment from the syntactic point of view. We may analyse *þa hine se broga angeat* as a subclause, but the main clause seems to lack a subject: "An indefinite subject, 'any one,' 'the one in question' is understood" (Klaeber 1950: 181). Klaeber's wording is ambiguous because 'anyone' and 'the one in question' are by no means synonymous. Usually the first suggestion, namely the indefinite 'anyone', is adopted by editors and commentators. But the second suggestion, namely a definite 'the one in question' seems in fact superior here: 'the one in question', namely Æschere, did not think of putting on helmet and mail-coat because there was absolutely no time for him to do so when the ogress seized him. The unexpressed subject of the main clause is identical with *hine*, the object of the subordinate clause. Kemble's translation is acceptable in this respect: "*he* [i.e. the warrior] remembered not his helmet, *nor* his wide mail-shirt, when the terror fell upon him" (Kemble 1837: 53).

If we follow in the main Elder's rendering, but work in the above considerations, then the passage may be translated: 'Then in the hall the hard-edged sword was drawn above the benches, many a broad shield was raised fast in hand; the one in question [Æschere] did not think of helmet and wide mail-coat when the monster seized him. When she was discovered, she was in haste; she wanted to get out of there to save her life. Swiftly she had taken one of the noblemen firmly in her grasp; then she went to the fen'.

8   *on fæder stæle* (1479b)

Before setting out for his fight against Grendel's mother Beowulf addresses King Hrothgar and makes final arrangements in case he should succumb in the enterprise:

Geþenc nu, se mæra   maga Healfdenes,
snottra fengel,   nu ic eom siðes fus,
goldwine gumena,   hwæt wit geo spræcon,
gif ic æt þearfe   þinre scolde
aldre linnan,   þæt ðu me a wære
forðgewitenum   on fæder stæle.

(Beo 1474–9)

The vocabulary of this passage does not present any particular problems. Kemble translates the last three lines of the quoted text as "if I at thy need should cease to live, that thou wouldst ever be in the place of a father to me, *when I had* departed" (Kemble 1837: 61). Subsequent translations are similar, as may be seen from Liuzza's recent rendering: "if ever in your service I should lose my life, that you would always be in a father's place to me when I have passed away" (Liuzza 2000: 98).

One difficulty with these lines evidently lies in the conclusion of the *þæt*-clause, because it is by no means obvious in what ways Hrothgar could 'be in the place of a father to me', that is to the then-dead hero Beowulf. Swanton wants *fæder* to refer to Beowulf's father: "that if I should relinquish life in your cause, you should always take the role of my father when I passed away" (Swanton 1978: 105). It is completely unclear, however, how Hrothgar could possibly assume the role of Beowulf's father in the circumstances envisaged by the Geat: Beowulf's father Ecgþeow is mentioned by name in the epic text but is dead by the time of the fight against Grendel and Grendel's mother, and plays no role of any significance in the action. The prepositional phrase *on fæder stæle* occurs once in Old English prose: *Cristenum cyninge gebyrað swiðe rihte, þæt he sy on fæder stæle cristenra þeode* (Jost 1959: 40), and here its function is clear: 'for a Christian king it is right that he should be in the function of a father [protector] to Christian people.' The meaning 'in the function of a father [protector]' is definitely suitable also in the quoted *Beowulf* passage, and the immediately following lines make clear what Beowulf's intentions are:

Wes þu mundbora   minum magoþegnum,
hondgesellum,   gif mec hild nime;
swylce þu ða madmas,   þe þu me sealdest,
Hroðgar leofa,   Higelace onsend.

(Beo 1480–3)

Some grammatical and contextual details must now be dealt with. The sequence *me . . . forðgewitenum* in the *þæt*-clause (*Beo* 1478b–9a) is possibly to be interpreted as an absolute construction meaning 'if I am dead' (literally '[with] me departed'); an adverbial rendering would be 'after my death' (on absolute constructions in Old English see in particular Mitchell 1985: 914–40). It is likely that *me* is not a dative object belonging somehow to *wære*. The *gif*-clause may then be translated as follows: 'If I should lose my life in your need then you should after my death forever assume the function of a father [protector]'. The following four lines indicate wherein this function lies: 'Be a protector for my followers, my companions if the battle should carry me away; and, dear Hrothgar, also send the treasures that you have given me to Higelac'. The word *fæder* is used in a metaphorical sense. Should Beowulf die, Hrothgar is requested to assume legal functions that are Beowulf's as long as the Geatish hero is alive: Hrothgar is asked to adopt Beowulf's companions into his household and to pass on to Higelac the gifts that were bestowed on Beowulf in recognition of his victorious fight against Grendel.

References and Further Reading

Andrew, O. S. (1948). *Postscript on* Beowulf. Cambridge: Cambridge University Press.

Buck, C. D. (1949). *A Dictionary of Selected Synonyms in the Principal Indo-European Languages: a contribution to the history of ideas.* Chicago, IL: University of Chicago Press.

Bugge, S. (1887). Studien über das Beowulfepos. *BGDSL*, XII, 1–112.

Elder, S. M. (2002). A note on the meaning of *Beowulf*, lines 1288–1295. *N&Q*, CCXLVII, 315–16.

Grein, C. W. M. (1974). *Sprachschatz der angelsächsischen Dichter* (repr. of the 2nd edn). Heidelberg: Carl Winter.

Holtzmann, A. (1863). Zu *Beowulf*. *Germania*, 8, 489–97.

Hoops, J. (1932a). *Beowulfstudien.* Heidelberg: Carl Winter.

Hoops, J. (1932b). *Kommentar zum* Beowulf. Heidelberg: Carl Winter.

Isaacs, N. D. (1963). Six *Beowulf* cruces. *JEGP*, LXII, 119–128.

Kuhn, S. M. (1979). Old English *aglæca*–Middle Irish óclach. In I. Rauch & G. F. Carr (eds), *Linguistic Method. Essays in honor of Herbert Penzl* (pp. 213–30). The Hague: Mouton.

Malone, K. (1930). Three notes on *Beowulf*. *JEGP*, XXIX, 233–6.

Malone, K. (1933). Beowulfiana. *MÆvum*, II, 58–64.

Mitchell, B. (1992). Literary lapses: six notes on *Beowulf* and its critics. *RES*, 43, 1–17.

Nicholls, A. (1991). Bede 'awe-inspiring' not 'monstrous': some problems with Old English *aglæca*. *N&Q*, 236 [n.s. 38], 147–8.

Penttilä, E. (1956). *The Old English Verbs of Vision: a semantic study*. Helsinki: Société Néophilologique.

Schaubert E. von (1961). *Heyne-Schückings Beowulf*, 2. Teil: *Kommentar*. Paderborn: Schöningh.

Sievers, E. (1904). Zum *Beowulf*. *BGDSL*, XXIX, 305–31.

Stanley, E. G. (1966). Beowulf. In Stanley (pp. 104–40). Repr. in P. S. Baker (ed.) (1995). *Beowulf. Basic readings* (pp. 3–34). New York: Garland.

Stanley E. G. (1979). Two Old English poetic phrases insufficiently understood for literary criticism: *þing gehegan* and *seonoþ gehegan*. In D. G. Calder (ed.), *Old English Poetry: essays on style* (pp. 67–90). Berkeley, CA: University of California Press.

Sweet, H. (1896). *The Student's Dictionary of Anglo-Saxon*. Oxford: Clarendon Press.

Chapter 2

A Point Well Taken: Manuscript Punctuation and Old English Poems

Daniel Donoghue

No one has done more than Bruce Mitchell to call attention to the poor fit between Old English poems and the modern punctuation that accompanies them in our printed editions. At the very least Mitchell's admonitions should lead us to question whether a system of punctuation that matured well after the advent of printing is congenial to an oral tradition that matured long before the first Old English poem was written down (Mitchell 1980). Yet with few exceptions the medieval poems have been edited with the commas, semicolons, periods, quotation marks and other visual cues familiar to us from modern languages. The editorial decision to use these marks, however, has gone largely unexamined. It is almost as though their use is considered to be as transparent and unobtrusive as substituting the modern letter <w> for the old runic *wynn* in the manuscripts. For their part, modern readers have found it convenient and reassuring to see a familiar system of visual cues sprinkled over an edited Old English poem: here is where a sentence begins, here it ends.

One sign that something is not quite right in this conspiracy of convenience between editors and readers has been the inordinate use of the semicolon. The modern semicolon has a loosely defined identity somewhere between a comma and a full stop. "Though the semicolon is less frequently employed today than in the past," observes the *Chicago Manual of Style*, "it is still occasionally useful to mark a more important break in sentence flow than that marked by a comma" (Anon. 1982: 5.68). In other words, its function hovers in a nebulous area between syntax ('sentence') and rhetoric ('flow'). While modern texts use it only infrequently, the editors of Old English poems have gravitated toward the semicolon precisely because of the ambiguity of the break it introduces in the "sentence flow". Thus if an editor is unsure whether the end of a clause also signals the end of a sentence, the semicolon can come to the rescue. In Klaeber's *Beowulf*, for example, approximately five semicolons appear on each of the 120 pages of text, and while Klaeber is but one example, his *Beowulf* has been the most influential edition among the generations of Anglo-Saxonists working today (Klaeber 1950). We cut our scholarly teeth on it. Other editors may use the semicolon more sparingly, but its frequency in Klaeber's edition still far outstrips what can be found in other kinds of writing from Modern English or any other period.

The semicolon thus becomes an index of the editor's struggles to accommodate the modern system of punctuation to the seemingly idiosyncratic syntax of Old English poetry. Similar observations could be made regarding parenthetic clauses, which modern editions separate out with parentheses or dashes, but with a frequency far greater than that found in other kinds of writing. But taken altogether, the modern marks of punctuation are not so incompatible that their presence in Old English poems becomes an obstacle to readers, especially readers less attuned to syntactic complexity. In fact, the long-unexamined presence of modern punctuation in modern editions can be explained at least in part by the combination of its utility and familiarity. If the fit is poor, it is not as painful as a pinching shoe.

Since 1980 Mitchell has proposed several alternate systems of punctuation for Old English poetry, and has more recently put them to the test with editions of *The Dream of the Rood* (Mitchell 1998) and *Beowulf*, in collaboration with Susan Irvine (Mitchell & Irvine 2000). The key virtues of the version in *Beowulf* are its simplicity and its consistency. The marks of punctuation indicate syntactic units, but because the system works in tandem with the metrical half-line spacing on the page, it can afford to be relatively sparing so as not to impede the "sentence flow", or more precisely "the flow of the verse paragraph" (Mitchell & Robinson 1998: 172). In Mitchell's system this larger and more flexible unit of syntax, the verse paragraph, is marked off by a capital letter at the beginning and at the end by a period. A raised point, borrowed from the punctuation of Old English manuscripts, marks off clauses within the verse paragraph, and commas separate units within clauses. The other marks are easy to recognize from their modern conventional use. But a major innovation of Mitchell's system is the absence of punctuation if the sense is clear without it. Thus one of the first impressions to strike those who look over the newly repunctuated texts is the sparseness of the marks, as though the editors had taken advice from Hippocrates: "First, do no harm".

Although Mitchell and his collaborators do not mention it, the restrained use of punctuation has an authoritative precedent in the manuscript copies of Old English poems. The general features of the scribal practices are well known. Typically, words are copied across the folio from margin to margin and not lineated as verse (that is, one line of verse for each line of writing, with an irregular right-hand edge). Capitals are used sparingly, as is the primary mark of punctuation, a raised point. The scholarly consensus concerning the placement of the capitals and punctuation has been that it is not quite systematic and not quite random. The scribes' practice is regular enough to tantalize, in other words, but sporadic enough to frustrate anyone looking for a consistent pattern. Its inscrutability has made it easy to neglect; many editions of Old English poems itemize the manuscripts' capitals and accent marks, but dismiss the punctuation with passing generalizations.

Taking Mitchell's revised editorial punctuation as a starting point, this article re-examines manuscript punctuation to argue that it may be more systematic than we have recognized. But first it puts the problem in a larger context by surveying the kinds of punctuation available to Anglo-Saxon scribes. If they lacked the array of marks available in our modern typographic convention, what *did* they have at their disposal? It turns out that a number of options was available, but the practice employed in transcribing Old English poems differs from that of Latin poetry, Old English prose, and other kinds of writing found in Anglo-Saxon England. The final part of this article places the punctuation of Old English poetry in a more purposeful, complementary role with a convention of poetic language known as verse grammar.

Other Conventions of Punctuation

In her comprehensive study of the visual cues employed in manuscript copies of Old English poems, Katherine O'Brien O'Keeffe draws attention to the significance of direct translations from Latin sources (O'Brien O'Keeffe 1990). The section of O'Brien O'Keeffe's book that would contextualize my topic most clearly is her discussion of *Riddle 40* from the Exeter Book. The Old English poem is a translation of Aldhelm's

Enigma C, which is the one hundredth and culminating riddle in his collection, with *"Creatura"* as its solution. Not only is the source riddle known, but O'Brien O'Keeffe is able to identify the exact manuscript of the Latin riddles from which the Old English translator worked: it is Oxford, Bodleian, Rawlinson C 697, in which Aldhelm's lengthy *Enigma C* is carefully copied. The Latin poem begins with a large red capital; smaller red capitals are lined up along the left margin at the beginning of each verse; each verse is given a separate line; and each line ends with a mark of punctuation. Given the close relation to the Rawlinson copy, observes O'Brien O'Keeffe, "if any Old English poem should show traces of Latin conventions of formatting, it should be this one" (O'Brien O'Keeffe 1990: 140). Yet the similarities are hard to find: the Old English is written out in the usual continuous lines from margin to margin; there are few capitals and an average of one point for every three lines in printed editions. (Here and elsewhere the term "capital" refers to any larger letter form, sometimes called *littera notabilior*, or 'more notable letter'.) Although the Old English poem breaks off abruptly in the middle of a line because of a missing folio from the Exeter Book, it is nevertheless quite long for a riddle (107 lines). A comparison with the source text makes it clear that the poet-translator's practice was to rework one line of Latin into two of Old English verse (Williamson 1977: 265–8). As if to demarcate this two-for-one ratio, for some stretches of the Old English a raised point comes at the end of every second line, illustrated in the passage reproduced here with lineation from a standard edition (Krapp & Dobbie 1936: 201):

> hyrre ic eom heofone   hateþ mec heahcyning
> his deagol þing   dyre bihealdan ·
> eac ic under eorþan   eal sceawige   40
> wom wraðscrafu   wraþra gesta ·
> micle yldra   þonne ymbhwyrft þæs
> oþþe þes middangeard   meahte geweorþan ·
> ond ic giestron wæs   geong acenned
> mære to monnum   þurh minre modor hrif ·   45
> ic eom fægerre   frætwum goldes
> þeah hit mon awerge   wirum utan ·
> ic eom wyrslicre   þonne þes wudu fula
> oððe þis waroð   þe her aworpen ligeð
> ic eorþan eom   æghwær brædre   50
> ond widgielra   þonne þes wong grena ·

> I am higher than heaven. The high king commands me to hold his precious hidden things. Likewise I look at everything under the earth, the evil foul dens of hostile spirits. I am much older than this world or this middle-earth could become, and yesterday I was born young from the womb of my mother, famous among people. I am fairer than ornaments of gold even if one filigrees it. I am more vile than this foul wood or this seaweed that lies here cast down. Everywhere I am broader than the earth and wider than this green world.

Even though a point seems to be "missing" from the end of line 49, the pointing of this passage is more consistent than that for most stretches of the poem. But in the light of the model that the Rawlinson manuscript offers, the question is not why a scribe omitted a point here or there. Rather it is why the Old English does not avail itself more of the practice of pointing found in the immediate source copy, to say nothing of its lineation and capitalization. A raised point appears after roughly half of the Old English verse lines where one might be expected, an expectation that could only increase in light of the source copy's presentation on the page. Why is the Old English punctuation apparently haphazard? It is as though a deliberate choice was made to remove visual cues that might otherwise assist the reader.

If *Riddle 40* retains few of the visual cues from its Latin original, then one might guess that Old English prose, with its less demanding syntax, would have even less punctuation. But such is not the case. The British Library manuscript Royal 7 C xii is a late tenth-century compilation of Ælfric's *Catholic Homilies*, first series. It is an early copy, close to the author's draft, and Ælfric himself (d. *circa* 1010) may have entered some corrections (Clemoes 1997: 65). More to our purpose here, the two scribes who copied it maintained a remarkably extensive and consistent system of punctuation, called *positurae*. It uses four marks, three of which are reproduced below: a *punctus versus* (resembling today's semicolon), a *punctus circumflexus* (a raised point) and the *punctus elevatus* (a point with an angled mark above). The *punctus versus* ends a *sententia*; the *punctus circumflexus* separates shorter syntactic units, often phrases; the *punctus elevatus* separates longer synctactic units, often clauses (Clemoes 1980; Parkes 1993: 35–6). The following passage provides examples of three of these marks from Ælfric's homily on the Nativity of the Innocents in the Royal manuscript, folios 26r–26v:

Matheus awrat on þære forman cristes bec þysum wordum be þæs hælendes gebyrdtide 7 cwæð ; Ða þa se hælend acenned wæs · on þære iudeiscan bethleem · on herodes dagum cyninges ⫶ efne þa comon fram eastdæle middaneardes þry tungelwitegan to þære byrig hierusalem · þus befrinende ; Hwær is iudeiscra leoda cyning · se þe acenned is ; we gesawon soðlice his steorran on eastdæle ⫶ 7 we comon to þy þæt we us to him gebiddan ; hwæt ða herodes cyning þis gehyrende wearð micclum ástyred 7 eal seo burhwaru samod mid him ;

Matthew wrote in the first book of Christ these words about the Saviour's nativity and said: "When the Saviour was born in Bethlehem of Judea in the days of King Herod, just then there came from the eastern regions of the earth three astronomers to the city of Jerusalem, thus inquiring, 'Where is the king of the Jewish people, who is born? Truly we saw his star in the east and we have come in order to pray to him.' Indeed then King Herod, hearing this, became greatly agitated and all the citizenry with him".

The punctuation in the Royal manuscript is more extensive than that in most homiliaries, even though there is no *punctus interrogativus* for the question *"Hwær is . . ."* or any special marks for direct speech. Even the simpler systems, however, had far greater regularity than what is found in the poetry. In fact, some printed editions, such as the two volumes for Ælfric's first and second series of the *Catholic Homilies*, simply reproduce one manuscript's punctuation, which takes relatively little effort to get used to (Clemoes 1997; Godden 1979).

The sparse punctuation in Old English poetic codices also contrasts with the scribal practices for other Germanic literature. The Old Saxon *Genesis*, for example, uses the *punctus circumflexus* (·) and the *punctus versus* (;) along with capitals, to divide the text into more "reader-friendly" units. (Among Anglo-Saxonists this manuscript is famous for confirming the theory that the Old English *Genesis B* was translated from an Old Saxon original.) The *punctus versus* in the Old Saxon manuscript usually ends a verse paragraph, almost always at the end of an alliterative long line and preceding a capital. The simple raised point is more frequent, and seems to have had a variety of uses, as illustrated in the following brief passage from the manuscript, Vatican, Biblioteca Apostolica, Palatinus Latinus 1447, 2r (Doane 1991, lines 159–63):

Thuo sea obar mambra   mahtige fuorun ·
thuo fundun sia abrahama   bi enum ala standan ·

> uuaran enna uuihstedi ·   endi scolda usas uualdandas
> geld gifrummian   endi scolda thar goda theonan
> an middean dag   manna thie bezto ;

When the mighty ones proceeded through Mambre, they found Abraham standing near a certain shrine, watching over a holy place, and he was offering our Lord's sacrifice, and there the best of men was serving God at noon.

Altogether, the marks of punctuation average about one per each alliterative line, with about twice as many coming at the end of the long line as in the middle. The pointing is more elaborate and systematic than the purely metrical pointing of the Old English version of the same poem, *Genesis B*, where points are used to separate half-lines without regard to syntactic structure.

Another Old Saxon poem with close ties to Anglo-Saxon England is the copy of *The Heliand* found in the British Library, manuscript Cotton Caligula A.vii, copied in the second half of the tenth century, most likely in England by an Anglo-Saxon scribe. It uses fewer marks of punctuation than the Vatican *Genesis*, but consistently uses capitals to mark off sense units, as if they were intended to take the place of punctuation. Many of these units correspond to the sentence boundaries in modern editions and usually consist of one to three clauses, sometimes more. The effect of these recurring capitals is to break up the narrative into intelligible chunks, which must have been a great aid in a poem of nearly 6,000 lines.

What is most striking from this survey is the indifference of Anglo-Saxon scribes to visual cues like punctuation *only* when they were copying Old English verse. When they copied Latin verse they adopted lineation, capitals and punctuation. When they copied Old English *prose*, they employed a hierarchical system of punctuation. The Anglo-Saxon scribe who copied *The Heliand* used frequent capitals and some punctuation. In translating from a Latin or an Old Saxon poem in manuscript, scribes and translators failed to retain most of the visual cues present in the original. Punctuation is never eliminated altogether, but it seems to be vestigial, or casually added as an afterthought. Why should Old English poetry be conspicuously resistant even when it had every opportunity to adopt visual cues? How could the scribes afford to be so indifferent? It is not as though the available scribal conventions were too primitive. Nor is it sufficient to say that because Old English was their native language, the Anglo-Saxons were able to do without visual cues. If that were the case, then the punctuation of Old English prose and of Old Saxon verse would be an extravagance. For some reason, in turning from any other kind of writing to the copying of Old English verse, Anglo-Saxon scribes deprived themselves of a readily available set of graphic cues.

Most discussions of manuscript punctuation for the poetry assume that Anglo-Saxon readers could get by with less because they recognized formulas and metrical patterns. Certainly this familiarity was an important part of the process of reading, but only a part, because even though the reading of medieval manuscripts was a slower process, it is doubtful that metre and formulas made the poems immediately comprehensible. It would be counterproductive in any period, medieval or modern, if the act of reading required too much mental energy to decipher the written forms. Punctuation was added to medieval texts precisely to facilitate reading, because its "primary function is to resolve structural uncertainties in a text, and to signal nuances of semantic significance which might otherwise not be conveyed at all, or would at best be much more difficult for a reader to figure out" (Parkes 1993: 1). We must assume that Old English poems were transcribed so that new readers, unfamiliar with the text, could understand them. Yet even if Anglo-Saxon readers developed a deep familiarity through a lifetime of acquaintance with the conventions of Old English poetry, much room for ambiguity and thus a need for graphic cues remains.

Punctuation and Verse Grammar

What has come to be known as Old English verse grammar seems to be more closely linked to manuscript punctuation than has previously been recognized. Where Latin poems relied heavily on visual cues, such as lineation, punctuation and capitalization, Old English poems relied on a more complex and complementary set of cues, some graphic, some metrical, some syntactic, some formulaic, which together rendered the poems in manuscript intelligible to their first readers. In other words verse grammar in poems like *Beowulf*, which will be the main test case, may have mitigated the need for fuller punctuation.

Before turning to verse grammar, however, I would like to comment more on the purpose of punctuation, which was particularly important to early Irish and Anglo-Saxon scribes because their vernaculars were not Latinate languages. As Malcolm Parkes observes, "From the ninth century onwards punctuation became in terms of pragmatics a more important component of a written text: it contributed directly to the communicative intention embodied within a text, although the intention communicated often reflected the interpretation of a scribe or corrector" (Parkes 1987: 29). Parkes describes these conventions as a "grammar of legibility", which consists of a generally accepted system of graphic cues including, besides pointing, capitalization and lineation. This grammar renders the text understandable for "an indeterminate audience disseminated over distance or time, or both" (Parkes 1987: 16, 1993: 23). A kind of economy guided the graphic conventions of Latin texts: "Medieval scribes and correctors punctuate where confusion is likely to arise," Parkes observes, "and do not always punctuate where confusion is not likely to arise, even when they are concerned with the *sententia litterae* . . . One is sorely tempted to measure medieval punctuation in terms of units of confusibles" (Parkes 1978: 139).

For my purposes, the two most applicable concepts in these observations are the "grammar of legibility" and the tempting "units of confusibles". In a grammar of legibility, punctuation is systematic; it is applied according to consistent, established conventions. The units of confusibles in an Old English poem might be difficult metrical or syntactic patterns, verse paragraphs, or larger rhetorical patterns. The enigma of the pointing of the *Beowulf* manuscript, to take a well-documented example, is that it seems to be neither systematic nor to coincide with what we might expect as confusibles. The punctuation, usually a simple raised point, is sparse. The total number of marks in O'Brien O'Keeffe's tally is 624, or about twenty every 100 lines. They follow a well-noted pattern in their distribution. The great majority end a full line in modern editions; that is, they come after the second half-line. Only 45, or 7 per cent, come in the middle of the line (O'Brien O'Keeffe 1990: 175). In other words, on average a point falls at the end of every fifth line, and in the middle about once every seventy lines. Many of the points, though not all, also come at the end of a clause. These two characteristics – at the end of a line, at the end of a clause – seem to describe the distribution of the pointing in *Beowulf*. The extended passage below (see also Figures 2.1 and 2.2), which gives the conventional word and half-line divisions (with some emendations from Klaeber 1950), demonstrates this pattern:

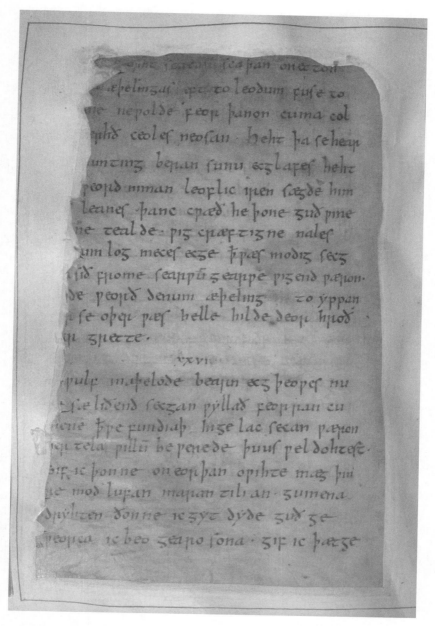

Figure 2.1   Cotton Vitellius A.xv, fol. 172v

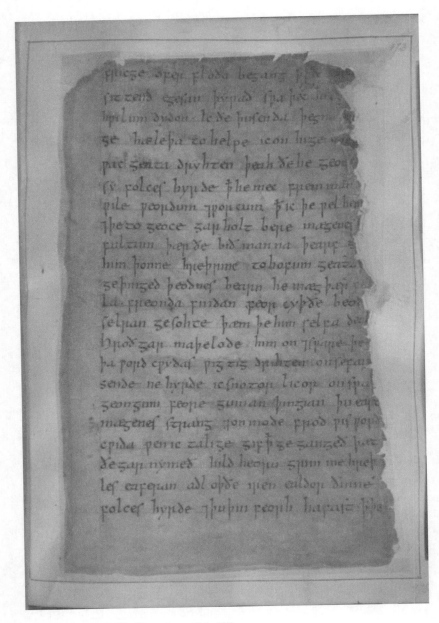

Figure 2.2   Cotton Vitellius A.xv, fol. 173r

· Ic þære socne   singales wæg
modceare micle   þæs sig metode þanc
ecean dryhtne   þæs ðe ic on aldre gebad
1780 þæt ic on þone hafelan   heorodreorigne
ofer eald gewin   eagum starige ·
ga nu to setle   symbelwynne dreoh
wiggeweorþad   unc sceal worn fela
maþma gemænra   siþðan morgen bið ·
1785 geat wæs glædmod   geong sona to
setles neosan   swa se snottra heht ·
þa wæs eft swa ær   ellenrofum
fletsittendum   fægere gereorded
niowan stefne   nihthelm geswearc
1790 deorc ofer dryhtgumum   duguð eal aras
wolde blondenfeax   beddes neosan
gamela scylding   geat unigmetes wel ·
rofne randwigan   restan lyste
sona him seleþegn   siðes wergum
1795 feorrancundum   forð wisade
se for andrysnum   ealle beweotede
þegnes þearfe   swylce þy dogore
heaþoliðende   habban scoldon ·
reste hine þa rumheort   reced hliuade
1800 geap ond goldfah   gæst inne swæf
oþ þæt hrefn blaca   heofones wynne
bliðheort bodode /   ða com beorht scacan   fol.
          . . .   scaþan onetton
wæron æþelingas   eft to leodum
1805 fuse to farenne   wolde feor þanon
cuma collenferhð   ceoles neosan ·
Heht þa se hearda   hrunting beran
sunu ecglafes   heht his sweord niman
leoflic iren   sægde him þæs leanes þanc
1810 cwæð he þone guðwine   godne tealde ·
wigcræftigne   nales wordum log
meces ecge   þæt wæs modig secg
ond þa siðfrome   searwum gearwe
wigend wæron ·   Eode weorð denum
1815 æþeling to yppan   þær se oþer wæs
hæle hildedeor   hroðgar grette ·

XXVI ·

        Beowulf maþelode   bearn ecgþeowes
        nu we sæliðend   secgan wyllað
        feorran cumene   þæt we fundiaþ
1820   higelac secan   wæron her tela
        willum bewenede   þu us wel dohtest ·
        Gif ic þonne on eorþan   owihte mæg
        þinre modlufan   maran tilian ·
        gumena dryhten   ðonne ic gyt dyde
1825   guðgeweorca   ic beo gearo sona ·
        gif ic þæt ge/fricge   ofer floda begang   fol.
        þæt þec ymbsittend   egesan þywað
        swa þec hetende   hwilum dydon ·
        Ic ðe þusenda   þegna bringe
1830   hæleþa to helpe   ic on higelac wat
        geata dryhten   þeah ðe he geong sy
        folces hyrde   þæt he mec fremman wile
        wordum ond worcum   þæt ic þe wel herige
        ond þe to geoce   garholt bere
1835   mægenes fultum   þær ðe bið manna þearf
        gif him þonne hreþric   to hofum geata
        geþingeð þeodnes bearn   he mæg þær fela ·
        freonda findan   feorcyþðe beoð
        selran gesohte   þæm þe him selfa deah ·
1840   Hroðgar maþelode   him on ondsware
        þe þa wordcwydas   wigtig drihten
        on sefan sende   ne hyrde ic snotorlicor
        on swa geongum feore   guman þingian
        þu eart mægenes strang   ond on mode frod
1845   wis wordcwida   wen ic talige
        gif þæt gegangeð   þæt ðe gar nymeð
        hild heorugrimme   hreþles eaferan
        adl oþðe iren   ealdor ðinne
        folces hyrde   ond þu þin feorh hafast ·
                            (London, British Library,
                Cotton Vitellius A.xv, fols. 172r–173r)

Of the eighteen total points, one is simply graphic (after the Roman numeral) and another is placed mid-line, line 1814. The rest come at the end of an alliterative line, with all but four coming at the end of a clause. Even this limited description, however, is useful as a starting point because it shows that most points come at a specific juncture of metre (end of the second half-line) and syntax (end of clause). In this passage, about two out of three points come at this position. On the other hand, the points do not come after any particular kind of clause (e.g. subordinate or principal) nor do they come after a specific metrical pattern. If Parkes's association of pointing and units of confusibles is applicable, then *Beowulf* has surprisingly few confusibles, and what precedes the point does not seem very confusing.

One of the more obvious advantages of the *Beowulf* pointing is that it facilitates scansion. In the prosody of classical Old English verse some pairs of half-lines are linked by three alliterating words and others by two, so at first glance a reader – even an experienced Anglo-Saxon reader – might not be certain where to end the first half-line, but the limits of both half-lines would be clear once the end of the second half-line were reached. It could save a good deal of backtracking and correction. Another advantage of the end-of-the-line points is that they give a fixed mark where the reader's eye can pause as it surveys the half-lines that come before and after. Perhaps the most significant feature about habits of reading suggested by the pointing is that where the basic unit of composition is the half-line (as revealed by formulas) the basic unit of reading may be the full line. If lines, rather than half-lines, were recited as complete units, the rhythm could give an interesting interplay between metrical phrasing and syntactic phrasing, especially where the syntax spills over from one line to the next, as it often does in enjambed clauses of *Beowulf*.

Most studies of pointing pay attention to what precedes the point, because we naturally think of punctuation as ending a passage. But where every half-line ends another one begins, and where every clause ends another clause begins. While this observation may seem like a statement of the obvious, when we shift our perspective and observe what comes *after* the manuscript points, even more interesting patterns emerge.

Clause-Initial Dips

In the *Beowulf* manuscript, many points fall just before a recognizable metrical and syntactic pattern at the beginning of the alliterative line. There are, on the average, about 20 points every 100 lines. In every 100 lines there are also about 35 clauses that begin with the first half-line rather than in the middle of the line. I call these **a**-clauses. If the points were distributed randomly at the end of verse lines, which is also to say at the beginning of verse lines, then we could expect roughly 7 points per 100 lines to coincide with the beginning of an **a**-clause. Instead we have over 14 points. In other words, more than 14 out of the 20 points per 100 lines fall at the beginning of a half-line at the beginning of a clause. The proportion is far more than what could be expected from random distribution.

This position can be defined further. Of all points that come before an **a**-clause, 7 out of 10 precede a clause dip. A clause dip can briefly be defined as a run of metrically unstressed syllables at the beginning of a clause, and it typically contains semantically light words such as conjunctions, personal pronouns, adverbs and auxiliaries. Old English prosody favours the semantically weighty nominals and their equivalents for the metrically stressed and alliterating positions, and it groups together the semantically lighter words into one position at the beginning of the clause (Kuhn 1933; Momma 1997). The semantically light words in this position are most often metrically unstressed. The syntax of the clause immediately following a point can also be characterized. About 7 out of 10 points begin principal clauses, and many in our standard editions begin new paragraphs.

The text of *Beowulf* was transcribed by two hands, now identified by the unpoetic names of Scribe A and Scribe B, and the passage reproduced here comes near the end of Scribe A's stint. Altogether it has eighteen points, only one breaking up the full line. Twelve come before clause openings; ten of these before metrical dips. Three examples would be the very first line in the sample passage, 1777, line 1787 and line 1829. They illustrate the three most common kinds of half-lines with a clause dip. However, not every clause dip is preceded by a point (for example 1780a).

Of the other points in the sample passage, two separate elements in apposition, one breaks up an alliterative run-on, and one follows the roman numeral at the beginning of a fitt. I will return to these later. I should mention that even in placing points before certain kinds of half-lines, the scribes still marked the point as belonging to the preceding clause, for the simple reason that no point begins a manuscript line, though many end one. One can draw a parallel with the modern colon: graphically it belongs to the anterior clause, but it anticipates something following it.

A special kind of clause dip is illustrated in the very first line: *Ic þære socne* (*Beo* 1777a). Half-lines like these, commonly known as Type A3 after the system of scansion developed by Eduard Sievers, are limited to the on-verse (also called the a-verse) and postpone the alliterating syllable to the second of the two possible positions (Sievers 1893). Sievers would assign metrical stress to the first syllable to give the half-line two stresses, but Bliss calls them metrically light verses, with stress only on the alliterating syllable (Bliss 1967). Other metrists generally adopt one scansion or the other, but however scanned, such half-lines are often preceded by a point; in this passage other examples are lines 1782, 1799, 1807, 1822 and 1826. One of the more controversial elements of Bliss's system of scansion is his treatment of clauses with an initial alliterating verb such as those in line 1799 (*reste hine þa rumheort*) and line 1807 (*Heht þa se hearda*). For these he argues that the alliteration of the initial verb is ornamental, that the verb does not bear metrical stress, and that they too are what he calls light verses. These "light" half-lines are especially likely to be preceded by a point, as the two examples cited here show, although what that coincidence means is not clear. Some have detected a more specific association between half-lines of Sievers' metrical Type A3 and the beginning of *principal* clauses – as opposed to clauses in general (Stanley 1992).

The association of the pointing with metrical and syntactical features in the *Beowulf* manuscript shows up even more clearly in the differences in the pointing of Scribe A, who copied up to line 1939, and Scribe B, who copied the rest. Their general similarity is well known (Malone 1963: 29–32; O'Brien O'Keeffe 1990: 175–9). Both scribes point at approximately equal rates, and both avoid mid-line pointing, which suggests that they simply carried over the punctuation from their copytext. Despite the similar rates, however, they show specific differences in the placement of the points. Scribe A is considerably more consistent in pointing before **a**-clauses, and places over 70 per cent of the points at the end of one clause and the beginning of another. Scribe B's rate is only about 50 per cent. Scribe B is also responsible for six folios with twice the average number of points, many of which do not come at the end of a clause. This variation is a reminder that scribes did not all point alike, and we will very likely never know how their copytext affected their pointing.

The inceptive half-lines with clause dips make up an important part of Old English verse grammar, which seeks to explain the features of poetry in a way that combines metre and syntax. Thus half-lines like *þa wæs eft swa ær* are the focus of much recent work on verse grammar, but it is not necessary to go into a technical discussion to demonstrate the importance of the semantically light words in such constructions. They concentrate a significant amount of grammatical information in one position at the beginning of the clause. The crucial role of this position was formulated in a seminal article about seventy years ago by Hans Kuhn, and in the intervening years his observations or laws have undergone a good deal of revision and criticism (Blockley 2001; Donoghue 1997; Kendall 1991; Kuhn 1933; Momma 1997). What remains clear, however, is the correlation between the initial clause dips and a category of words that includes clausal conjunctions, personal pronouns, adverbs, the verb of being and auxiliary verbs. When these are grouped together at the beginning of the clause, they remain unstressed. If any such word appears anywhere else it is found in a metrically stressed position. Of course clausal conjunctions and subject pronouns can be expected at the beginning, so Kuhn's *Gesetz* is of no great consequence to them. It has important consequences, however, on the others: adverbs, non-lexical verbs and personal pronouns in oblique cases. At the same time the role of initial clause dips helps explain why certain element orders fail to appear in the poetry. Line 1841 provides a clear illustration:

> þe þa wordcwydas   wigtig drihten
> on sefan sende

> the wise Lord sent these utterances into your mind.

The first word is the dative pronoun *þē*, and is unstressed at the beginning of the clause. Its location and lack of metrical stress are typical. But what we never find, or almost never find, in Old English poetry is an element order that reverses the sequence of two initial half-lines:

> *wigtig drihten   þe þa wordcwydas

The new element order would be Subject, Indirect Object, Object, Verb, a more conventional (or prose-like) order than the poem's IndO O S V (Mitchell 1985: 10). The key to the workings of verse grammar is the unstressed pronoun *þē*. Neither the rules of syntax by themselves nor the rules of metre by themselves are able to account for the absence of clauses like the hypothetical *wigtig drihten þē þa wordcwydas*. Whenever a word like the pronoun *þē* is bumped from the initial unstressed position, it lands in a position of metrical stress, as illustrated by the line just before the last example, line 1840:

> Hroðgar maþelode   him on ondsware

> Hrothgar spoke in answer to him.

where the displaced dative pronoun *him* participates in the alliteration and stress. A displaced and stressed pronoun like *him* in 1841 is unusual, but a displaced and unstressed pronoun like my hypothetical *þē* is quite rare. The same goes for other words in this category, such as auxiliaries, the verb of being and many adverbs.

The relevance of this discussion to punctuation is that an Anglo-Saxon reader, coming across a cluster of these unstressed words, would immediately detect the beginning of a clause. The same reader, coming across my hypothetical line, might assume, mistakenly, that the clause begins with *þē*, because verse grammar would condition such an interpretation.

Thus the clause dips can serve two functions for a reader: they signal clause boundaries and (as individual words) provide grammatical information. Because graphic cues like punctuation also signal clause boundaries and provide grammatical information, verse grammar may make graphic cues less necessary. But there remains a need for punctuation, which still has an important, complementary role to play. Even if the points are too unsystematic and too sparse to constitute what Parkes calls a "grammar of legibility", their features make them hard to dismiss. If they make sense within a context of grammar at all, it is a more comprehensive context, one that works together with verse grammar.

Other Uses for Punctuation

Even after incorporating the pointing into my expanded notion of system, however, quite a few marks of punctuation remain unaccounted for. I am not concerned with pointing that is solely graphic – for example, those around roman numerals or around runic signs or multiplied at the end of a poem. While the remaining textual points cannot all be accommodated in a hierarchical syntactic system like that of modern English, many of them have a more localized function (Dunning & Bliss 1969: 11). One such function is to mark out adjacent elements in apposition, as in the passage reproduced from *Beowulf*, in line 1810, where *þone guðwine godne* is separated from the apposed adjective, *wigcræftigne*. Another example is on line 1792, *geat unigmetes wel · | rofne randwigan.* A second localized use is to mark half-line boundaries where the alliteration seems to continue from the end of one line to the beginning of the next, for example, the ð-alliteration between lines 1837 and 1838. A third localized use in *Beowulf* is pointing before the formula X *maþelode*, as for example in line 1840.

These five uses of the raised point – before clause-initial dips, to signal elements in apposition, to break up alliterative runs, before the formula X *maþelode* and graphical marks – account for all but three marks of punctuation in the passage reproduced above. Other passages in *Beowulf* have more stray points, especially on some folios where Scribe B suddenly increased the rate of pointing, as mentioned earlier. But for most of the poem, these five account for most of the points, with the bulk falling before a clause-initial dip. Thus clause-initial dips helped shape an incipient system of punctuation, but at the same time verse grammar reduced the need to make that system comprehensive.

Variance in Punctuation

I do not want to overstate the strength of the association between pointing and clause-initial dips. While other poetic manuscripts show similar patterns, the practice varies from one to the next. The Junius manuscript, for example, is unusual in its placement of a raised point after most half-lines, which reduces the pointing to a purely metrical function with little relevance to syntax. Another reminder of the variability of scribal practice can be found in the two *Soul and Body* poems from two composite manuscripts, the Exeter Book and the Vercelli Book (Moffat 1990). In the 120 or so lines that the two versions have in common, the placement of points coincides thirteen times. All but one come at the end of a long line and before an initial clause dip. This coincidence may suggest that the scribes recognized the usefulness of pointing before clause dips, but the number of instances where the points do not coincide obscures the picture. The Exeter version has another thirteen points, all of which come at the end of the line, and the Vercelli version has another forty, many of which come in the middle of the long line. What we see in the Vercelli version may be the cumulative effect of changes introduced by a succession of scribes, where the addition of points has weakened the association with verse grammar.

Nonetheless, the incidence of pointing before clause-initial dips in *Beowulf* and other poems is significant. The pattern does not answer all our questions – it is not systematic enough to make up a grammar of legibility – but the scribal marks work in a complementary fashion with verse grammar, and together they contribute to the oral/literary matrix that has been the focus of much recent work. This explanation goes some distance towards making sense of what otherwise would appear to be needlessly vestigial. Modern readers cannot rely on a native speaker's intuitive knowledge of verse grammar. However, the scribal practices employed in *Beowulf* and other manuscripts support Mitchell's fundamental insights that our edited texts can benefit from lighter punctuation and that a specially designed system can bring out the richness of the poetry that might otherwise escape the modern reader. In fact most manuscript points in *Beowulf* coincide with some mark of punctuation in Mitchell and Irvine's edition. The manuscript is so sparingly marked, however, that it makes the "light" punctuation in Mitchell-Irvine seem copious in comparison. The consensus about manuscript punctuation that I mentioned at the beginning – that it is not quite systematic, not quite random – may still hold, but it is clearly more systematic than we have supposed.

References and Further Reading

Anon. (1982). *The Chicago Manual of Style: for authors, editors, and copywriters*, 13th edn. Chicago, IL: University of Chicago Press.

Bliss, A. J. (1967). *The Metre of Beowulf*, rev. edn. Oxford: Basil Blackwell.

Clemoes, P. (1980). *Liturgical Influence on Punctuation in Late Old English and Early Middle English Manuscripts*. Binghamton, NY: CEMERS SUNY-Binghamton (repr. of 1952 paper).

Donoghue, D. (1997). Language matters. In K. O'Brien O'Keeffe (ed.), *Reading Old English Texts* (pp. 59–78). Cambridge: Cambridge University Press.

Kendall, C. B. (1991). *The Metrical Grammar of* Beowulf. Cambridge: Cambridge University Press.

Mitchell, B. (1998). *The Dream of the Rood* repunctuated. In P. S. Baker & N. Howe (eds) (pp. 143–58).

Moffat, D. (ed.) (1990). *The Old English Soul and Body*. Wolfeboro, NH: D. S. Brewer.

Parkes, M. B. (1978). Punctuation, or pause and effect. In J. J. Murphy (ed.), *Medieval Eloquence: studies in the theory and practice of medieval rhetoric* (pp. 127–42). Berkeley, CA: University of California Press.

Parkes, M. B. (1987). Contributions of insular scribes of the seventh and eighth centuries to the 'grammar of legibility'. In A. Maierù (ed.), *Grafia e Interpunzione del Latino nel Medioevo* (pp. 15–30). Rome: Edizioni dell'Ateneo.

Parkes, M. B. (1993). *Pause and Effect: an introduction to the history of punctuation in the west*. Berkeley, CA: University of California Press.

Parkes, M. B. (1997). *Rædan, Areccan, Smeagan*: how the Anglo-Saxons read. *ASE*, 26, 1–22.

Stanley, E. G. (1992). Initial clusters of unstressed syllables in half-lines of *Beowulf*. In M. Korhammer (ed.), *Words, Texts and Manuscripts: studies in Anglo-Saxon culture presented to Helmut Gneuss* (pp. 263–84). Cambridge: D. S. Brewer.

Chapter 3

The Incomparable Wryness of Old English Poetry

Roberta Frank

English conversation thrives on understatement. Guidebooks to the English "way of life" still alert non-native speakers to curiosities such as: "Do you want a lift home?" "I wouldn't mind." "A piece of chocolate?" "I won't say no." "Are you happy at Harvard?" "Not entirely." "I have a headache." "You don't say." "That's his new wife." "Not bad." "He has had *a bit* to drink" = 'He's plastered.' "Jason has eaten *enough*" = 'too much'. One cultural critic puts understatement first in his list of 77 phenomena exposing the peculiar character of the British. Peter Ackroyd, searching in Anglo-Saxon England for the origins of the English imagination, speaks knowingly of a common "fierce reticence", a "brevity or understatement, fading into silence". "Instead of asking what is 'modern' about the Anglo-Saxons", he urges, "inquire instead what is Anglo-Saxon about 'the modern'".

How Anglo-Saxons actually spoke to one another in byre and tavern is forever lost. Perhaps they were exquisitely restrained and reserved; perhaps they were mean windbags, confusing nastiness with smarts. Speakers in Old English poetry, however, even the villains, display excruciatingly good manners. In *Beowulf*, a beefy breaker-of-rings gives a king his deathblow and the narrator does not say with Seamus Heaney "he swung his arm", but instead observes drily: "[his] hand did not hold back the blow" (*Beo* 1520). In *ChristA*, the speaker politely begs Christ "Don't tarry too long" (*ChristA* 373) – meaning 'Hurry up'. The wolf in *Maxims I* "does not weep over the slaughtered" (*Max I* 150), a wry way of noting that the prospect of dining makes that carrion beast deliriously happy. This distinctive tone is largely absent from Old English prose. Indeed, the presence in homiletic discourse of a reticent, negative observation such as "that plan *did not profit* them" (= it was a total disaster) indicates that the speaker is here quoting vernacular poetry (Wright 2002). Two centuries later, Old Norse prose is famous for its understated rhetoric. Hrefna in *Laxdœla saga* explains delicately to her mother-in-law why she doesn't want to wear that headdress to the party: "Many people say that it is not unexpected that I may come to places where I have fewer folk to envy me than at Laugar." Saga understatements range from extended compliments ("Your troop seems not altogether unpromising nor altogether certain of being annihilated") to stiff-upper-lip responses to danger, as when Sinfjötli (in *Beowulf*, Fitela) finds a poisonous snake in his bread-dough and kneads it in: "I am not without suspicion that there was not something alive in the meal." For some reason, Anglo-Saxon England restricted this tone to vernacular poetry.

Much else separated Old English poetry from prose. Bruce Mitchell refers in the final sections of his magisterial *Old English Syntax* (1985) to "problems peculiar to the poetry" (*OES*: §§3944–7), "problems related to the poetry" (ch. 10) and "problems affecting the poetry" ("Conclusion"). Studies over the last 20 years have confirmed his belief that verse syntax follows a different drummer (Donoghue 1987; Momma 1997; Blockley 2001). Vernacular poetry and prose also differ in vocabulary. Some words occur only in prose (Stanley 1971); many occur exclusively or almost exclusively in verse. Compounds in which the first element does not modify the second ("battle-warrior") and kennings in which the first element clarifies a mysterious second ("bone-vessel" = body) are typical of verse. The presence of such poetic words in a piece of rhythmical discourse helps to push it over the edge, into the leafy-green region of verse (Stanley 1985; Frank 1994). Orthography and morphology also distinguish the two modes. Poetry has a pervasive northern colouring: the West-Saxon scribe of the prose *Boethius* writes normal West-Saxon *ceald* 'cold' and *adwæscð* 'he quenches'; the same passages subsequently turned into verse have the differently spelled and pronounced *cald* and *adwæsceð* (Stanley 1994: 159–63). Poetry is also distinguished by the use of variation or apposition, the repetition in different words of the same sentence-element, as well as by the use of formulaic diction and themes. And then there is tone, a speaker's attitude to his audience. That of Old English prose is quite variable, ranging as it does from laws and medical recipes to history and romance. But verse, like a *New Yorker* editor, seems to have imposed a distinct house-style on its contributors.

A Predilection for Understatement

It does not take long for beginning students of Old English to encounter the term "litotes", a device "not uncommon in Anglo-Saxon poetry", as Roy Liuzza has litotically observed (Liuzza 2000: 54). In their *Guide to Old English*, Bruce Mitchell and Fred Robinson speak of "the Anglo-Saxons' predilection for understatement" (Mitchell & Robinson 2001: 273). Eric Stanley refers to "litotes, common in Old English" (Stanley 1994: 195). Even general handbooks to literature know that litotes is one of the "characteristic figures of speech of Old English poetry" (Harmon & Holman 1996: 293). Yet the terse, evaluative comments that punctuate every longer Old English poem have inspired only one general study, that of Frederick Bracher (1937), based on his unpublished 1934 Berkeley doctoral dissertation.

Given the range of hypothetical possibilities, the kinds of understatement actually allowed in Old English verse are severely restricted. The most frequent type in modern English and classical Latin epic – the denied negative – is avoided by Anglo-Saxon poets. One searches through the verse corpus in vain for the vernacular equivalent of *vir non indoctus*. There is no certain example in the thirty-thousand lines of Old English poetry of "a not unlearned man", "a not uninteresting essay", "a not unjustifiable assumption" or "my lips are not yet unsealed" (said by British Prime Minister Stanley Baldwin in 1935 when questioned about the crisis in Ethiopia and usually misquoted). This fastidiousness of the Anglo-Saxon poet would have gratified George Orwell, who famously recommended as cure for this verbal disease memorizing the sentence: "A not unblack dog was chasing a not unsmall rabbit across a not ungreen field." Nor did the verse of the Anglo-Saxons provide a home for that *bête-noire* of the Fowlers, the placing of a qualifying adverb before an emphatic word: "somewhat filthy", "a little extraordinary", "a trifle appalled", "a shade dismayed". In the novel *Mr Golightly's Holiday* (2003), God indulges in just this kind of verbal tentativeness, confessing at one point to being "slightly trepidatious". Anglo-Saxon poets would not have allowed anyone, even a woman, to speak in this lily-livered way. They did have a weakness for undenied negative modifiers such as *unfæger* 'unbeautiful' (= hideous) or *unleof* 'unloved' (= despised), a fondness shared by Seamus Heaney. But while Heaney's poetic coinages –

unstingable, unscarfing, unshiftably, un-get-roundable, unkindled, unclenched, unroofed, unbleeding, undrowned – evoke for us the absence of something, we cannot determine which Old English *un*-words would have struck contemporaries as "positives", like "unhappy" (= sad or miserable rather than 'not happy') in current English.

The basic type of Old English poetic understatement is *negatio contrarii,* 'denying the opposite': "that is not a fair joy" (= [hell] is indescribably awful); "that is not an excellent dwelling-place" (= hell is a real hole). An important subtype ("understating the contrary") substitutes for "not" a minimalizing adjective or adverb: a chatterbox is "little silent" (meaning *'not at all* silent' = voluble); a killing flood supplies "water enough" (= an immense quantity); the Egyptians experience "few worldly joys" (= total devastation). Context in each instance indicates that the poet is understating a situation and not simply reporting a fact. There is an inherent fuzziness or imprecision in such evaluations, foreshadowing the basic fact of modern physics that "nothing can ever be measured with perfect accuracy" (Gell-Mann 1994: 26).

The Old English verse rendition of *Boethius* uses both types of understatement. Having accused the Arian Theodoric of beheading Pope John, the poet asserts: *næs ðæt hærlic dæd* 'that was not a noble deed' (*Met* meter 1, 43). But how bad was it? A few pages later, naughty Nero sets Rome afire for the fun of it: *næs þæt herlic dæd* 'that was not a noble deed' (*Met* meter 9, 18), notes the speaker, again leaving the degree of depravity open – anything in the range from "rather" wicked to "exceedingly" so. When Boethius points out that men, unlike animals, possess the faculty of reason, the highest of the three Platonic properties of the soul, the Old English poet enthusiastically interjects: *nis ðæt scandlic cræft* 'that is not a shameful power' (*Met* meter 20, 188). And when Boethius proposes that men do not fish for salmon on mountains or hunt for deer in the seas, the Old English poet uses a minimalizing adverb to give this argument some bite: "You might think that you will seek them [the deer] *oftor micle* 'far more often' (= always) in the woods than out at sea" (*Met* meter 19, 17–19). None of these four sardonic observations is found in Boethius's original Latin nor in the Old English prose translation from which the verse was derived. Like make-up and high heels, the poet's negations and diminutions intimate without being specific, keeping things sane and funny.

Some understatements convey polite contempt towards an enemy. As Saint Andrew drowns a city of cannibals, the *Andreas* poet gloats: "The cupbearers, the serving-men, did not delay; there was at once enough drink ready for everyone" (*And* 1533–5). We are assured that the saint's slayer "did not end up surrounded by laughter" (*And* 1702–3). Saint Juliana refuses to marry her passionately pagan suitor "unless", she says sardonically, "he more eagerly worships the God of hosts than he has yet done" (*Jul* 109–10). The narrator continues: "Her father in his fury replied to her angrily – not at all did he promise ornaments" (*Jul* 117–18); indeed, he swore to feed her to wild beasts. A pagan judge commands Juliana's head to be cut off and the poet observes: "That death did not profit him" (*Jul* 605). The poem concludes with the saint's tormenters on their way to hell: "The warriors in that dark house, the band of comrades in that low pit, had no need to expect appointed treasures from that lord, that they, on the ale-bench of a wine-hall, might receive rings, burnished gold" (*Jul* 683–8). To convey indescribable suffering, the poet calls a more pleasant situation to mind – and then cancels it through negation, leaving all other possibilities weakly asserted. Old Norse skalds used such negative comparisons to convey grim amusement at their own situation: "In battle it was *not* at all like laying a beautiful woman beside oneself on the bed", or "in battle it was *not* like kissing a young widow on the high seat." Famously, the first translators of these verses did not recognize that an *-at* suffixed to the verb meant 'not', that the skald was recording absence, not presence. The image of the Viking has never been the same.

"Bygone Politesse" in *Beowulf*

Readers have long marvelled at the "non-heroic reflectiveness" of *Beowulf*. The poem is rich in terse, negative evaluations that surface every 30 lines or so. (Its 3182 lines represent about one-tenth of the entire Old English poetic corpus, but they contain almost a third of its "na"s, "no"s and "nealles"s, plus 64 examples of *ne* + verb.) The narrator and his male characters practise ostentatious self-restraint. "Hrothgar did not fail to carry out his vow" (= he distributed rings as if there were no tomorrow; *Beo* 80). "Cain did not rejoice in that crime" (= God sent him packing; *Beo* 109). Grendel "mourned not at all for his crimes" (= he was a happy camper; *Beo* 136–7); "he didn't want to sue for peace or pay wergild" (= he preferred to eat and run; *Beo* 154–8); "his life was not useful to men" (*Beo* 793–4), "nor did his death seem painful to them" (= it was party-time at Heorot; *Beo* 841–2). "None of the counsellors needed to expect bright compensation from the killer's hands" (= a gaping wound was more likely; *Beo* 841–2). "The sea-monsters got no joy at feasting" (= they were slain before the first course; *Beo* 563). There are almost a hundred such "denials of the contrary" in *Beowulf*. Scyld's funeral ship is "loaded with no fewer treasures than had come with him over the waves" (*Beo* 43–6). "Death is not easy (= impossible) to avoid" (*Beo* 1002–3). Hrothgar's men "did not at all find fault with their king" (= they praised him to the skies; *Beo* 862). Grendel's mother seized Hrothgar's favourite: "that was not a good exchange" (*Beo* 1304). The hellish mere is "not a pleasant place" (*Beo* 1372), its brave conqueror, not "slow of valour" (*Beo* 1529), his legendary sword, not "the smallest of powerful helps" (*Beo* 1455). Beowulf decapitates Grendel with a giant sword: "the edge was not useless" (*Beo* 1595). The coastguard did not greet the departing Beowulf "with insults" (*Beo* 1892): hugs and kisses would have been more in order. The fair wind by no means hindered the ship in its journey (*Beo* 1907–8). Young Beowulf was not more hated by Hrethel than any of the latter's sons (= the king loved him as his own child; *Beo* 2432–3). Grown up, he did not lack rewards (*Beo* 660) or have to be ashamed of them (*Beo* 1025–6). Hildeburh had no need to praise the good faith of the Jutes (= their treachery destroyed all she loved; *Beo* 1071–2). Hygd was not stingy or too sparing of gifts (*Beo* 1929–30); Thryth's was not queenly behaviour (*Beo* 940); Beowulf's was not that of a coward (*Beo* 541); Eofor did not hold back the mortal blow (*Beo* 2489). Looking back at his long life, Beowulf boasts that, with him around, Hygelac had no need to search far afield for a worse warrior (= he already had the greatest; *Beo* 2493–6). In the fight with the dragon, Beowulf did not boast of glorious victory (= death was imminent; *Beo* 2583). Wiglaf reports that his first venture inside the mound had been granted "not at all pleasantly" (= a resident dragon had first to be overcome; *Beo* 3089). Like Homer ("not then would you divine Atrides see inactive, nor yet loath to fight"), the narrator regularly bestows praise not by adding up virtues but by subtracting faults. Beowulf by no means slew his closest companions at their drink – his heart was not savage (*Beo* 2179–80). As death approaches, the hero recites a do-it-yourself obituary: he never caused the death of kinsmen (*Beo* 2742) and never engaged in military adventurism (*Beo* 2738). He leaves it to others to supply what remains unsaid.

Characters in the poem sometimes say "never" or "always" indirectly, through adverbs such as "not much" "little" and "often". Enumerating his feats, Beowulf boasts that he does "not brag about it *much*" (*Beo* 586), meaning 'not at all'. When the messenger reports the king's death to his followers, "*little* (= not at all) was he silent with his news" (*Beo* 2897); "he did not lie *much* (= at all) in words or facts" (*Beo* 3029–30). Among Beowulf's last words: "I did not seek treacherous quarrels, nor did I *much* (= at all) perjure myself" (*Beo* 2738–9). Beowulf sets out for Denmark: "wise men *little* (= not at all) dissuaded him from that journey" (*Beo* 202–3). Warriors rush to haul out the dragon's gold: "*little* (= not at all) did anyone mourn that they quickly carried the loot from the vault" (*Beo* 3129–30). Beowulf survives a raging ocean: "fate *often* (= always) protects the undoomed man" (*Beo* 572–3). He praises his sword, which "early and late *often* (= always) stood by [him]" (*Beo* 2499–500). It was the custom of the Geats that they "*often* (= always) were ready for action" (*Beo* 1247). Beowulf relates that Eofor's hand "remembered *enough* (= many) hostile acts" and "did not hold back the mortal blow" (*Beo* 488–9). Wiglaf assures those accompanying him into the cave that they will there see *enough* (= many) treasures from close up (*Beo* 3104). Such verbal restraint is, as Stanley observed, "redolent of what appears to be, for the poet and his contemporaries, a bygone politesse" (Stanley 1998: 96).

Down-toners like "not ... much", "little", "often" and "enough" are an essential part of the fabric of *Beowulf*. When Seamus Heaney (2000) boldly translates Old English *no ic þæs fela gylpe* ('I don't brag about it much') as "I don't boast", or removes "often" from "the sword that often stood me in good stead late and soon", the earlier poet's voice seems muffled. When Heaney renders Old English *lyt ænig mearn* ('little did anyone mourn') as "it was no trouble", or *snotere ceorlas lythwon logon* ('wise men little dissuaded him') as "nobody tried to keep him from going", the urbanity of the original begins to dissolve. Shades of meaning vanish when a negative construction such as *ne wæs þæt gewrixle til* ('that was not a good exchange') becomes "the bargain was hard". Sometimes ignoring an understatement fatally injures the sense. Heaney renders the Anglo-Saxon narrator's dry observation *feorhsweng ne ofteah* ('[Eofor's hand] did not hold back the mortal blow' (= he struck hard; *Beo* 2489) as "his [Ongentheow's] feud-calloused hand could not stave off the fatal stroke." Without the anchors of litotes and meiosis, even the finest of translators slowly drifts away from "the Anglo-Saxon sea-floor".

Decorous Self-Restraint in Other Old English Poems

An adverbial down-toner appears in what may be the earliest surviving Old English poem. The two-line *Proverb from Winfrid's Time*, embedded in an early eighth-century Latin letter, is introduced with the words "remember the Anglo-Saxon saying: The man slow in action often (= always) puts off glory, puts off every victorious exploit; therefore he dies alone" (Stanley 1974). Datable poems from the end of the Anglo-Saxon period are notably rich in understatement. *The Battle of Brunanburh* (after 937) includes a number of sarcastic asides, including "the Mercians did not refuse battle to the Northmen" (= they jumped at the opportunity, *Brun* 24–8) and "the defeated had no need to boast, to exult, or to rejoice at that battle" (= laments were the order of the day for them, *Brun* 39–40 and 44–7). In *The Battle of Maldon* (after 991), Byrhtferth scornfully answers the Viking invaders: "We'll give you payment in war-gear that will not benefit you in battle" (= it will cost you your lives, *Mald* 48). Edward, reports the poet, "did not withhold the blow" (*Mald* 118). The English deserters "did not care for the battle" (= they ran like rabbits, *Mald* 192). Both Ælfwine and Leofsunu declare that the folks back home "will not be able to reproach [them]" for retreating from the fray (= their choice to fight and die will bring public praise; *Mald* 220 and 249–52). In Old English verse, the speech of the best and the brightest, as well as of the worst and the foulest, drips with rhetorical reserve. God in *Genesis B* pleads with the first couple to behave: "there will not be a lack of good things for you" (*GenB* 236). A little later, Satan is tempting Eve, humankind is about to fall, but the narrator, translating from Old Saxon, keeps his perspective: "Not at all did [the devil] preach what was advantageous" (*GenB* 610). Christ in the Old Saxon *Heliand* uses similar language to scold the Pharisees: "That will not turn out to your benefit" (3818).

Anglo-Saxon poets take for granted that their audiences are acquainted with Judaeo-Christian story. "That was not a one-day hostility" (*Max I* 193) dryly notes *Maxims I* with reference to Cain's slaying of Abel. In *Genesis A*, Abimelech discreetly asks Abraham for a return favour: "Show me kindness, since I was not grudging to you of land and delights" (*GenA* 2824–5). The narrator of *The Fates of the Apostles* expects his hearers to know that James was the first apostle to suffer martyrdom: "Nor was his brother [James] slow, sluggish in the journey [to death]" (*Fates* 33–4). He soon praises Simon and Thaddeus in similar terms: "These two were not sluggish with respect to the battle" (*Fates* 75). Similarly, a basic knowledge of northern legend is prerequisite for enjoying the understatements of *Widsith, Deor, Waldere* and *Beowulf*. As with biblical lore, there is the pleasure of sharing in an erudite game. Widsith names the celebrated hero Guthhere, famed over a wide area and for a long time: "That was not a sluggish king" (*Wid* 67). The speaker visits Ermanaric's esteemed companions Widia and Hama and reports: "They were not the worst of retainers" (*Wid* 125). We hear that Widia's illustrious but unlucky father, Weland the smith, "often (= continually) endured misery" (*Deor* 4). Unferth's sword Hrunting, famous for its excellence, "was not the smallest of powerful helps" (*Beo* 1455). Northern legend was something people had to know, like claret, cricket and chess, if they wanted to be thought cultivated.

The massing of adverbial down-toners like "often", "few", "much", "enough" quickly colours a speaker "aristocratic", as in the following passage from *The Wanderer* (see also Chapter 5):

> Wat se þe cunnað,
> 30 hu sliþen bið   sorg to geferan,
> þam þe him *lyt* hafað   leofra geholena ...

> Forþon wat se þe   sceal his winedryhtnes
> leofes larcwidum   *longe* forþolian:
> ðonne sorg ond slæp   somod ætgædre
> 40 earmne anhogan   *oft* gebindað ...

> swimmað *oft* on weg.
> Fleotendra ferð   *no* þær *fela* bringeð
> 55 cuðra cwidegiedda.   Cearo bið geniwad
> þam þe sendan sceal   *swiþe geneahhe*
> ofer waþema gebind   werigne sefan.

This reticent speaker, described by Fred Robinson and Bruce Mitchell as a "heroic-age nobleman" (Mitchell & Robinson 2001: 268), muses over his painful lot. He has "few (= no) dear companions" (*Wan* 31); he speaks as one who "must long (= forever) do without his beloved lord's counsels" (*Wan* 38); in his dreams, "when sorrow and sleep both together often (continually?) bind the wretched solitary one" (*Wan* 40), the imagined, remembered kinsmen "often (= always) drift away" (*Wan* 53), like the seabirds; they bring there "not many (= no) known utterances" (*Wan* 55).

"Sorrow is renewed for the one who must often enough (= always) send his exhausted mind over the binding of the waves" (*Wan* 55–7). The Wanderer's stiff upper lip, his self-restraint, is portrayed as class-specific: "I know indeed," he says, "that it is an aristocratic custom for a noble-man to bind tight his heart ..." (*Wan* 11–14). His decorous, insistent down-toners, about one every five lines, support a vision of human life as bounded and needy; no lament is adequate. The stoic hero of Tennyson's *Ulysses* is almost as reticent: he says "not to fail" for "succeed splendidly", "not unbecoming" for "completely appropriate", "not least" for "greatest" and "it little profits" for "it profits not at all". The voice of the Viking-age Norse poet conveys a similar reserve.

Reticence in Viking-Age Skaldic Poetry

The skalds who flocked to Cnut's court in southern England seem addicted to the terse, the ironic, the negatively put. There is an intimate tone, implying a personal relationship, a watchfulness, between speaker and audience. They evaluate Cnut's achievements cautiously and vaguely. Too much clarity could prove counterproductive: in the late Viking Age it did not take much to turn a gift-giving prince into a homicidal maniac.

"The sailing of the warrior was not wretched" is how one skald describes the splendour of Cnut's glistening armada; a second skald confides: "Svein's son was not sluggish in the test" (in other words, Cnut was a real tiger); "He gave to helmets not a little difficulty" (= he smashed skulls right and left); "few ring-givers," observes Sighvatr of his prince, "will have thus measured with feet the road south" (no northern king ever before walked to Rome). When Cnut fought battles "ravens did not starve" (understatement for 'corpses were piled high as far as the eye could see').

Cnut's skalds do their best to avoid boorish frankness, dogmatism, grandiloquence or heated assertions when addressing the king directly. Óttarr the Black offers such temperate compliments as: "no great delight, I think, you took in quiet, king"; "No mean battle you won by Thames bank"; and "you got yourself enough of a name there." There is respect, along with an overt lack of commitment. The court poets of Viking-age Scandinavia speak with self-deprecating wryness of themselves. After a great slaughter, the skald says: "I think the prince won a victory there", meaning: 'It couldn't be clearer, I saw with my own eyes that . . .'; the same poet's dry observation "I don't think gold will diminish for the king's troops" predicts that their reward will be great indeed.

If Norse poets are not usually thought of as understated and self-effacing, it is not their fault. Translators of skaldic poetry have done their best to remove negatives and minimalizing adverbs from the texts. The skald Bragi Boddason described Thor's fishing for the world-serpent, a myth portrayed in several Viking-age stones. The monster when hooked gave such a tug on the line that the god's foot went through the bottom of the boat. Bragi's stanza says urbanely: "The fishing-line of Viðrir's [Odin's] heir [Thor] lay by no means slack on Eynæfir's ski [ship]." This has been translated as 'His line was strained hard on to the gunwale.' Another early skald, Þjóðólfr of Hvin, speaks of a goddess whose apples kept the gods young. She was abducted and brought to the home of the "dwellers of the steep cliffs" (giants), who, says the skald, "were not upset at that" (= they were deliriously happy). The standard translation reads: "the giants were joyful." Another skald, Illugi, describes that famous moment in northern legend when Sigurd penetrated the wall of flame around Brynhild's hall: "The valiant prince did not have a swift ride to the woman's dwelling." The Old English poet describes the equally pivotal moment when Beowulf is forced to back off from the dragon: "That was not an easy journey" (*Beo* 2586).

A pride of understatements runs through skaldic court poetry of the late tenth and early eleventh centuries: "the raven's beak was not lacking in blood" (= corpses were everywhere); "Harald's death did not bring me wealth" (= I lost my lord and patron); "they did not give way in battle" (= they rushed the enemy); "treachery was not hidden" (= there was open warfare); "they did not ask again for such an outcome for themselves" (= they couldn't after being slain); "I drank not altogether joyful a drink at Yule" (= I was miserable – I lost my best friend); "the all-ruler did not pay back the Danes scantily for their deceit" (= he wiped them out). Minimalizing adjectives and adverbs, where circumstances call for a maximum, are everywhere: "enough (= great) battle was there"; "most (= all) see"; "few (= no one) waited for wounds from him" (= everyone ran away); "not a few (= a multitude of) corpses floated along the shore"; "the flight of spears was little (= not at all) restrained"; "middling-free of deceit (= deceitful)"; "late (= never) will my grief let up"; "the dull sword bit least (= not at all)". A particular poetics encourages or reinforces a particular take on reality. In the Old English *Soul and*

Body poem, a soul, released from hell to visit his decayed body, quietly sums things up: *Nis nu se ende to god* 'the end is not now too good.' He sounds like a northern gentleman.

Applications

Increasing our sensitivity to Old English poetic understatement can have practical benefits. Sometimes light is shed on the interpretation of a puzzling passage. Saturn's complaint about "fate" in *Solomon and Saturn II* (*Hwæt, hie wile lifigende late aðreotan | ðæt heo ðurh fyrena geflitu fæhðo ne tydre*; *Sol* 449–50) contains an adverb, *late* 'slowly' (= never) long misread by editors. Faulty translations include Kemble's "Lo! She [i.e. fate] will the living slowly oppress, that she through conflict of crimes feud engender not" and Dobbie's "Lo, it living, will be wearied at last, so that it will not propagate enmity through the conflict of crimes." Menner was first to grasp the meaning of Saturn's sad litotes: "Lo, as long as she [i.e. fate] lives, she will be slow to tire [i.e. she will never tire] of engendering enmity by means of sinful disputes." Old Saturn knows of what he speaks.

Sometimes the particular effect that an author sought through understatement becomes a little clearer. When *The Wanderer* says "a wise man must not be too hot-hearted or too hasty of speech" (*Wan* 66), it is talking about traits not merely undesirable in excess, as Mitchell pointed out 35 years ago (1968). When the narrator of *Guthlac B* says of Adam and Eve that "they wearied *too soon* of performing the will of God" (*GuthB* 844), he is not suggesting that they should have waited another hour or two before their fatal *déjeuner sur l'herbe*. The poet of *Judgement Day I* is urging haste when he tells his audience: "He who wishes to live with God must not be too slow or too sluggish concerning these teachings" (*JDay I* 88). The Deity is exquisitely polite when he reassures Saint Matthew: "Don't be *too* (= at all) afraid" (*And* 97). One and only one Anglo-Saxon prose writer used this type of understatement – and did so non-stop. Wulfstan, archbishop of York until his death in 1023, was exceptionally fond of urbane assertions like "we anger God *more than we need to*" and "wrongdoing . . . happens *too widely* among men on earth." When he says "be neither *too* deceitful nor *too* untrustworthy", he means, like the Wanderer, "not at all." His lament that "*too* many sins reigned in the land" does not champion evil in moderation. Wulfstan is especially attached to the formula *ealles to swiðe | ealles to gelome* 'All too often', adding it to the familiar words of the Lord's Prayer ("do not lead us into temptation *all too often*" (= never). His rewriting of Ælfric's injunction ("don't drink in a tavern, nor be drunk") as "don't drink in taverns *all too often*, nor be *too* drunk" does not commend the occasional pub-crawl. Nor does his reworking of an earlier law against enslavement ("let not Christians and innocents be sold out of the country") as "let not Christians be sold out of the country *all too often*" give permission to do so once in a while. Adverbial phrases like these not only distinguish Wulfstan's prose style from that of his contemporaries, but associate it with the oral tradition of vernacular verse (Orchard 1992, 2002).

A third productive approach to Old English poetic understatement is to examine the distribution of individual litotic expressions. A poet who hit upon a pleasing formulation was likely to repeat it. At least two of Cynewulf's "denials of the opposite" are unique to his signed poems – and to *Guthlac B*. In *Elene*, the narrator refers to a ravenous wolf that *wælrune ne mað* 'did not hide its murderous intent' (*El* 28) and to a praying bishop who *hygerune ne mað* 'did not hide his heart's intent' (*El* 1098). The only other *x ne mað* in the entire corpus occurs when a weeping servant reports Guthlac's death: *he þa wyrd ne mað* 'he did not hide that event' (*GuthB* 1345). The litotic sentence *ic ne þearf behlyhhan . . .* 'I have no need to rejoice over . . .' has a similar distribution. The devil overcome by Saint Juliana laments: *ic bihlyhhan ne þearf . . . siðfæt þisne* 'I have no need to rejoice . . . over this venture' (*Jul* 526). Saint Guthlac's servant announces (bizarrely to our ears) his sorrow over that saint's death: *Huru ic swiðe ne þearf hinsið behlehhan* 'Indeed, I have no need to rejoice greatly at [his] departure' (*GuthB* 1357). Just as Cynewulf's evocative plays on *rod* 'cross' and *rodor* 'heaven' serve to sign three poems irrevocably his (Frank 1972: 210–11), so, too, the presence of sets of parallel understatements suggests a relationship between his two poetic saints' lives and *Guthlac B*.

Reading Wryness

Immodesty now has cachet in the sports arena, in personal ads, and in contemporary trash-talk and hip-hop braggadocio. Beowulf wore his bigness differently. Horace's much quoted lines about the immortality of poetry begin with a boast: "I have executed a memorial longer lasting than bronze . . ." The northern poet shared this hope but expressed it modestly and wryly: an Old Norse ode is "a not eager-to-be-broken (= strong, solid) praise pile"; it is a "slow-to-grow-old (= unforgettable, lasting) ship of the dwarves [poem]." Like these skalds, the characters of Old English poetry, whether Old Testament patriarchs, Christian saints or Roman villains, have a sense of proportion. Their insouciance and panache, indirections and reticences, their tentative asides and aristocratic disdain for heroics, are northernisms for which there is no northern name. To appreciate the distance between our expectations and those of an Anglo-Saxon audience is a first step in increasing our sensitivity to a major aspect of Old English style.

References and Further Reading

Bracher, F. (1937). Understatement in Old English poetry. *PMLA*, 52, 915–34. Repr. in J. B. Bessinger & S. J. Kahrl (eds) (1968) (pp. 228–54).

Donoghue, D. (1987). *Style in Old English Poetry: the test of the auxiliary*, Yale Studies in English, 196. New Haven, CT: Yale University Press.

Frank, R. (1972). Some uses of paronomasia in Old English scriptural verse. *Speculum*, 47, 207–26. Repr. in R. M. Liuzza (ed.) (2002). *The Poems of MS Junius 11* (pp. 69–98). London: Routledge.

Frank, R. (1994). Poetic words in late Old English prose. In M. Godden, D. Gray & T. Hoad (eds) (pp. 87–107).

Gell-Mann, M. (1994). *The Quark and the Jaguar: adventures in the simple and the complex*. New York: W. H. Freeman.

Harmon, W. & Holman, C. H. (1996). *A Handbook to Literature*, 7th edn. Upper Saddle River, NJ: Prentice Hall.

Harris, A. L. (1988). Litotes and superlative in *Beowulf*. *ES*, 69, 1–11.

Heaney, S. (2000). *Beowulf: a new verse translation*. New York: Farrar, Straus & Giroux.

Hoffmann, M. E. (1987). *Negatio Contrarii: a study of Latin litotes*. Assen/Maastricht, Netherlands: Van Gorcum.

Hollander, L. M. (1938). Litotes in Old Norse. *PMLA*, 53, 1–33.

Hübner, A. (1930). *Die 'mhd. Ironie' oder die Litotes im Altdeutschen* (Palaestra, 170). Leipzig: Mayer & Müller.

Orchard, A. (1992). Crying wolf: oral style and the *Sermones Lupi*. *ASE*, 21, 239–64.

Orchard, A. (2002). On editing Wulfstan. In E. Treharne & S. Rosser (eds) (pp. 311–40).

Stanley, E. G. (1971). Studies in the prosaic vocabulary of Old English verse. *NM*, 72, 385–418.

Stanley, E. G. (1974). The oldest English poetry now extant. *Poetica* (Tokyo), 2, 1–24. Repr. in E. G. Stanley (1987). *A Collection of Papers with Emphasis on Old English Literature* (pp. 115–38), Publications of the Dictionary of Old English, 3. Toronto: Pontifical Institute of Mediaeval Studies Press.

Stanley, E. G. (1985). *The Judgement of the Damned*, from Corpus Christi College, Cambridge 201 and other manuscripts, and the definition of Old English verse. In M. Lapidge & H. Gneuss (eds) (pp. 363–91). Repr. in E. G. Stanley (1987). *A Collection of Papers with Emphasis on Old English Literature* (pp. 352–83), Publications of the Dictionary of Old English, 3. Toronto: Pontifical Institute of Mediaeval Studies.

Stanley, E. G. (1998). Courtliness and courtesy in *Beowulf*. In P. S. Baker & N. Howe (eds) (pp. 67–103).

Wright, C. D. (2002). More Old English poetry in Vercelli Homily XXI. In E. Treharne & S. Rosser (eds) (pp. 245–62).

Chapter 4

Straining Words and Striving Voices: Polysemy and Ambiguity and the Importance of Context in the Disclosure of Meaning

Antonette diPaolo Healey

The first business of a dictionary . . . is to give the meanings of the words in plain Modern English, discriminating clearly the different meanings of each word . . . The ambiguity of many English words makes it difficult to define meanings with certainty without full quotations. The best method is to add part of the context.

(Sweet 1896: ix)

Words strain,
Crack and sometimes break, under the burden,
Under the tension, slip, slide, perish,
Decay with imprecision, will not stay in place,
Will not stay still.

(T. S. Eliot 1962: "Burnt Norton" V)

Henry Sweet, irascible but brilliant, understood the critical role of context in determining meaning. Although he had no high opinion of the Anglo-Saxon lexicography of his day and earlier, with the notable exceptions of Clark Hall's "great industry", of Toller's work and of his own (Sweet 1896: v–vi, xi), he recognized that his little *Student's Dictionary of Anglo-Saxon* was necessarily a compromise too. Intended to be an authorized abridgement of Bosworth and Toller for the beginner, its terms of reference did not allow space for full quotation (Sweet 1896: v). This was obviously a concern, for while acknowledging that extensive quotation is "quite incompatible with the nature of a concise dictionary", he also noted that "quotations are next in importance to definitions" (Sweet 1896: ix). Indeed, he was no doubt aware, as are all practising lexicographers, that meaning and sense distinctions are not only illustrated by but are discerned from the quotations, those segments of text which furnish the basis for our verbal taxonomies (Silva 2000: 89). Sweet's pragmatic solution for complex words was to contextualize his definitions by listing their referents enclosed within parentheses. So, for example, under the adjective *fæst*, we find, among others, the definitions 'firm, fixed, stiff (soil)', 'heavy (sleep)', 'steadfast, firm (mind, faith)' and 'religious, Christian (book)'. Or again under the verb *feallan*, we discover the metaphoric sense 'fall (into vice)' together with 'flow (*of* river)', 'come to an end, decay (*of* kingdom)' and 'fall (in battle)'. Sweet's practice, in fact, anticipated the emphasis of modern linguistics on the influence of context (Ullmann 1962: 168). He knew both intuitively and experientially, without the guidance of a fully articulated theory of semantics, that we determine the meaning of a word primarily through analysis of its context. This principle has now the nature of a "general truth" articulated in standard histories of the language: "words are defined by their relationship to other words" (Smith 1996: 116), and in encyclopedias of language: "meaning is studied by making detailed analyses of the way words . . . are used in specific contexts" (Crystal 1997: 102). It follows that polysemy, the ability of a word to have more than one conceptual meaning, will not lead to confusion as long as only one meaning makes sense in any given context.

"Making sense" was Sweet's enterprise. Lacking Toller's characteristic self-effacement and modesty (Bankert 2003: 301; Proud 2003: 343), Sweet viewed his own lexicographic foray, despite its narrower compass, as an unparalleled advance: "In conclusion, I venture to say that, whatever may be the faults and defects of this work, I believe it to be the most trustworthy Anglo-Saxon dictionary that has yet appeared" (Sweet 1896: xi). His confidence arose from his avoidance of the most flagrant errors of his predecessors. The particular objects of his disdain were those Anglo-Saxon dictionaries, such as Leo's *Angelsächsisches Glossar*, which, with seeming abandon (Sweet's term was "recklessness"), invent "new forms and meanings" or embody "an enormous number of spurious words and meanings" (Sweet 1896: v–vi). Their "uncritical" stance offended his exact scholarship, one based on original research on the manuscripts and the testing of the evidence of his predecessors. Drawing upon the parable of the wheat and the chaff, he laments the labour required in separating the *"grains* of wheat" from the *"mass* of chaff" (Sweet 1896: vi; my emphasis). The gleaning of lexical items in earlier dictionaries succinctly images Sweet's point: dictionaries composed largely of fabrications have little value. He resolved that his dictionary would be different from the others through his exercise of judgement from the first moment of compilation: "I have tried, as a general rule, to keep doubtful matter out of the dictionary" (Sweet 1896: vii). If ghost words never entered the dictionary at the outset, they could not import spurious meanings. Sweet's penchant for exclusion perhaps arose from a deep concern for the authority wielded by dictionaries of English and their makers, for from the seventeenth century on they had come to define not only individual words but what constituted "the language" itself (Curzan 2000: 96).

The essence of scholarship, as Peter Baker has recently reminded us in speaking of Toller's deep engagement with the lexicographic conversation of his own day and of the past, is the "listening, accepting, modifying, rejecting, giving all back in a new form" (Baker 2003: 294). Although we would probably view Sweet's posture towards his predecessors and contemporaries as less benign than Toller's, more "rejecting" than "accepting", his brief Preface to his *Student's Dictionary of Anglo-Saxon* shows an acute understanding of the heart of lexicography, the distinguishing of meaning. This was certainly not a new concern for him, but one of long standing. It emerged clearly 25 years earlier in the Preface to his edition of King Alfred's translation of Gregory the Great's *Pastoral Care*, a prose text which he considered lexicographically "of high importance" because of the number of rare words, many of which, apparently, occurred nowhere else. According to Sweet, much of this vocabulary had made its way into dictionaries, although, unfortunately, "often in a corrupt form, or with inaccurate renderings" (Sweet 1871: vi). And, as Sweet was quick to point out, some of the vocabulary was recorded now only by him for the first time.

It is instructive to look at Sweet's theory of translation, articulated in the Preface to his edition and translation of the *Pastoral Care*, to comprehend how he would arrive at definitions for his *Dictionary*. Tellingly, Sweet had little use for an English translation of the Old English text, as required at the time by the Early English Text Society series. His dismissal is not out of idiosyncratic pique but from scholarly rectitude. To acquire proper competence in a language, he states, a grammar and dictionary are required (Sweet 1871: ix); no mere translation will suffice. However, if a translation must be provided, his will be based on the Old English text and not the Latin source:

> My principle throughout has been to ask myself the question, What ideas would this sentence suggest to a ninth century Englishman, unacquainted with the original? and to frame my translation accordingly. In many obscure passages, however, I have been obliged to consider what meaning the translators themselves intended to convey, and only as a last resource have I occasionally translated from the Latin. (Sweet 1871: ix–x)

The self-portrait of Sweet imaginatively entering into the world of his "ninth century Englishman", trying to understand his language and habit of mind, as it were, from the inside, is remarkable.

This manifest sensitivity to Anglo-Saxon culture, one which acknowledges difference between then and now and accepts the difference sympathetically, cannot have been arrived at easily. Eric Stanley, writing nearly 125 years after Sweet, describes the "deliberate act of imagining" (Stanley 1994: 246) required on his own part to re-enact the sense of wonder at the divine which, he argues, permeates the literature of the Anglo-Saxons. In turn, Katherine O'Brien O'Keeffe has reminded us of the crucial, but sometimes neglected, fact that we are not the audience for whom these early medieval texts were written (O'Brien O'Keeffe 1994: 148–9). Others have remarked on the strangeness or distance of the voices (Frank 1997: 491–2), or cautioned against reading into this literature of old our contemporary concerns and seeing it simply as a reflection of our present selves (Healey 2003: 254), or questioned specifically whether the Anglo-Saxons had our kind of social conscience (the answer is "no", Stanley 2003: 264). Sweet, as editor, translator and lexicographer, presciently anticipated some of the current attitudes toward our literary past, especially our concern with "understanding the texts on their own terms" (Robinson 1997: 8). We have come to expect no less from his original mind, justly praised for its ability "to look at any linguistic topic . . . in a new theoretical light" (MacMahon 1998: 170). No doubt Sweet would have concurred with his posthumous reputation, for while alive, he judged himself as "wider and more original" than Napier (to whom he lost the Merton Professorship) – although "less accurate", he admitted, with characteristically unflinching candour (Ker 1970: 154). Sweet's cogent assessment of the importance of context, both immediate and, more broadly, cultural, for the discrimination of sense gives to his little

dictionary an astonishing authority still today. Even his selection of
the dominant West-Saxon dialect, although of the earlier period, for his
headword spellings was a pioneering influence on the selection of late
West-Saxon as the preferred spelling for headwords in the *Dictionary of
Old English* (*DOE*).

The Power of Context

Following the lexicographic tradition of Sweet in paying particular
attention to context, I wish to describe a few types of semantic development – shifts in application, specialization of meaning, figurative language,
wordplay – and their treatment in the *Dictionary of Old English*. Unless
otherwise noted, editions, short titles, and systems of reference for Old
English texts are those given in *DOE*. Most of my examples are drawn
from the recently published letter *F* (Cameron et al. 2003). As lexicographers, we are indebted to scholars in various fields of our discipline
for charting particular areas of uncertainty and ambiguity. We certainly
will not be able to resolve all difficulties, but by attending closely to the
formulation of the problem by experts from their individual perspectives,
we may see more clearly the parameters within which useful inquiry
can progress. Syntacticians, for instance, have alerted us to their own
minefields of ambiguity. Bruce Mitchell, propelled by his research to the
interface between syntax and lexicography, has helpfully focused the
discussion on specific questions of polysemy. His enabling remarks,
encompassing a wide sweep, provide new directions for further lexicographic inquiry: are real distinctions being made in translating *self* as
'self' or 'very' or 'same' (*OES*: §494)? Is it ever possible for *oþþe* 'or',
which marks exclusion, to carry the sense 'and', which marks no exclusion
(*OES*: §1751)? As a translation of *hwilc* 'every, each', when is 'any one'
possible or even preferable (*OES*: §422)? Can *mōdig* in poetry tolerate a
translation such as 'in the mood/of a mind' in addition to 'brave' (*OES*:
§3474)? How does one capture the various meanings of *eornostlīce, sōþlīce,
witodlīce*, given the range of Latin words they translate (*OES*: §3168)? So
far, only the last question has been partly addressed by the editors of the
DOE through their treatment of *eornostlīce*. Here we have taken guidance
from Mitchell's articulation of the problem: it is through looking at the
Latin terms which *eornostlīce* translates that we can approximate its
semantic range. Such directed challenges from experts help lexicographers

of Old English to interrogate more precisely the words before them, and perhaps advance our understanding of the language.

Shifts in application

One productive source of polysemy in Old English, as in present day English, is shifts in the application of a word. In dictionaries, senses are often clearly demarcated, perhaps with an exactness that may be unwarranted. Frequently, meanings simply shade into one another, as lexicographers look for the appropriate translation terms for individual contexts. Although shifts in application can be found among various word-classes, it is a particularly effective agent of polysemy among adjectives. To take a very simple example, the adjective *fals* 'false', occurring seven times in the Old English corpus, can be variously translated, depending on the noun it modifies. When applied to weights, it means 'violating legal standards', i.e. 'not truly adjusted'; when describing money, it means 'counterfeit', i.e. 'spurious, not genuine'; when depicting people, it means 'intending to defraud', i.e. 'deceitful', so that a *fals mynetere*, literally a 'false minter' is a 'counterfeiter' (*DOE* s.v. *fals* adj.). Although each of these applications can be described as 'false' in some way, it is the noun which controls the precise shade of meaning. As a result, we come to regard each of these applications as different senses.

A more complex example is the adjective *fæst*, one of the adjectives for which Sweet in his little *Dictionary* indicated referents. If we reconfigure the *DOE* entry for *fæst* 'firm' according to the nouns it modifies, its semantic richness becomes apparent. As the outline below shows, four main groupings can be discerned: People, Concretes, Abstracts and States.

I   People, their attributes, feelings, etc.

   1a   steadfast, constant (positive)
   1b   stubborn, unyielding, obstinate (negative)
   2   fast (on a deathbed/in a grave/in torments)
   3   strong, secure, ?impenetrable (band of soldiers in battle array)

II   Concretes

   1   firmly fixed in place or position (stone, anchor, wall, star, etc.)
   2   attached/bound to a spot
   2a   firmly attached/held fast to or by something (tent, tree, sail, ship, hair of the head, etc.)

2b firmly tied, not easily loosed (band, knot, fetter, etc.)

    2b(i) constipated (bowels)

    2b(ii) fast (clasp, embrace)

    2b(iii) solid, hard (frost)

3 shut fast, secured (door, lock)

4a firm, solid; not readily yielding to pressure or impact (column, wall, building, a joining, etc.)

4b firm, dense, having a close consistency (ground, soil)

5 strong, fortified, secure from intrusion (island, house, city, fortification, refuge, etc.)

5a shut up, shut tight (room, enclosure)

5b watertight (vessel/bottle)

5c dense (grove, wood)

III Abstracts

1a unchangeable, permanent, enduring (positive)

1b stubborn, intractable (negative)

2a firm, fast (alliance)

2b binding, immutable (legal settlement/agreement)

2c strict (principle, rule)

IV States

1 deep, sound (sleep)

2 permanent (residence)

There are two striking features in this display of senses. First, there is no evidence in the Old English period of *fæst* branching into a second main meaning, the one which predominates today, 'rapid, quick'. This other branch arose only in the Middle English period and, according to the OED (s.v. *fast* a. sense II), it apparently developed in the adverb first and then transferred to the adjective. The earliest quotation for the sense 'quick, speedy, swift (movement or process)' cited by the *MED* is from c. 1395 and is found in the Franklin's Tale, F.1066: *Prey hire she go no* **faster** *cours than ye*. The second notable feature in the outline above is how heavily weighted is the evidence towards concrete nouns. As we move from one category of concrete noun to the next, we can see the adjective taking on precise colourings. Although each of these senses can be classified as 'firm' in some way, it is the noun which gives exactitude to the adjective. The collocation which presented the greatest uncertainty, and which is not represented above under the classification of "concretes", was *fæst boc*, which Sweet rendered as 'religious, Christian book'.

However, there is no evidence that the simplex *fæst* ever means 'religious' or 'Christian'. The expression is found in the Old English *Orosius*, Book 6, Chapter 31: *þa wæs he [Iulianus] sona geornfull þæt he wolde diegellice þone cristendom onwendan, 7 forbead openlice þæt mon nane* **fæste** *boc ne leornode* 'then was he [Julian] immediately eager to subvert Christianity secretly and he openly forbid any man to learn the "fast-book"' (Bately 1980: 150.14). There is no corresponding Latin at this point for 'fast-book' to help us understand what may have been intended; however, Bately's note on this point is illuminating. She suggests that the text may be corrupt and could be an error for either of two words meaning 'pious' – *ārfæst* or *ǣfæst* (Bately 1980: 335). The phrase has elsewhere been interpreted as 'fast-book, penitential' with *fæst* equivalent to or an endingless form of *fæsten*[2] 'fast, abstinence', for which there is no other evidence in Old English. The *DOE*, also uncertain about the meaning of the phrase, but assuming the manuscript reading is correct, gives it a separate sense, and suggests three possibilities for *fæst boc*: ?reputable, ?serious, ?standard book. These adjectives as renderings of *fæst* are only guesses, attempts at suggesting how *fæst* and *boc* might be construed together, informed solely by the range of meanings listed earlier. None of the concrete applications above, however, offers any secure guidance, because *fæst* does not modify any other item comparable with "book". Does *fæst* refer to the content of the book ('serious')? Or to its reception ('reputable', 'standard')? Our effort to make sense of the manuscript reading underscores the importance of the noun in determining the appropriate meaning of the adjective. Shift in application is the primary agent in the development of meaning in adjectives like *fæst*.

Specialization of meaning

William Safire has recently called attention to the fact that the meaning of a word may change, depending upon the profession or environment in which it is spoken (Safire 2004: 15). For each category of professional, specialist, etc. a word may convey one meaning that will naturally arise before all the others. Safire's example is the word "actionable", which to lawyers means 'subject or liable to an action at law' or, in other words, 'providing grounds for a lawsuit'. Safire cites the first quotation given under the headword in the *OED*, William Lambarde's 1591 complaint that his client had been "[b]aited, and bitten with libells and slanders that be not actionable". However, as Safire has noticed, "actionable" has now broadened and undergone a semantic shift, apparently under the press of military duty, so that today it also means 'that which can be acted on' as in the phrase "actionable intelligence".

This feature of specialization has been present in English from the start. Old English provides us with many examples of words that have developed specialized senses within a particular sphere from the more general framework of ordinary language. The noun *fyll²*, occurring 55 times in the Old English corpus and conveying various senses meaning 'fall', from 'fall from a height' to 'collapse (of a wall, building, structure)', to 'death specifically by a fall (in battle)', to 'downfall, ruin, destruction', etc., also carries a specialized grammatical sense, 'case, inflection' (*DOE fyll²* sense 8), as does its rarer cognate form *feall* (*DOE feall* sense 2). Similarly, the past participle *gefēged* conveying the general sense 'put together, joined, united', when used as a grammatical term means 'compounded' (*DOE gefēged* sense 1.b.i), so that Ælfric in his *Grammar* can write "from *fido* is **compounded** *confido*". Its cognate forms *gefēgednes, (ge)fēging, gefēgnes*, all of which in general mean either 'framework' or 'joining', have, in addition, the specifically grammatical sense 'conjunction'. Historical records of various sorts are particularly productive, though not the only, sources of specialized legal senses. In a tenth-century will, Ælfgar can use the verb *forwyrcan¹* in a legal sense as he urges his children not 'to set aside' or 'annul' his will (*DOE forwyrcan¹* sense B.2.a) against the verb's more general meanings 'to misuse, hurt, destroy'. Or *flēam*, used to denote 'fleeing' of various sorts, such as in cowardice or defeat, in captivity or danger, can be appropriated by the legal system in *Law II Cnut* to describe the hardest flight of all, 'the banishment, exile (of an outlaw)' (*DOE flēam* sense 4.b). The one so exiled is labelled a *flȳma*, as is a 'fugitive from justice' (*DOE flȳma* sense 4), a specifically legal development from a general term for any fugitive fleeing danger, persecution, etc. This outlaw, wherever possible, might seek *friþstōw*, here 'a place of refuge for a fugitive, sanctuary' (*DOE friþstōw* sense a), a technical development of the personal sense 'refuge, asylum' in this Alfredian compound. In the restricted sphere of medicine, ordinary verbs such as *flēogan* and *flēon*, both of which can mean 'to flee', have developed the specific sense 'to avoid some foods/deleterious substance'; *forhabban*, usually 'to restrain, hold in check', describes a medical condition in the phrase *beon innan forhæfd* 'to be constipated'. Similarly, the phrase *fyr settan on*, literally 'to set fire on', in a medical context means 'to cauterize' (*DOE fȳr* sense 10).

Specialization pushed to its limits occurs when a common noun becomes a place name. Some well-known examples are *bæþ* "Bath", *blæcpōl* "Blackpool", *burh* "Peterborough" and "Borough Green, Cambridgeshire", *ceaster* "Chester" from the noun for 'fortification; town' (from the *castrum* of the Roman legions in Britain), and from the evidence of fourteenth-century documents, *cēapstōw* "Cheapstow" from the noun for 'market-place'. We have not yet discovered in the Old English corpus evidence for the type of specialization noticed by Ullmann for a later period of English where "a common noun virtually becomes a proper name denoting a single object in a particular environment" (Ullmann 1962: 162), such as in many well-known London landmarks: the Abbey, the House, the Tower, the Yard, etc. Nevertheless, the previous examples from the restricted categories of grammar, law and medicine, to take but a few, indicate how productive specialization is, in the creation of polysemous words.

Figurative language

Polysemy based on metaphor can be seen in Old English in many expressions which still survive in Modern English: **floor** of ice (*DOE flōr* sense 1.f.), **flood** of blood or tears (*DOE flōd* sense 5.b), **field** of study (*DOE feld* sense 2.b), **bosom** of the earth (*DOE fæþm* sense 1.a), **vessel** of death (*DOE fæt* sense 1.e.iii), etc. However, we may be unfamiliar with the expression "**fatness** of mind" (*DOE fǣttnes* sense 1) as a metaphor for wisdom, or "**feet** of the soul" (*DOE fōt* sense 1.a.iv) as a bold Augustinian metaphor for the love of God and men, imported into the language of the Anglo-Saxons (Healey 2004: 143–4). We all may know that Satan is the "**father**" of lies (*DOE fæder* sense B.3), but be unaware that Fate is the "**father** (and mother)" of sins (*DOE fæder* sense B.5). In each case the metaphorical transposition works because we are conscious at some level of the literal meaning of the word.

Even the most prosaic verbs in the language provide examples of figurative uses. The phrase "to fare on" in the sense 'to rush upon, assault (someone)' is uniquely recorded for 1535 in a literal sense by *OED* (s.v. *fare* v.[1] sense I.1.d) in William Stewart's *The Buik of the Croniclis of Scotland*. (I.10.342), where Gathelus "rushes upon" his enemies: *He . . .* **fuir on** *thame with sic a felloun force.* However, more than five centuries earlier, Old English poetry furnishes a figurative use of the phrase in *Seafarer* 91 where "old age advances upon/assails [each man], his face turns pale, gray-haired he mourns": *yldo him* **on fareð**, *onsyn blacað, gomelfeax gnornað* (with the preposition preceding rather than following the verb). *MED* s.v. *fāren* does not record anything comparable. The Old English example (*DOE faran* sense I.C.4.a) not only antedates the *OED* citation but fills out the history of the phrase by supplying a clearly figurative attestation. However, it is important to notice that this figurative citation in Old English coexists with literal examples in the early period where an assailant, an army, a commander etc. "advances upon (with hostility), moves forward against, i.e. attacks (someone)" (*DOE faran* sense I.C.4). Both senses exist side by side and enlarge our understanding of the meaning of the verb.

Another surprising figurative usage was identified by *DOE* under the noun "frost" (*DOE forst* sense 1.d). In the late tenth century, Ælfric uses the expression *ehtnesse forst* 'frost of persecution' in an extended metaphorical passage in which he depicts the plight of the Holy Innocents, those "blossoms of martyrs" growing up amid the "chill of unbelief":

> hi [the Innocents] sind gehatene martyra blostman. for ðan ðe hi wæron swa swa upaspringende blostman · on middeweardan cyle ungeleaffulnysse. swilce mid sumere ehtnysse **forste** forsodene
>
> they are called blossoms of martyrs because they were as blossoms springing up amid the chill of unbelief, consumed, as it were, by the frost of some persecution.
>
> (*ÆCHom* I, 5 220.105–7)

Although Ælfric is indebted to *Sermo 222* of Caesarius of Arles for the metaphor (*quaedam persecutionis* **pruina**), this is the first appearance in English of a figurative sense of "frost". Eric Stanley has noted (personal communication) that there is nothing quite like this, according to the *OED*, until late in the sixteenth century, with "frost of cares" appearing in the 1595 edition of *Caxton's Blanchardyn and Eglantine* (Kellner 1890: 214.16). The *DOE* has distinguished the Old English metaphor from the other literal senses of "frost", and recorded a figurative sense which will have a later and longer history.

Metonymy, a figure of speech where an attribute stands for the whole, is another source of polysemy. In the Anglo-Saxon Laws a "free hearth" means a 'household of or belonging to a free man' (*DOE frēo* adj. sense A.1.b.iv) where "hearth" is used as typical of the 'household' or 'home'. The Old English examples anticipate Coriolanus to Aufidius: "Now this extremity / Hath brought me to thy hearth" (*Cor* IV.v.85). This near identification of "hearth" with "home", begun in the Old English period, eventually gives rise in the mid-nineteenth century to the alliterative phrase "hearth and home", first cited by the *OED* for 1857, an expression now cloyingly familiar. The Victorian phrase makes explicit what in Old English is metonymically implied. Both cases, however, enlarge the concept of "hearth" to a wider domestic relationship, and the noun acquires an additional meaning.

Words in play

To fix meaning in a language not spoken for almost a thousand years is never easy. Frequently, composers of Old English, especially the poets, make the work of lexicographers even more challenging by deliberately playing on ambiguity. Which word is precisely meant? Is it this word? Or another? Or more usually, both? Is the ambiguity purposely left unresolved so that listeners/readers are compelled to approximate the meaning by holding the alternatives in the mind simultaneously? For lexicographers this conflicted state, a twilight space of indecision and uneasy balance, has to be resolved in some measure – at least sufficiently to file the intractable quotation under a headword. Roberta Frank's "reasoned plausibility" (Frank 1997: 497) is perhaps the most we can expect to achieve, given our lack of native informants. Yet even when a decision is reached, signs of its arbitrary nature trace a pattern of uncertainty in the *Dictionary*. Perhaps Anatoly Liberman's depiction of etymologists may apply in equal fashion to lexicographers: "Hesitations and discord beset [them], and being uncertain is their lot" (Liberman 2003: 111).

Homonyms, where etymologically unrelated words share the same form, are especially difficult. Traditionally, they are treated as separate words in the dictionaries because of their different etymologies (Healey 2004: 138). The *DOE*, for example, distinguishes the adjectives *fāh*[1] 'at feud, hostile' (related to *fæhþ* 'feud') and *fāh*[2] with its three main senses 'variegated; stained; shining' (related to *fæn, fǣgan* 'to colour/paint'). Stanley has recently cited this particular pair of adjectives as early examples of the "untranslatableness" of wordplay in English because there is aural/visual wordplay as well as play upon sense (Stanley 2001: 348). Their separation is, at times, problematic, as the following two examples illustrate. In *Genesis A*, the serpent of Eden is described as a **fah** *wyrm* which speaks *þurh fægir word* (*GenA* 899). Is this a 'hostile' worm

(*DOE fāh*[1] [related to 'feud'] sense *e*), which deceives Eve by masking its enmity with fair words? Or is it a 'shining' serpent (*DOE fāh*[2] [related to 'to colour/paint'] sense 3), which lures Eve not only by its speech but also through its coruscating sinuousness? The *DOE* placed this particular example under *fāh*[1] 'hostile', yet we marked the text's (and our) ambivalence by suggesting that there might be a pun on *fāh*[2] in the sense 'shining'. Or again in *Christ and Satan*, fallen Lucifer depicts himself as *dædum* **fah**, *gewundod mid wommum* (*Sat* 155). Is he 'hostile' by deeds (i.e. actively hostile [cf. *DOE fāh*[1] sense a.iii]) as well as wounded by evils? Or is he 'stained' by deeds (*DOE fāh*[2] sense 2), besmirched and sullied by them, a state parallel to being wounded by wrongs? These juxtaposed senses from two different adjectives, "hostile" or "stained" (by deeds), are especially vexing because scholars have taken both to mean 'guilty' and have therefore blurred the original distinctions in sense and etymology. Yet this blurring may be a truer indication of the poet's intent where both "enmity" and "staining" blend in the minds of auditors/readers, and perhaps resolve themselves conceptually into the notion of guilt. The *DOE* filed this citation under *fāh*[2] in the sense 'stained' but commented that it has also been taken under *fāh*[1] 'hostile' and that the concept of guilt has been attached to both.

Deliberate punning, however, is not confined to homonyms in Old English. Even among the separate senses of an individual word, verbal play is evident. Again if we look at *fāh*[2], we notice that sense 2 'discoloured, stained, marked' and sense 3 'bright, shining, gleaming; adorned' are restricted to poetry. At times it is difficult to distinguish which of the two meanings is intended. Is Heorot, the best of houses, "stained" with blood or "shining" with blood (*Beo* 934) because of Grendel's ravages? When Beowulf rises from the mere with Grendel's head, is the surface of the water "discoloured" with blood or "bright" with blood (*Beo* 1631)? Is the sword which cuts through the opposing boar helmet "marked" with blood or "gleaming" with blood (*Beo* 1286)? Probably the *Beowulf* poet intended both and we ought not to limit his artistry by privileging only one interpretation. Although the *DOE* assigned these three examples to sense 2 'stained', we drew attention to the likely play on sense 3 'shining'.

Another intriguingly ambiguous pairing involves *fyrn*(-) 'ancient' and *firen*(-) 'sin(ful)'. Fred Robinson has offered tantalizing readings that suggest that the word-element *fyrn*(-) 'ancient, of old' may carry in some poetic contexts a specific sub-sense 'pre-Christian', referring either to the "heathen" period of the Germanic tribes, a semantic development found in cognate ON *forn*, or to the specifically pre-Christian period of the Old Testament (Robinson 1999). If Robinson's argument is accepted, this may help to explain the paronomastic punning which seems to occur between the *fyrn*(-) 'ancient' and *firen*(-) 'sin(ful)' word-families recently discussed by Samantha Zacher in her study of Cynewulfian orality (Zacher 2002: 366–7). In the *DOE* we found the orthographic and semantic convergence of *firenlic* with *fyrnlic*, for example, so complete – both adjectives being used attributively of sins and deeds – that we had difficulty distinguishing whether the acts/actions were 'sinful, wicked' (*firenlic*) or were 'committed in the past' (*fyrnlic*). An editorial note at the start of each entry signals the ambiguity.

Moreover, the Anglo-Saxon penchant for punning is not restricted to literary monuments. Even in the historical records, such as the *Anglo-Saxon Chronicle*, verbal play can refine the meaning of a word. I quote the passage in question from the Peterborough annal for 1086 [*recte* 1087] with the words in play bolded:

> Swylc coðe com on mannum. þæt fullneah æfre þe oðer man wearð on þam wyrrestan yfele. þet is on ðam **drife**. ⁊ þet swa stranglice. þæt mænige menn swulton on ðam yfele; . . . eala hu earmlice ⁊ hu reowlic tid wæs ða, ða ða wreccæ men lægen **fordrifene** fullneah to deaðe. ⁊ syððan com se scearpa hungor ⁊ adyde hi mid ealle.

> Such disease came on the people that very nearly every other person became ill with the worst disease, that is, with **fever**, and that so seriously that many people died of that disease . . . Oh, how miserable and how piteous a time it was then, when wretched people lay **fever-stricken** nearly to the point of death and afterwards sharp famine came and killed them off completely.

> (*ChronE* 1086.5–14)

Cecily Clark was the first to notice a "grim pun" in the chronicler's choice of participial *fordrifene* 'afflicted' and the noun *drif* 'fever' which precedes it at a little distance (which my ellipsis masks; Clark 1970: 74). She renders the participle as 'exhausted', focusing on the effect of fever. However, the question for the lexicographer is how explicit should we be in drawing the connection between the two words? Is it sufficient to note that there may be wordplay, and cautiously provide only an intensive definition such as Clark's 'exhausted' or Whitelock's earlier 'lay driven'

(Whitelock et al. 1961: 162), or Earle and Plummer's even earlier but less satisfactory 'drive[n] away' (Earle & Plummer 1892: I.334)? Or are we confident enough of the full context and the verbal punning to offer a bolder definition, one which incorporates the concept of fever into the very sense of *fordrifene* in this particular example? Although the distance between the two terms gave us momentary pause, we chose the latter strategy. We found Clark's suggestion of wordplay convincing (as has Stanley; 2003: 245 n. 17), and have gone further than she by defining the participle in this instance as 'ill with fever, fever-stricken', creating for it a separate sense (*DOE fordrīfan* sense 6), and supporting our reading with a cross-reference to the noun *drȳf*.

Conclusions

Shifts in application, specialization, figurative language and wordplay all suggest the inherent flexibility of language to accommodate itself to changing contexts, giving rise both to polysemy and, at times, ambiguity. The epigraph quoted from "Burnt Norton" at the start of this essay expresses in an uncommonly succinct way a particular kind of linguistic change. Although Eliot here seems to focus on the historical degradation of language rather than its innovation, he has captured the central fact of its movement. The pre-Modernist "development and decay" model which he seems to reflect would soon be followed by the "evolutionary" model of the Neo-grammarians with their universalizing principles (McMahon 2003: 140–1). Poised as we are at the start of the twenty-first century, looking back at a language of a thousand years ago and more, we have retreated from both objectivist certainty and generalizing hypotheses. Especially in the semantic analysis of a language as distant as Old English, circumspection is required. Sweet's principle of trying to understand Old English from the Anglo-Saxon point of view seems a good place to begin, if possible.

References and Further Reading

Baker, P. (2003). Toller at school: Joseph Bosworth, T. Northcote Toller, and the progress of Old English lexicography in the nineteenth century. In D. G. Scragg (ed.). *Textual and Material Culture in Anglo-Saxon England: Thomas*

Northcote Toller and the Toller Memorial Lectures (pp. 283–300). Cambridge: D. S. Brewer.

Bankert, D. A. (2003). T. Northcote Toller and the making of the *Supplement* to the *Anglo-Saxon Dictionary*. In D. G. Scragg (ed.). *Textual and Material Culture in Anglo-Saxon England: Thomas Northcote Toller and the Toller Memorial Lectures* (pp. 301–21). Cambridge: D. S. Brewer.

Crystal, D. (1997). *The Cambridge Encyclopedia of Language*, 2nd edn. Cambridge: Cambridge University Press.

Curzan, A. (2000). The compass of the vocabulary. In L. Mugglestone (ed.) (pp. 96–109).

Frank, R. (1997). The unbearable lightness of being a philologist. *JEGP*, 96, 486–513.

Healey, A. diP. (2003). Questions of fairness: fair, not fair, and foul. In M. C. Amodio & K. O'Brien O'Keeffe (eds), *Unlocking the Wordhord: Anglo-Saxon studies in memory of Edward B. Irving, Jr* (pp. 252–73). Toronto: University of Toronto Press.

Healey, A. diP. (2004). Polysemy and the *Dictionary of Old English*. In J. Coleman & A. McDermott (eds), *Historical Dictionaries and Historical Dictionary Research: papers from the International Conference on Historical Lexicography and Lexicology, at the University of Leicester, 2002* (Lexicographica Series Maior, 123) (pp. 137–47). Tübingen: Niemeyer.

Ker, N. R. (1970). A. S. Napier, 1853–1916. In J. L. Rosier (ed.) (pp. 152–81).

Liberman, A. (2003). Origin unknown. In D. Minkova & R. Stockwell (eds), *Studies in the History of the English Language: a millennial perspective* (pp. 109–23). Berlin: Mouton de Gruyter.

MacMahon, M. K. C. (1998). Henry Sweet (1845–1912). In H. Damico (ed.) with D. Fennema & K. Lenz, *Medieval Scholarship: biographical studies on the formation of a discipline*, vol. 2: *Literature and Philology* (pp. 167–75). New York: Garland.

McMahon, A. (2003). Language: "History is a nightmare from which I am trying to awake". In D. Bradshaw (ed.), *A Concise Companion to Modernism* (pp. 138–57). Oxford: Blackwell.

O'Brien O'Keeffe, K. (1994). Editing and the material text. In D. G. Scragg & P. E. Szarmach (eds), *The Editing of Old English: papers from the 1990 Manchester Conference* (pp. 147–54). Cambridge: D. S. Brewer.

Proud, J. (2003). Thomas Northcote Toller "This fearless and self-sacrificing knight of scholarship". In D. G. Scragg (ed.), *Textual and Material Culture in Anglo-Saxon England: Thomas Northcote Toller and the Toller Memorial Lectures* (pp. 333–45). Cambridge: D. S. Brewer.

Robinson, F. C. (1997). Introduction: transmitting what is preserved: how are we doing? In P. E. Szarmach & J. T. Rosenthal (eds) (pp. 1–10).

Robinson, F. C. (1999). A sub-sense of Old English *fyrn*(-). *NM*, C, 471–5.

Safire, W. (2004). Janus strikes again. *The New York Times Magazine*, 11 January, 15.

Silva, P. (2000). Time and meaning: sense and definition in the OED. In L. Mugglestone (ed.) (pp. 77–95).

Smith, J. (1996). *An Historical Study of English: function, form and change*. London: Routledge.

Stanley, E. G. (2001). Playing upon words, I. *NM*, CII, 339–56.

Stanley, E. G. (2003). Did the Anglo-Saxons have a social conscience like us? *Anglia*, 121, 238–64.

Sweet, H. (1896). *The Student's Dictionary of Anglo-Saxon*. Oxford: Clarendon Press.

Ullmann, S. (1962). *Semantics: an introduction to the science of meaning*. Oxford: Basil Blackwell.

Whitelock, D. with D. C. Douglas & S. I. Tucker (1961). *The Anglo-Saxon Chronicle: a revised translation*. London: Eyre & Spottiswoode.

Zacher, S. (2002). Cynewulf at the interface of literacy and orality: the evidence of the puns in *Elene*. *Oral Traditions*, 17, 346–87.

Chapter 5

"Eala, geferan and gode wyrhtan": On Interjections in Old English

Risto Hiltunen

Ælfric's Latin *Colloquy* and its Old English translation, from which the quotation above is taken ('Oh, companions and good workmen' – *Coll* 41), indicates that Ælfric was aware of the role and significance of interjections in language. He discusses interjections in some detail in his Latin grammar, where he introduces the term *betwuxtalegednys* as a calque of the Latin *interiectio*. He recognizes that interjections constitute a part of speech and that they can have several meanings: *forðan ðe he getacnað hwilon ðæs modes blisse, hwilon sarnysse, hwilon wundrunge and gehwæt* (*ÆGram* 278). He goes on to gloss individual Latin items in English, noting the connection between the meaning of the word and the way it is pronounced. He also points out that not all meanings translate into English. On the other hand, sometimes Latin and English have the same item for the same sense, as when *haha and hehe getacnjað hlehter on leden and on englisc, forðan ðe hi beoð hlichende geclypode* (*ÆGram* 279).

Even though such properties of interjections as those mentioned by Ælfric have probably always been acknowledged by grammarians, their full significance for communication does not appear to have been sufficiently appreciated by all of their successors, at least if we are to believe some of the most recent writers on this subject. According for example to Felix Ameka, editor of a special issue of the *Journal of Pragmatics* (vol. 18; 1992) devoted entirely to interjections, these have for the most part been ignored in theoretical linguistics, in spite of the fact that they form "a significant subset of those seemingly irrational devices that constitute the essence of communication" (Ameka 1992: 101). Such a statement reflects the upsurge of the study of spoken language in real time, and the modern technologies that have made this development possible. The results have indeed opened up new vistas into how inter-jections function in speech and what they contribute to the message in the contexts in which they occur.

In contrast to what contemporary spoken language has to offer to the investigator, the written texts of the distant past, such as the surviving corpus of Old English texts, can give us only a limited view of the factors governing communication. Even the most basic contextual information as to time and place of production often has to be reconstructed on the basis of incidental – and accidental – information. The lack of direct evidence as to authentic pronunciation, intonation and stress patterns is another serious limitation, as Bruce Mitchell has repeatedly emphasized (e.g. *OES*: *passim*; Mitchell 1995: §42). On the other hand, we do know for example that interjections most probably occur in all natural languages, implying that there are shared features regarding the motivation of their use on a general communicative level. Within the history of a particu-lar language, the established method of comparing different stages of development helps us to identify parallels and diachronic changes over time in terms of a single language. We will return to this question towards the end of this paper, but before that our main concerns will be:

1 to examine the occurrence of interjections in different varieties (genres) of OE writing in the light of the material included in the Old English part of the *Helsinki Corpus of Historical Texts* (henceforth *HC*);
2 to discuss the major uses and functions of interjections in particu-lar genres and contexts, focusing on the most frequent items in the corpus.

The present investigation draws on several earlier studies of English interjections. For OE, Offerberg (1967) provides the most comprehensive discussion in terms of data and findings. The Middle English (ME) and Early Modern English (EModE) situation is discussed in two papers by Taavitsainen (1995, 1997), using the *HC* as data. These studies are important both methodologically and in terms of findings, suggesting parallels and points of comparison for the present analysis. As regards interjections in the contemporary language, Aijmer's recent empirical work on English discourse particles in the London-Lund Corpus of Spoken English (Aijmer 2002) provides interesting insights into the subject that are relevant in a historical context as well.

Some Preliminaries

According to Crystal, interjections constitute a class of words which are unproductive, do not enter into syntactic relationships with other classes and have a purely emotive function (e.g. *Yuk! Strewth! Blast! Tut tut!* – Crystal 1997: 200). He points out that there is an unclear boundary between these items and other types of exclamation, where some refer-ential meaning may be involved and which may consist of more than one word, e.g. *Excellent! Lucky devil! Cheers! Well, well!* Traditionally, a distinction has been drawn in terms of primary and secondary interjec-tions, the former referring to items which do not have any other function, such as *oh!*, while the latter refer to those adopted from another grammatical category, e.g. *what!* (cf. Mustanoja 1960: 621; *OES*: §1235; Taavitsainen 1997: 574). In this paper the emphasis will be on primary interjections. In most grammatical descriptions of Modern English, inter-jections are usually dealt with only briefly. There are obvious reasons for their peripheral status. As explained by Quirk et al., interjections can be considered a closed class and those that are fully lexicalized are few in number (Quirk et al. 1985: §2.42). The brevity of the discussion in Quirk et al. (1985) confirms the marginal status of interjections in grammar, though at the same time drawing attention to their most salient commun-icative properties, such as emotive meanings (Quirk et al. 1985: §11.55) and the capacity to convey emotive emphasis (Quirk et al. 1985: §18.55).

When we turn to grammatical descriptions of English in earlier periods, the attention paid to interjections diminishes even further, due to the fact – already referred to – that interjections are primarily characteristic of the spoken rather than the written medium and that for any past period we are deprived of authentic records of the spoken idiom. The written language deliberately tends to avoid any traits of overtly casual speech, which is where interjections are probably most likely to occur (cf. Aijmer 2002). As Cassidy (1996: 45) points out, interjections in OE probably had similar functions and uses as today; they are simply poorly recorded in the texts. Since they are marginal in the primary data, it is to be expected that they will also appear so in descriptions of these data. In view of this background, we should not expect to find many instances of interjections in texts written as far back as Anglo-Saxon times. However, the situation is not as desperate as might be assumed on the basis of some OE grammars, such as Quirk and Wrenn (1957) or Campbell (1959), which do not discuss interjections at all. Mitchell (1985) devotes a short but extremely informative section to the subject, in spite of the fact that interjections play "no part in the syntax of the sentence" (*OES*: §1234). His account also contains an alphabetical list of the items in OE (*OES*: §§1234–8).

However, there are some specific studies of particular authors and texts which have paid attention to OE interjections. An example is Wülfing (1901), who discusses the interjections occurring in Alfredian texts in terms of a semantic classification and gives examples of individual items, including *la, eala, hwæt, wa, hu, wel, efne, gea la gea, gise la gise, nese la nese* (Wülfing 1901: §§1110–25). The most comprehensive section consists of examples of *hwæt* (Wülfing: §1118). It will be in order to conclude this brief survey by referring, once again, to Offerberg (1967). This is a most useful source for OE interjections, including information about their etymologies and the occurrence of related items in other Germanic languages. Offerberg included the following items in her study: (1) the primary interjections *eala, eglæg, eow, hela, higla, huig, la, o, tæg tæg, wa, wæ, weilawei, wila wei*; (2) the secondary interjections *georstu, sehðe* (verbs), *nu, nu la, nu nu, wella* (adverbs), *hwæt* (interrogative pronoun), and *afæstla, one, welga* (uncertain). Before taking a look at the data of the present study, let us briefly consider some recent theoretical developments in the study of English that are relevant to the present discussion.

Current Trends

In the past few decades, the study of various "marginal" features of language use has received increasing attention in research, at first in terms of the contemporary language and subsequently also in the language of earlier periods. The theoretical impetus for such an approach is derived from discourse analysis and pragmatics. In Modern English the study of so-called discourse markers paved the way for a functional approach to "peripheral" items (cf. Schiffrin 1987). Discourse markers (or discourse particles) refer to elements such as *oh, well, I mean,* and the like, whose principal function is to signal units of speech. According to Aijmer, there is a cline between discourse particles and interjections: both can function "as signposts in the communication facilitating the hearer's interpretation of the utterance on the basis of various contextual cues" (Aijmer 2002: 2).

In the historical domain, Brinton provides the most comprehensive discussion of the "mystery features" of English medieval texts, i.e. items that resemble discourse markers in Modern English. She points out that rather than seeing them as meaningless or merely stylistic, discourse analysts recognize a number of global functions in them, on a textual level: these include (a) marking various kinds of boundaries (initiating or ending a discourse or effecting a shift in topic); (b) assisting in turn-taking in oral discourse or "chunking" (marking of episode or para-graph) in written discourse; and on the interpersonal level, (c) subjectively, expressing speaker attitude, and interactively, achieving intimacy between speaker and addressee (Brinton 1996: 6). Interjections may have similar functions. The OE exclamatory *hwæt!*, which is one of the items studied by Brinton, is a case in point (Brinton 1996: 181–210).

Another way of looking at the communicative impact of interjections is to relate them to the roles of speaker and addressee. Ameka speaks of "expressive interjections" in referring to items that place the focus on the speaker's mental state (Ameka 1992: 113–14). According to him, these may be of two kinds: emotive (e.g. *Wow!* 'I am surprised') and cognitive (*Aha!* 'I know this'). On the other hand, interjections that are directed at an auditor and that aim at getting someone's attention or demand an action or response from the hearer – e.g. *sh!* 'I want silence here' – he calls "conative interjections". This distinction is also helpful in the analysis of historical material (cf. Taavitsainen 1997: 574). In the same vein, we may also assume that the use of interjections is analogous in all periods of English and that interjections constitute a trait of the spoken language in written English in all periods, in spite of the fact that the items them-selves may be different at different times. All this means that interjections are a significant element of communication in all periods. According to Taavitsainen, they may be the most important category for showing personal involvement and affect in texts (Taavitsainen 1997: 573).

Data and Method

The OE section of the *HC* (Kytö 1996) is divided into four chronological sections: OE1 (–850), OE2 (850–950), OE3 (950–1050) and OE4 (1050–1150). Each section contains samples of varying length from the major texts of the period in question, as follows: OE1: documents; verse; OE2: law, documents, handbooks (medicine), philosophy, religious treatises, prefaces, history, Bible, verse; OE3: law, documents, handbooks (medi-cine), science (astronomy), homilies, rules, religious treatises, prefaces, history, geography, travelogues, lives, Bible, verse; and OE4: law, docu-ments, handbooks (astronomy), philosophy, homilies, rules, religious treatises, prefaces, history, lives.

In collecting the data, all genres and texts were included in the search, except for glossed texts. These were excluded because of their heavy dependence on the Latin text. The list of primary interjections was compiled on the basis of the secondary sources mentioned above. The resulting text examples were then scrutinized manually to screen out any irrelevant instances from the data. As the present investigation is a corpus study, the results will be valid outside the data only insofar as the *HC* itself may be said to represent OE. The general nature of OE texts at large also needs to be borne in mind. OE texts tend to be formal rather than spontaneous, and a great deal of what would be relevant for a complete understanding of the language is not recorded in the written text. There is therefore an inherent imbalance in the basic material in favour of religious texts, which tend to be relatively formal, at the expense of other subjects; this will naturally be reflected in the results. In the initial stage all OE interjections were included in the search. However, as several of them are rare in OE, even including some hapax legomena, a number of items yielded no examples in the *HC*, including *æ, afæstla, ea, eow, haha, hehe, hig, tæg tæg* and *weilawei*. Due to the focus on primary interjections the secondary ones were excluded, except for *hwæt*; this was included because of its distinctive and frequent exclamatory usage in OE. As a result, the following five items were included in the present corpus: *eala, efne, hwæt, la* and *wa*. The total number of tokens of interjec-tions in the corpus is 228. We next take a closer look at these items.

Results

Eala

Eala is the most frequent primary interjection in the data. Its 66 occurrences are distributed between genres and individual texts as shown in Table 5.1. The table gives information about the following parameters: period of OE (1–4); the genre of the texts, as indicated in the *HC*; number of occurrences per genre (N); normalized frequency per 1,000 words (NF);

Table 5.1 Frequency and distribution of OE *eala*

Period	Genre	N	NF	Occurrences
OE2	philosophy	1	0.09	*Bo*
OE2–4	religious treatises	4	0.11	*CP* (1); *ÆLetW2* (1); *ÆLetS* (2)
OE3	verse	22	1.30	*And* (1); *Christ* (12); *Met* (6); *Wan* (3)
OE3	scientific	1	0.25	*ByrM*
OE3	Bible	5	0.49	*OldT*
OE3–4	homilies	16	0.66	*BlHom* (3); *ÆHom* (1); *WHomI* (7); *HomS* (2); *WHomII* (3)
OE3	lives	4	0.18	*GDH* (1); *ÆLS* (2); *Mart* (1)
OE3–4	rules	4	0.27	*BenR* (1); *WPol* (3)
OE3	fiction	6	0.92	*ApT*
OE4	history	3	0.35	*Chr*
Total		66	0.43	

and the individual text samples in which the examples occur, with the number of occurrences in brackets. Where no figure appears in brackets after the short title, this means that all instances are found in the text mentioned. The short titles of OE texts follow those suggested in Mitchell, Ball and Cameron (1975), with a few exceptions. The full titles of the texts are given in Appendix I, which also contains a summary account of the whole material.

Distribution and genres Table 5.1 indicates that *eala* occurs in a fairly broad range of texts. The genre designations in the *HC* are to be seen as approximations, most of them comprising texts that are not necessarily analogous in all their characteristics. On the other hand, several genres represented in the *HC*, including laws and documents, handbooks and prefaces, show no instances at all. There is a concentration of occurrences in verse and religious texts. About half of the examples (N = 33) are derived from various kinds of religious writing (treatises, homilies, saints' lives, rules, the Bible). In comparing the frequencies it has to be kept in mind that the text samples vary in length, and the relative frequency is therefore expressed as the ratio per 1,000 running words. The highest ratio occurs in verse texts (1.30), followed by fiction (0.92) and homilies (0.66). Although religious texts as a whole contain most of the examples, it is interesting that the only representative of "fiction" (*ApT*) should have the second highest relative figure for *eala*. With regard to verse texts, Offerberg has already drawn attention to the fact that the distribution of *eala* is uneven there in the sense that most of the occurrences are found in texts that are either translated or adapted from Latin Christian models. She found no examples in native texts treating non-Christian themes, such as *The Battle of Maldon*, the Riddles or the OE Charms. From this she concluded that *eala*, when it first appeared in poetry, was an emotional interjection of decidedly literary, especially Christian, associations (Offerberg 1967: 26).

Uses and functions in prose   The Latin and/or Christian background is also shared by most of the prose texts containing *eala*. In addition, they also share the feature of interactivity, best illustrated by the homilies, which actively seek to involve their audiences. This may happen through various rhetorical devices such as the use of first- and second-person pronouns, specific forms of address, mental verbs and direct discourse. Passages of direct discourse in a text either claim to represent speech or are themselves instances of it, as in dialogue. Representations of speech are characteristic of narrative writing, where *eala* typically occurs in the frame [V + *eala* + NP]. Here V stands for a reporting verb, often the preterite form *cwæð*, and NP for a noun of address, cf. (1) and (2) below. The page reference after the short title refers to the edition used as the source for the *HC* (see Kytö, 1996). A Modern English translation of the examples is given in Appendix III at the end of this paper.

(1)   Drihten andwyrde. þam chananeiscum wife. and *cwæð;* **Eala** *ðu wif.* micel is ðin geleafa. (*ÆCHom* 70)

(2)   Apollonius *cwæð:* **Eala** *ðu goda cyngc*, gif ðu me gelifst, ic secge þæt ic ongite þæt soðlice þin dohtor gefeol on swegcræft. (*ApT* 26)

There are altogether 18 (28 per cent) examples of this type in the material, including all the instances in *ApT*. The noun of address may be a simple or complex NP. In religious texts it is very often "God", with or without a relevant epithet, unless God has already been mentioned as the subject of *cwæð*, as in (1).

Instances of direct discourse proper are typical of homilies representing oral delivery. In such instances too *eala* has a conative meaning by virtue of the expression including a reference to the addressee. In Wulfstan's homilies the reference is often expressed collectively by *leofan men*, as for instance in (3).

(3)   *Eala, leofan men,* ne latiað na, ne latiað, ac ofstlice efstað & to Gode wendað. (*WHom* 10c 206)

A reference to the audience may occur whenever its involvement needs to be specially invoked. In such instances, the interjection typically has both anaphoric and cataphoric reference. It draws attention to what the homilist is about to say next, but with reference to what has been stated in the context immediately preceding. The sentence before (3) urges the audience to turn away from evil and observe God's law, while (3) contains a proposed course of action to this end, highlighted by *eala*. There are altogether 26 (40 per cent) instances of *eala* followed by an explicit reference to the addressee in the data. Thus more than half of the examples (N = 44; 68 per cent) belong to the groups exemplified by (1) and (2).

These figures are given additional validity by comparison with Offerberg's statistics for *eala*. One of the types she distinguishes is *"eala + vocatives"* (Offerberg 1967: 25). The other types consist of "absolute" use; *"eala + statements/questions"*; *"eala + exclamatory clauses"*; and *"eala + absolute noun"*. Offerberg does not indicate relative frequencies, but calculation of the proportion of the "vocative" type in her figures yields a figure of 64 per cent. In the summary in Table 5.2, the figures for the glossed texts included in Offerberg's material have been excluded from the count to make the comparison more reliable.

In the *HC* we find more examples in verse than in homilies, while in the reference data the opposite is true. In terms of verse texts and

Table 5.2   "*Eala* + vocative" in Offerberg (1967) and the *HC*

Data	Offerberg (1967)	HC
All texts	144	65
Verse	31 (22%)	22 (34%)
Homilies	61 (42%)	16 (25%)
Verse and homilies	92 (64%)	38 (58%)

homilies combined, however, the results are comparable, with total relative frequencies fairly close to each other. Both materials indicate the importance of *eala* for signalling audience attention to the message being conveyed.

The semantic colouring of *eala* depends on the meaning of the clause following it, whether statement, question, command or conditional clause. The interjection in a way encapsulates the sense expressed by the following clause. The examples below illustrate *eala* in some of these contexts. In (4), the interjection may be taken to emphasize the content of the statement following, while in (5) and (6), where it is followed by an exclamatory question, it may indicate sadness and praise, respectively. Statements constitute the most numerous group in this context (24 instances), followed by questions (13 instances) and commands and conditional clauses (3 instances each).

(4) *Eala*, rihte gedafenað cristenum mannum þæ hi Crist sylfne geefenlæcan georne (*WHom*10c 202)

(5) *Eala* hu earmlice & hu reowlic tid wæs ða. (*Chr* 1086 217)

(6) *Eala* hu manful man þu eart, ðu þe wast þæt þu æfter axast. (*ApT* 10)

Uses and functions in verse   Among the verse texts in the HC, the poem *Christ* provides most of the instances of *eala*. As in the prose texts, the interjection followed by an address form is a recurrent pattern; all but one instance represent this type. The use of the interjection in *Christ* is interesting. All instances occur in the first part of the poem, where the emphasis is on Christ's incarnation for the redemption of man. According to Raw, this part of the poem is based on a series of antiphons sung at the *Magnificat* during the day immediately before Christmas (Raw 1991: 233). Each occurrence of *eala* signals a new theme in the poem. Examples (7)–(9) are the first three occurrences:

(7) **Eala** þu reccend ond þu riht cyning, / se þe locan healdeð, lif ontyneð, / eadga upwegas, oþrum forwyrneð / wlitigan wilsiþes, gif his weorc ne deag. (*Christ* 3)

(8) **Eala** sibbe gesihð, sancta Hierusalem, / cynestola cyst, Cristes burglond, / engla eþelstol, ond þa ane in þe / saule soðfæstra simle gerestað, wuldrum hremge. (*Christ* 4)

(9) **Eala** wifa wynn geond wuldres þrym, fæmne freolicast ofer ealne foldan sceat þæs þe æfre sundbuend secgan hyrdon (*Christ* 5)

In line with the thematic progression, the prose translation (Gordon 1954) introduces a new paragraph with each new occurrence of *eala*. Another interesting feature in the poem is the dialogue between Joseph and Mary, the earliest dramatic scene in English literature (Gordon 1954: 133). It too makes use of *eala*. At the beginning of the short dialogue Mary first addresses Joseph (10) and he answers her (11):

(10) **Eala** Ioseph min, Iacobes bearn, / mæg Dauides, mæran cyninges, / nu þu freode scealt fæste gedælan, alætan / lufan mine. (*Christ* 7)

(11) Ic lungre eam / deope gedrefed, dome bereafod, / forðon ic worn for þe worde hæbbe / sidra sorga ond sarcwida . . . **Eala** fæmne geong, / mægð Maria. (*Christ* 8)

In (10) *eala* indicates the beginning of the dialogue after a long speech by the poet in praise of God and the Virgin Mary. Joseph's reply ends with *eala* in an exclamatory expression of sorrow and devotion, much as in Mary's opening line. The choice of *eala* in the dialogue echoes an attempt to represent genuine verbal exchange.

Emphasis *Eala*, like other interjections, as such draws attention to what is being said, but it may also be used with repetition for a distinctly emphatic effect. There are a few such examples in the present data, both prose and verse:

(12) **Eala, eala,** fela is þæra, þe sacerdhades on unriht gyrnað (*WPol* 97)

(13) **Eala, eala,** soð is þæt ic eow secge, swær is seo byrðen þe Godes bydel beran mot (*WHom* 17 244)

(14) ða bæd he eaðmodlice ðæt he hiene ne sende & cuæð: **Eala eala eala** Dryhten, ic eom cnioht; hwæt conn ic sprecan? (*CP* 49)

(15) **Eala** beorht bune. **Eala** byrnwiga. / **Eala** þeodnes þrym. (*Wan* 136)

In (12) and (13), from Wulfstan, the item is repeated twice, while in (14), from *CP*, it is repeated three times in succession. The example from *Wan*

Table 5.3 Frequency and distribution of OE *la*

Period	Genre	N	NF	Occurrences
OE2	philosophy	1	0.09	*Bo*
OE3	verse	5	0.17	*Beo* (2); *El* (1); *Met* (2)
OE3	scientific	3	0.32	*ByrM* (2); *ÆTemp* (1)
OE3	Bible	9	0.32	*OldT* (5); *OldT (PPs)* (2); *NewT* (2)
OE3–4	homilies	11	0.82	*ÆCHom* (2); *WHomI* (8); *WHomII* (1)
OE3	lives	5	0.18	*GDH* (1); *GDC* (1); *ÆLS* (2); *Mart* (1)
OE4	rel. treatises	3	0.30	*ÆLetS*
OE4	rules	5	1.05	*WPol*
Total		42	0.33	

is different in that *eala* is repeated in consecutive half-lines, each time preceding a different noun. In all instances great emotional intensity is involved.

La

On the basis of her analysis of the interjection *la* in OE, Offerberg (1967: 64) comes to the conclusion that (unlike *eala*) *la* must have been idiomatic and belonged to the spoken language. As one indication of this she notes that in translated OE texts there is usually nothing corresponding to *la* in the Latin. Moreover, it survived into ME, where *lo* is used in very much the same way as OE *la*. The distribution of *la* in the genres of the *HC* is set out in Table 5.3.

The occurrences of *la* are fewer than those of *eala*, but there is a similar concentration in homilies, and religious texts generally, in both sets of data. However, whereas *eala* also occurs fairly frequently in verse texts, there are only five examples of *la* in the poetry. Among the religious texts, most of the examples occur in the Bible and the homilies of Wulfstan.

In contrast to the general pattern of interjections occurring sentence/ clause-initially or before an address form, *la* may also be inserted inside a clause after an address form or even placed in final position in the sentence. When inserted, it tends to be associated with the preceding word (cf. Offerberg 1967: 55). The examples below illustrate the following uses and syntactic patterns of *la*: independent use in sentence-initial position (16), preceding a noun of address (17), following a noun of address (18), and independent use in sentence-final position (19).

(16)   **La**, hu mæg man eaðost gehwyrfan fram yfele & fram unrihte, butan þæt man deofol georne forbuge & his undæda ealle oferhogie (*WHom* 20 202)

(17)   Ac, **la** Drihten, ne afyr þinne fultum fram me, ac loca to minre generennesse. (*OldT(PPs)* 45)

(18)   Hwi læddest ðu, **la**, us of Egypta lande, þæt we swulton on þisum westene. (*OldT* XXI 5)

(19)   ða cwæð ic: Hwæt is þæt, **la**? (*Bo* 86)

There are minor variations of the above patterns. For example, in initial position *la* may be preceded by the conjunction *and/ac*, connecting the expression to the preceding discourse. In the present material, Wulfstan's homilies offer several examples of this, reflecting the oral background of their delivery. In terms of frequencies, the preposed type, exemplified by (16) and (17), has 24 (62 per cent) occurrences, while the postposed type, exemplified by (18) and (19), has 15 (38 per cent) occurrences in the total of 39 instances. Comparing the figures with those of Offerberg, it appears that in her data the postpositional type is more frequent. Counting from her statistics, there are 81 (45 per cent) instances of the preposed type (Offerberg 1967: 62), mostly occurring in the *WS Gospels* (33 per cent), *GHC* (15 per cent), *GDH* (14 per cent) and *WHom* (17 per cent). Correspondingly, there are 97 (55 per cent) instances of postpositional *la* (p. 63). Most of these examples occur in *Bo* (11 per cent), Ælfric's homilies (13 per cent) and *GDC* (51 per cent). In the latter group, however, one text (*GDH*) has far more examples than any of the others.

As regards the uses of *la*, we find similar patterns as with *eala*. In absolute use (16), it draws the listener's attention to what is being said. Before a noun of address (17), it establishes contact with the addressee. Inserted within the clause or in clause- or sentence-final position it is emphatic, as in (18) and (19). In narrative texts, *la* occurs in direct discourse after a reporting verb; cf. (19). To these we may add the cases where *la* occurs in collocation with another exclamatory word, e.g. (20)–(24).

(20) Farao ða het clypian Abram, & cwæð him to: **Hwæt la**, hwi dydest ðu swa wið me; hwi noldest ðu secgan þæt heo þin wif ys. (*OldT* XII, 1)

(21) **La hwæt**, we witan ful georne þæt to miclan bryce sceal micel bot nyde, & to miclan bryne wæter unlytel, gif man þæt fyr sceal to ahte acwencan. (*WHom* 20 268)

(22) Heo þa gefeonde cwæþ, Ecce dominus meus, **Hona la** min hlaford. (*Mart* 29)

(23) **Nu la**, leofan men, gelyfað huru georne & anrædlice beþencað þæt annes & ðrynnes on godcundnesse an is; ðæt is fæder & sunu & frofergast. (*WHom* 10c 207)

(24) **Wel la**, monna bearn geond middangeard, friora æghwilc fundie to þæm ecum gode þe we ymb sprecað (*Met* 185)

In such examples, the collocating word adds emphasis to *la*. As a rule the collocating word precedes *la*, but with *hwæt* we find positional variation, as indicated by (20) and (21). In (22), the combination of *la* and the interjection *heonu* translates Latin *ecce* 'behold'. In (23) *la* appears in conjunction with *nu*, functioning as a discourse marker and indicating a topic change. At this point in the homily the speaker is addressing his audience about the consequences of a preceding expository passage in the text. In (24), we have one of the few instances of *wel* with *la* in the present material. Offerberg's material contains more examples of this combination, all from *Bo* and *Met*; according to her, it is used in direct address indicating "faint approval or encouragement or merely serving to attract attention or give emphasis" (Offerberg 1967: 105).

Hwæt

Hwæt belongs unquestionably to the secondary interjections. It functions primarily as an interrogative pronoun, but is also used as an interjection, although the difference between these meanings is not always easy to tell. The fact that the non-interrogative use is quite typical of certain kinds of OE writing justifies including it in the discussion. As an interjection, *hwæt* functions above all as an "attention-getter", and the usage must be ultimately connected with oral delivery. It is most familiar

Table 5.4 Frequency and distribution of OE *hwæt*

Period	Genre	N	NF	Occurrences
OE2	philosophy	12	1.10	*Bo*
OE2	history	1	0.12	*Or*
OE2/4	rel. treatises	9	0.33	*CP* (5); *ÆLetS* (4)
OE3	verse	46	0.75	*And* (5); *Beo* (6); *Christ* (3); *Dream* (2); *El* (7); *Exo* (2); *Fates* (3); *Gen* (2); *Jul* (4); *Met* (8); *MPs* (4)
OE3	Bible	4	0.39	*OldT*
OE3–4	homilies	3	0.61	*WHomI* (2); *HomS* (1)
OE3–4	lives	10	0.61	*GDH* (3); *ÆLS* (5); *PstMarg* (2)
OE3	fiction	1	0.15	*ApT*
Total		86	0.59	

from the poetry. Altogether nine OE poems begin with this word, which indicates that the usage was in keeping with the traditional style of Germanic poetry (Offerberg 1967: 108). The precise meaning and function of exclamatory *hwæt* have been discussed extensively in the scholarly literature (for a recent survey see Brinton 1996). Brinton observes that almost every occurrence of *hwæt* in verse is accompanied by a first- or second-person pronoun (Brinton 1996: 185). In prose, this item is much less frequent, as the figures in Table 5.4 testify. Brinton thinks that this may be because of the more "literary" and less "oral" nature of much OE prose (p. 192).

The figure for verse texts indicates that *hwæt* is found in a number of poems, none of which, however, has very many examples. Even in *Beo* there are only six instances. On the other hand, in the much shorter poems *El* and *Met* there are seven and eight examples, respectively. The titles of the verse texts in Table 5.4 indicate that both poems dealing predominantly with traditional Germanic themes and those that deal predominantly with Christian themes contain examples of non-interrogative *hwæt*. However, only *Beo* represents the former group. The following examples illustrate some of the most typical uses in poetry:

(25) **Hwæt**. We gefrunan on fyrndagum / twelfe under tunglum tireadige hæleð, / þeodnes þegnas. (*And* 3)

(26)   Beowulf maþelode, bearn Ecgþeowes: / **Hwæt**. þu worn fela, wine
       min Unferð, / beore druncen ymb Brecan spræce, / sægdest from
       his siðe. (*Beo* 529)

(27)   **Eala hwæt**, þæt is wræclic wrixl in wera life, / þætte moncynnes
       milde scyppend / onfeng æt fæmnan flæsc unwemme, / ond sio
       weres friga wiht ne cuþe, / ne þurh sæd ne cwom sigores agend /
       monnes ofer moldan. (*Christ* 14)

The first example is from the opening of *And*, perhaps calling attention
to the performance of the poem. The next example illustrates the fact that
the interjection belongs to direct discourse. In narrative texts, such as *Beo*,
direct discourse is signalled by a reporting verb preceding *hwæt*. The
interjection itself introduces an emphatic statement. Narrative poems vary
in terms of how much direct discourse they contain. That instances of
hwæt and other interjections appear to be fewer in poems dealing with
traditional Germanic subject matter as opposed to those based on Latin
tradition and Christian themes may be due in part to the fact that the
latter groups offer more instances of dialogue and direct discourse than
the former. Example (27), from *Christ*, illustrates a collocation with *eala*.
As we saw earlier, *eala* is used several times in the first part of the poem.
This collocation occurs at the end of the first part, where *hwæt* is
added to further heighten the poet's words in praise of Christ and his
Immaculate Conception.
    The distribution of the examples in the prose texts is rather uneven,
with some of the texts containing very few examples; for instance *ApT*
has just one instance. On the other hand, "lives" has ten instances. The
text that has by far the highest absolute and relative frequency of *hwæt* is
Bo. Although this text contains long passages of dialogue, it is interesting
that none of the other interjections is nearly as prominent in it as *hwæt*.
Offerberg thinks that *hwæt* in *Bo* "creates the impression that it was a
mere expletive, which had been taken over from verbose spoken language"
(Offerberg 1967: 108). The usage in the metrical version of the text (*Met*)
is in line with the prose *Bo* in having an even higher relative frequency
(1.51) for the exclamatory *hwæt*.

Other items: efne *and* wa

The only other items in the present corpus represented by ten or more
instances are *efne* and *wa*. Their frequencies are given in Tables 5.5 and 5.6.

Table 5.5 Frequency and distribution of OE *efne*

Period	Genre	N	NF	Occurrences
OE3	Bible	7	0.68	*OldT*
OE3	scientific	2	0.49	*ByrM*
OE3	religious treatises	1	0.13	*ÆLetW1*
Total		10	0.45	

Table 5.6 Frequency and distribution of OE *wa*

Period	Genre	N	NF	Occurrences
OE3	verse	3	0.11	*Beo* (1); *Jul* (1); *Rid* (1)
OE3–4	homilies	12	0.77	*BlHom* (1); *HomS* (8); *WHomII* (3)
OE3	religious treatises	1	0.13	*ÆLetW2*
OE4	rules	8	1.68	*WPol*
Total		24	0.44	

OE *efne* appears normally as a gloss to Latin *ecce* (Offerberg 1967: 98–9), and this is also the case in the instances of Table 5.5; for example:

(28) God cwæð ða: **Efne** ic forgyfe eow eall gærs & wyrta sæd berende ofer eorðan & ealle treowa (*OldT* I 29)

(29) **Efne** nu ic sette min wed to eow & to eowrum ofspringe. (*OldT* IX 9)

The normalized frequencies are rather high, but only three texts are involved. *Wa*, on the other hand, is much more frequent. All instances in the present corpus follow the pattern: [*wa* + (V) + pron.], where the verb is an optional element:

(30) **Wa** þam witodlice, þe godcunde heorde underfehð and naþer gehealdan ne can ne hine sylfine ne þa heorde (*WPol* 97)

Table 5.7 Interjections in the genres

Genre	N	NF
philosophy	14	1.28
religious treatises	18	0.51
verse	76	1.13
scientific	6	0.64
Bible	25	0.87
homilies	42	1.54
lives	19	0.60
rules	17	1.15
fiction	7	1.18
history	4	0.23
Total	228	0.92

(31) **Wa** is me nu, forþam þe ic þa toweardan þinc ne gemunde. (*HomS* 167)

(32) **Wa** me, forþam þe ic sceal to helle for þinum yfeldædum and þu hafast gedon, þæt ic eom deofles bearn and deoflum gelic. (*HomS* 167)

In these examples, the above frame is followed by a relative clause in (30), and an adverbial clause in (31) and (32). In all of them, *wa* seems to indicate what Offerberg calls the "mental agony" of "grief, longing, fear, and so on" (Offerberg 1967: 83). The figures indicate that this interjection is most common in the homiletic style and in Wulfstan's writings.

Some trends

Table 5.7 gives the frequencies for all the interjections discussed according to the genre designations of the *HC*. Naturally, in drawing conclusions such conflated figures need to be related to the nature of the material, taking into account for instance the fact that the distribution of the material in terms of genres is uneven, and that in such limited material as this the results may be skewed by the idiosyncratic properties of individual texts.

Some trends are apparent in the light of the figures. The highest rate of occurrence (1.54) occurs in the homilies. Comparing the major homilists of the period, Ælfric and Wulfstan, and taking into account all their writings, Wulfstan uses interjections approximately twice as frequently as Ælfric (2.67 vs. 0.71). Wulfstan's style also affects the figures for "rules", as a result of the inclusion of *WPol*. Religious treatises and lives are fairly close to each other in tone. Verse has a somewhat higher rate of incidence of interjections than prose (1.13 vs. 0.84). "Philosophy" has relatively high frequencies due to the fact that *Bo* contains a great deal of dialogue. As a primarily narrative genre, on the other hand, "history" has very few examples. The genres also differ in terms of which interjections are represented in the texts. Only religious treatises have examples of all five items. The Bible and the homilies have instances of four, while most genres have examples of three items. Only fiction and history have instances of just two interjections. Without going into detail, the overall picture seems by and large consistent with the profiles of individual texts in these groups.

After Old English

We have seen above that interjections are part of the expressive capacity of written OE. The purpose of this section is to add a postscript by briefly considering developments in later periods. Bearing in mind the processes involved in the transition from Old to Middle English, it is to be expected that interjections too will be affected. The most apparent change in ME is that the items themselves have changed or have been replaced entirely. In the Early Middle English (EME) section of the *HC* (ME1; 1150–1250), there are still some occurrences of OE interjections. For example *eala* has thirteen occurrences – four instances in the *HVesp* and nine in *HRoodT*. OE *hwæt* has six occurrences, three in the *HVesp* and three in *HBod*. OE *la* occurs just once (in *HVesp*). On the other hand, ME *lo* has ten instances in ME1, all in the texts of the Katherine Group. It is noteworthy that the surviving OE items in EME are all found in texts based on OE originals. The only OE interjection in the present corpus that is still fairly frequent in EME is *wa*. It occurs in a variety of religious texts, especially *Sawles Warde* and *Vices and Virtues*, where it is repeated several times in succession in certain passages of these texts.

After the EME period the changes become more apparent, as indicated by Taavitsainen's study of ME interjections. These items, with a few exceptions, are not attested in OE at all, including for instance *a/ah, o/oo, ey, alas* (cf. Taavitsainen 1997: 599–600). OE *hwæt, la* and *wa*, however, survive in ME as *what, lo* and *wo*. The overall contexts favouring the use of interjections remain similar in ME. For example, Taavitsainen notes that her examples occur chiefly in direct speech quotations imitating spoken language (Taavitsainen 1997: 575). But it is not only the word types of interjections that change in ME; the range of available genres changes as well. In particular the role of "imaginative" texts becomes much more prominent in ME. In the *HC* this expansion is seen in the emergence of such genres as metrical romance, letters and drama, as well as in the considerable growth of prose fiction. The variety of emotions and affective meanings relevant to such genres creates a productive environment for the use of interjections. Taavitsainen's material shows how such contexts also contribute to increased reader involvement. In EModE this trend is further strengthened, with most of the interjections occurring in comedy and fiction, where they are most typically found in direct speech quotations (cf. Taavitsainen 1995: 444).

Conclusions

In the light of the present study, interjections form a fairly small but stable component of written OE. They are essentially emotive words capable of expressing a variety of moods and sentiments. They occur in both prose and poetry. In both varieties they may have a cognitive function, with the focus on the speaker's own mind and mental processes, as well as a conative function, with the focus on the interaction between the participants in the communicative situation. The latter function is the predominant one and a distinctive sign of the interactive purpose of the text. The typical locus for the occurrence of interjections in OE texts is in direct discourse, including direct speech quotes as well as dialogue. Such passages may occur in many kinds of writing, but they are most frequent in instructive and narrative texts. Among the former, texts of religious instruction, especially homilies, are specifically constructed as discourse with the purpose of influencing the audience. One of the verbal means to this end is to draw the audience's attention to the content and its delivery at different stages by means of interjections. Functionally, interjections may signal a variety of discourse phenomena, including boundaries between direct and indirect discourse, topic shift and text structuring, turn-taking in dialogue, and speaker's meanings and attitudes of different kinds, such as assigning special prominence to a particular topic in the discourse. A comparison of the OE data with that for later periods reveals that the frequency of interjections increases significantly with the emergence of new genres of imaginative writing in ME and EModE. However, it is the items and contexts that change; the basic functions of interjections persist. The roots of the uses and function of English interjections are already present in OE. In the words of Bruce Mitchell – words he uses to describe the "Englishness" of Old English: "Continuity then – not discontinuity – is my theme" (Mitchell 1994: 169).

Note

I would like to acknowledge financial support for the research reported here from the Academy of Finland (decision numbers 203930 and 205426). I also wish to thank Anneli Bergholm for help with the compilation of the data, Inga Offerberg for permission to consult her unpublished thesis on OE interjections, and Ellen Valle for her comments on the style of this paper. Any errors and shortcomings are entirely my own responsibility.

References and Further Reading

Aijmer, K. (2002). *English Discourse Particles: evidence from a corpus*. Amsterdam: John Benjamins.

Ameka, F. (1992). Interjections: the universal yet neglected part of speech. *Journal of Pragmatics*, 18, 101–18.

Brinton, L. (1996). *Pragmatic Markers in English: grammaticalization and discourse functions*. Berlin: Mouton de Gruyter.

Cassidy, F. C. (1996). The Anglo-Saxon interjection. In C. Pollner, H. Rohlfing & F. R. Hausmann (eds), *Bright is the Ring of Words: Festschrift für Horst Weinstock* (pp. 45–8). Bonn: Romanistischer Verlag.

Crystal, D. (1997). *A Dictionary of Linguistics and Phonetics*, 4th edn. Oxford: Blackwell.

Garmonsway, G. N. (1975). *The Anglo-Saxon Chronicle. Translated with an introduction*, new edn. London: Dent (1st edn 1953).

Gordon, R. K. (1954). *Anglo-Saxon Poetry*, rev. and reset. London: Dent.

Offerberg, I. (1967). A Study of Old English Interjections. Unpublished thesis, University of Stockholm.

Quirk, R. & Wrenn, C. L. (1957). *An Old English Grammar*. London: Methuen (1st edn 1955).

Quirk, R., Greenbaum, S., Leech, G. & Svartvik, J. (eds) (1985). *A Comprehensive Grammar of the English Language*. London: Longman.

Raw, B. C. (1991). Biblical literature: the New Testament. In M. Godden & M. Lapidge (eds), *The Cambridge Companion to Old English Literature* (pp. 227–42). Cambridge: Cambridge University Press.

Schiffrin, D. (1987). *Discourse Markers*. Cambridge: Cambridge University Press.

Taavitsainen, I. (1995). Interjections in Early Modern English: from imitation of spoken to conventions of written language. In A. Jucker (ed.), *Historical Pragmatics: pragmatic developments in the history of English* (pp. 439–65). Amsterdam: John Benjamins.

Taavitsainen, I. (1997). Exclamations in Late Middle English. In J. Fisiak (ed.), *Studies in Middle English Linguistics* (pp. 573–607). Berlin: Mouton de Gruyter.

Wülfing, E. (1901). *Die Syntax in den Werken Alfreds des Grossen*. Zweiter Teil. Bonn: P. Hanstein's Verlag.

Appendix I: Abbreviated titles

Except for those listed below, abbreviations in the paper are as in Mitchell, Ball & Cameron (1975: 213–19; 1979).

ÆGram (*Ælfrics Grammatik und Glossar*, J. Zupitza (ed.), 1880); *ÆLetS* (Ælfric's Letter to Sigeweard); *ÆLetW1/2* (Ælfric's First/Second Letter to Wulfstan); *Chron* (Chronicle ms. E); *Coll* (*Ælfric's Colloquy*, G. N. Garmonsway (ed.), 2nd edn, 1947); *GDC* (Gregory's Dialogues ms. C); *GDH* (Gregory's Dialogues ms. H); *HomB* (The Bodley Homilies); *HRoodT* (History of the Holy Rood-Tree); *HomS* (Homilies for specified occasions; A Homily for the Sixth (or Fourth) Sunday after Epiphany); *HomV* (The Vespasian Homilies); *MPs* (The Metrical Psalms of the Paris Psalter); *NewT* (West-Saxon Gospels); *OldT* (The Old English Version of the Heptateuch); *OldT (PPs)* (The Paris Psalter); *PstMarg* (A Passion of St Margaret); *WHomI* (Wulfstan's Homilies 8c, 10c, 13, 20); *WHomII* (Wulfstan's Homilies 1b, 2, 3, 7, 17).

Appendix II

Abbreviations

G	Genre of text in the *HC*
HC	*Helsinki corpus*
HC abbr.	Abbreviation of text in the *HC*
N	Number of instances
NF	Normalized frequency
PTC	Prototypical text category in the *HC*
WordC	Word count

Appendix IIa: Statistical analysis of OE texts to c. 1150

Text	[HC abbr.]	WordC	N	NF	PTC	G
ÆCHom	[AELFR]	3,130	2	0.639	IR	HOM
Æ Hom	[AELFR15]	1,720	1	0.581	IR	HOM
ÆLetS	[LSIGEW]	10,180	9	0.884	IR	RELT
ÆLetW1, 2	[LWSTAN1,2]	7,960	3	0.377	IR	RELT
ÆLS	[AELIVES]	6,980	9	1.290	NN	BIL
ÆTemp	[TEMP]	5,360	1	0.187	EX	SCIA
And	[AND]	4,860	6	1.235	XX	XX
ApT	[APOLL]	6,530	7	1.072	NI	FICT
BenR	[BENEDOE]	9,970	1	0.100	IR	RULE
Beo	[BEOW]	17,310	9	0.520	XX	XX
BlHom	[BLICK]	10,670	4	0.375	IR	HOM
Bo	[BOETHAL]	10,920	14	1.282	XX	PHILO
ByrM	[BYRHTF]	4,070	5	1.229	IS	SCIA
Christ	[CHRI]	6,130	15	2.447	XX	XX
Chr	[CHRONE2]	8,490	3	0.353	NN	HIST
CP	[CP]	17,140	6	0.350	IR	RELT
Dream	[DREAM]	1,110	2	1.802	XX	XX
El	[ELENE]	7,310	8	1.094	XX	XX
Exo	[EXOD]	2,980	2	0.671	XX	XX
Fates	[APOST]	670	3	4.478	XX	XX
GDC	[GDC]	5,100	1	0.196	NN	BIL
GDH	[GDC]	5,170	5	0.967	NN	BIL
Gen	[GEN]	4,840	2	0.413	XX	XX
HomS	[SUND6]	1,610	11	6.832	IR	HOM
Jul	[JULOE]	4,130	5	1.211	XX	XX
Mart	[MART]	10,270	2	0.195	NN	BIL
Met	[MBO]	5,270	16	3.036	XX	XX
MPs	[MPS]	6,720	4	0.595	XX	XX
NewT	[WSNEW]	9,920	2	0.202	XX	NEWT
OldT	[AELFOLD]	10,240	21	2.051	XX	OLDT
OldT(PPs)	[PPS]	8,450	2	0.237	XX	OLDT
Or	[OROS]	8,640	1	0.116	NN	HIST
PstMarg	[MARGOE]	4,200	2	0.476	NN	BIL
Rid	[RIDDL]	5,090	1	0.196	XX	XX
Wan	[WAND]	690	3	4.348	XX	XX
WHomI	[WULF03]	6,950	6	0.863	IR	HOM
WHomII	[WULF03/4]	3,290	18	5.471	IR	HOM
WPol	[POLITY]	4,760	16	3.361	IR	RULE
Total		248,831	228	0.916		

Appendix IIb: Statistical analysis of ME1 texts 1150–1250
excluding wa

Text	[*HC* abbr.]	WordC	N	NF	PTC	G
HBod	[BOD]	5,880	3	0.510	IR	HOM
HRoodT	[HROOD]	6,920	9	1.301	NN	RELT
HVesp	[VESP]	5,880	8	1.361	IR	HOM

Appendix III: Translations of the examples

Note: Where a translation is taken from a published source, the reference is provided in brackets. In some such cases the translation has been slightly modernized, e.g. by substituting "you" for "thou" and "-s" for "-th" as third-person singular verbal ending.

(1) The Lord replied to the woman from Canaan and said, O you woman, great is your faith.

(2) Apollonius said, O you good king, if you allow me I will say what I feel that truly your daughter has failed in her music.

(3) Oh, beloved men, do not delay, do not delay, but speedily make haste and turn to God.

(4) Alas, it is truly befitting for Christian people that they should desire to be like Christ himself.

(5) Alas! how wretched and how unhappy the times were then! (Garmonsway 1975: 217)

(6) Oh, how wicked a man you are, you who know what you are asking for.

(7) O you ruler and you righteous king, who hold the key, who open life; gladden us with victory, with glorious success, denied to another if his work is not well done. (Gordon 1954: 133)

(8) O vision of peace, holy Jerusalem, best of thrones, city of Christ, habitation of angels, and in you the souls of righteous men alone rest eternally, rejoicing in glory. (Gordon 1954: 134)

(9) O joy of women in heavenly glory, fairest maid on the whole face of the earth, of whom dwellers by the sea ever heard tell. (Gordon 1954: 134)

(10) O my Joseph, son of Jacob, descendant of David the glorious king, must you now break off steadfast love, forsake my fondness? (Gordon 1954: 136)

(11) I am this instant deeply distressed, reft of repute, because I have heard on your account many words, great griefs [. . .] O young maiden, Virgin Mary! (Gordon 1954: 136)

(12) Alas, alas, many are they who strive for priesthood unjustly.

(13) Alas, alas, it is true what I tell you, heavy is the burden that God's minister must carry.

(14) [H]e then prayed humbly that he would not send him and said: Alas, alas, alas, Lord, I am a boy, what can I say?

(15) Alas, the bright cup! Alas, the warrior in his corslet! Alas, the glory of the prince! (Gordon 1954: 74)

(16) Lo, how can one most readily turn away from evil and wickedness, except by completely avoiding the devil and by despising all his wicked deeds.

(17) But, oh Lord, do not withdraw your help from me but look upon my deliverance.

(18) Alas, why did you lead us out of the land of Egypt to die in this desert?

(19) [T]hen I said: Lo, what is it?

(20) Then Pharaoh ordered Abraham to be called, and said to him: Alas, why have you done this to me; why did you not tell me that she was your wife?

(21) Oh, alas, we are fully aware that a great breach will require great compensation and a great fire a great deal of water to be extinguished at all.

(22) She said to the rejoicing, Ecce dominus meus: Lo, behold my Lord.

(23) Now, oh dear men, at all events do readily believe, and resolutely bear in mind, that oneness and trinity are united in divinity, that is Father and Son and the Holy Ghost.

(24) Well, children of men throughout the world, let every free man aspire to the eternal good that we are speaking about.

(25) Lo! we have heard in distant days of twelve glorious heroes, servants of the Lord, under the stars. (Gordon 1954: 181)

(26) Beowulf spoke, son of Ecgtheow: Lo! you have spoken a great deal, friend Unferth, about Breca, drunken as you are with beer; you have told about his journey. (Gordon 1954: 13)

(27) O! what a marvellous new thing is this in the life of men, that the merciful Creator of mankind should receive from the Maiden, flesh without spot; nor knew she aught of man's embraces; nor did the Lord of victory come by the seed of any man on earth. (Gordon 1954: 140)

(28) Then God said: Lo! I give you all the grass and every herb bearing seed and all the trees in the whole earth.

(29) Lo and behold, I now/herewith establish my covenant with you and with your offspring.

(30) Woe to him, verily, who receives the spiritual flock and cannot keep either, neither himself nor the flock.

(31) Woe is me, now, for not remembering the things to come.

(32) Woe is me, for I must go to hell for your evil deeds, and you have made me the devil's son and like the devil.

Chapter 6

Speaking One's Mind
in *The Wanderer*

Susan Irvine

Bruce Mitchell's seminal article "The dangers of disguise: Old English texts in modern punctuation" draws attention to the distorting effects of modern punctuation on the flow and meaning of Old English prose and poetry. Mitchell cites *The Wanderer* lines 37–57 to exemplify the way that poetic insights can be denied by the use of modern punctuation:

> (To put it in grammatical terms) *secga geseldan* may be used *apo koinou* as both the object of *greteð* and *geondsceawað* and also the subject of *swimmað*. Or (to put it 'poetically') *secga geseldan* can refer to both the Wanderer's former companions and to the birds as the grip of *sorg ond slæp* tightens and loosens, and his focus shifts: is he asleep? or awake? In the reverie? or out? Which are they? Birds or men or men or birds or both? Any rigid modern punctuation tends to prevent or inhibit or destroy a proper reaction to the poet's triumph in these lines. And this is not an isolated example. (Mitchell 1980: 396)

As Mitchell suggests, the complexity of response demanded by the passage clearly relies on a fluidity in syntactical structure which modern punctuation belies. Building on Mitchell's work, this essay will begin by readdressing the implications of the syntax of *The Wanderer* lines 50b–57, focusing first on the passage itself (and especially the phrase *ferð fleotendra*), and then on its place in the poem as a whole. Through its representation of an image of failed communication, the passage can be seen to play a pivotal role in the poem's development. The poet's self-conscious attention to spoken discourse means, this essay will suggest, that interpretation of the poem may also be enhanced by considering it in relation to the idea of a fiction of orality.

The Wanderer, Lines 50b–57

Lines 50b–57 of *The Wanderer* (which appear on folio 77 recto of the Exeter Book) are arguably the most enigmatic in the poem. They are cited here with no punctuation or translation, since the controversial nature of these will be discussed below:

> sorg bið geniwad
> þonne maga gemynd   mod geondhweorfeð
> greteð gliwstafum   georne geondsceawað
> secga geseldan   swimmað oft on weg
> fleotendra ferð   no þær fela bringeð
> cuðra cwidegiedda   cearo bið geniwad
> þam þe sendan sceal   swiþe geneahhe
> ofer waþema gebind   werigne sefan

Clearly these lines focus on the activity of the mind, its association with memory, and its potential separation from the body. Exactly how they are constructed, however, is a more contentious issue. The question raised by Stanley Greenfield gives some indication of how fundamental the uncertainties are:

> One major difficulty lies in lines 50b–5a, as to exactly what or whom the exile-wanderer greets and finds no consolation in: Are the *secga geseldan* and the *fleotendra ferð* references to sailors on ship or in port, or fantasies of the speaker's imagination, or . . . sea-birds akin to those who substitute for human company in *The Seafarer*? (Greenfield 1966: 152)

And even before the phrase *secga geseldan* ('companions of men', line 53a) occurs, questions arise. First, what is the subject of the verb *geondhweorfeð* ('visits every part of'): is it *maga gemynd* ('memory of kinsmen', line 51a) or *mod* ('mind', line 51b)? Roy Leslie, along with most earlier editors of the poem, takes *gemynd* as subject and *mod* as object (Leslie 1985: 80). Dunning and Bliss agree with Leslie that the verbs *greteð* ('greets') and *geondsceawað* ('examines every part of') in line 52 parallel *geondhweorfeð*; these editors, however, take *mod* as subject and *gemynd* as object, translating lines 51–2 as: ". . . when his imagination calls his kinsmen to mind one by one, greets them joyfully, gazes at them eagerly" (Dunning & Bliss 1969: 22). Peter Clemoes, in his article *"Mens absentia cogitans* in *The Seafarer* and *The Wanderer"* similarly takes *mod* as the subject of these three verbs, and argues further that it "is also the subject of *bringeð* in line 54b" (Clemoes 1969: 75). Clemoes's argument that *mod* is the subject of *bringeð* ('brings') is interesting and will be addressed again later in this essay.

The phrase *secga geseldan* is obscure both in meaning and in grammatical function (see Dunning & Bliss 1969: 114–15). Although its literal translation 'companions of men' seems straightforward, various explanations have been offered for who or what these companions might be. Early critics were generally agreed that the phrase refers to the spirits of absent or dead comrades who appear, and then fade away. A multitude of other possibilities have been suggested since, however: for example, that the Wanderer is staying in a sea-port and that the phrase refers to visiting sailors who sail away again (Owen 1950), or that the *secga geseldan* are seagulls (see Dunning & Bliss 1969: 114–15). Leslie translates *geseldan* as a singular rather than plural noun, and interprets the 'companion of men' as *mod*, the Wanderer's imagination (Leslie 1985: 80–1). Mitchell, in the passage cited at the opening of this essay, suggests that *secga geseldan*, referring to both the Wanderer's former companions and sea-birds, can be taken *apo koinou*, making it both the object of *greteð* and *geondsceawað* and also the subject of *swimmað* ('swims').

There is some constraint on the fluidity of syntactical structure in this passage, which is entailed by the curious half-line *fleotendra ferð* (*Wan* 54a). The previous half-line (*Wan* 53b) includes a finite verb in the present plural form (*swimmað*); the subsequent half-line (*Wan* 54b) includes a finite verb in the third person present singular form (*bringeð*). It is inconceivable in terms of Old English concord (see *OES*: I.13–14) that the noun *ferð* could be the subject simultaneously of both a plural verb and a singular one. However one interprets *ferð*, it has to look either backwards or forwards, but not both.

Two different interpretations have been offered of the noun *ferð*, 'mind/spirit' (used as a collective singular) and 'host/troop'. The meaning 'host/troop' was dismissed by Leslie and by Dunning and Bliss in their editions of the poem, but has been revived in a more recent edition of the poem by Anne Klinck (Klinck 1992: 116–17). There is no need, however, to posit the more unusual meaning 'host/troop' for *ferð*, since the meaning 'mind/spirit' makes sense and is more resonant in the poem as a whole.

Does *fleotendra ferð* belong with what comes before or after? Leslie, treating *ferð* as a plural noun, takes *fleotendra ferð* as the subject of *swimmað* (*Wan* 53b) and translates "the spirits of seafarers often swim away"; he suggests that "the effect of the whole clause is to give a parenthetic explanation of the strange illusions described in lines 50–53a, which can overtake a lonely suffering man at sea" (Leslie 1985: 82). Dunning and Bliss, for whom *ferð* is a singular noun, make *fleotendra ferð* the subject of *bringeð*, and translate: "The companions of men [i.e. the sea-birds of line 47] swim away again, the minds of the floating ones [again the sea-birds] do not bring there any familiar spoken utterances" (Dunning & Bliss 1969: 25, 115).

Another interpretation, however, may be considered. If, as Clemoes argues, *mod* in line 51b may be the subject of *bringeð*, then a possible corollary of this interpretation is that *ferð* in line 54a, in apposition to *mod*, is also the subject of *bringeð*. The mind wanders through its memories of kinsmen, greeting them joyfully, scrutinizing them eagerly, but ultimately it fails to bring back many familiar sayings (presumably implying none at all – see Chapter 3). And this, the speaker concludes (at lines 55–7), renews the sorrow of those who must send out their weary mind across the sea in this way. If the mind of the Wanderer (and of others like him) does not bring back familiar utterances then the fallibility of the mind is implied: sorrow is renewed (*Wan* 50b), Clemoes suggests, "because of the limitations of memories, perhaps . . . because they are fading. The pathos of the inadequacy of memory would indeed contribute to the sadness of repeatedly sending a weary mind in loneliness across an expanse of ocean" (Clemoes 1969: 75). Not only is the inadequacy of memory implied, but also the ephemerality of spoken words: they continue to exist only through the mind's ability to recall them.

An interpretation in which *ferð* is treated as apposed to *mod* in line 51b would imply that *fleotendra* could refer to solitary travellers such as the Wanderer. This raises some difficulties. The word *fleotendra* seems to link semantically to *swimmað* in the previous line, itself apparently referring to the swimming away of sea-birds whom the Wanderer imagines to be his kinsmen. And the verb *fleotan* with an animate subject normally means either 'float' or 'swim', not 'sail' (though the latter applies where a ship is the subject). The passage as a whole, however, expresses the disorientation of the Wanderer through its syntactic ambiguity, which reflects the confusion of sea-birds and kinsmen in his mind. In this context, it seems possible that the use of *fleotendra* reflects the merging of the physical and metaphysical realms which the poem depicts at this point: just as the imagined kinsmen do not literally swim, so too those on a sea-journey do not literally float.

The speaker in this passage, then, envisages how the lonely seafarer, like the Wanderer himself, focuses his mind on the memories from his past, and imagines them recreated in his surroundings. But the mind, when it is sent out over the sea (as in lines 56–7), does not bring back familiar utterances, whether from the memories of kinsmen or from the sea-birds or from both (depending on how loosely one interprets *secga geseldan*). The representation of the mind as separate from the self is, as Malcolm Godden has noted, characteristic of the poem as a whole (Godden 1985: 291–3), and in this passage the mind ranges widely, intensifying the self's sorrow through its inability to bring any intelligible utterances.

In its assertion that the comfort of meaningful communication is not available to the lonely Wanderer, the passage takes a different direction from the portion of Ambrose's *Hexaemeron* which may have been its source (Clemoes 1969: 74–5). Ambrose describes how thought can lead to communication with the absent or dead:

> sequimur proficiscentes, inhaeremus peregrinantibus, copulamur absentibus, alloquimur separatos, defunctos quoque ad colloquium resuscitamus, eosque ut viventes complectimur et tenemus, et vitae officia his usumque deferimus.

> We follow them [those known to us] when they are setting out, we keep with them when they are journeying, we are united with them when they are absent, we speak to them when they are separated, when they are dead we revive them to talk to, and we embrace and hold them as we would living people and accord them the courtesies and usage of life.
>
> (Text and translation cited from Clemoes 1969: 66–7)

For Ambrose this process is to be compared to God's all-seeing perception; for the speaker in *The Wanderer* the attempt to engage with memories in this way only leads to frustration. Unable to recall familiar utterances, the mind is seen to be disconnected from comprehensible speech. It is with this image of failed communication and the ephemerality of spoken words that the poet, at the very centre of the poem, chooses to express the sorrow that isolation can bring.

Thinking and Speech in the Poem as a Whole

However one interprets *fleotendra ferð*, the passage discussed above clearly privileges the role of words in providing comfort, even as it paradoxically implies the transience of those words. By envisaging the sorrow which the unavailability of familiar speech through the memory can bring, the poet points inversely to the power of spoken words to provide consolation. The connection between the act of thinking and that of communication with others is highlighted in this passage by the semantic juxtaposition between words denoting thought (*mod, ferð* and *sefan*) and words denoting speech (*cuðra cwidegiedda*). Collocation of these kinds of words is found elsewhere in the poem as well. On ten separate occasions in the poem words associated with speech or speaking are collocated with words for thought or thinking (*Wan* 6, 10–11, 37–8, 50b–57, 65b–66, 69, 70–2, 88–91, 111, 112b–113). Indeed, there is no instance of a word relating to speech which is not collocated with a word relating to thought.

In repeatedly connecting thought and speech in this way, the poet sets up a pattern of "cross-references" characteristic of his technique elsewhere in the poem (Orchard 2002). Such a technique can be seen to reflect more generally the intertextuality of Old English poetry, an intertextuality which may itself be rooted in the oral-formulaic tradition (Pasternack 1995). As the work of John Miles Foley and Alain Renoir has shown, a particular idiom or theme can take on an added dimension in its context by reference to its traditional or formulaic meaning. Thus Foley writes of a "network of signification" offered by Old English poetic diction, which "provides the individual poet not with a ready-made collection of prefabricated phrases but with a ready-made method of communicating his artistic vision" (Foley 1991: 153). Foley compares this to the effect of narrative metonyms such as the "Beasts of Battle": they "do much more than fill out the narrative; they help to create it in full extratextual resonance, bringing the immanence of tradition to the individual text and individual moment" (Foley 1991: 153). In using the idiom of the link between thought and speech, the *Wanderer* poet is drawing on tradition and thus bringing to bear just such an "extratextual resonance". Other Old English poets use the same idiom, particularly the authors of what is known as wisdom poetry (*Maxims I, The Order of the World* and *Precepts* all provide a number of examples). The *Wanderer* poet, however, has made the complex nature of the discourse between mind and speech central to the meaning of the poem. The poet offers various perspectives on this idea which have wider implications for the poem.

The sorrow felt by the Wanderer is, as has been seen, expressed through his inability to bring to mind familiar spoken utterances. This is an apt image of desolation, given that earlier in the poem the speaker describes how he himself is unable or unwilling to voice his thoughts to others:

> Nis nu cwicra nan
> þe ic him modsefan   minne durre
> sweotule asecgan.   Ic to soþe wat
> þæt biþ in eorle   indryhten þeaw,
> þæt he his ferðlocan   fæste binde,
> healde his hordcofan,   hycge swa he wille.

There is now no one living to whom I dare speak my mind openly. I know in truth that it is an excellent custom in a nobleman that he bind fast his life-enclosure [breast], guard his hoard-chamber [heart], let him think as he will.

(Wan 9b–14)

The Wanderer, not daring to speak his mind openly to any living person, advocates keeping one's thoughts to oneself. The verb *durre* in line 10 is interesting: it is not just because of his physical isolation that the Wanderer does not speak his mind, but because he does not dare to. The implication here may perhaps be that the Wanderer has some guilty secret, or that he would somehow place himself or others in jeopardy merely by the act of talking. At any rate the Wanderer knows that the heroic code encourages such restraint as a counterbalance to the mind's frailty:

> Ne mæg werig mod   wyrde wiðstondan,
> ne se hreo hyge   helpe gefremman

The weary mind cannot withstand fate, nor the troubled spirit provide help.

(Wan 15–16)

The Wanderer describes how he acted in consonance with such heroic precepts. Binding his thoughts with fetters (*Wan* 19–21), he proceeds to search for another treasure-giver (*Wan* 25–9). But his attempt to exercise mental restraint is shown to be far from successful. The syntax of the poem becomes increasingly ambiguous and complex (Greenfield 1963). The convoluted structure of lines 17–29a is evident from the analysis by Dunning and Bliss, who identify eight interrelated clauses:

a principle clause, *forðon . . . fæste*; a clause of comparison, *swa . . . sælan*; a temporal clause, *siþþan . . . biwrah*; a syndetic co-ordinate clause, *ond . . . gebind*; an asyndetic co-ordinate clause, *sohte . . . bryttan*; a noun clause, *hwær . . . meahte*; a relative clause, *(þone) þe . . . wisse*; and a syndetic co-ordinate clause, *oþþe . . . wynnum.* (Dunning & Bliss 1969: 17)

The syntax alerts us to the Wanderer's uncertainty, even before it becomes evident that his attempt to control his thoughts by silently repressing them has failed. At line 29b, the pronouns change from first to third person as the Wanderer begins to generalize from his experience. The continuing syntactic ambiguity extends the uncertainty to embrace all those who have undergone a similar experience. The word *wat* used in lines 29 and 37 suggests a degree of certainty which is undermined by the difficulty of ascertaining exactly what is known (Mitchell 1968b: 178–82; Dunning & Bliss 1969: 28–30). In particular, line 37 introduces a sequence of clauses which seems almost impossible to understand on any rational level in terms of both syntax and meaning. Syntactically, the problem is one of identifying which clauses are to be treated as principal and which as subordinate (Mitchell 1968b: 187–91; Dunning & Bliss 1969: 19–21). However editors may choose to punctuate these lines, their syntactically convoluted structure cannot be ignored. The repetition of *þonne* (*Wan* 39, 45, 49, 51) conveys the idea of an inevitable cause-and-effect progression which reflects the nature of earthly existence. The obscurity in syntactic function of clauses mimetically enacts the gradual disintegration of mental clarity. The mind's struggle to cope with the alternation of its thoughts, whether in memory, dream or hallucination, with the grim reality of the surrounding landscape is vividly evoked. Syntactic ambiguity is as much part of the fabric of the poem as the cumulative power of diction and imagery.

The ambiguity of syntax and indeed its gradual decadence may imply not only the Wanderer's mental torment but also an awareness of the futility of attempting to maintain the kind of restraint advocated earlier in the poem. Certainly such reticence provides no relief for the Wanderer. Unable to express its sorrow, his mind continues to exacerbate it nevertheless: *Gemon he selesecgas ond sincþege* ('he remembers hall-retainers and the receiving of treasure', *Wan* 34). Deprived of his beloved lord's speech (*his winedryhtnes / leofes larcwidum*, 'the spoken counsels of his beloved friendly lord', *Wan* 37–8), he imagines him present: *þinceð him on mode þæt he his mondryhten / clyppe ond cysse* ('it seems to him in his mind that he embraces and kisses his liege lord', *Wan* 41–2). In memory and dream the mind continually reverts to its former happiness, creating a strong contrast with the resurfacing reality.

At the climax of the Wanderer's reverie (*Wan* 50b–57), he finds not only that his own reticence fails to assuage his sorrow but also that he is unable to bring to mind any familiar utterances. The *Wanderer* poet uses the absence of communication between oneself and others to express poignantly the meaninglessness of man's existence without Christian consolation. One might argue that for a poet, whose role is to communicate, this is a particularly apt image. And ironically the poem itself counters this image, since inherent in the very existence of a poem is the idea of communication.

Although sending the mind out over the sea leads to renewed sorrow in lines 55–7, the subsequent lines of the poem offer a more optimistic perspective:

> Forþon ic geþencan ne mæg   geond þas woruld
> for hwan modsefa   min ne gesweorce,
> þonne ic eorla lif   eal geondþence

Therefore I cannot think throughout this world why my mind should not become dark when I meditate on all the life of noblemen.

> (*Wan* 58–60)

To the puzzlement of the speaker, his mind is not dark (an interpretation which is valid, as Mitchell points out, whether the second line here is translated as 'why my mind does not become dark' or 'why my mind may not become dark' – Mitchell 1968a: 55–9). But wisdom, the speaker goes on to say, lies in understanding the direction of one's mind, and when this has been attained speaking out is to be encouraged. Thus at line 69 the speaker includes speech accompanied by knowledge as one of the qualities pertaining to a wise man: *ne næfre gielpes to georn, ær he geare cunne* ('nor ever too eager for boasting, before he fully understands', where 'nor . . . too' probably implies 'not at all' – see, for example, Mitchell 1968: 191–8; see also Chapter 3, this volume). The speaker then elaborates:

> Beorn sceal gebidan   þonne he beot spriceð,
> oþþæt collenferð   cunne gearwe
> hwider hreþra gehygd   hweorfan wille

A man must wait when he utters a vow until, bold-spirited, he really
understands where the thoughts of his heart will turn.

(*Wan* 70–2)

Through careful thought, the right to speak out can be earned. The clause
ær he geare cunne ('before he really understands', *Wan* 69b) may, as Mitchell
has noted, be taken with line 69a, or with lines 70–2, or *apo koinou* (Mitchell
1980: 407). The repetition of *cunne gearwe* in line 71 emphasizes the
importance of speaking out only when the direction of the mind is
understood. When the mind's direction and purpose are understood, the
speaker implies, then meaningful communication can result.

Lines 112–14 of the poem also suggest that speaking out is justified
when one has constructive advice to give:

Til biþ se þe his treowe gehealdeþ,   ne sceal næfre his torn to rycene
beorn of his breostum acyþan,   nemþe he ær þa bote cunne,
eorl mid elne gefremman.

He is good who keeps his faith, nor must a man ever disclose his grief too
quickly from his breast, unless that nobleman has thought out previously
how to bring about the remedy with courage.

(*Wan* 112–14)

To speak of one's feelings is acceptable, but only in a constructive context.
The poet, in advocating such a compromise through his speaker, perhaps
simultaneously justifies his own poem.

Three other passages in the poem point in a different way to the poet's
focus on spoken discourse and its relation to thought. Lines 6–7, 88–91
and 111 all act as a kind of framework to what precedes or follows them.
In the first and last of these, both of which begin *swa cwæð*, the poet
speaks in his own voice; lines 88–91 may on the other hand be spoken by
either the poet or the Wanderer.

It has been long acknowledged that the *swa cwæð* construction, which
is used at lines 6 and 111 of the poem, seems to carry a significance
which has nothing to do with the question of speakers. Rosemary Woolf
sums up this puzzling feature of the poem:

In a personal response to the poem it seems that the *swa cwæþ* construction
at lines 6 and 111 is so conspicuously intrusive that it must serve an
important function, whilst paradoxically the question of who is speaking at
the beginning of the poem . . . and at the end . . . seems scarcely to affect
one's understanding of the poem. (Woolf 1975: 197)

The construction may be, as Woolf suggests, a blocking device to separate out the first and last passages about the consolation of God's mercy from the main body of the poem, but it is also a tangible manifestation of the *Wanderer* poet's self-conscious focus on the act of speaking out. The construction can be compared in its function with *ond þas word acwið* (*Wan* 91), again used to introduce a speaker in the poem. In each case the act of speaking out is explicitly linked to the process of thought. In each case the narrator describes a speaker who represents the effective inter-action of a wise mind and speaking out.

In lines 6–7 the Wanderer's speech is linked to his being *gemyndig*, or 'mindful':

> Swa cwæð eardstapa,   earfeþa gemyndig,
> wraþra wælsleahta,   winemæga hryre.

Thus said the Wanderer, mindful of adversities, of cruel slaughters, of the fall of kinsmen.

(*Wan* 6–7)

The Wanderer's memories prompt the words which he speaks. Indeed the act of speaking thoughts aloud can be said to underlie the very exist-ence of the poem.

At lines 88–91 a wise man is introduced in terms strikingly similar to lines 6–7:

> Se þonne þisne wealsteal   wise geþohte
> ond þis deorce lif   deope geondþenceð,
> frod in ferðe,   feor oft gemon
> wælsleahta worn,   ond þas word acwið.

He, then, who has wisely thought about this foundation and deeply meditates on this dark life, wise in mind, often remembers from long ago a multitude of slaughters, and utters these words.

(*Wan* 88–91)

Like lines 6–7, these present a speaker drawing on the memory of harsh experiences to present a viewpoint on existence in this world. In this passage, however, there is a particular emphasis on the wisdom and profundity of the speaker's mind, as the aggregation of words associated with mind and thought suggest: *wise geþohte* ('has wisely thought about'), *deope geondþenceð* ('deeply meditates on'), *frod in ferðe* ('wise in mind') and *gemon* ('remembers'). The mind's wisdom is resolved in the spoken word: *ond þas word acwið* ('and utters these words'). Speech represents a way of passing on understanding.

Finally, echoing its previous use in the poem, *swa cwæð* recurs in line 111: *Swa cwæð snottor on mode, gesæt him sundor æt rune.* This is usually translated as: 'Thus said the one wise in mind, he sat apart in secret meditation.' Line 111a is, however, curiously ambiguous; it might also, as Gerald Richman has suggested (Richman 1982), mean: 'Thus said the wise one in his mind' (that is, he said it to himself). Both interpretations are feasible: in the first *snottor on mode* ('wise in mind') parallels *frod in ferðe* ('wise in mind') at line 90; in the second there is a more effective link with the second half of the line. This syntactic ambiguity, I suggest, is not accidental. Thinking and saying interact in syntax and meaning, even as the poem resolves into its conclusion where the message of eternal hope and comfort is finally explicit, and the possibility of a true conjunction of communication and understanding is offered.

Part of the development of *The Wanderer*'s meaning rests on the idea that when the mind engages constructively with experience, truths emerge which can be exchanged with others through speech. First the poem presents a fictionalized persona who speaks out about the need not to speak out, but who fails to find comfort from such taciturnity. The second half of the poem suggests that speaking out when understanding has been attained is justifiable. Simultaneously the poem is justifying its own utterances; it parallels the wise man's and Wanderer's own speeches in that it is itself a speaking out, self-consciously reflecting its own message about the right to express one's feelings. Its freedom of speech, it implies, has been earned.

The Wanderer and the Fiction of Orality

In the course of its exploration of speech in relation to thought, the poem self-consciously draws attention to the act of speaking out. This suggests that it might be fruitfully considered in relation to the idea of the fiction of orality, which has been seen as an important element of Old English poetry. John Niles writes of Old English poetry that it "regularly 'speaks' to its 'audience' as if it were being voiced aloud in a social situation" (Niles 1998: 202). Old English poets exploit this fiction of orality in sophisticated ways, some of which can be seen to have interesting parallels with *The Wanderer*. In *Maxims I* the poetic persona begins by directly addressing the audience, demanding an exchange of knowledge:

> Frige mec frodum wordum!   Ne læt þinne ferð onhælne,
> degol þæt þu deopost cunne!   Nelle ic þe min dyrne gesecgan,
> gif þu me þinne hygecræft hylest   ond þine heortan geþohtas.
> Gleawe men sceolon gieddum wrixlan

Question me with wise words. Do not let your mind be hidden, or what you know most deeply be obscure. I will not tell you my secret if you conceal from me the wisdom of your mind and your heart's thoughts. Wise men ought to exchange sayings.

(*Max I* 1–4a)

The *Maxims I* poet, like the *Wanderer* poet, incorporates a range of words relating to speaking out and the mind. In this passage the imperative verbs in line 1 themselves draw attention to the act of speaking out, and the pile-up of first-person and second-person pronouns points to the mutual benefits of verbal exchange. Whereas *The Wanderer* makes no direct reference to its addressee, *Maxims I* exploits the fictional situation of one speaker (*ic*) directly addressing another (*þu*) to enhance its particular emphasis on the need to share knowledge.

The fiction of orality is exploited by other poets in different ways. Thus, for example, the *Beowulf* poet describes a poet reciting, perhaps even composing orally, a poem about Beowulf:

>   Hwilum cyninges þegn
> guma gilphlæden   gidda gemyndig
> se ðe ealfela   ealdgesegena
> worn gemunde,   word oþer fand
> soðe gebunden;   secg eft ongan
> sið Beowulfes   snyttrum styrian
> ond on sped wrecan   spel gerade,
> wordum wrixlan.

Sometimes the king's retainer, a man gifted with eloquence and with the memory for lays, one who remembered a whole host of ancient tales, devised other words truly linked; that man then set out to relate Beowulf's exploit skilfully, to recite successfully a well-wrought tale, varying his words.

(*Beo* 867–74)

Whether or not this passage actually describes the innovative oral composition of poetry rather than just its recital (see Chapter 1), it clearly
draws attention to the voicing aloud of poetry. Its effect is to alert *Beowulf*'s
audience to the idea that a poem about Beowulf was composed and
recited before a different audience, one made up of the characters in
Beowulf itself. A fictional image of a poet speaking out to his audience
about Beowulf is embedded within a poem which, right from its arresting
opening word *Hwæt*, exploits the fiction of a poet speaking out to his
audience about Beowulf.

The Book-Moth Riddle of the Exeter Book (Krapp & Dobbie no. 47,
Williamson no. 45) uses the perspective of a first-person speaker (*ic*) to
describe the destruction of written words by a book-moth. Through a
complex series of puns it plays on the relationship between written and
spoken words in order to represent "the simultaneous reality and insub-
stantiality of language" (Robinson 1975: 362):

> Moððe word fræt.   Me þæt þuhte
> wrætlicu wyrd,   þa ic þæt wundor gefrægn,
> þæt se wyrm forswealg   wera gied sumes,
> þeof in þystro,   þrymfæstne cwide
> ond þæs strangan staþol.   Stælgiest ne wæs
> wihte þy gleawra,   þe he þam wordum swealg.

A moth ate the words. That seemed to me a strange event, when I heard of
that wonder, that the worm swallowed the speech of a certain man, thief in
the darkness, the glorious statement and the foundation of that mighty
(utterance). The thieving guest was not at all the wiser in that he had
swallowed those words. (see also Chapter 1)

The paradoxical idea that words are both substantial and insubstantial
is enhanced by the series of puns relating to speech. *Word* in the first
half-line, as Craig Williamson notes, can be taken in the sense of 'spoken
words' or 'speech': "neither moths nor worms can eat spoken words –
that is the paradox of the riddle" (Williamson 1977: 286). *Wyrd* meaning
'event/fate' in the second line may be a pun on *gewyrd* meaning 'speech/
conversation'. *Gied* (line 3) and *cwide* (line 4) reinforce the reference to
spoken language. And the insistent repetition in the riddle of the metaphor of devouring words (lines 1, 3 and 6) emphasizes its implicitly
paradoxical quality: words are normally spoken by the mouth rather

than devoured by it. The transience of spoken words is as much the subject of this riddle as the transience of words on vellum.

Old English poets, it seems, exploited the oral culture which may have provided the conditions from which their works ultimately derived. Seth Lerer argues for "the fundamentally self-referential quality of many Anglo-Saxon works, that is, for their thematic interest in the methods of their own composition, transmission, and understanding" (Lerer 1991: 4). Of poetry he writes more specifically:

> What we have come to think of as the inherently 'oral' quality of early English poetry – its origins in formulaic composition or its transmission in the public contexts of instruction or entertainment – may, as I suggest, be a literary fiction of its own. (Lerer 1991: 4)

The Wanderer explores the image of voice and mind interacting within the context of a fiction of orality in particularly imaginative ways. In his own speaking out, the poet parallels the speaking out by the speaker or speakers within his poem, in which the act of speaking out in certain circumstances is advocated. The poet justifies the existence of his own poem. And yet paradoxically, in the central image of the poem the poet also addresses the possibility that spoken words have no substantial existence: the Wanderer, when he most needs words of consolation, can find no familiar utterances. The poet incorporates orality into his meaning, fictionalizing and analysing the art of oral expression. The work brings to the fore the issue of oral discourse. The spoken word and its function are integral to the meaning of *The Wanderer*.

The spoken word is inherently ephemeral. This being so, it is appropriate that a poet whose overriding theme is earthly transience should choose to focus on this aspect of human communication. The poet draws for much of his imagery on a pre-literate heroic world when spoken utterances were the only means of communication and were crucial for the survival of the whole culture. The mind, the memory, were the only means by which spoken utterances could be given a kind of continuity beyond the present. As Franz Bäuml succinctly expresses it:

> The spoken word is heard, and, as sound, it is ephemeral. It therefore is limited to two modes of existence: its utterance and its remembrance. Its utterance being ephemeral, its remembrance is critical. (Bäuml 1980: 247)

Like the spoken word, the poet shows, the mind and its memories are ultimately transient and unreliable. Spoken words can be beneficial, but only when thought and speech are seen to cohere in their recognition that the meaning of existence is to be found in the eternal *fæstnung* of heaven. The critique of oral discourse which the poet offers in the poem enhances his message: even the art of poetry has relevance and meaning only insofar as it relates to and promotes the universal search for God's comfort and stability.

The *Wanderer* poet uses spoken words as an image of earthly transience. The scanty survival of writings in Old English also attests to such transience: *The Wanderer* itself is extant only in a unique copy in the Exeter Book. By speaking his own mind, both through his inspirational teaching and through his formidable body of scholarship, Bruce Mitchell has been pre-eminent in fostering our understanding of Old English texts, and thus in counteracting some of the ravages of time which have afflicted them.

References and Further Reading

Bäuml, F. H. (1980). Varieties and consequences of medieval literacy and illiteracy. *Speculum*, 55, 237–65.

Clemoes, P. (1969). *Mens absentia cogitans* in *The Seafarer* and *The Wanderer*. In D. A. Pearsall & R. A. Waldron (eds), *Medieval Literature and Civilization: studies in memory of G. N. Garmonsway* (pp. 62–77). London: Athlone Press.

Foley, J. M. (1991). Texts that speak to readers who hear: Old English poetry and the languages of oral tradition. In A. J. Frantzen (ed.) (pp. 141–56).

Godden, M. R. (1985). Anglo-Saxons on the mind. In M. Lapidge & H. Gneuss (eds) (pp. 271–98).

Greenfield, S. B. (1963). Syntactic analysis and Old English poetry. *NM*, LXIV, 373–8.

Greenfield, S. B. (1966). The Old English elegies. In E. G. Stanley (ed.) (pp. 147–72).

Lerer, S. (1991). *Literacy and Power in Anglo-Saxon Literature*. Lincoln, NB: University of Nebraska Press.

Mitchell, B. (1968a). More musings on Old English syntax. *NM*, LXIX, 53–63. Repr. in B. Mitchell (ed.) (1988) (pp. 126–33).

Mitchell, B. (1968b). Some syntactical problems in *The Wanderer*, *NM*, LXIX, 172–98.

Michell, B. (1980). The dangers of disguise: Old English texts in modern punctuation. *RES*, XXXI, 385–413.

Niles, J. D. (1998). Exeter Book Riddle 74 and the play of the text. *ASE*, 27, 169–207.

Orchard, A. (2002). Re-reading *The Wanderer*: the value of cross-references. In T. N. Hall (ed.), *Via Crucis: essays on early medieval sources and ideas in memory of J. E. Cross*. Morgantown, WV: West Virginia University Press.

Owen, W. J. B. (1950). *Wanderer*, lines 50–57. *MLN*, LXV, 161–5.

Pasternack, C. B. (1995). *The Textuality of Old English Poetry* (CSASE, 13). Cambridge: Cambridge University Press.

Renoir, A. (1988). *A Key to Old Poems: the oral-formulaic approach to the interpretation of West-Germanic verse*. University Park, PA: Pennsylvania State University Press.

Richman, G. (1982). Speaker and speech boundaries in *The Wanderer*. *JEGP*, LXXXI, 469–79. Repr. in K. O'Brien O'Keeffe (ed.) (1994). *Old English Shorter Poems: basic readings* (pp. 303–18). New York: Garland.

Robinson, F. C. (1975). Artful ambiguities in the Old English 'book-moth' riddle. In L. E. Nicholson & D. W. Frese (eds) (pp. 355–62).

Shippey, T. A. (1994) *The Wanderer* and *The Seafarer* as wisdom poetry. In H. Aertsen & R. H. Bremmer, Jr (eds), *Companion to Old English Poetry*. Amsterdam: VU University Press.

Woolf, R. (1975). *The Wanderer, The Seafarer*, and the genre of *Planctus*. In L. E. Nicholson & D. W. Frese (eds) (pp. 192–207). Repr. in H. O'Donoghue (ed) (1986). *Art and Doctrine: essays on medieval literature: Rosemary Woolf* (pp. 157–73). London: Hambledon Press.

Chapter 7

Wulfstan's Scandinavian Loanword Usage: An Aspect of the Linguistic Situation in the Late Old English Danelaw

Tadao Kubouchi

The question of "the continuity of English prose" or that of "the English-ness of Old English" has recently acquired a new urgency. Mitchell (1994) cogently demonstrates the continuity and furnishes a guide as to what remains to be done. However, linguistic evidence of Scandinavian influence, datable to the transition period between Late Old English and Early Middle English and localizable to the Danelaw area, still lacks a corpus of sufficient size. Old Norse-derived loanword studies, at least related to pre-Early Middle English, are deplorably fated to be limited by this insufficiency. Although the situation has changed little, however, there are signs of attempts from different viewpoints which promise to throw new or renewed light on the linguistic situation in the tenth- and eleventh-century Danelaw, as testified by Townend (2000, 2002). In what follows I will review firstly the status of Scandinavian loanwords in the history of the English language and secondly Wulfstan's Scandinavian loanword usage as it changes over his lifetime.

Wulfstan's works done while he was Archbishop of York (1002–1023) and plurally Bishop of Worcester (1002–1016) outnumber those done while he was Bishop of London (996–1002). York then was at the heart of Scandinavian settlement, where there was a bilingual society. Figure 7.1 shows how densely parish names of Scandinavian origin are distributed within the Danelaw. The line connecting London and Chester marks the

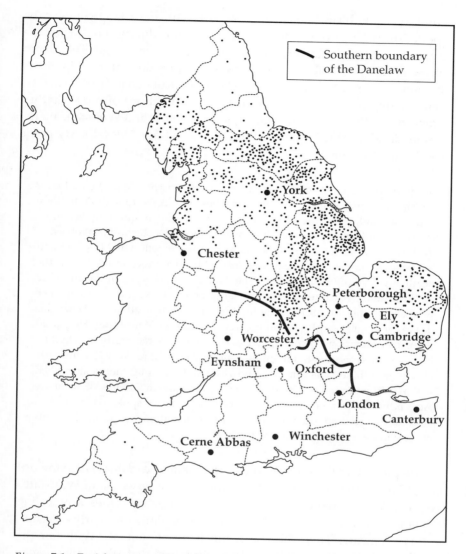

Figure 7.1 Parish names of Scandinavian origin in early eleventh-century England (county boundaries 1970)

boundary of the Danelaw. In this respect Wulfstan's language can be expected to provide the material of more than ordinary interest for the assessment of Scandinavian influence at its beginning stage. This paper represents another attempt to unravel the question of the linguistic situation in the Late Old English Danelaw. Kubouchi (1983) was an attempt along the same lines in terms of the alterations of prose rhythm as reflected in the manuscript punctuation of Ælfric and Wulfstan, alterations made when Wulfstan rewrote Ælfric's *De Falsis Diis* [*sic*]. My point includes the following:

> But perhaps the most important factors are the purpose and the audience which the authors had – or their scribes and correctors thought they had – in mind, when they wrote or rewrote the text in question. When he rewrote, Wulfstan was Archbishop of York as well as Bishop of Worcester. York then was at the heart of Scandinavian settlement. His York seat and his position as Primate must have made him deeply concerned with the heathen worship prevailing there. He had as his audience in the churches of York (and Worcester as well) a large and "not very subtle audience whose capacities for abstruse thought he did not overestimate." Hence his desire for greater emphasis and greater clarification of meaning. He placed these considerations before that for adherence to regularity in rhythm. His version shows his intention in a rather conspicuous way. Its strength, clarity, multifariousness in tone and rhythm are among the most marked features. The version we have in T [i.e. T_C, Bethurum's E; for MS sigla see Appendix] is a product designed, in the first place, for spoken delivery to a large audience. Our examination of the punctuation of the manuscripts bears witness to this. (Kubouchi 1983: 70)

Can we prove that the same is true of Wulfstan's Scandinavian loanword usage? That is the main aim of this paper. The observation of Wulfstan's Scandinavian loanword usage, at the same time, provides a revealing insight into Wulfstan's role in the linguistic situation of the early eleventh-century Danelaw. There has been much discussion of "Wulfstan the homilist and statesman". Observation will reveal that Wulfstan's role as educator also deserves some attention. Before we enter into the discussion of Wulfstan's changing vocabulary, it would be useful to reconsider what the status of Old Norse-derived loanwords in the history of the English language is like. A general survey follows.

The number of Scandinavian loanwords in English looks far smaller than we expect in comparison with those from Latin and French. This reminds us that the distinction between "open-class" items and "closed-system" items must be considered in the discussion of foreign influence on vocabulary, especially in the case of Old Norse-derived loanwords. In other words, any analysis of Old Norse loans in terms of "types" only might be an imperfect and misleading one. "Tokens" should also be considered at the same time.

Finkenstaedt and Wolff (1973: table 28) came up with the following figures for four major sources, i.e. Germanic, Latin, French (including Old French and Anglo-French) and Old Norse: 16,130 (20.13%), 22,633 (28.25%), 22,699 (28.34%), 1,471 (1.83%) for the 80,096 entries of the *Shorter Oxford English Dictionary* (*SOED*) (1968 version, without Addenda of 1,086 entries); 5,007 (21.53%), 5,616 (24.14%), 8,263 (35.53%), 471 (2.02%) for Hornby et al. (1963 – *ALD*); and 1,825 (45.81%), 381 (9.56%), 1,514 (38%), 123 (3.09%) for West (1965 – *GSL*). The entries which *ALD* and *GSL* have in common with *SOED* – and which are therefore relevant to the statistical comparison – are 23,257 and 3,984, respectively. Native words, i.e. words inherited from Germanic roots, represent the core of the language and the acutely rising curve is natural. The curves for the foreign languages are remarkable: the one for Latin shows a sharp drop, and those for French and Old Norse steadily rising curves. This indicates that those loanwords from the latter two languages are distributed closer to the core of the English vocabulary. Which is closer? It is a hard question to answer, but we can point out that Old Norse-derived words are, in some crucial cases, distributed where words from French and Latin are not distributed.

Grammar is said to form a closed system, vocabulary an open one. Vocabulary, however, does not in every respect form an open system: classes like nouns, adjectives, verbs and adverbs are open classes whose membership is "indefinite and unlimited" (Biber et al. 1999: 56); and those like articles, pronouns (demonstrative, personal, interrogative, relative, reflexive, indefinite), auxiliaries, prepositions and conjunctions are groups of closed systems, whose membership is definite and limited. Some other groups, i.e. numerals, intensifiers, conjunctive adverbs and interjections or "inserts", cannot be easily classified as closed or open, and new members of closed systems can, although quite rarely and slowly, be created or borrowed: a newly revived and Latin-derived preposition *re* is a good example. Even open-class groups form closed subgroups within themselves. Words denoting basic things like body-parts, father–mother and brother–sister relationships, basic motion, and so forth form closed sub-groups. Another example would be the above-mentioned intensifiers: they are derived from original adverbs. Although these pose problems, the point of view focusing on the "open-class" vs. "closed-system" distinction is a well-grounded and significant one.

What percentages do the open-class items occupy in the vocabulary? According to Finkenstaedt and Wolff (1973: table 21), and to take *ALD* figures as an example, nouns occupy 59.14% (13,751 words), adjectives 20.43% (4,749 words), verbs 18.26% (4,245 words) and adverbs 1.43% (332 words), the total of the open-class items being 99.26% (23,077 words). The remaining 0.74% account for the closed-system items in *ALD*. The "article" slot in the table is left blank and the total is 173. However, the number of these should be 180 (23,257 − 23,077 = 180). These closed groups largely comprise the so-called "function words". On the type-level, the open-class items, which are called lexical words, are predominant and the closed-system items only a few, but on the token-level the distribution of lexical words and function words is roughly equal, although the distribution varies from one register or genre to another. According to the frequency list of grammatical word classes in Leech et al. (2001: 296, list 6.1.2), which is based on the two-million-word Sampler Corpus of the British National Corpus, occurrences of nouns (21.5%), adjectives (5.9%), verbs (10.9%) and adverbs (6.9%) account for 45.2% of lemmatized tokens (the figures are normed to a frequency per million words). The remaining 50% account for the closed-system items, tokens of which are made up by pronouns (9%), determiners (11.2%, which include articles), anomalous finites and verbals (9.3%), prepositions (11%), conjunctions (5.6%), numerals (2.2%) and interjections (1.6%). There may be a margin of error especially owing to terminological differences, and intensifiers, for example, are counted as open-class here. All the same the dramatic leap from 0.74% (on the type-level) to 49.9% (on the token-level) is especially noteworthy and it represents what closed-system words are grammatically responsible for.

Old English frequency analysis does not yet seem to have gone beyond that of poetical vocabulary, and we have to wait for the appearance of lemmatized concordances based on Healey and Venezky (1980) and Venezky and Butler (1985). One of the most useful word-lists so far published is that of Madden and Magoun (1972). The work is based on "a count of the 168,500-plus running words used in the 30,000-plus lines or, better, verse-pairs of the Anglo-Saxon poetical corpus". The following observation, nevertheless, might be read as applicable to the frequency profile of Old English prose vocabulary, which emphasizes the equal predominance of the closed-system items, and matches, though only approximately, the profile that Modern English frequency analysis gives: "A glance at the beginning of this list will show that the first five entries (i.e. (1) 15,974 pers. and poss. pron. *ic, þu, he*; (2) 10,458 dem. pron., def. art. *se, sio, þæt.* rel. particle *þe*; (3) 5,001 *and* 'and'; (4) 4,747 *on/in* prep., adv.; *inn(e), innan* adv.; (5) 4,189 *wesan/bion* 'to be') add up to 41,269 running words, providing the learner with nearly 25 per cent of all words used, while the three inflected items among these with a total of 30,621 account for nearly 20 per cent of words used. The combined forms of the personal pronoun alone constitute almost 10 per cent of words used" (Madden & Magoun 1972: vi).

Old Norse-derived closed-system words include prepositions such as *fro* 'from' (?c1200 *Orm.* – ON *frá*), *like* (?c1200 *Orm.* – ON *glíkr*), *thwart* 'across' (?a1425 MS. Htrn.95 *thwerte* – ON *þvert* (neut.) ← *þverr* 'athwart, transverse'), *till* 'to, till' (OE *til* 'to', ?c1200 *Orm. till* 'till' – ON *til* 'to, till'), *until* (?c1200 *Orm.* – ON **und + til*); conjunctions such as *and* 'if' (a1225 (?OE) *Lamb. Hom.* cf. ON *enda*), *both(e)* (as a correlative conjunction) (?c1200 *Orm. baþe* – ON *baþir*), *though* (?c1200 *Orm. þohh* – ON *þó*), *till* (?a1121–60 *Peterb. Chron.* – ON *til* 'to, till' [prep.]), *until* (?c1200 *Orm.* ← *til* [prep.]). On *and* 'if', *OED* (s.v. *and* C. conj. conditional, = if) says that the suggestion by Vigfusson et al. (cf. Cleasby & Vigfusson, s.v. *enda*) that the English use was derived from that of Norse *enda* is very doubtful. But the alternative suggestion on the other hand is not wholly acceptable either. The earliest Norse-derived examples cited in *MED* include those from *Ancr.* (Corp-C) dated c1230 (?a1200) and Laȝamon's *Brut* dated a1225 (?a1200), under whose MS provenance *Lambeth Homilies* also falls. Vigfusson's suggestion thus can be said to be still tenable.

Pronouns include "pronominal adjectives" on the one hand, such as *bothe* 'both' (a1131 *Peterb. Chron.* an. 1127 *baðe* – ON *báðir*) and *same* (a1375 *WPal. same* ← [adj.]: ?c1200 *Orm. same* – ON *samr, sami* [masc.], *sama* [fem., neut.]), and personal pronouns on the other, such as *they* (c1150 [?OE] *PDidax. þæȝe* – ON *þeir*), *their(s)* (?c1200 *Orm. þeȝȝre* – ON *þeira*), *them* (?c1200 *Orm. þeȝȝm* – ON *þeim* [dat.]). The third person feminine personal pronoun *she* is "of difficult etymology". Hoad (1986) and *MED* seem to have restricted their proposals to the following: "All types [*scæ* [?a1160 *Peterb. Chron.* an. 1140], *sȝe, sse, sche* (XIII); *scho, sho* and *ȝho, ȝhe*] appear to be developments [with LOE stress shift in the diphthongs] of the OE fem. pers. pron. *heo*, acc. *hie*" (Hoad 1986). However, we are not able to deny the possibility as a whole of developments of the OE fem. demonstrative pronoun *sío, séo, síe*. It is to be noted, as *OED* says (s.v. *she*), that "the districts in which *she* or *sho* first appears in the place of *heo* are marked by the abundance of Scandinavian elements in the dialect and place-names; and in Old Norse the dem. pron. (of all genders) is often used as a personal pron." Despite the *OED*'s unfavourable verdict, it is still arguable that ON *sjá* 'this', although its reference included nom. sing. masc. as well as nom. sing. fem., had a role to play in preparing the way for *scæ*'s appearance in the *Peterborough Chronicle* as a fem. nom. sg. pers. pron. and that the role was significant.

There is one more point to be added about the pronouns and this concerns the development in English of the definite article. Old English had two sets of demonstrative pronouns and no separate definite article. Old Norse had both sets of demonstrative pronouns and a definite article set, although "the definite article *inn* was normally suffixed to its nouns, unless an adjective preceded the noun" (Gordon 1957: 312). Fisiak points out that the appearance of a definite article as distinct from the demonstrative pronouns in Middle English must have been due to the constant contact with Scandinavian (Fisiak 1977: 251).

Auxiliaries which might safely be said to be closely connected to Old Norse include a present indicative 1–3 pl. *are*. OE *earun, aron, earan* are restricted to Northumbrian and Mercian texts. West-Saxon texts usually had *sindon, sint* and *beoþ*. Old Norse forms are *erum, eruð* and *eru*, and this phonetic similarity must have played some role in the development of the northern forms into the standard forms in the Middle English period.

As we have seen, Old Norse-derived closed-system words include prepositions, conjunctions, pronouns and auxiliaries. Latin and Old French-derived closed-system words, on the other hand, include only prepositions and conjunctions. This feature should not be downplayed when we set out to estimate the extent of the Old Norse influence on English vocabulary. Even in the cases of open-class items, it is their depth and homogeneity that examinations of Old Norse words in English in many cases impress on us. They largely belong to common "Lebenswelt" vocabulary smelling of everyday life. A glance at such words as *anger, angry, bag, band, cast, die, dirt, egg, flat, happy, hit, husband, ill, knife, low, root, scurf, sister, skill, skin, skirt, take, Thursday, ugly, want, window, wrong* will suffice for confirmation. Phonological homogeneity includes monosyllabism and consonant cluster features; and morphological homogeneity includes the two-type verbal conjugation system. So-called irregular verbs mainly comprise reflexes of OE strong verbs, which are smaller in total number than "regular" weak verbs, but are for the most part commoner and of higher frequency on the practical level. *SOED* records 260 irregular verbs, of which 28 are of foreign origin. Of 28 borrowed verbs 20 are from Old Norse: *cast, fling, get, rid, rive, take,* etc., 7 from Old French (e.g. *catch, cost, pay, strive,* etc.) and one from Dutch (*split*).

What is also striking is the conspicuous presence of the vocabulary shared between Old English and Old Norse, with more or less distinctive and systematic differences of pronunciation. This feature results in the coexistence and/or rivalry of such pairs as: (ON /sk/: OE /ʃ/) *scatter / shatter, skirt / shirt*; (ON /k/: OE /tʃ/) *call* / OE *ceallian, kirk /church*; (ON /g/: OE /j/) *give* / OE *ģiefan, gift* / OE *ģift*, ME *egges* / ME *eyren*, and so forth. This partly explains the possible success with which the Icelandic poet Gunnlaug was able to recite his poem in his language to Ethelred the Unready at the latter's court and another possible success with which the messenger of the Vikings, standing on the shore at Maldon in 991, made himself understood when he tried to announce "the message of the seafarers" to the English ealdorman Byrhtnoth and his men. Words such as OE *fæder* (ON *faðer, -ir*), OE *módor* (ON *móðer-ir*) represent the cases in which it is hard to tell which language the modern forms come from. *OED* says (s.v. *father*), "The mod. Eng *-ther* for OE *-der, -dor* in *father* and *mother* is often wrongly said to be due to the analogy of *brother*, or to Scandinavian influence; it is really the result of a phonetic law common to the great majority of Eng. dialects." But no one could utterly deny the possibility of the Old Norse influence, especially when it comes to Danelaw usage. Danelaw, at least as it was in the Viking Age, was a bilingual society.

Date could be another indicator. Although the evidence peak comes lamentably late (the thirteenth century), it precedes that of Old French (the fourteenth century). As for the delayed emergence into written English of Scandinavian loanwords, Burnley explains: "Contact between the two languages took place in the spoken mode, and largely with reference to questions of immediate interest only to the local community. Most Scandinavian terms were adopted into English at the level of everyday communication and were barred from written expression both by the existence of a standardized form of written English, the West-Saxon *Schriftsprache*, which was the official administrative language of the Anglo-Saxon state, and by the perception of Scandinavian-derived forms as belonging to comparatively non-literary registers" (Burnley 1992: 419).

Infiltration at the level of everyday communication in the earlier period could account for the closeness to the inner core of the language.

Now we may turn to an examination of Wulfstan's Scandinavian loanword usage. As our concern is about the usage as shown in his oral-delivery-oriented prose, we have to confine ourselves to Wulfstan's homiletic texts: homilies collected in Bethurum's edition (1957) and his revision of Ælfric's first Old English Pastoral Letter for Wulfstan (Fehr II). Hans Peters (1981a, b) gives a list of 148 Old Norse-derived words evidenced in Old English works, although this list includes 35 words of still undetermined origin. Of 148 ON loanwords at least 10 appear in our Wulfstan corpus (Roman numerals indicate homily numbers in Bethurum (1957); for MS sigla see Appendix. B_B stands for Bethurum's B; $C_B = D_F$ Bethurum's C, Fehr's D; $E_B = T_C$ Bethurum's E, Clemoes' [or Pope's] T, and so on): *fes(i)an* 'to drive away' (XX [E_BI_B]), *grið* 'peace, protection, sanctuary' (Xc, XIX, XX [B_BH_B, C_B, E_BI_B]), *lagu* 'law' (Ib, III, V, VI, VIIIc, IX, Xa, Xc, XI, XII, XIII, XV, XVII, XIX, XX [B_BH_B, C_B], XXI, Fehr II [D_F]), *nydgyld* 'exaction, tribute' (XX [C_B, E_BI_B]), *nydmæg* 'blood-relation, cousin' (XX [C_B, E_BI_B], Fehr II [D_F]), *þegengilde* 'legal money value of a thane' (XX [C_B, E_BI_B]]), *þræl(l)* 'serf, thrall' (IX, XX [C_B, E_BI_B]), *unlagu* 'injustice, bad law' (ON *úlög* [pl.]; XI, XX [B_BH_B, C_B, E_BI_B]), *wælcyrie* 'walkyrie, lit. chooser of the slain' (XX [E_BI_B]), *wicing* 'sea-robber, Viking' (XX [C_B, E_BI_B)]). To Peters' list the following derivatives may be added: *ungyld* 'excessive tax' (XX [B_BH_B, C_B, E_BI_B]), *griðian* 'to protect' (Xc, XX [C_B, E_BI_B]), *griðleas* 'unprotected' (XX [B_BH_B, C_B, E_BI_B]), *lahbryce* 'breach of law' (XX [B_BH_B, C_B, E_BI_B]; cf. OE *æwbryce* 'adultery' (VIIIc, Xc, XX [B_BH_B, C_B, E_BI_B])), *lahgewrit* 'legal writing' (Xa), *lahlice* 'lawfully' (XX [B_BH_B, C_B, E_BI_B], Fehr II [D_F]), *þrælriht* 'the rights of a slave' (XX [B_BH_B, C_B, E_BI_B]). The Scandinavian names of Germanic deities such as *Oðon* (ON *Óðenn* 'Odin, Woden, Mercury'; OE *Woden*) (XII) and *Þor* (ON *Þórr* 'Thor, thunder'; OE *Þunor*) (XII), too, may be added. It should be noted here that they are all open-class items, especially nouns, and yet they exhibit a bias towards legal terms and do not belong to aspects of everyday life. This suggests that the Old Norse influence on Wulfstan's vocabulary on the whole remained not very profound. But we know that at the same time side by side with such tendencies in Wulfstan the Anglo-Saxon educator, there must have been tendencies which ultimately resulted in more profound influence evidenced by the infiltration of closed-system changes. This shows that in regard to the linguistic situation of the early eleventh-century Danelaw, we should bear in mind that what Wulfstan's loanword usage gives us is no more than one aspect, and that there must have been various other aspects, although in Wulfstan himself we see multifarious sub-aspects or aspects within aspects.

The chronological distribution of the Wulfstan loanwords is illuminating. According to Bethurum's chronology (Bethurum 1957: 101–4), the order of Wulfstan's homiletic works is as follows. First comes the group called "Eschatological homilies", which were written mainly when he was Bishop of London (996–1002): II, III, Ia (in Latin), Ib, IV, V. The following nine texts, which deal with "the Christian Faith", are assumed to have been written after he was appointed Archbishop of York (1002) and Bishop of Worcester (1002) and before his *Canons of Edgar* (1005–1007): Xa, VI, VII, IX, XI, VIIIa (in Latin), VIIIb, Xb (in Latin), Xc, VIIIc. About the order of the other homilies, XIII–XXI, Bethurum says, "The order is less clear" (Bethurum 1957: 104). But in view of the contents and elsewhere the order in her mind seems to be: XIV, XV, XVI, XVII, XVIII, XIX, XX (c. 1014), XIII, XXI. She says, "Certainly late in his career are XX and XIII . . . On stylistic grounds I should be inclined to put XIV and XV in the early period, and XXI for its concentrated and skilful indictment of evil leaders of the people fairly late" (Bethurum 1957: 104).

Bethurum XII contains *De Falsis Dies* [sic], which is a revision by Wulfstan of the roughly first 100-line portion of the later and expanded version of Ælfric's *De Falsis Diis* [sic] printed in Pope (1967–68: 667–724). MS T_C (i.e. E_B; ff. 58v–61r) represents Wulfstan's version. MS R_C (pp. 142–47) and MS S_C (pp. 365–72) are manuscripts representing Ælfric's expanded version, the issue of which Clemoes (1959) puts in the period 1006–1010. About Fehr II Clemoes is specific and puts it in 1006. Fehr II is Ælfric's First Old English Pastoral Letter for Wulfstan printed in Fehr (1914, 1966: 68–145). MS O_F (pp. 320–36), MS Oz_F (ff. 133r–37r) and MS V_F (f. 75r–v) are manuscripts representing Ælfric's original version. MS D_F (i.e. C_B; pp. 31–40) represents the version revised by Wulfstan. So we could conclude, so far as our Wulfstan corpus is concerned, that in the case of Wulfstan the distribution of all the Old Norse-derived loanwords except for *lagu* started after his York translation. There is a noteworthy correspondence between the chronological assumption and the distribution of the ON loanwords. The dependability of the assumption is proved even by the loanword distribution. This in turn reflects the linguistic situation of the early eleventh-century Danelaw and Wulfstan's understanding of his position and his world.

OE *lagu* appears four times in the London homilies. But in all the instances *lagu* has *Godes* as its pre-modifier: Ib 9 *Godes lage*, III 30 *Godes lage*, V 82 *Godes lage*, V 115 *Godes lagum*. It is from Wulfstan that *OED* cites the earliest use of OE *lagu* in the sense of 'divine law', which suggests that OE *lagu* had acquired the religious sense of 'God's law'. Wulfstan's use of *lagu* in this sense must reflect the usage of pre-1000 London and it must be Wulfstan himself who contributed to making this use prevalent in the central Danelaw. It was not long before Abbot Ælfric adopted *lagu*. About this Godden explains lucidly: "In his earliest writings, in the early 990s, Ælfric excluded *lagu* from his vocabulary altogether. He then began to use it very occasionally in a specific and secular sense but subsequently, not long before he became abbot of Eynsham in 1005, took to using it quite frequently as an exact equivalent of the native word *æ* in the religious sense, with reference to the law of the Old Testament or the New. It may be significant that this more widespread use began at about the same time as our first evidence of contact between Ælfric and Wulfstan, who uses *lagu* very regularly. For some readers either *æ* or *lagu* must have been still unfamiliar, for Ælfric occasionally uses the two words in tandem" (Godden 1980: 216–17).

Table 7.1 shows the distribution of the four Old Norse loanwords and their West-Saxon equivalents over our texts arranged in their assumed chronological order. What we see in the table is not a simple historical picture of adoption and discarding; that is, the gradual adoption of Scandinavian loanwords and the subsequent discarding of Old English native words. Wulfstan's effort to keep using the OE native words when possible is noteworthy. A comparison of Wulfstan texts with those of Ælfric enables us to have an idea of where Wulfstan's effort was directed. The comparison also indicates the different dialectal and functional milieus in which the two religious figures are placed in terms of linguistic situation. Wulfstan presumably spent most of his life within the Danelaw area after he was appointed Archbishop of York. He died in York in 1023 and was buried at Ely. Peterborough was said to be one of the candidates claiming his burial place. Ælfric (c. 950–c. 1010), on the other hand, spent most of his life outside the Danelaw. He was educated under Bishop Æthelwold in the monastic school at Winchester, and after becoming a monk and priest was sent around 987 to the abbey of Cerne Abbas (see Figure 7.1), newly founded by the thegn Æthelmær, son of Ealdorman Æthelweard. In 1005 Æthelmær refounded the abbey

Table 7.1   The distribution of four Old Norse loanwords and their West Saxon equivalents

	ON	OE	ON	OE	ON	OE	ON	OE
	grið	*frið*	*lagu*	*æ(w)*	*Oðon*	*Woden*	*þræl*	*þeow*
(996–1002)								
II								
III			1					
Ib			1					
IV								
V			2					
(1002–07)								
Xa			1	1				1
VI			2					
VII								
VIIa								
IX			3				1	
XI			1					
VIIIb								1
Xb								
Xc	1		9					
VIIIc			5					
(1007–1014)								
Fehr II(D$_F$)			8	5				2
XII			1		2			
XIV								
XV			2					
XVIb								
XVII			2					
XVIII								
XIX	1	1	4					
(c. 1014)								
XX (B$_B$H$_B$)	1		5					2
XX (C$_B$)	1		6				7	3
XX (E$_B$I$_B$)	1		8				6	3
XIII			1					
XXI			1					

of Eynsham and Ælfric became the first abbot (Lapidge et al. 1999). The
locus of Ælfric's life remained largely within Wessex and his language
represents the West-Saxon *Schriftsprache*. His audience, in comparison to
Wulfstan's, would consist of relatively more learned listeners.

The first point that I would like to highlight is the ON *lagu*–OE
æ alternation witnessed in Fehr II. Ælfric manuscript O_F invariably has
æ (13 times), the later twelfth-century manuscript Oz_F *æ* except for three
cases (Fehr II 8a (twice), 10) and V_F *æ* (Fehr II 34). Wulfstan's version in
D_F has *æ* (Fehr II 8a, 19 (2×), 34, 134–35) as well as *lagu* (Fehr II 8a, 10 (2×),
19, 119, 128, 134–5, 146). There seems to be no hard and fast rule as to
which to use. When *godes, moyses* or *eald* comes as a pre-modifier, *æ* as
well as *lagu* is used almost interchangeably. (Braces { } indicate an addition or emendation.)

Fehr II 8a

O_F: Þreo tyda synd   on þisse worulde .   An tyd wæs
        ær godes .ǽ.

Oz_F: Ðreo tid   beoð   on ðissere weorlde .   Án tid   wæs
        ær godes lagæ .

D_F: Þry timan sind getealde   on þissere worlde .   An tima wæs {o}
        ær godes .ǽ.

Fehr II 8a

O_F: on þære   heah fædera tyman .   Oþer under godes .ǽ.
        on moyses tyman .

Oz_F: on þare   heah fadera timan .   oðer under godes lage
        on moyses timan .

D_F: on þar{a}   heah fædera timan .   þa iéo wæron . Oðer under
        godes lage .   on moyses . Ᵹ on ðare wítegena timan .

> There are assigned three ages in this world: one age was before God's law,
> in the time of the patriarchs, who once existed; the second under God's law
> in the time of Moses and the prophets.

Here again, incidentally, Wulfstan seems to have been more concerned
with expanding the text than with concision or alterations in rhythm.
As for the *lagu–æ* lexical alternation, he seems to have intentionally left
Ælfric's *æ* untouched. The function of pastoral letters suggests that the
audience differs from that of homilies. Wulfstan's homilies were first

and foremost addressed to a lay congregation. The audience here may be classified as a more learned audience. What this suggests is that Wulfstan the Anglo-Saxon educator stood in the foreground. It seems that he wanted to remind his audience of the presence of Old English equivalents, old familiar words. It seems that the same is true of the following example:

Fehr II 134–135

O$_F$: 7 hit stod æfre swa on þære ealdan .æ. Nu is seo ealde .æ.
geendod æfter cristes tocyme .

Oz$_F$: 7 hit stod æffre þus on þare ealde .æ. Nú is þeo ealde æ.
íendod . æfter cristes to cyme .

D$_F$: 7 hit stod æfre þus on ðare ealdan æ. Nu is seo ealde lagu
geendod . æfter cristes to cyme .

> And it stood ever thus in the old law. Now the old law is ended after Christ's coming.

By "ealdan æ" and "seo ealde lagu" the law of the Old Testament is referred to. This kind of equation is used often and the aim can be said to be instructive. The following case may be counted as of the same kind: Bethurum XIX 50 *ge orsorge wuniaþ on lande on griðe 7 on friðe under minre munde* ('You will live in this land without any anxiety in peace under my guardianship in the Danish way as well as in the English way.') "On griðe" and "on friðe" are used in tandem.

Bethurum XII is a revision by Wulfstan of Ælfric's *De Falsis Diis* [sic]. It is noteworthy that Wulfstan follows Ælfric's use of Scandinavian forms (*Oðon, Þor*) for Germanic deities, and he does not try to change Ælfric's originals. In her *Pelican History of England* (1952) Whitelock says, "Gradually, however, they were forgotten, so that when, at the end of the tenth century, the homilist Abbot Ælfric repeats the normal equation of classical and Germanic deities, he uses the Scandinavian forms of the names of the latter. Presumably the fresh influx of heathen settlers in the Viking age had made these forms more familiar to an English audience than those used in their own, long distant, heathen past" (Whitelock 1952: 23). Would there have been any need to change them, especially when dealing with heathen gods one is trying to denounce? T$_C$ represents Wulfstan's version. The other example of *Þor* occurs in Bethurum XII 56.

Bethurum XII 72

R_C: ㄱ he is óðon gehÄten { ⁊} oðru*m* naman on denisc ; Nu
S_C: ㄱ he oþon { ⁊} gehaten oðru*m* naman on denisc . Nu
T_C: ㄱ he is oðon gehaten oðrum naman on denisce wisan . Nu

Bethurum XII 73

R_C: secgað þa deniscan on heora gedwylde . þæt se iouis
S_C: secgað þa deniscan on heora gedwilde . þæt se iouis
T_C: secgað sume þa denísce men on heora gedwylde . þæt se iouis

Bethurum XII 74

R_C: wære {⁊} þe hi þór hátað {.} mercuries sunu {.} þe hi oðon
hatað ⁊
S_C: wære {:} þe hi þór hataþ . mercuries sunu . þe hi óþon { ⁊}
hataþ .
T_C: wære þe hy þor hatað . mercuries sunu . þe hi oðon
namíað .

> and in the Danish manner he is called by the other name Odin. Now some
> of those Danish men say in their error that Jove, whom they call Thor, was
> the son of Mercury, whom they name Odin.

The ON *þræl*–OE *þeow* relationship seen in Xa, IX, VIIIb, Fehr II and XX
calls for a brief comment. The amelioration that we see in the case of *lagu*
('godes lagu'; see above), *grið* 'sanctuary' (Bethurum XX [E_BI_B] 82: 'Godes
grið') is also to be found in the case of OE *þeow*, whose original meaning
is 'a slave, bondman, thrall'. In our corpus *godes* is always attached to
þeow, except for one instance (Bethurum VIIIb 59). *Þræll* has as its pre-
modifier *Antecristes* in Bethurum IX 128.

We started from the question of "the continuity of English prose" or "the
Englishness of Old English". My theme is also the continuity of English
prose, especially orally delivered prose. What Wulfstan's vocabulary and
his Scandinavian loanword usage suggest is in no way opposed to this
tendency. Instead we see in his usage his intention to enlighten and edu-
cate, which includes his use of the English language. To him the English
language was West-Saxon. Wulfstan the educator deserves greater attention. He carefully refrains from making linguistic compromises. His loanword adoption seems to have been reduced to a minimum and he made
the most of a minimum of means.

Wulfstan's Scandinavian loanword usage suggests what his audience was like. It goes without saying that his audience might have been bilingual. Hansen says, "it is agreed that there must have been at least a limited degree of mutual intelligibility between the two languages owing to their Common Germanic past, and that this hastened the bilingualism among the Danish settlers and possibly among the English population of the Danelaw as well, as bilingualism is a prerequisite for linguistic borrowing of any kind" (Hansen 1984: 66). In this respect it is noteworthy that Wulfstan's concern was more with Scandinavian loanwords than with Northern dialect forms. Franz Wenisch gives a list of 57 Northumbrian words (Wenisch 1979: 325). The list does not contain any of Wulfstan's vocabulary listed in Dobyns (1973). The evidence as a whole points to the following conclusion: what we saw when we dealt with prose rhythm in Wulfstan's works might be applicable, *mutatis mutandis*, to Wulfstan's Scandinavian loanword usage. The evidence also confirms that Wulfstan's understanding of his role as Anglo-Saxon educator deserves much attention.

Note

This paper is a revised version of my Japanese article "Changing Wulfstan's vocabulary: an aspect of Old Norse loanword usage in the late Old English Danelaw", in Y. Terasawa & S. Takebayashi (eds) (1988). *Aspects of English Vocabulary* (pp. 113–33). Tokyo: Kenkyusha. My special thanks are due to Professor John Scahill of Keio University, who read through my manuscript and as always gave me constructive and valuable criticisms, and Dr Heiner Gillmeister of the University of Bonn, who kindly helped by making accessible to me works otherwise hard to obtain.

References and Further Reading

Arngart, O. S. A. (1948). Some aspects of the relation between the English and the Danish elements in the Danelaw. *Studia Neophilologica*, 20, 73–87.

Biber, D., Johansson, S., Leech, G., Conrad, S. & Finegan, E. (1999). *Longman Grammar of Spoken and Written English*. Harlow: Pearson Educational.

Björkman, E. (1900–1902). *Scandinavian Loan-Words in Middle English* (2 vols) (Studien zur englischen Philologie, 7 and 11). Halle: Max Niemeyer. Repr. New York: Greenwood, 1969.

Brown, G. H. (1996). *Bede the Educator*. Jarrow Lecture 1996.

Burnley, D. (1992). Lexis and semantics. In N. Blake (ed.), *The Cambridge History of the English Language*, vol. II: *1066–1476* (pp. 409–499). Cambridge: Cambridge University Press.

Cleasby, R. & Vigfusson, G. (eds) (1957). *An Icelandic–English Dictionary*, 2nd edn with a supplement by Sir William A. Craigie. Oxford: Clarendon Press (1st edn 1874).

Clemoes, P. A. M. (1959). The chronology of Ælfric's works. In P. A. M. Clemoes, *The Anglo-Saxons: studies in some aspects of their history and culture presented to Bruce Dickins* (pp. 212–247). London: Bowes. Repr. as *Old English Newsletter* (Subsidia, 5). CEMERS, SUNY-Binghamton, 1980.

Dance, R. (2002). Interpreting Laȝamon: linguistic diversity and some cruces in Cotton Caligula A. ix, with particular regard to Norse-derived words. In R. Allen, L. Perry & J. Roberts (eds), *Laȝamon: contexts, language, and interpretation* (pp. 187–202). London: King's College London, Centre for Late Antique and Medieval Studies.

Dobyns, M. F. (1973). Wulfstan's vocabulary: a glossary of the homilies with commentary. PhD diss., University of Illinois.

Finkenstaedt, T. & Wolff, D. (1973). *Ordered Profusion: studies in dictionaries and the English lexicon*. Heidelberg: Carl Winter.

Fischer, A. (1989). Lexical change in late Old English: from *æ* to *lagu*. In A. Fischer, *The History and the Dialects of English: Festschrift for Eduard Kolb* (Anglistische Forschungen, 203) (pp. 103–114). Heidelberg: Carl Winter.

Fisiak, J. (1977). Sociolinguistics and Middle English: some socially motivated changes in the history of English. *Kwartalnik Neofilologiczny*, 24, 247–59.

Fisiak, J. (ed.) (1995). *Linguistic Change under Contact Conditions* (Trends in Linguistics: Studies and Monographs, 81). Berlin: Mouton de Gruyter.

Godden, M. (1980). Ælfric's changing vocabulary. *ES*, 61, 206–23.

Gordon, E. V. (1957). *An Introduction to Old Norse*, 2nd edn, rev. A. R. Taylor. Oxford: Clarendon Press.

Hadley, D. M. & Richards, J. D. (eds) (2000). *Cultures in Contact: Scandinavian settlement in England in the ninth and tenth centuries* (Studies in the Early Middle Ages, 2). Turnhout: Brepols.

Hansen, B. H. (1984). The historical implications of the Scandinavian linguistic element in English: a theoretical evaluation. *North-Western European Language Evolution* (Odense), 4, 53–95.

Hoad, T. F. (ed.) (1986). *The Concise Oxford Dictionary of English Etymology*. Oxford: Clarendon Press.

Hofmann, D. (1955). *Nordisch-Englische Lehnbeziehungen der Wikingerzeit* (Bibliotheca Arnamagnæana, 14). Copenhagen: Munksgaard.

Hornby, A. S., Gatenby, E. V. & Wakefield, H. (1963). *Advanced Learner's Dictionary of Current English*, 2nd edn. London: Oxford University Press (1st edn 1948) (*ALD*).

Jost, K. (1950). *Wulfstanstudien* (Schweizer Anglistische Arbeiten, 23). Bern: Francke.

Keller, W. (1925). Skandinavischer Einfluss in der englischen Flexion. In W. Keller (ed.), *Probleme der englischen Sprache und Kultur: Festschrift Johannes Hoops zum 60. Geburtstag überreicht von Freunden und Kollegen* (pp. 80–7). Heidelberg: Carl Winter.

Kirch, M. S. (1959). Scandinavian influence on English syntax. *PMLA*, 74, 503–10.

Kolb, E. (1925). Skandinavisches in den nordenglischen Dialekten. *Anglia*, 83, 127–53.

Kubouchi, T. (1983). A note on prose rhythm in Wulfstan's *De Falsis Dies* [*sic*]. *Poetica* (Tokyo: Shubun International), 15/16, 57–106. Repr. in T. Kubouchi (1999). *From Wulfstan to Richard Rolle: papers exploring the continuity of English prose* (pp. 33–46). Cambridge: D. S. Brewer.

Lapidge, M., Blair, J., Keynes, S. & Scragg, D. (eds) (1999). *The Blackwell Encyclopaedia of Anglo-Saxon England*. Oxford: Blackwell.

Leech, G., Rayson, P. & Wilson, A. (2001). *Word Frequencies in Written and Spoken English: based on the British National Corpus*. Harlow: Pearson Education.

Madden, J. F. & Magoun, F. P. (1972). *A Grouped Frequency Word-List of Anglo-Saxon Poetry* (Harvard Old English Series, 2). 9th printing. Cambridge, MA: Harvard University Press.

Mawer, A. (1933). The Scandinavian settlements in England as reflected in English place-names. *Acta Philologica Scandinavia*, 7, 1–30.

Meaney, A. L. (1970). Æthelweard, Ælfric, the Norse gods and Northumbria. *Journal of Religious History*, 6, 105–32.

Menner, R. J. (1948). Anglian and Saxon elements in Wulfstan's vocabulary. *MLN*, LXIII, 1–9.

Moskowich-Spiegel Fandiño, I. (1996). Scandinavian loanwords during the Middle English period: geographical distribution. In S. G. Fernández-Corugedo et al. (eds), *Some Sundry Wits Gathered Together: i congreso de filoloxía inglesa* (pp. 155–62). Poznan.

Page, R. I. (1971). How long did the Scandinavian language survive in England? The epigraphical evidence. In P. Clemoes & K. Hughes (eds) (pp. 165–81).

Page, R. I. (1981). The audience of *Beowulf* and the Vikings. In C. Chase (ed.), *The Dating of Beowulf* (pp. 113–22). Toronto: University of Toronto Press.

Peitz, A. (1933). *Der Einfluss des nördlichen Dialektes im Mittelenglischen auf die entstehende Hochsprache* (Bonner Studien zur Englischen Philologie, 20). Bonn: Peter Hanstein.

Peters, H. (1981a). Zum skandinavischen Lehngut im Altenglischen. *Sprachwissenschaft*, 6, 85–124.

Peters, H. (1981b). Onomasiologische Untersuchungen: Zum skandinavischen Lehngut im Altenglischen. *Sprachwissenschaft*, 6, 169–85.

Serjeantson, M. S. (1935). *A History of Foreign Words in English*. London: Routledge & Kegan Paul.

Thorson, P. (1936). *Anglo-Norse Studies: an inquiry into the Scandinavian elements in the modern English dialects*, part 1. Amsterdam: N.V. Swets en Zeitlinger.

Townend, M. (2000). Viking age England as a bilingual society. In D. M. Hadley & J. D. Richards (eds), *Cultures in Contact: Scandinavian settlement in England in the ninth and tenth centuries* (Studies in the Early Middle Ages, 2) (pp. 89–105). Turnhout: Brepols.

Townend, M. (2002). *Language and History in Viking Age England: linguistic relations between speakers of Old Norse and Old English* (Studies in the Early Middle Ages, 6). Turnhout: Brepols.

Tuso, J. F. (1966). An analysis and glossary of dialectal variations in the vocabularies of three late tenth-century Old English texts, the *Corpus*, *Lindisfarne*, and *Rushworth Gospels*. PhD diss., University of Arizona.

Wenisch, F. (1979). *Spezifisch anglisches Wortgut in den nordhumbrischen Interlinearglossierungen des Lukasevangeliums* (Anglistische Forschungen, 132). Heidelberg: Carl Winter.

West, M. (1965). *A General Service List of English Words*. London: Longmans, Green & Co. (*GSL*).

Whitelock, D. (1952). *The Beginnings of English Society* (The Pelican History of England, 2). Harmondsworth: Penguin Books.

Whitelock, D. (1981). *History, Law and Literature in 10th–11th Century England*. London: Variorum Reprints.

Wilcox, J. (1992). The dissemination of Wulfstan's homilies: the Wulfstan tradition in eleventh-century vernacular preaching. In C. Hicks (ed.), *England in the Eleventh-Century: proceedings of the 1990 Harlaxton Symposium* (Harlaxton Medieval Studies, 2) (pp. 199–217). Stamford, CA: Paul Watkins.

Xandry, G. (1914). *Das skandinavische Element in den neuenglischen Dialekten*. Neu-Isenburg: August Koch.

Appendix: Manuscript Sigla

B_B	Cambridge, Corpus Christi College, 419
$C_B = D_F$	Cambridge, Corpus Christi College, 201
$E_B = T_C$	Oxford, Bodleian Library, Hatton 113
$H_B = Oz_F$	Oxford, Bodleian Library, Bodley 343
I_B	London, British Library, Cotton Nero A. i
O_F	Cambridge, Corpus Christi College, 190
R_C	Cambridge, Corpus Christi College, 178
S_C	Oxford, Bodleian Library, Hatton 116
V_F	London, British Library, Cotton Vespasian D. xiv

Chapter 8

An Aspect of Old English Poetic Diction: The Postpositioning of Prepositions

Michael Lapidge

During the nearly two centuries that Old English has been taught in universities as an academic discipline, there has been a series of milestones marking out progress in the subject: Kemble's edition of *Beowulf* (1833; 2nd edn 1835), Sievers's demonstration of the laws of Old English metre (1893) and his grammar of Old English (1898; rev. edn 1942), Toller's revision and supplement to Bosworth's dictionary of Old English (1898–1921), Liebermann's edition of the Anglo-Saxon laws (1903–16), Klaeber's edition of *Beowulf* (1922; 3rd edn 1950), Holthausen's etymological dictionary of Old English (1934), Ker's catalogue of manuscripts containing Old English (1957), Greenfield and Robinson's bibliography of Old English literature (1980), Gneuss's handlist of Anglo-Saxon manuscripts (2001), to name only a few. One of these great milestones was undoubtedly the publication, in 1985, of Bruce Mitchell's *Old English Syntax* (*OES*). This massive work, in two volumes containing nearly 2,000 pages divided into 4,000 numbered paragraphs, describes every significant feature of normal Old English syntax. But even a vast compendium such as *OES* leaves open many paths for further exploration. At the very end of the work Mitchell lists, among "some paths worth pursuing", the study "of syntax and element order for the appreciation of poetic effect" (*OES*: §3976). What follows is an attempt to explore one minor aspect of syntactical poeticism.

A distinctive feature of the poetic diction of most (perhaps all) Indo-European languages is the use of hyperbaton, that is to say, the placement of words in unusual, often striking, positions, thereby to accentuate the difference between the poetic register and that of normal speech. When Shelley, for example, wrote in his sonnet *Ozymandias* of an ancient statue lying shattered in the desert, he used a striking example of hyperbaton to describe the features of the statue's face, which:

> Tell that its sculptor well those passions read,

whereas normal English syntax would require the inversion of the adverb and the verb: "(the features) tell that its sculptor read those passions well". If hyperbaton is a feature of the poetic diction of an analytic language like Modern English, it is evidently more so in the case of synthetic languages like Greek and Latin and Old English, where the relationship between words is signified by desinences. A comprehensive study of hyperbaton in Old English, particularly in verse, is a great desideratum, but obviously lies far beyond the scope of a brief essay. I therefore limit my discussion to one (relatively minor) feature of hyperbaton in Old English verse, namely the postpositioning of prepositions. This feature is also well attested in Greek and Latin verse, where it is described by the rhetorical term "anastrophe" (literally 'inversion': see Martin 1974: 309–10). As far as I am aware, students of Old English have never used the term anastrophe in describing this feature of Old English; I therefore retain the more familiar term "postpositioning". Although postpositioning of prepositions is a well-known feature of Old English verse (see Wullen 1911; Wende 1915: 142–216; Fakundiny 1970: 139–42; Mitchell 1978: 248–55), many questions still remain. How common a practice was it? Why were some prepositions postpositioned, but not others? Why did some poets employ postpositioning, but not others? And where and when and why did the practice originate?

In order to attempt to answer these questions, the first task is the compilation of a record of all occurrences of postpositioning of prepositions in Old English verse. One begins with the list of Old English prepositions, attested in both prose and verse, compiled by Bruce Mitchell (*OES*: §1178); then, for each preposition (and variant spelling forms thereof), one consults the occurrences listed in Bessinger and Smith's concordance to *The Anglo-Saxon Poetic Records* (Bessinger & Smith 1978). Unfortunately, this task is not as straightforward as one might wish, because on inspection, many apparent cases of postposited prepositions turn out to be adverbs. In other words, the context of every occurrence listed in the concordance needs to be checked in scholarly editions, commentaries and glossaries where these are available. In what follows, with the exception of *Beo*, which is cited from the third edition of Klaeber (1950), and *Instr*, which is cited from Rosier (1964), all poetic texts are cited from *The Anglo-Saxon Poetic Records*. I also refer to the following editions of individual poems: *GenA* (Doane 1978), *GenB* (Doane 1991), *Exo* (Lucas 1994), *Dan* (Farrell 1974), *And* (Brooks 1961), *Dream* (Swanton 1970), *El* (Gradon 1958), *Guth* (Roberts 1979), *Phoen* (Blake 1964), *Jul* (Woolf 1966), *Jud* (Griffith 1997), *Mald* (Scragg 1981) and *MSol* (Menner 1941). In each case I distinguish between discussion found in the commentary ("comm.") and glossary ("gloss."). Two texts crucial to the present study have not, alas, been the subject of detailed philological commentary: *PPs* and *Met*. For reasons which may have bearing on questions of Old English metre, I distinguish between monosyllabic and polysyllabic prepositions, a distinction which overlaps with Mitchell's distinction between "simple" and "compound" prepositions (*OES*: §1177(1)). I underline the first letter of a preposition when (and only when) it participates in alliteration, in order to distinguish between stressed alliterating and stressed non-alliterating usage. Note that the lists are intended to be complete (total numbers of occurrences of each preposition within the poetic corpus are given in parentheses).

The Postpositioning of Monosyllabic Prepositions in Old English Verse

æt (358×)

þe me **æt** wunað   awa to feore (*PPs* 90.1)

þu me **æt** byst   efne rihte (*PPs* 138.6)

ic þe **æt** stande   ær on morgen (*PsFr* 5.3)

bi (51×), *be* (146×), *big* (2×) [cf. *OES*: §§1183–4]

him **big** stodan   bunan ond orcas (*Beo* 3047)

and begen þa beornas   þe him **big** stodon (*Mald* 182)

eac (376×)

ac þa mægenþreatas   meredeað geswealh / **spellbodan eac**. (*Exo* 514)

[Lucas (gloss.) understands *eac* throughout *Exo* as a preposition (+ dat.),
and cites no example of adverbial *eac*; accordingly, line 514 is presumably
to be included in his specification of "245, 374, 381, etc."; the lines
mean, 'but a sea-death swallowed the mighty hosts together with the
messenger'.]

ealle æfæste ðry;   **him eac** þær wæs / . . . engel ælmihtiges. (*Dan* 271)

fram (132×), *from* (104×) [cf. Wullen 1908: 24; *OES*: §§1188–9]

fæder æt frymðe   þeah þe hie **him from** swicen (*GenA* 954)

Ne syndon **me** on ferhðe freo   **from** gewitene (*GenA* 1255)

folcgestreonum,   ac **him from** swicon (*GenA* 1981)

freondrædenne   hu heo **from** hogde (*Jul* 34)

hyldo to halgum,   beoð þe ahylded **fram** / . . . wita unrim. (*Jul* 171)

metod for þy mane   **mancynne fram** (*Beo* 110)

mære þeoden   **mondreamum from** (*Beo* 1715)

us fram afyrde   æghwær symble (*PPs* 102.12)

Ða **me** eac frecne **fram**   fleam gedydan (*PPs* 141.5)

þe þeos **eorðe from**   æfter groweð (*PPs* 146.8)

heora bacu bitere, and heora **blisse from** (*Met* 2.15)

in (986×) [cf. *OES*: §§1190–3]
There are several occurrences in the poetic corpus where the preposition
in is used in combination with the adverb *innan*, so as to create a kind of

adverbial phrase; I do not reckon these occurrences as simple instances of postpositioning, because it is not clear in these instances whether it is *in* or *innan* which is functioning as the adverb.

þæt he grenes fond   **goldburgum in** (*GenA* 2551)

flihte lacan   **friðgeardum in** (*ChristA* 399)

wyllestreama   **wuduholtum in** (*Phoen* 362)

winburgum in,   gif þas word sind soþ (*Jul* 83)

wlonce wigsmiþas   **winburgum in** (*Vain* 14)

ic **him in** wunige   a þenden ic lifge (*Rid* 85.6)

Scyldes eafora   **Scedelandum in** (*Beo* 19)

þær Sicilia   **sæstreamum in** (*Met* 1. 15)

mid (1195×) [cf. *OES*: §§1194–8]

hine cneowmæcgas / . . . **mid** siðedon (*GenA* 1733–4)

freonda feasceaft.   **Him** ferede **mid** / . . . sinces hyrde (*GenA* 2100)

þe **me mid** sceoldon   mearce healdan (*GenA* 2135)

lastas lecgan   and þe læde **mid** / þin agen bearn (*GenA* 2851)

heht **hine** geonge twegen / men **mid** siðian (*GenA* 2868–9)

ne on mode ne murn.   Ic þe **mid** wunige (*And* 99)

ond ealle þa menigo   þe þe **mid** wunað (*And* 101)

ond eal þæt mancynn   þe **him mid** wunige (*And* 945)

mirce manslaga.   Ic þe **mid** wunige (*And* 1218)

þurh meahta sped.   Ic **eow mid** wunige (*ChristB* 488)

wiga wælgifre.   **Hine** wunade **mid** / an ombehtþegn (*GuthB* 999)

ofnes æled,   ac **him** is engel **mid** (*Az* 177)

maþmum mislicum   þæt **hine mid** wille (*Sea* 99)

madma mænigo   þa **him mid** scoldon (*Beo* 41)

frecne dæde,   ne wæs **him** Fitela **mid** (*Beo* 889)

mægenbyrþenne   þara þe he **him mid** hæfde (*Beo* 1625)

þa **me** symble **mid**   sæton ond eodon (*PPs* 100.6)

eallne þære mænige   þe **hire mid** wunodeð (*Met* 26.61)

manna gehwylcum   þe **him mid** reste (*MRune* 9)

winburgum mid   weolan unmete (*Instr* 136)

neah (63×), *neh* (11×)

In practice it is often immensely difficult to distinguish between the use of *neah* as an adjective, adverb or preposition, and I have been guided by the opinions of editors, notably Brooks (gloss.), who takes *ne(a)h* in "*And* 359, 821, 833 etc." as *prep. w. d.*; Klaeber (gloss.), who takes all the cited examples from *Beo* as *prep. w. dat.*; and Woolf (gloss.), who takes the example in *Jul* 635 as *prep. w. dat.* But even here there are discrepancies: for example, Gradon (gloss.) takes *neah* in *El* 66 to be an "adv.", although the analogues indicate that Cynewulf employed it as a preposition.

hildewulfas   **herewicum neh** (*GenA* 2051)

hwonne siðboda   **sæstreamum neah** (*Exo* 250)

gesæt him þa se halga   **holmwearde neah** (*And* 359)

on hronrade   **heofoncyninge neh** (*And* 821)

bliðne bidan   **burhwealle neh** (*And* 833)

Cristes cempa   **carcerne neh** (*And* 991)

standan **stræte neah,**   stapul ærenne (*And* 1062)

eorlas ymb æðeling   **egstreame neah** (*El* 66)

duguða dryhten.   Is þam **dome neah** (*ChristB* 782)

ecan lifes.   **Him** wæs engel **neah** (*GuthA* 172)

frasunga fela.   **Him** wæs fultum **neah** (*GuthA* 189)

oft eahtade   (wæs **him** engel **neah**) (*GuthA* 336)

hat, **heortan neah,**   hildescurum (*GuthB* 1143)

Ða wæs gelæded   **landmearce neah** (*Jul* 635)

arum bregdað   **yðborde neah** (*Gifts* 57)

nydbysgum neah;   gewiteð nihtes in fleah (*Rim* 44)

þæt hy gemittað   **mearclonde neah** (*Rid* 3.23)

leolc on lyfte,   hwilum **londe neah** (*Rid* 56.8)

ic wæs be sonde,   **sæwealle neah** (*Rid* 60.1)

symbel ymbsæton   **sægrunde neah** (*Beo* 564)

selfa mid gesiðum   **sæwealle neah** (*Beo* 1924)

wunode on wonge   **wæteryðum neah** (*Beo* 2242)

dyrnan cræfte   dracan **heafde neah** (*Beo* 2290)

hlæw under hrusan   **holmwylme neah** (*Beo* 2411)

heaðofyrum hat,   ne meahte **horde neah** (*Beo* 2547)

hreas on hrusan   **hordærne neah** (*Beo* 2831)

feðecempa   frean **eaxlum neah** (*Beo* 2853)

hige **heortan neah**   hædre wealleð (*MSol* 62)

stæf **stræte neah**   stille bideæð (*MSol* 137)

in Cantwarum   **cynestole neah** (*Men* 105)

of (683×) [cf. *OES*: §§1199–1203]

eardode ic þe on innan   ne meahte ic ðe **of** cuman (*Soul I* 33)

werigra wraþu   **worulddreamum of** (*GuthB* 1363)

eardode ic þe on innan.   No ic þe **of** meahte (*Soul II* 30)

ða he **him of** dyde   isernbyrnan (*Beo* 671)

[Klaeber (gloss.) interprets this as a "prep. postposit. (stressed)". However, the occurrence of a similar phrase in *Beo* 2809 raises the possibility that in *Beo* 671 *him* is a reflexive pronoun, in which case *of* is being used adverbially. Cf. also *OES*: §1078.]

ealle þa telgan   ðe **him of** hlidað (*PPs* 79.11)

forðon he **him** his yrre   **of** acyrde (*PPs* 105.19)

þu **me** scealt edwitt min   **of** awyrpan (*PPs* 118.39)

þæt hi hi æfre **him**   **of** aslepen (*Met* 13.9)

gif mon þonne wolde   **him** awindan **of** (*Met* 25.22)

on (4401×), *an* (122×) [cf. *OES*: §§1204–6]

For examples where the preposition follows the relative particle *þe*, see *Dream* 98, *ChristB* 521 and 570, *GuthA* 256 and *Beo* 2796. See also discussion by Mitchell 1978: 248–9 (esp. §28), and *OES*: §§1062, 1079. I omit from the present discussion the few examples of postpositioning involving relatives in Old English verse.

aldre beneoteð   **hine on** cymeð (*GenA* 1041)

wite æfter weorce.   **Hine** waldend **on** (*GenA* 1043)

eastlandum on,   eðelstowe (*GenA* 1052)

and ealle þa wocre   þe ic **wægþrea on** / liðe nerede (*GenA* 1490)

[Doane (comm.) construes *on* with *liðe* in the preceding line; in my understanding of the syntax, *liðe* is being used adverbially here: the line means 'I graciously saved all the progeny in the wave-punishment (*wægþrea*)'.]

mid wean greteð   ic **hine** wergðo **on** (*GenA* 1775)

magum sinum;   **hine** monige **on** / wraðe winnað (*GenA* 2291)

[I take *on* as governing *hine*, and would translate, 'against him many shall fight angrily'; cf., however, Mason 1915: 91.]

hine Abraham **on**   mid his agene hand / beacen sette (*GenA* 2768)

legde **him** lustas **on**   ond mid listum speon (*GenB* 687)

mægnes mæste   **mearclandum on** (*Exo* 67)

ofne on innan   aldre generede (*Dan* 258)

[The fact that *on* is here construed with the adverb *innan* raises the possibility that *on innan* was employed by OE poets as a sort of adverbial phrase (for the similar use of *in innan*, cf. *in* (above); cf. also *And* 1241 and *Soul I* 33. It is also possible that *on* + *innan* are to be understood as a single word, the compound preposition *oninnan*: cf. *PPs* 147.2 (without postpositioning), *Alms* 1 and *Met* 5.16.]

efstan elne mycle   þæt he **me** wolde **on** gestigan (*Dream* 34)

ricra ne heanra,   ac **hine** ræseð **on** (*GuthB* 995)

eastdælum on   æþelast londa (*Phoen* 2)

gewiten under waþeman   **wæstdælas on** (*Phoen* 97)

yldo **him on** fareð,   onsyn blacað (*Sea* 91)

maþmas ond meaduful   **mægburge on** (*Fort* 62)

firum freamærne   **feorlondum on** (*Pan* 10)

þæt **him** þa ferend   **on** fæste wuniaþ (*Whale* 25)

æt þæm edwylme   þa þe **him on** cleofiað (*Whale* 73)

siþþan **hine** Niðhad **on**   nede legde (*Deor* 5)

efne swa mec wisaþ   se **mec** wræde **on** (*Rid* 3.13)

se **mec** geara **on** / bende legde (*Rid* 20.29)

þæt **me on** fealleð   ufan þær ic stonde (*Rid* 93.26)

yfles ondgiet,   ær hit **hine on** fealleð (*JDay I* 72)

þæt **hire an** dæges   eagum starede (*Beo* 1935)

freawine folca   **Freslondum on** (*Beo* 2357)

oreðes ond attres;   forðon ic **me on** hafu (*Beo* 2523)

him on efn ligeð   ealdorgewinna (*Beo* 2903)

forðam **me on** sah   unrihtes feala (*PPs* 54.3)

and **me** fealleð **on**   fyrhtu deaðes (*PPs* 54.4)

wordum weorðinge;   ne **me** wiht **an** siteð (*PPs* 55.9) ne **me** unrihtes **on**   awiht wistan (*PPs* 58.3)

side sæflodes   on þa **him** syndon **on** (*PPs* 68.34)

þa **him on** becwom   yrre drihtnes (*PPs* 77.30)

us an nimeð   ece drihten (*PPs* 88.16)

Hwæt, **me** ealne dæg   edwitspræce **on** / mine feondas . . . brohtan (*PPs* 101.6)

þara eardendra   þe **hire on** lifdan (*PPs* 106.33)

and **hine** seo ylce **on**   eft gesette (*PPs* 108.17)

is **me** heorte **on**   hearde gedrefed (*PPs* 108.22)

þe **him on** standeð   egsa dryhtnes (*PPs* 117.4)

Nymþe **us on** wese   ece drihten . . .
nymþe **us** eardige **on**   awa drihten (*PPs* 123.1)

þe **me** woldan yrre   **on** acyðan (*PPs* 137.7)

and **me** is heorte **on**   hearde gedrefet (*PPs* 142.4)

and ealle þa þe **him on**   ahwær syndon (*PPs* 145.5)

longe gelæstan   forðæm **him** lungre **on** / swift wind swaþeð (*Met* 7.19)

gemen gæle,   þonne **him** grimme **on** / woruldsælða wind . . . blaweð (*Met* 7.51)

for ðæm earfoðum   þe **him on** sæton (*Met* 26.97)

ðeah **him** feohtan **on**   firas monige (*MRune* 83)

ðæt hiene **him** scyle eall ðeod   **on** genæman (*MSol* 259)

ðæt sindon <ða feondas> ða **usic** feohtað **on** (*MSol* 460) *to* (1831×) [cf. *OES*: §§1209–16]

torn niwiað   and **him** **to** nimað (*GenA* 1258)

trymede tilmodigne   and **him** **to** reordode (*GenA* 2167)

swiðor stepan   and **him** soðe **to** (*GenA* 2367)

on woruldrice;   he **him** þæs worhte **to** (*GenA* 2379)

torn þrowigean,   ac **him** **to** sende (*GenA* 2424)

druncnum eode / seo yldre **to** (*GenA* 2600–1)

forht folces weard.   Heht **him** fetigean **to** (*GenA* 2667)

him þa Abraham **to**   ofstum miclum (*GenA* 2673)

stiðum wordum   spræc **him** stefne **to** (*GenA* 2849)

on þære stowe   þe **him** se strange **to** (*GenA* 2900)

him þa ofstum **to**   ufan of roderum (*GenA* 2912)

hio spræc **him** þicce **to**   and speon hine ealne dæg (*GenB* 684)

hwæt ge nu **eagum to**   on lociað (*Exo* 278)

boldes bidað.   Oft **him** brogan **to** (*GuthA* 84)

þæt **me** engel **to**   ealle gelædeð (*GuthA* 253)

ond **him** anum **to**   eal biþence (*Jul* 155)

torht getæhte   þæt hie **him** **to** mihton (*Beo* 313)

se þe **him** bealwa **to**   bote gelyfde (*Beo* 909)

[For this and the following example, see also *OES*: §1078.]

weana gehwylces,   swa ic **þe** wene **to** (*Beo* 1396)

þe **us** seceað **to**   Sweona leoda (*Beo* 3001)

feonda minra,   ðe **me** feohtað **to** (*PPs* 58.1)

þeah þe **eow** wealan **to**   wearnum flowen (*PPs* 61.11)

God min, God min,   ic **þe** gearuwe **to** / . . . lustum wacie (*PPs* 62.1)

forþan **me** feondas **to**   feohtað geneahhe (*PPs* 68.17)

asete **him** þa unriht **to**   þe hi geearnodon (*PPs* 68.27)

ahyld **me** þin eare **to**   holde mode (*PPs* 70.2)

þe **me** yfel **to**   ær gesohton (*PPs* 70.22)

hæl þinne scealc   forþon ic **ðe** hihte **to** (*PPs* 85.2)

on þam þu **us to**   eadmedum ealle gebrohtest (*PPs* 89.17)

spræc **him** wordum **to**   þurh wolcnes swyr (*PPs* 98.7)

on unwemmum wege   hwænne þu **me** wylle **to** (*PPs* 100.1)

þæt **me** cuðlice **to**   acweden syndon (*PPs* 121.1)

oft **me** fuhtan **to**   fynd on geoguðe (*PPs* 128.1)

ic **þe**, drihten, **to**   dyrum clypige (*PPs* 140.1)

Romwara bearn   and **him** recene **to** (*Met* 1.34)

truwian scolde.   Hi **me** t̲o wendon (*Met* 2.14)

tunglu genedest   þæt hi **ðe** t̲o herað (*Met* 4.5)

afeoht swylce   þe **me** fuhtan **to** (*PsFr* 34.1)

feonda minra,   þe **me** feohtað **to** (*PsFr* 58.1)

wið (451×) [cf. *OES*: §1217]

wite wealdeð   þonne he **him wið** mæge (*Dan* 522)

him þa ofstlice   Andreas **wið** / . . . wordum mælde (*And* 299)

[There are three further instances of *wið* in *Andreas* which Brooks (gloss.) treats as "postposited": 263, 305–6 and 632. However, since *þingian* is normally construed with the dative, in each of these cases *him* could be the indirect object of *þingian*, *wið* being used adverbially. Note also that earlier editors resolved the problem by understanding *wiðþingian* as a compound verb. Cf. also *El* 76–7 and *Jul* 260.]

and **mec** stiþne **wið**   stanas moton / fæste gehabban (*Rid* 16.9)

þæt þu **him** aht **wið**   æfre hæfdest (*PPs* 143.4)

ymb (178×) [cf. *OES*: §§ 1218–19]

Note: *Ymbe* is treated with polysyllabic prepositions, below.

me seredon **ymb**   secgas monige (*Sat* 496)

tid wæs toweard;   **hine** twegen **ymb** (*GuthA* 114)

eorles andwlitan,   ond **hine ymb** monig (*Beo* 689)

forð on **me** manige **ymb**   mægene syrewað (*PPs* 54.17)

The Postpositioning of Polysyllabic
Prepositions in Old English Verse

æfter (396×) [cf. *OES*: §§1179–82]

him æfter heold,   þa he of worulde gewat (*GenA* 1143)

[The line as transmitted lacks alliteration; if Holthausen's conjecture – that *worulde* be emended to *earde* – be accepted, alliteration would be restored, and *æfter* would participate in the alliteration, as in all the other examples cited.]

ænegum minra,   ac **me æfter** sculon (*GenA* 2178)

ingeþancum   þæt **me æfter** sie (*GenA* 2184)

mine aldorlege,   swa **me æfter** wearð (*Dan* 139)

eorles on elne;   ic **him æfter** sceal (*Beo* 2816)

[Klaeber (gloss.) understands this usage as "semi-adv. (verb of motion understood: 'follow')".]

beforan (25×)

nys **unc** wuht **beforan** / to scursceade (*GenB* 812)

[Doane (comm.) translates, 'there is nothing in front of us as a protection against storms', and describes the construction (gloss.) as an "adverbial preposition with dative" (whatever that is).]

him beforan foron   fyr and wolcen (*Exo* 93)

him beforan fereð   fægere leoht (*Sat* 387)

frætre **þeode   beforan** cyðde (*And* 571)

him beforan ferian   on feonda gemang (*El* 108)

þe **him beforan** fremede   freobearn godes (*ChristB* 643)

þu **him** weg **beforan**   worhtest rihtne (*PPs* 79.9)

we beoð færinge   **him beforan** brohte (*JDay II* 119)

behindan (7×)

ne læt **þe behindan**   þonne þu heonan cyrre (*ChristA* 155)

ðe ðone hehstan heofon   **behindan** lætst (*Met* 24.29)

he let **him behindan**   hyrnde ciolas (*Met* 26.23)

leoht on lyfte   ligeð **him behindan** (*Met* 29.51)

letan **him behindan**   hræw bryttian (*Brun* 60)

beneoðan (1×)

hio bið swiðe fior   **hire selfre beneoðan** (*Met* 20.222)

betweonan (2×), **betweonum** (3×), **betwinum** (1×), **bitweon** (2×), **bitweonum** (1×)

ne sceolon **unc betweonan**   teonan weaxan (*GenA* 1902)

leton **him þa betweonum**   taan wisian (*And* 1099)

hæðengildum / teledon **betwinum**. Ða se tan gehwearf. (*And* 1103)

ond sybbe swa same   **sylfra betweonum** (*El* 1206)

frið **freondum bitweon**   forð butan æfestum (*ChristC* 1658)

dægwoman bitweon   ond þære deorcan niht (*GuthB* 1218)

hornum bitweonum   huþe lædan (*Rid* 29.2)

betweox (7×), **betwuh** (2×), **betwyx** (3×), **betweoh** (2×)

heofenes tunglu, hu hi **him**   healdað **betwuh** / sibbe singale (*Met* 29.4)

fore (151×) [cf. *OES*: §§1185–7]

mid fæcne gefice   þe **me fore** standaþ (*El* 577)

frodra ond godra   þe **us fore** wæron (*El* 637)

ne eam ic swa fealog / swa ic **eow fore** stonde (*GuthA* 246)

cempa, gecyðeð   þæt **him** Crist **fore** (*GuthA* 402)

ealra þara bisena   þe **us** bec **fore** (*GuthA* 528)

Cumað **him fore**   and cneow bigeað
on ansyne   ures drihtnes
ond **him** wepan **fore**   ðe us worhte ær (*PPs* 94.64)

gif **him** wan **fore**   wolcen hangað (*Met* 5.4)

ofer (654×) [cf. Wullen 1911: 461]

Hi **<u>o</u>fer** cume   unþinged deað (*Ps* 54.13)

wese **us** beorhtnes **ofer**   bliðan drihtnes (*PPs* 89.19)

and **me <u>o</u>fer** cume,   ece dryhten (*PPs* 118.41)

ongean (29×), *ongen* (3×)

ongeotan gastlice!   **us on<u>g</u>ean** cumað (*Sat* 300)

forþon he hine tredne **him** / **on<u>g</u>ean** gyrede (*ChristC* 1166)

open ond oðeawed,   **alogum ongean** (*ChristC* 1604)

Guðlac **him ongean** þingode   cwæð þæt hy gielpan ne þorftan (*GuthA* 239)

sigeleasne sið.   no ic **eow** sweord **ongean** (*GuthA* 302)

þæt ic **him** monigfealde   modes gælsan / **ongean** bere (*Jul* 367)

wið wuldorcyning.   **him** se awyrgda **ongean** (*Whale* 67)

sona þæt onfindeð   se þe **mec** fehð **ongean** (*Rid* 27.9)

fleogað mid þam feondum.   **him** biþ fyr **ongean** (*JDay I* 18)

synfull sawel,   þæt **hyre** sie swegl **ongean** (*JDay I* 69)

oft ic **flode ongean** / muð ontynde (*Rid* 77.3)

oft ic begine   þæt **me ongean** sticað (*Rid* 91.3)

nat he þara goda   þæt he **me ongean** slea (*Beo* 681)

[Klaeber (gloss.) cites *Beo* 2364 as an example of *ongean* postpositioned, the assumption then being that *foran* is an adverb (thus Klaeber [gloss.], s.v. *foran*); but it is equally possible that *foran* is the postposited preposition, and that *ongean* here is adverbial. For an example of *ongean* used adverbially in *Beo*, cf. 747–8.]

togeanes (19×), *togenes* (8×)

him þa **togeanes**   mid guðþræce (*GenA* 1973)

gastum togeanes   gretan eode (*GenA* 2432)

eodon **him** þa **togenes**   garum gehyrsted (*And* 45)

ðær **him togenes**   god herigende (*And* 657)

him þa **togenes**   þa gleawestan (*El* 536)

nu ge fromlice   **freondum togeanes** (*ChristB* 575)

ðær bið oft open   **eadgum togeanes** (*Phoen* 11)

swinsað ond singeð   **swegle togeanes** (*Phoen* 124)

þurh his hidercyme   **halgum togeanes** (*Phoen* 421)

sunnan togeanes   þær hi siþþan forð (*Phoen* 579)

deorum dædum   **deofle togeanes** (*Sea* 76)

Grendle togeanes   swa guman gefrungon (*Beo* 666)

grimman grapum   ond **him togeanes** feng (*Beo* 1542)

eodon **him** þa **togeanes**   Gode þancodon (*Beo* 1626)

gæstas grette,   ac **him togeanes** rad (*Beo* 1893)

godum togenes   nu sceal gled fretan (*Beo* 3114)

of ðære ginnan byrig   **hyre togeanes** gan (*Jud* 149)

tomiddes (8×)

hatne heaðowelm   **helle tomiddes** (*GenB* 324)

holte tomiddes   hraðe bioð forsewene (*Met* 13.37)

mid hettendum   **helle tomiddes** (*MSol* 172)

stylenne stan;   sticað **him tomiddes** (*MSol* 506)

mid helme beþeht   **holte tomiddes** (*JDay II* 2)

swiðe hat and ceald   **helle tomiddes** (*JDay II* 193)

blissiendum modum   **byrgum tomiddes** (*JDay II* 286)

toweard (8×)

As in the case of *neah* (above) it is often difficult to distinguish pre-positional from adjectival *toweard*. Doane (gloss.) takes *toweard* in *GenA* 1318 as an adj. The other seven instances cited in Bessinger and Smith are either adverbial or adjectival.

þæt wæs þrealic þing **þeodum toweard** (*GenA* 1318)

towiþre (1×)

wig towiþre   wicfreoþa healdan (*Max I* 128)

under (353×) [Wullen 1908: 51]

In my opinion the occurrence of *under* cited by Wullen in *Rid* 22.11 (*recte* 22.10) is not a case of postpositioning (*under hrunge*), and that in *ChristC* 1332 is adverbial.

siððan wide rad   **wolcnum under** (*GenA* 1392)

rim miclian   **roderum under** (*GenA* 2223)

siððan þu **usic under**   Abrahame þine (*GenA* 2677)

gesæliglic   **swegle under** (*GenA* 2845)

uppan (3×)

oððæt **him uppan**   æðelinges wæs (*El* 885)

ymbe (41×)

ac licgað **me ymbe**   irenbenda (*GenB* 371)

of þissum lioðobendum.   licgað **me ymbe** (*GenB* 382)

lufan and lissa.   angan þa **listum ymbe** (*Met* 1.59)

mare geferað   þa hire **middre ymbe** (*Met* 28.24)

ymbutan (18×)

ond **hine ymbutan**   æþelduguð betast (*ChristC* 1011)

hu widgil sint   **wolcnum ymbutan** / heofones hwealfe (*Met* 10.6)

middelgemærum   munt is **hine ymbutan** (*MSol* 256)

Some Preliminary Observations

One fact which emerges from the evidence cited above is that certain of the prepositions listed by Mitchell (*OES* §1078) are never found in verse. These include the following:

abutan, andlang, andlanges, begeondan, beheonan, bufan, (ge)hende, gemang, geondan, onbutan, onforeweardan, ongemang (ongemong), onmiddan, onufan, onuppan, toeacen, toefenes (toemnes), toweardes, þurhut, underneoþan, wiþæftan, wiþforan, wiþgeondan, wiþhindan, wiþinnan, wiþufan, wiþutan.

Were these prepositions somehow felt to be prosaic?

More importantly, certain prepositions attested in the poetic corpus are never postpositioned (in the lists which follow, I supply in parentheses the number of occurrences listed in Bessinger and Smith (1978). Note that the *Concordance* does not distinguish between prepositions and adverbs, nor indeed between homonyms, and hence that its statistics can provide only the roughest of guides to the frequency of prepositions in OE verse). These include:

Monosyllabic prepositions

ær (511×), for (448×), geond (197×), oþ (56×) and þurh (661×; also þuruh, 11×).

Polysyllabic prepositions

ætforan (1×), beæftan (1×), beutan (3×), binnan (2×), butan (103×; also buton, 31×), foran (26×), innan (80×), into (1×), onemn (1×), onforan (1×), samed (14×; also samod, 40×; somed, 15×; somod, 35×), toforan (1×), ufan (39×), ufenan (3×), utan (56×), wiþer (1×).

I am at a loss to understand why some prepositions were frequently postpositioned by Old English poets, but others apparently never were. Why *from* and *mid*, but not *geond* and *þurh*? Why *æfter* and *under*, but not *innan* and *utan*? (See above s.v. *on: ofne on innan . . .*). This is an aspect of "poetic effect" (Mitchell's words) which remains masked from us.

What is clear from the above evidence, however, is that prepositions, when removed from their normal position before the noun or pronoun which they govern, and then postpositioned, came almost invariably to acquire metrical stress (an apparent exception being *an* in *PPs* 55.9, but that text is badly edited and, as Rob Fulk points out to me (personal communication) we should probably read *ansiteð*, 'oppresses' here). Furthermore, having become stress-bearing particles, they frequently, but not invariably, participated in the verse's alliteration. The phenomenon is a widely recognized feature of Old English verse composition, and the regulation of stress on words according to their position in the clause is described in detail in a famous article by Hans Kuhn (1933; cf. Momma 1997: 28–54). According to Kuhn, certain words of variable stress, known as particles (*Satzpartikeln*), are normally stressed, but they may go unstressed in the first unstressed position of the clause; later in the clause they are always unstressed. Words that are normally dependent upon a following word, known as clitics (*Satzteilpartikeln*, including prepositions), are usually unstressed, but if they are moved from their position of dependence on the following word, they are treated in the same way particles are, and thus they are stressed. This is what happens to prepositions when they are postpositioned. For example, in the first line of *Beowulf*, the preposition *in* precedes the noun which it governs (*geardagum*) and is accordingly unstressed:

Hwæt we Gar-Dena   *in* geardagum (*Beo* 1)

Some lines later, however, the preposition *in* has been displaced or postpositioned so that it follows the noun which it governs (*Scedelandum*), and in this new position it acquires metrical stress (thus constituting a verse of type E1: / \ x /):

Scyldes eafera   **Scedelandum in** (*Beo* 19)

Because it occupies the second stress of the b-verse, *in* here obviously cannot participate in the alliteration; but postposited prepositions, especially when placed in the a-verse, often do participate in the alliteration. In keeping with the previous examples involving *in*, note the following line from the *Riddles*:

ic **him in** wunige   a þenden ic life (*Rid* 85.6)

Here the postpositioned preposition *in* both carries metrical stress and participates in the alliteration (with *in* in the a-verse alliterating with *a* in the b-verse).

According to the evidence presented above, Old English poets employed postpositioning of prepositions on 273 occasions (monosyllables 183×, polysyllables 90×). Of monosyllabic prepositions, there are 67 occurrences of postpositioning in the a-verse (of which 25 participate in the alliteration), and 116 in the b-verse (of which 39 participate in the alliteration). Of polysyllabic prepositions, there are 40 occurrences in the a-verse (of which 27 participate in the alliteration), and 50 in the b-verse (of which 17 participate in the alliteration).

Which poets practised the postpositioning of prepositions? With one exception (to be discussed below), the greatest number of postpositions, involving the largest number of prepositions, is found in two poems which, on my understanding of the evidence, date from the earlier eighth century and stand at the beginning of recorded Old English poetic tradition, rather than at its end (see Fulk 1992: 348–51, 381–92): *Genesis A* and *Beowulf*, which each have 33 occurrences of postpositioning. Behind these two poems, but at some distance, come poems which are conventionally assigned to the ninth century: Cynewulf, with 15 occurrences (*El* 6×, *Jul* 5×, *ChristB* 4×) and King Alfred's metrical versions of the metres of Boethius (19 occurrences). In his use of postpositioning, at least, the poet of *Andreas* stands close to the practice of Cynewulf and King Alfred. At the other end of the scale, postpositioning scarcely figures at all in those Old English poems which are commonly studied in university courses: the *Seafarer* (3×), the *Dream of the Rood* (1×) and the *Battle of Maldon* (1×); there is no occurrence of postpositioning in the *Wanderer*.

The one striking exception to this pattern (which in some respects might be a reflex of the chronology) is the high incidence of postpositioning in the metrical psalms of the Paris Psalter, where (according once again to the evidence assembled above) there are some 47 occurrences of postpositioning. The metrical psalms are regarded as a "pedestrian and unimaginative piece of poetic translation" (Griffith 1991: 167), and their metrical faults have often attracted comment (Fulk 1992: 410). For these reasons, the metrical psalms are assumed to date from the end of the Anglo-Saxon period. Yet in respect at least of the postpositioning of prepositions, the poet of the metrical psalms was apparently attempting to emulate the diction of earlier poetic tradition; and in certain respects, such as the postpositioning of *æt*, *on*, *to* and *ofer*, he went well beyond it. Whether such usage succeeds in imparting an elevated tone to his verse is difficult to say.

The one poet who clearly was attempting an elevated stylistic register, and who may have been the pioneer in this field, was the poet of *Genesis A*. Not only was he apparently the first poet to use postpositioned monosyllabic prepositions in combination with trisyllabic nouns in order to constitute an entire verse (i.e. half-line) at a stroke – for example, *eastlandum on* (1052), *herewicum neh* (2051), *goldburgum in* (2551) – but he was the only poet to use postpositioned *under* (1392, 2223, 2677, 2845). On one striking occasion, the postpositioned preposition was separated from its noun over a line break, as when the eldest daughter of Loth goes in to copulate with her drunken and naked father:

> Hie dydon swa;   **druncnum** eode
> seo yldre **to**,   ær on reste
> heora bega fæder . . .
>
> (*GenA* 2600–2)

The dramatic postpositioning here emphasizes the shock experienced by the daughter on approaching her naked father.

The Origin of Postpositioning in Old English Verse: A Hypothesis

As is obvious from his work of biblical translation, the poet of *Genesis A* was skilled in Latin, and it has been demonstrated convincingly that he had read at least one Latin poem in hexameters, namely Aldhelm's *Carmen de uirginitate* (Wright 1996). The process of learning Latin in an Anglo-Saxon school will have involved the minute study of a curriculum of Christian-Latin poets, and the poetry of Vergil as well (Lapidge 1996: 455–98). Because anastrophe, or the postpositioning of prepositions, was a marked stylistic feature of Latin poetic diction (Marouzeau 1922–53: 3.44–57; Hofmann and Szantyr 1965: 216–17; Maurach 1995: 36), it is worth at least asking whether Anglo-Saxon poets such as the author of *Genesis A* had learned this stylistic device from their study of Latin poetry. To answer this question would require a thorough study of all the Latin verse which Anglo-Saxon poets read and composed. Such a study lies far beyond the scope of the present discussion, but it may be worthwhile briefly to show how Roman poets employed the anastrophe of prepositions.

The first Roman poet to employ this kind of anastrophe, probably in imitation of the diction of Hellenistic verse, was Lucretius (d. 55 BC) in his cosmological epic *De rerum natura* (*DRN*). Some of Lucretius's postpositionings are striking indeed:

nec quae nigra cluent de nigris sed **uariis ex** (*DRN* ii.791) scilicet haec ideo **terris ex** omnia surgant (*DRN* vi.788)

multa siti prostrata **uiam per** proque uoluta (*DRN* vi.1264)

However, since there is very little evidence that Lucretius was ever studied in Anglo-Saxon England, it is more appropriate to consider a poet who was undoubtedly studied by all those Anglo-Saxons who had acquired expertise in Latin: namely Vergil. Vergil was deeply indebted to the diction of Lucretius, and this debt is reflected in Vergil's use of post-positioned prepositions:

saxa per et scopulos et depressas conuallis (*Georg.* iii.276)

turbam inter fremitumque Gyas; quem deinde Cloanthus (*Aen.* v.152)

his magnum **Alciden contra** stetit, his ego suetus (*Aen.* v.414)

transtra per et remos et pictas abiete puppis (*Aen.* v.663)

corpus in Aeacidae, magnas obeuntia terras (*Aen.* vi.58)

fata per Aeneae iuro dextramque potentem (*Aen.* vii.234)

But whereas Vergil (unlike Lucretius) only rarely postpositions a mono-syllabic preposition – the above-listed examples of *in* and *per* are unusual in Vergilian usage – he very frequently postpositions polysyllabic pre-positions, especially *circum, contra, inter* and *iuxta*:

quam pius arquitenens oras et **litora circum** (*Aen.* iii.75)

prouehimur pelago uicina **Ceraunia iuxta** (*Aen.* iii.506)

uictori chlamydem auratam, quam **plurima circum** (*Aen.* v.250)

solus qui **Paridem** solitus contendere **contra** (*Aen.* v.370)

dant sonitus, erratque auris et **tempora circum** (*Aen.* v.435)

pectoribusque arsisse, Iouis cum **fulmina contra** (*Aen.* x.566) uertite ad Aenean. stetimus **tela** aspera **contra** (*Aen.* xi.282)

solaque Tyrrhenos **equites** ire obuia **contra** (*Aen.* xi.504)

ossa sed **inter** / ferreus ad costas alto stat uulnere mucro (*Aen.* xi.816–17)

These are only a few of the many postpositionings of prepositions which are found throughout Vergil's *Aeneid*, particularly in the second half (books vii–xii). It will be seen from the above examples that in each case Vergil has placed the displaced polysyllabic preposition in the final foot of the hexameter. This practice closely resembles that of the Old English poets, who similarly placed polysyllabic prepositions at the end of their verses (indeed some prepositions, such as *tomiddes, toweard* and *under*, are invariably placed there). Thus when the poet of *Genesis A* places the preposition *under* at the end of a verse – *siððan wide rad* **wolcnum** **under** (1392), *rim miclian* **roderum under** (2223), etc. – he can be seen to be following Vergilian practice. We have seen that the poet of *Genesis A* on one occasion, and in order to achieve a dramatic effect, placed the post-positioned preposition in the following line. This kind of displacement, too, could have been inspired by Vergil:

feretro **Pallanta** reposto / procubuit **super** atque haeret lacrimansque gemensque (*Aen.* xi.149–50)

sed nunc, est **omnia** quando / iste animus **supra**, mecum partire laborem (*Aen.* xi.509–10)

It is a plausible hypothesis, therefore, that the postpositioning of prepositions in Old English poetry could have been modelled on similar practice in Latin poets such as Vergil. The hypothesis needs of course to be tested, not least by the examination of the Latin curriculum-poets other than Vergil who were studied in Anglo-Saxon schools. One objection is that postpositioning is found in Old Saxon and Old Icelandic verse as well (Kuhn 1933), and might arguably be an aboriginal feature of Germanic verse; yet it could be argued that Latin influence reinforced and extended a tendency already present. And the objection will also be raised that, unlike Latin, the postpositioning of prepositions is widely attested in Old English prose, in phrases such as *comon him to* (Wende 1915: 23–141; Mitchell 1978: 248–55; *OES*: §1062). But this is not an insuperable objection either, for no surviving Old English prose dates from earlier than the end of the ninth century, whereas some Old English poetry, notably *Genesis A* and *Beowulf*, dates from at least a century earlier. In other words, it could be argued that the use of postpositioned prepositions in Old English prose is to be explained as a poeticism adopted from the practice of Old English poets (Campbell 1970). Pending further investigation, the use of postpositioned prepositions in Old English verse may well turn out to be an example of Latin influence on (one minor aspect of) Old English syntax.

Note

I should like to express my warmest thanks to Rob Fulk and Mechthild Gretsch for constructive comments on an earlier version of the article.

References and Further Reading

Campbell, A. (1970). Verse influences in Old English prose. In J. L. Rosier (ed.) (pp. 93–8).

Fakundiny, L. (1970). The art of Old English verse composition. *RES*, XXI, 129–42, 257–66.

Fulk, R. D. (1992). *A History of Old English Meter.* Philadelphia, PA: University of Pennsylvania Press.

Griffith, M. S. (1991). Poetic language and the Paris Psalter: the decay of the Old English tradition. *ASE*, 20, 167–86.

Hofmann, J. B. & A. Szantyr (1965). *Lateinische Syntax und Stilistik.* Munich: Beck.

Lapidge, M. (1993–96). *Anglo-Latin Literature, 600–1066* (2 vols). London: Hambledon Press.

Marouzeau, J. (1922–53). *L'ordre des mots dans la phrase latine* (4 vols). Paris: Champion.

Martin, J. (1974). *Antike Rhetorik: Technik und Methode.* Munich: Beck.

Mason, L. (1915). *Genesis A. translated from the Old English* (Yale Studies in English, 45). New York: Holt.

Maurach, G. (1995). *Lateinische Dichtersprache.* Darmstadt: Wissenschaftliche Buchgesellschaft.

Mitchell, B. (1978). Prepositions, adverbs, prepositional adverbs, postpositions, separable prefixes or inseparable prefixes, in Old English? *NM*, 79, 240–57.

Wende, F. (1915). *Über die nachgestellten Präpositionen im Angelsächsischen.* (Palaestra, 70). Berlin: Mayer & Müller.

Wright, C. D. (1996). The blood of Abel and the branches of sin: *Genesis A, Maxims I* and Aldhelm's *Carmen de uirginitate. ASE*, 25, 7–19.

Wullen, F. (1908). *Der syntaktische Gebrauch der Präpositionen fram, under, ofer, þurh in der angelsächsischen Poesie*, I. Kiel: Ehlers.

Wullen, F. (1911). Der syntaktische Gebrauch der Präpositionen *fram, under, ofer, þurh* in der angelsächsischen Poesie. *Anglia*, 34, 423–97.

Chapter 9

Issues for Editors of Anglo-Saxon Poetry in Manuscript Form

Bernard J. Muir

This paper is concerned with reviewing what Anglo-Saxon manuscripts can tell us about the transmission and reception of vernacular poetry. It will examine the evidence for how the surviving poetic codices were compiled, and the roles of those involved in this process – the poets, anthologists, scribes and correctors. This evidence, however, proves on inspection to be a tangled web, making linear discussion problematic: for example, in discussing the anthologist, you discover that at times he may have been performing as poet by adapting the received poetry to suit his compilation; in discussing the scribe, you may discover that he too has altered the text during transmission, and so is also effectively the poet of the final recorded version of the text. But that is the nature of textual reception and transmission in the Middle Ages, a time when, in the wake and influence of oral traditions, texts were not sacrosanct, but living, dynamic entities that were regularly adapted during the process of trans-mission: on the vernacular literary scene, there was no awareness of the *verbatim* transmission of a text, nor of its potential merits (see Jabbour 1969).

There are only four major witnesses to these events, so their testimony is crucial to our understanding of poetic activity in Anglo-Saxon England. At first glance, the fact that *only* four manuscripts survive seems to suggest that there may not have been many such compilations made in the first place, or that the vernacular poetic tradition was not flourishing and dynamic; but a closer examination of the poems and the manuscripts themselves suggests otherwise (for a more sceptical view, see Sisam 1953: 99–100). Not only is there considerable evidence for purposeful anthologizing, but the texts themselves have been subject to extensive revision and correction by scribes and subsequent readers. The first part of this study focuses on the roles of the compiler or anthologist and poet, and the relationship between them, with specific reference to the Exeter, Dean and Chapter MS 3501 and Oxford, Bodleian Library MS Junius 11, the two Anglo-Saxon poetic compilations that can properly be described as *poetic* anthologies. Neither the Vercelli Book nor the so-called *Beowulf* manuscript was originally compiled as an anthology. The six poems in the former are in three discrete groups situated randomly, it seems, among a collection of twenty-three Anglo-Saxon homilies; nor does there appear to be an organizing rationale within any of the groupings. The compilation and subsequent history of the *Beowulf* manuscript have been the subject of intense critical debate during the past two decades, as is well known (see Kiernan 1996: 133–69 and Orchard 1995 for detailed discussions of these and related issues). Kiernan argues that the poem *Judith* was originally unrelated to *Beowulf* and was appended to it some time after it had first been copied out, whereas Ker and Lucas suggest that the acephalous *Judith* may have originally been positioned at the beginning rather than the end of the composite manuscript known as the Nowell Codex, which also includes three prose works, *The Passion of Saint Christopher*, *The Wonders of the East* and *The Letter of Alexander to Aristotle* (these are now bound first in the codex; see Orchard 1995: 3–27 for a summary of critical views concerning its structure). The Nowell Codex was subsequently bound together with the so-called Southwick Codex by their bibliophile owner, Sir Robert Cotton (1571–1631), which complicates the discussion of the history of this manuscript, which is now known as London, BL Cotton MS Vitellius A.XV. In the second part of this paper, representative alterations made to Exeter D&C 3501 by its scribe and subsequent correctors are briefly examined to determine what they can reveal about how scribes worked, whether or not they were "competent", and how the poetry was received and transmitted during the Anglo-Saxon period.

Anthologists and Poets

The starting point for discussions of scribal competence and the nature of the Anglo-Saxon poetic compilations is often the seminal work of Kenneth Sisam, whose essays were collected and published as *Studies in the*

History of Old English Literature. Of particular interest for the present study are his papers on the "Exeter Book" and the "*Beowulf* manuscript" (Sisam 1953: 29–44, 61–4, 65–96, 97–108, 291–2). Sisam rightly points out that many difficult readings may require emendation rather than a tortured defence by a conservative editor who wishes to defend the manuscript and tenaciously uphold its authority (Sisam 1953: 30). There can be no doubt that conjectural emendation is a useful and necessary tool for editors, especially when a text survives in a unique witness which is defective, as is the case with most of the surviving Anglo-Saxon poetry. Sisam also notes that we cannot be certain to what degree the extant witnesses record the original words of the poets – as we shall see later, there is ample evidence that vernacular texts were freely modified during transmission and that this could happen in a relatively short period of time; it is left to editors to determine, so far as it is possible from an assessment of all the evidence, whether such changes were made by anthologists (who are thus also assuming the role of poet and scribe) or subsequent readers, skilled enough in their native verse to modify texts as they read them (and thus also becoming the "poet" of the newly configured text).

Since Sisam first focused attention on the question of scribal competence and the authority of the surviving manuscripts there have been a number of important investigations of individual texts by other scholars that have improved our understanding of the Anglo-Saxon poetic tradition, and some of these will be reviewed here. But recent codicological and paleographical analyses have led to the discovery of hundreds of previously unnoticed alterations to the texts in these manuscripts which provide us with new insights into the techniques used by scribes and readers to correct, modify and update the surviving texts; thus the validity of previous observations on scribal competence and the authority of the manuscripts must be reconsidered. The textual notes in *The Exeter Anthology* (Muir 2000) alone document over four hundred previously unnoticed alterations to the texts, and there are a considerable number in the other collections as well. Given the attention that has been focused on this relatively small body of vernacular poetry, which consists of a total of slightly more than 35,000 lines, it may seem extraordinary that such a large number of alterations had gone unnoticed for so long. This new body of evidence indicates that scribes were very attentive to their tasks and that they took considerable care to ensure that they were transmitting the texts of their exemplars as accurately as possible. How then do we account for the large number of nonsensical readings that remain in the manuscripts, sometimes even after words have been "corrected" by the scribe as he was copying from his exemplar? A response to this puzzling question will be offered below.

The use of digital technology to reproduce and analyse manuscript texts is contributing to a resurgence of interest in codicological and paleographical issues and leading to a reconsideration of the authority of the manuscripts and the work habits of scribes and reader-correctors. Three of the four poetic compilations have now been made available as digital facsimiles – the "*Beowulf* Manuscript" (one part of London, British Library Cotton MS Vitellius A.XV) by Kiernan (1996), and Junius 11 (Oxford, Bodleian Library, MS Junius 11) and *The Exeter Anthology* (Exeter, Dean and Chapter MS 3501), both by Muir (2004, 2005) – and there is a project afoot to do the fourth, the "Vercelli Book" (Vercelli, Cathedral Library, Codex CXVII; see URL: Rosselli Del Turco). Thus scholars and students will soon have unprecedented access to high-resolution images of all the poetic compilations and be able to evaluate better for themselves the evidence and conclusions presented here and in other similar studies. It seems inevitable that this will ensure a long and lively debate on these issues.

Interestingly, many dozens of the alterations made to Exeter 3501 are clearly visible in the earlier photographic facsimile (Chambers et al. 1933), yet they still went unnoticed in subsequent critical discussion. That Krapp and Dobbie were content to use the then newly released photographic facsimile instead of examining the manuscript itself when preparing their edition of Exeter D&C 3501 for publication as *Anglo-Saxon Poetic Records III* is indicative of this lack of attention to paleographical and codicological matters (Krapp also based his edition of Junius 11 on a facsimile reproduction); this is even more remarkable in that Krapp and Dobbie's commentary is essentially textual rather than literary. It will be interesting to see if the new digital facsimiles come to be regarded as authoritative enough to make personal examination of the manuscript itself again seem unnecessary – it is clearly expected by libraries involved in the digital reproduction of manuscript materials that this will be the case, and that these irreplaceable cultural treasures will consequently suffer less stress to their fabric in the future. Recent experience suggests that digital facsimiles are now good enough to allow readers to resolve most paleographical questions, but that *in situ* examination will remain essential for addressing codicological issues, as would be expected.

Sisam referred to Exeter D&C 3501, the so-called "Exeter Book", as a "miscellany" (Sisam 1953: 97). In a field where so many editors and critics have a stake in so small a body of evidence, even nomenclature becomes an issue. In order to stimulate discussion of the nature of these collections and to reflect my own perceptions, when publishing the new edition of this manuscript I purposely called it *The Exeter **Anthology** of Old English Poetry* (Muir 2000), knowing full well that there would initially be strong resistance to changing the "name" of the manuscript, since it has been universally referred to as the "Exeter Book" for nearly a century. But such changes are healthy for the discipline when they lead to reconsideration of accepted ideas which may have become outdated. Thanks to the collective insight of the many scholars who have written on these issues during the past 50 years, we now have a better understanding of how Anglo-Saxon poets and scribes worked. I also assigned new titles to a number of poems – in view of the importance of the issue of "political correctness" in contemporary society, titles such as *The Gifts of Men* and *The Fortunes of Men* seemed quaint, if not potentially offensive, and in need of updating; these were replaced with *God's Gifts to Humankind* and *The Fates of Mortals*. *Azarias* was renamed *The Canticles of the Three Youths*, which reflects its subject matter better, and other titles were made more descriptive, so that *Juliana*, for example, was rechristened *The Passion of Saint Juliana*.

Even if scholars agree, however, that the new *Canticles* title serves the poem better than *Azarias*, it is difficult to adopt because of the convention of using the "short titles" introduced by the publication of the new *Dictionary of Old English* in order to standardize references to the poetry in criticism (Mitchell et al. 1979). In a recent article on *Canticles*, the author rejects the title *Azarias*, following *The Exeter Anthology*, but introduces a modified version of the title proposed there, calling the Exeter poem *The Three Youths* (Remley 2002). This sort of fastidious tinkering with names serves only to complicate matters further and should be avoided – if a new edition is adopted, then so too should its terms of reference. The new title will from now on exist side by side with the old, just as *Christ I – The Advent Lyrics*, *Christ II – The Ascension* and *Christ III – Christ in Judgement* already do. *The Exeter Anthology* acknowledges and clearly signals that the three *Christ* and two *Guthlac* poems are all by different poets, and by its use of dual line-numbering allows for ease of reference to earlier critical writings that used the continuous numbering of the *Anglo-Saxon Poetic Records*; Krapp confused the issue unnecessarily in *ASPR III* by first acknowledging that the three *Christ* and two *Guthlac* poems were by different authors and then numbering each set consecutively instead of restarting the numbering with each new poem. The naming and re-naming of manuscripts and poems may at first appear to be a minor issue, but it is clear that this is not so; editors will continue to be confronted by the tension between tradition and convention and the need to update terms of reference so that they reflect evolving critical perceptions.

As already noted, Exeter D&C 3501 and Junius 11 differ from the Vercelli Book and the *Beowulf* manuscript in that they were created specifically as *poetic anthologies*. In its present form Junius 11 contains just four poems – *Genesis* (*A* and *B*), *Exodus*, *Daniel* and *Christ and Satan* – but these were carefully selected, arranged and perhaps modified by the anthologist as he assembled his compilation. *Genesis B* is a partially illustrated translation of an earlier Old Saxon poem, which has been interpolated into the Anglo-Saxon *Genesis A*. *Christ and Satan* was fashioned from three poems on the topics of "The Fall of the Angels", "The Harrowing of Hell" and "The Temptation of Christ", but it is not known if this was done specifically for the Junius 11 anthology or if *Christ and Satan* was already a composite poem when it was copied into the manuscript; that is, the existing poem may have been created by adapting three pre-existing texts *by the Junius 11 anthologist-poet*. The Junius 11 texts explore incidents and themes that are particularly relevant for the Easter liturgy and which are the subject of its readings – creation, freedom from bondage and servitude, triumph over temptation and the powers of evil, and the journey towards a promised land – and critics today regard this as the organizing principle of the anthology (see Muir 2004: Introduction, The Work). There is no way of knowing for certain if the anthologist of Junius 11 was the person who first interpolated *Genesis B* into *Genesis A*, or if the two poems were already integrated in his exemplar; if he was responsible for merging the texts (and perhaps even making the translation from Old Saxon), then he is effectively the poet of the extant unified *Genesis* poem. Raw (1976) argues compellingly that most of the illustrations in Junius 11 were derived from the original Old Saxon *Genesis* poem, but supplementary drawings were added to it in England, and the anthologist may well have also overseen this stage of the poem's transmission. Junius 11 originally included *Genesis A* and *B*, *Exodus* and *Daniel*; *Christ and Satan* was added to the original anthology soon after it had been made. *Christ and Satan* was evidently selected to supplement the first three poems because its themes were also relevant for Eastertide. This augmentation of the manuscript may well have been orchestrated by the original anthologist as new material came to hand, in which case it would be further evidence for the dynamic nature of the transmission of vernacular poetry.

In summary, during its evolution to its present form Junius 11 passed through *at least* the following stages, though their ordering remains open to debate and it is not known how many stages of transmission may lie behind the individual poems:

- The Old Saxon *Genesis* poem is composed and perhaps illustrated at the same time (if not, then during a separate stage of transmission); subsequently it was brought to England (see Raw 1976).
- *Genesis A, Exodus*, the three poems which comprise *Christ and Satan*, and a poem based on episodes from the biblical book of Daniel are composed at various times; this original "Daniel" poem lies at a distance behind both *Daniel* and *The Canticles of the Three Youths* (in Exeter D&C 3501; for a detailed discussion of the relationship between them see Remley 2002).
- *Daniel* is composed.
- The Old Saxon *Genesis* is translated into Old English (as the so-called *Genesis B*); some or all of its illustrations are also copied.
- *Genesis B* is interpolated into *Genesis A*. Either at this stage or subsequently, supplementary illustrations were added to the hybrid *Genesis* poem. The illustrations are sometimes seriously out of alignment with the text, suggesting that the artists either did not agree with the anthologist's or scribe's proposed cycle, or perhaps that they could not understand the text (i.e. they were foreigners), and the misalignment was accidental.
- The anthologist selects and arranges the first three poems to explore themes relevant for Eastertide. The poems were to be illustrated throughout, but for reasons unknown the cycle was never finished, so that blank spaces occur throughout this part of the manuscript.
- *Christ and Satan* is fashioned from three pre-existing poems.
- The anthologist of the first three poems, or another compiler, decides to add *Christ and Satan* to the manuscript and to have it illustrated with full-page drawings (which are now lost – see Muir 2004: Introduction, Codicology, Gathering 17).

The complexity of the evolution of the Junius 11 anthology is abundantly clear from this, as is the fact that we shall never be able to describe the stages of its development definitively.

In his discussion of the "arrangement" of Exeter D&C 3501, Sisam notes that "the first part contains all the longer poems, and that they are all religious" (Sisam 1953: 291), but he cannot see any other organizing principle in the manuscript. He further observes that "because the copy may be several times removed from the original miscellany, not much light on the method of compilation can be expected from the scribe as a copyist" (Sisam 1953: 97). Sisam is correct in noting that the *present* D&C MS 3501 is a copy of a pre-existing miscellany (or better, anthology), but the situation is more complex than this. It seems that the Exeter anthologist had before him *a number of pre-existing collections or anthologies* from which to select and arrange his material; the challenge for editors and critics is to make sense of what he has done with these "raw materials". Though the compilation may not have a single controlling structural rationale, the anthologist can be seen arranging the texts into meaningful groupings throughout.

As noted earlier, the anthology opens with eight substantial poems on Christian themes. The first folio of Exeter D&C 3501 is missing and the first lyric of *The Advent Lyrics* is acephalous; textual evidence suggests, however, that there is not much missing from this sequence of seasonal poems, so the opening of the present *Lyric I* plus perhaps one more lyric would easily have fit onto the lost folio. Seventeen shorter poems follow next, then the first set of riddles, eight more short poems, and finally, the second set of riddles. The original size of the present anthology is unclear, since whole gatherings may have been lost at its beginning and end, or within where there is evidence of the loss of text between existing gatherings (see Muir 2000: 11–12).

It has been observed elsewhere that the rationale for the arrangement may have been that each poem presents an ideal for some aspect or mode of Christian life (Muir 2000: 16–25). Christ, whose life is the subject of the first three poems, is *the* role-model for Christian living; Guthlac, represented by two poems, is the *male* role-model for an ideal Christian, fighting continually to oppose the forces of evil (*Guthlac A*) and dying in an exemplary fashion (*Guthlac B*); the three Hebrew youths, representing the Just in the Old Testament, are pre-Christian believers who are willing to die for their faith; the allegorized Phoenix represents "everyman", guaranteeing eternal life to all of Christ's present and future followers;

and Juliana presents the *female* role-model for contemporary Christians. Significantly, the word *had* (the New English suffix *-hood*), referring to a state of being or mode of life, occurs a number of times throughout these poems. The fact that there *are* three *Christ* poems, arranged sequentially to describe his life chronologically in the manuscript, reveals the hand of the anthologist and encourages such an interpretation.

In light of this argument the absence of a separate poem dedicated to Christ's passion and death may seem a glaring omission, but there simply might not have been one available to the anthologist when he needed it; the three existing poems do, however, deal with all aspects of Christ's life, not just his incarnation, ascension and coming in judgement, as suggested by their modern editorial titles. The series of "leaps" (*hlypas*) in *The Ascension*, for example, which the Anglo-Saxon poet increases to six from the five in his source (a homily by Pope Gregory I) as he composes (which is relevant for the present discussion), includes the incarnation, birth, crucifixion, burial, descent into hell and ascension.

The use of the word *nu* at the beginning of *The Ascension*, *The Whale* and *The Husband's Message* may be evidence that the texts are being adapted by an anthologist during transmission. *The Whale* is the second in a truncated series of bestiary poems in Exeter D&C 3501; its opening words "Now (*Nu*) by my wit I want to make known another poetic song about a kind of fish . . ." indicate that the anthologist-poet is using the adverb to link related poems together in a sequence. The adverb may have the same function at the beginning of *The Ascension*, and reveal the hand of the anthologist-poet adding a short transitional introductory and dedicatory passage to an existing signed poem by Cynewulf. A more radical reading of the evidence suggests that *The Ascension* was actually written as a transitional poem to link *The Advent Lyrics* to *Christ in Judgement*, and that it may have been composed by the anthologist-poet (see further Chase 1974; Liuzza 1990).

In the rare cases where a poem in Old English survives in more than one witness, the evidence suggests that poets and scribes were not overly concerned with the *verbatim* replication of existing poems, but that they felt free to reshape and adapt existing texts to meet their needs. The poem *Soul and Body*, versions of which occur in the Vercelli Book (*S&B I*) and Exeter D&C 3501 (*S&B II*), is the most striking example of this. Gyger (1969) argues that the difference between the two *Soul and Body* poems is evidence of the poems being adapted during oral transmission, whereas Moffat (1983, 1987, 1992) and Orton (1979a) demonstrate that the revisions took place "not in performance but on the page, the source of the variation presumably being the transcribers themselves" (Moffat 1987: 1). Not only does the textual evidence indicate that the poem has been freely modified and adapted during transmission, but the version in D&C 3501 has been truncated, presumably not accidentally, by the anthologist performing as editor. If this *was* done intentionally, then as it survives the poem reflects the anthologist's agenda – by eliminating the speech of the "Body", he transformed the poem from a dialogue into a monologue. It is now very homiletic in tone and thus fits quite well with the poem which precedes it in the manuscript, *Homiletic Fragment III*, formerly thought to be the conclusion of *The Partridge*. In effect, if this is accepted as a deliberate modification, then the Exeter text is actually a "different poem" and ought to be assigned a separate name; this, however, would obscure the relationship between the two poems and, once again, create an awkward situation with respect to the critical tradition.

Remley examines the relationship between the texts of *The Canticles of the Three Youths* and *Daniel*, poems which ostensibly recount the same biblical events while diverging considerably from each other at times. Challenging established views that the differences between the poems indicate either a careless and corrupt process of written transmission (for this line of argument see, for example, Sisam 1953: 31–9), or slippages more easily "attributable to the lapses of memory of an 'oral singer' than to anything else" (Jones 1966: 95–6), he argues that many of the passages in *Canticles* but not in *Daniel* were added by a poet (whom he designates the 'Canticle-Poet') who had an interest in botanical imagery (Remley 2002: 101–13). In her consideration of these poems, O'Brien O'Keeffe had earlier foreshadowed the problems addressed by Remley when she noted that the relationship between them illustrates "the complex problems in evaluating residual orality and literate transmission" (O'Brien O'Keeffe 1990: 138, n. 1). Critical attention has now clearly focused on the dynamic nature of the transmission of Anglo-Saxon poetry and the impact of the oral tradition on written texts. Remley believes that there are "as many as eight discernible transmissional stages" behind *The Canticles of the Three Youths* as recorded in Exeter D&C 3501 (Remley 2002: 140), further attesting to the intensity of poetic activity in Anglo-Saxon England.

Exeter D&C 3501 also contains two substantial collections of riddles. Due to the damage caused by fire to the end of the manuscript and the loss of the occasional folio, it is impossible to tell exactly how many riddles there are or might have been originally, but the number approximates one hundred and it seems that a century comprised of two collections of sixty and forty was intended. This is significant because there was a tradition of riddles being composed or collected and published in centuries, and in adding a second set of (approximately) forty to his original set of (approximately) sixty the anthologist appears to be aware of this convention. Editors and critics cannot agree on the number of riddles in the manuscript, however, because there is still disagreement about the boundaries between some of the texts. Even the question of exactly which poems *are* riddles remains an issue. The confusion derives from the manuscript itself and originates in the anthologist or scribe's exemplar. *Riddles* 42 and 43 are treated as one poem by the scribe, as are 47 and 48 (as numbered in Muir 2000); as Liuzza notes, the riddles were not carefully copied out (Liuzza 1988: 11). Riddles 1 to 3, though clearly treated as separate poems by the scribe, are sometimes edited as one long poem with three movements. *Wulf and Eadwacer*, the most enigmatic of all Anglo-Saxon poems, comes before the first set of riddles and is counted as a riddle by some early and more recent editors.

The second set of riddles presents more interesting problems. Most editions of Exeter D&C 3501 present the sequence of poems leading up to this group as *Riddle 30b, Riddle 60, The Husband's Message* and *The Ruin*, but the codicological and paleographical evidence suggests that this is not the way the original anthologist or scribe understood the texts in his exemplar. The anthologist or scribe thought that the second set of riddles began with *Riddle 30b*, which is then followed by *Riddle 60*. He mistook *The Husband's Message* for three riddles, as his layout and punctuation show; the formatting he used for the text was probably that of his exemplar. As can be seen in Figures 9.1–9.5 (fols 122v–124r), the scribe uses initials of the same size and style for the three sections of *The Husband's Message* and *The Ruin* as he does for the riddles before and after them. He also "right justifies" the last line of the first two sections of *The Husband's Message* and of *The Ruin*, on one occasion using a wrap-mark to offset the text (Figure 9.6), as he often does throughout the two sets of riddles. The use of runes in the closing section of *The Husband's Message* (Figure 9.7) may have suggested to him that it was a riddle, since they occur frequently in other riddles (which is evidence of their literary rather than oral origins, since runes are *visual* cues); this would have reinforced his perception that the first two sections were also short riddles. The scribe also uses a rune as "short-hand" in *The Ruin* (Figure 9.8, "M" for *mon-* in *mondreama*); this together with its opening word *wrætlic* ('wondrous'/

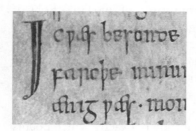

Figure 9.1

Figure 9.2

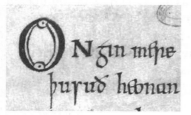

Figure 9.3

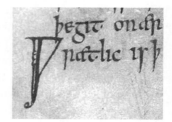

Figure 9.4

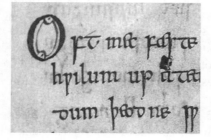

Figure 9.5

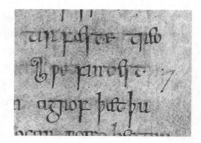

Figure 9.6

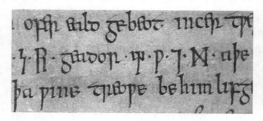

Figure 9.7

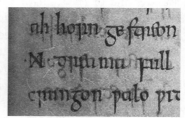

Figure 9.8

'wonderful') which is quite often used to describe the personified speaker in Exeter riddles, may have confirmed the scribe's perception that the second riddle sequence had started with *Riddle 30b*.

It has been argued that there is thematic unity in the sequence of poems *Judgement Day I* to *Homiletic Fragment II* in that they are all concerned with aspects of the Easter liturgical season (Muir 2000: 23–5). This accounts for all the poems between the first and second sets of riddles except for *The Wife's Lament*, if the second set is understood to begin with *Riddle 30b*. It has been argued, however, that *The Wife's Lament* is open to an allegorical reading which associates it with themes relevant for Eastertide (see Anderson 1986: 84–99). If this be the case, then the whole sequence between the two groups of riddles becomes a series of reflections on a unified theme (Easter), and was arranged purposely by the anthologist.

All that remains unaccounted for in this analysis of the work of the anthologist is the sequence of poems *The Wanderer* to *Homiletic Fragment III*. There is no apparent thematic unity among these poems, but the anthologist may have arranged them to be a sequence of Christian wisdom poetry (representing a number of genres – elegy, allegory, satire, didactic, catalogue). In such a scheme, however, it is hard to account for the presence of *Widsith*, unless it is understood to be an Anglo-Saxon "defence of poetry" or *ars poetica*, making it appropriate for inclusion in this sequence of didactic texts (see Rollman 1982).

Scribes, Correctors and Readers

Sisam has this to say about the scribe of Exeter D&C 3501:

> It might be inferred that such a well-trained hand would transcribe mechanically, bringing to English the habit of literal reproduction that was required in Latin. In fact his one consecutive scrap of Latin . . . is barbarous, probably because he had no thought of correcting a corrupt original. (Sisam 1953: 97–8)

and this about readers and correctors of Anglo-Saxon poetry:

> But it is certain that after the Exeter Book left the scriptorium, little was done by later readers to remove even crude errors from the text . . . No

doubt some readers of English poetry could not write, and others had not pen in hand. But when the few feeble glosses to the main hand of the Junius manuscript are taken into account, the likeliest explanation is that not many in the eleventh century understood the harder poetry well enough to read it critically. The few later corrections in the poetical manuscripts are usually concerned with variant forms, less often with patent errors. (pp. 98–9)

In his discussion of scribal "accuracy", based on a comparison of variant or divergent readings in the few texts preserved in more than one witness, Sisam assumes that the aim of all poet-scribes was to reproduce the texts of their exemplars as accurately as possible (Sisam 1953: 31–44). The discussion in the first part of this paper demonstrates that many critics today regard these points of divergence as evidence for the dynamic nature of vernacular textual transmission in the Middle Ages – that is, the norm seems to have been for texts to be modified freely as they were transmitted. Peoples not constrained by codified written traditions most likely regarded vernacular poetic texts as common or shared cultural artefacts.

Sisam's comments raise a number of issues about which more can be said in light of recent closer scrutiny of the four surviving poetic manuscripts. At the outset it is important to note that most medieval manuscripts are fraught with error. Moreover, often either contemporary or later correctors or readers have attempted to correct, annotate, update or punctuate them. These things are all evidence for the transmission and reception of Anglo-Saxon manuscripts, though the evidence is often difficult to interpret.

It seems logical to assume that the correcting of manuscripts did not usually happen spontaneously – special tools were required in order to correct a manuscript: a sharp knife, a quill or pen, ink, and perhaps water. It does not seem likely that an individual reading a text in private would have had these things at hand unless he were in a writing centre (that is, a scriptorium). Moreover, if the reader were correcting the text by comparing it to an exemplar, then it is even more likely that he would have been working in a scriptorium.

If the poetic manuscripts were used in such a way that one person read the poems to a group of listeners, as is often assumed, then it is unlikely that the reader would have made corrections to the text while he was reading – this would not have been practical. And yet if the manuscripts *were* used in this way, then the reader must have been able

Figure 9.9

to cope with errors encountered in the text as he was reading. If he were a native speaker, on discovering a lexical error he would immediately realize that the text made no sense and that there was no point in reading out the perceived error. For example, in Exeter D&C 3501, *Riddle* 56.7 (Figure 9.9), the scribe wrote *fæft* for *fæst*. Now *fæst* is a very common Old English word – in fact, it appears as an adverb (*fæste*) in the previous line of this poem (and in the *same* manuscript line) – whereas *fæft* is plain nonsense. How do we account for the scribe writing a nonsensical word, and how would a reader deal with it when he encountered it? And if such forms *were* read out, how did listeners cope with them?

The nonsensical form *fæft* may well have been in the scribe's exemplar, but it is difficult to account for why a native speaker would not correct such an obvious error while he was copying out the text. Certainly no one today would write, "That girl runs *faft*", and it is hard to believe that blind faithfulness to an exemplar would induce an Anglo-Saxon scribe to write out nonsensical forms in his own language (being a scribe required training and intelligence, after all – it was a serious undertaking). Certainly, a scribe could misconstrue a form when looking at it quickly, and mistake an Insular "s" for an "f" (since they are identical, except that the "f" has an additional final stroke, its tongue), but as he actually wrote the word out you would have expected him to correct it either immediately (and there are a lot of examples of words corrected "in progress" (*calamo currente*) in the poetic codices) or as soon as he had finished the word and looked at it (many words are also corrected after they have been written out by the principal scribe). What is most puzzling of all, is the situation where an Anglo-Saxon scribe wrote out a nonsensical word and then corrected it, but the corrected form as recorded in the manuscript is still not an acceptable Old English form. Such an example occurs in D&C 3501 in *The Phoenix* (l. 15a) where the scribe at first wrote *f*æft*

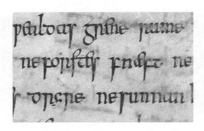

Figure 9.10

(Figure 9.10), where the asterisk represents a letter he erased and which can no longer be identified (but it was obviously wrong and unacceptable to him). Over the erasure he wrote his correction, an "n", so that the manuscript now has the reading *fnæft*. As can be seen immediately by anyone with even a modicum of knowledge of Old English, in its "corrected" form this is still a nonsense word. And yet the "corrector" or, as it seems, the scribe in this case has adjusted the word and decided to let it stand. He seems to have realized that he miscopied his exemplar, but not that the form in his exemplar was itself an error. Moreover, the word occurs in a rare situation where the "a" and "b" verses actually have end rhyme, in this case *fnæst–blæst*, so it is even more surprising that he left the reading *fnæft* to stand.

An identical situation is found in *God's Gifts to Humankind* (l. 109), where the manuscript reading is *þeaw fæft ne* (Figure 9.11), which is written over an erasure; though the scribe corrected part of the original reading here (*þeaw*), the recorded reading is a nonsense word. In *Maxims I(A)* l. 63b is the form *belihð*, which is fine; but in *Maxims I (B)* l. 30b, where the same form is required, the scribe writes *behlið* (Figure 9.12), which makes

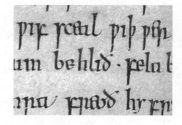

Figure 9.11   *Figure 9.12*

no sense in this context. In addition, it seems that the final stroke of the "h" has been altered (that is, the form has been corrected) near the baseline. The following list describes the nature and level of scribal activity (or inactivity) on folio 90v of Exeter D&C 3501, which contains part of *Maxims I (B)*:

- l. 3 (Figure 9.13): *linden bord*: the scribe originally made a descender for the first stroke of the final "n" of *linden*, which he subsequently scraped away; it seems that he may initially have written an "r", perhaps anticipating the "r" of *bord* (a form of audible memory lapse). This correction was made while the poem was first being copied out, not by a later corrector. Two words later he makes another error in a common word: for *wilcuma* he wrote *wul cu / ma* (divided by a line end); subsequently, either he or a corrector erased the second minim of the first "u" to produce the required form. This correction was not made "in progress", and because it is an erasure we cannot be sure when the correction was made.
- l. 4 (Figure 9.14): here we find that the much-discussed Frisian "wife" almost never made it into critical discussion: the scribe at first wrote either an "s" or an "f" as the first letter of this word. We cannot tell whether he immediately caught his error and altered the letter as he wrote (i.e. it is an "in progress" correction), or whether he wrote a nonsense word and only noticed and corrected it subsequently. The ink matches the rest of the text, so the alteration was made by the original scribe rather than later by a reader-corrector.
- l. 5 (Figure 9.15): *laðaþ*: "ð" has the usual shape of a "d", suggesting that the scribe first wrote a "d" and then crossed its upper arm to make the required letter; he frequently confuses these two letters.
- l. 8: *behlið*: (discussed above).
- l. 9: *fyrwet geonra*: for *fyrwetgeornra*; the recorded form *-geonra* is a nonsense form, but has not been corrected either by the scribe or by any subsequent reader.
- l. 13 (Figure 9.16): *holm*: "o" has been corrected from original "e" by scraping away its medial arm and closing its loop; *helm*, which the scribe initially wrote, is a perfectly good Old English word – it just makes no sense here. So, even though the form was noticed and subsequently corrected by the scribe, the nature of the error suggests the following scenarios: *helm* was in the exemplar and he copied it mechanically; or he subconsciously substituted one common word for

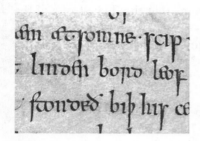

Figure 9.13

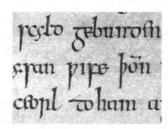

Figure 9.14

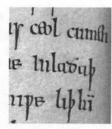

Figure 9.15

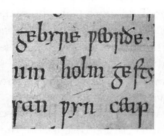

Figure 9.16

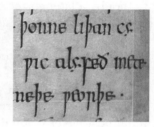

Figure 9.17

another because of their similar sound. In any case, he subsequently noticed the error and corrected it.

- l. 14: *mægð egsan wyn* (with *wyn* accented): this is apparently best restored to sense by reading *mægðes agen wyn*; as they stand, the words make no sense.
- l. 16 (Figure 9.17): *alyfeð*: the participle, *alyfed*, is required; this is perhaps another instance of mistaking "d" for "eth", but it is evidence of mechanical copying. If the scribe proofread this page, as some of the changes indicate he did, then why did he not notice this error?

There is nothing particularly unusual about the kinds of mistakes and corrections made on this folio, nor about their density. The point to be made is that the manuscript has been heavily corrected throughout.

It becomes clear as you study texts recorded in manuscript form that you need to develop a theory of reading in order to understand how these texts might have been useable: how would a listener or reader understand a corrupt text? The manuscript evidence indicates that medieval readers had a high level of tolerance of interruptions in the sense of particular phrases, which allowed them to read so that they supplied or restored what might be called a "micro-meaning" from context; that is, in a particular sequence of words the overall drift or logical progression of ideas would dictate that this problematic word must fit in thus. So, for example, when a reader came upon *fæfte* in his text, he would immediately substitute the appropriate correct form as suggested by common usage and context; in this case, he would read out *fæste* instead of the manuscript's nonsense form, *fæfte*. We must appreciate that in a manuscript culture which lasted for over 2,000 years, readers and listeners would have been very familiar with the error rate in texts and would probably have been quite adept at dealing with minor textual corruption; by comparison, in the age of print, people often get a small thrill from finding a typographical error in a polished publication and having the opportunity to cross through it with a pencil and write the correction in the margin – if nothing else, it proves to posterity that you have read the book closely! The use of variation, which is essential to the verse, and Anglo-Saxon poetry's formulaic character, whereby verse syntax makes certain grammatical forms predictable, would have assisted a native speaker in making minor restorations to the text as it was read or heard. It is also important to recall in this context that the poetic manuscripts, all from the late tenth or early eleventh centuries, exhibit quite an advanced stage of the "levelling of inflections", indicating that *even in the poetry*, which generally has more complex syntax than prose, a new set of expectations were at work that allowed readers to distinguish between words in different cases on grounds other than the specificity of their case endings; again, this indicates an increased tolerance among readers for what might at first appear to be ambiguity in the text.

Readers and listeners, as distinct groups, will have different experiences of a text and, of course, each person will understand the text in a unique way – no two encounters with the text will be identical, even for the same person returning periodically to the text. Thus the polysemous nature of any given (poetic) text also encourages tolerance in the listener or reader; it is enticing to imagine that as a person experiences a poem, the collage or sequence of images (and the formulaic expression of them) as they interact with each other has a "syntax" that can override the minutiae at the level of verbal syntax and ensure the text's meaning or intelligibility, should it falter momentarily. Greenfield (1955) discusses how the theme of exile is expressed formulaically in Anglo-Saxon poetry;

once again, traditional verbal collocations relating to the expression of essential ideas and themes would help an informed listener make sense of minor mistakes or inconsistencies in a text.

The scribe copying a text is in a unique position because he is at the same time a reader. His role as reader may at times interfere with his function as scribe, and cause him to alter, emend, update or otherwise change the text, either consciously or inadvertently. For example, he may substitute a synonym for a word in his original between the act of reading the exemplar and writing out his copy (e.g. *mere* for *sæ*), or a different spelling of the same word (e.g. *yrnan* for *rinnan* at Riddle 84.5, where the latter is required by the metre); alternatively, he may inadvertently substitute a word because it is suggested by the context. There are no surviving native speakers of Old English, so we can never be certain that our assumptions or conclusions are valid, but it may be that when an Anglo-Saxon heard a text read aloud in the tenth or eleventh century there would have been little distinction between the sound of the same word when pronounced in different dialects; in fact, the person reciting may well have standardized the dialect or updated the language of a poem as he read it.

Recent close study of the surviving Anglo-Saxon poetic manuscripts reveals that scribes and correctors made considerably more alterations to them than has been generally realized by editors and critics. The fact that so many nonsense words and grammatically unacceptable forms remain, even after the manuscripts have been subject to extensive proofreading and correction, suggests that in the late tenth century, when the monastic reform was at its height and there was extensive intellectual and cultural exchange between England and the Continent, some scribes and artists involved in manuscript production may have been non-native speakers.

It is perhaps remarkable that so many issues can arise from the study of such a small body of literature – and there are many others that have not been touched upon here. The whole question of the nature and status of "standard" editions in the digital age, for example, needs to be addressed. The manuscript evidence suggests that poetry was popular, and circulated widely in Anglo-Saxon England, though this begs the question of why so few compilations survive. The mutilated condition of Exeter D&C 3501 – slashed by knives, stained, burnt, and stripped of its covers – suggests that once these texts were no longer intelligible, they were discarded, if they could not be of use in the scriptorium. Junius 11 probably escaped a similar fate because its illustrations were of interest to subsequent ages.

References and Further Reading

Chase, C. (1974). God's presence through grace as the theme of Cynewulf's *Christ II* and the relation of this theme to *Christ I* and *Christ III. ASE*, 3, 87–101.

Greenfield, S. (1955). The formulaic expression of the theme of exile in Anglo-Saxon poetry. *Speculum*, 30, 200–6.

Gyger, A. (1969). The Old English *Soul and Body* as an example of oral transmission. *MÆvum*, 38, 239–44.

Jabbour, A. (1969). Memorial transmission in Old English poetry. *Chaucer Review*, 3, 174–90.

Jones, A. (1966). *Daniel* and *Azarias* as evidence for the oral-formulaic character of Old English poetry. *MÆvum*, 35, 95–102.

Kiernan, K. S. (1996). *Beowulf and the Beowulf Manuscript*. Ann Arbor, MI: University of Michigan Press.

Liuzza, R. M. (1988). The texts of the Old English *Riddle 30. JEGP*, 87, 1–15.

Liuzza, R. M. (1990). The Old English *Christ* and *Guthlac* texts, manuscripts, and critics. *RES*, 41, 1–11.

Lockett, L. (2002). An integrated re-examination of the dating of Oxford, Bodleian Library, Junius 11. *ASE*, 31, 81–140.

Moffat, D. (1983). The MS transmission of the OE *Soul and Body. MÆvum*, 52, 300–301.

Moffat, D. (1987). A case for scribal revision in the Old English *Soul and Body. JEGP*, 86, 1–8.

Moffat, D. (1992). Anglo-Saxon scribes and Old English verse. *Speculum*, 67, 805–27.

Muir, B. J. (1989). A preliminary report on a new edition of the Exeter Book. *Scriptorium*, 43, 273–88, Pls. 21–4.

Muir, B. J. (1991). Watching the Exeter Book scribe copy Old English and Latin texts. *Manuscripta*, 35, 3–15, Pls. 1–7.

Orchard, A. (1995). *Pride and Prodigies: studies in the monsters of the Beowulf manuscript*. Cambridge: D. S. Brewer.

Orton, P. R. (1979a). The OE 'Soul and Body': a further examination. *MÆvum*, 48, 173–97.

Orton, P. R. (1979b). Disunity in the Vercelli Book *Soul and Body. MÆvum*, 48, 173–97.

Pope, J. (1980). What the seraphim do in line 396a of the Old English *Advent*: a scribal cover uncovered. *Speculum*, 68, 1–5.

Raw, B. (1976). The probable derivation of most of the illustrations in Junius 11 from an illustrated Old Saxon *Genesis*. *ASE*, 5, 133–48.

Remley, P. G. (2002). *Daniel*, the *The Youths* fragment and the transmission of Old English verse. *ASE*, 31, 81–140.

Rollman, D. A. (1982). *Widsith* as an Anglo-Saxon defense of poetry. *Neophilologus*, 66, 431–9.

Saenger, P. (1997). *Space Between Words: the origins of silent reading*. Stanford, CA: Stanford University Press.

Sisam, K. (1953). *Studies in the History of Old English Literature*. Oxford: Clarendon Press.

Chapter 10

Language and Style in Two Anonymous Old English Easter Homilies

Hiroshi Ogawa

The present study deals with two Old English anonymous Easter Sunday homilies for which *HomS* 27 and *HomS* 28 are the *DOE* short titles. They are examples of the genre known as "composite homilies" – homilies "made up largely of passages drawn with little change from other Old English writings (usually homiletic) and not freshly composed or translated from Latin" (Godden 1975: 57) – and are both preserved only in one manuscript, *HomS* 27 in CCCC 162 (s. xi[in]) and *HomS* 28 in Junius 121 (s. xi 3rd quarter) (see Ker 1957: 51–6, 412–18), in which they are titled, respectively, *In Die Sancto Pasce* (as the manuscript rubric) and *De Descensu Christi ad Inferos* (as a note in the margin by a later hand: Ker 1957: 54; Fadda 1972: 998). As these titles suggest, the two homilies derive from distinct traditions of Easter Sunday homilies and show no evidence of connection with each other in textual transmission. What brings them together for discussion here is the fact that they both use Ælfric's homily as source material for part of the composite work. Moreover, as we shall see, the two homilies use different items in the *Catholic Homilies* and differ remarkably in the way they modify the borrowed passages for their use. To compare the methods and practices of these homilies is to examine an important facet of the history of the homilies in late Anglo-Saxon England, both in terms of language and style and attitudes to the preceding monuments in the tradition of vernacular prose in which they found themselves.

In Die Sancto Pasce

Our first text, *In Die Sancto Pasce* (*HomS* 27), is an Easter homily which is not based on a lection of the Bible assigned for the day. On the contrary, it is a concatenation of five major themes – the Earthly Paradise, the Evils of the Sixth Day, the Sunday List, the Harrowing of Hell and the Last Judgement, as Lees (1986: 125) calls them – which are thus treated methodically according to the Christian history of mankind but which lack, in that treatment, a consistent narrative or exegesis that would weld them into a continuous development of a single dominant subject. It is as if the homilist had selected the themes which, though they are not all associated particularly clearly with Easter, he finds useful to dwell upon on this particular occasion, with little evident attempt on his part to integrate them. In Lees's words:

> The accumulation of such a number of themes and motifs, the attraction to lists, and the treatment of the extracts from Ælfric . . . suggests an indiscriminate and unsophisticated selection of material. The homily is a mass of information loosely based on Easter without any clear message for its audience. (Lees 1986: 142)

This "loose" structure of the homily seems to have some consequences for its prose. This may be illustrated by the opening passage, which "assumes a kind of pulpit cadence the momentum of which seems to override some of the grammatical and logical inconsistencies of the text" (Schaefer 1972: 185):

> . . . And efne swa þa tida on hærfæst mid wæstmum and mid blostmum beoð gefyllede, swa him wæron ealle god gesealde oðða æt nextan he forheold Godes bebodu swa him Drihten ne bebead. Ac þurh unwisdom he gesyngode beforan Gode and þa æfter þam nænige hreowe he ne dyde þæs gyltes. Swa hit is awriten on halgum bocum, 'Se ðe synne deð and þa ne beteð se bið þære synne þeow' oð ðæt he hi eft gebeteð Gode to willan.
>
> Swa þonne, men ða leofestan, æfter þam þeowdome Drihten God wæs ariend and helpend menniscum cynne. And swa swa on ðam sixtan dæge Adam gesceapen wæs, and on þam sixtan dæge he gesyngode æfter þan. (*HomS* 27.9)

The inconsistencies are to be observed particularly clearly in the use of *swa swa* and *swa*, which dominates the entire passage. Grammatically, *swa . . . ne* (as in the manuscript) in the opening sentence (meaning literally '[he neglected God's commandments] as God did not command him') is irregular; Lees omits *ne*. But *ne bebead* might well be "a lax substitution for *forbead*" suggesting "a kind of colloquial understatement", as Schaefer thinks (Schaefer 1972: 85), paraphrasing the *swa*-clause as 'as God commanded him not to'. More blatant perhaps is the inconsistency of the *swa swa* in the last sentence. It is evidently a conjunction introducing a subordinate clause of manner but lacks a proper main clause, which would have run something like *swa on þam sixtan dæge gesyngode he . . .* , rather than *and on þam sixtan dæge he gesyngode*, as it stands in the manuscript. It looks as if the homilist lost sight of the syntax of the complex sentence, continuing instead in a compound sentence.

It is interesting to observe that this loose syntax occurs in what Schaefer refers to as "a non sequitur after the sentence [*Swa þonne . . . cynne.*]" (Schaefer 1972: 186). In fact, the non sequitur seems to originate with this latter sentence itself, where the initial adverb *swa* is not logically consistent. Unlike the other uses of *swa* and *swa swa* in the passage, it has no modal sense, since it has no statement about God's mercy and help to man to refer back to in the preceding sentences. It is apparently used, at what both Lees and Schaefer print as the beginning of a new paragraph, rather loosely, together with the empty word *þonne*, as a sentence connective, not unlike ModE *so* in a sentence like "So, that is what I mean", in the sense defined by the *OED* as "As an introductory particle, without a preceding statement (but freq[uently] implying one)" (s.v. *So* 10b). The use is not otherwise unknown in Old English (see Ericson 1932: 19). However, given that the usage is dated in the *OED* only from the eighteenth century, our homilist's apparent example might belong to the colloquialisms of his day, like *swa . . . ne bebead* mentioned above. So might another use of *swa* typical of the homilist, seen in *HomS* 27.82: "hi þa swa cwædon . . . and eac hi swa cwædon . . .". Introducing as it does a Biblical quotation each time, the *swa* obviously means 'in this way; thus; as follows' – a sense which the *OED* dates only from *a*.1250 (s.v. 2c). All these details may be another aspect of the prose which allows grammatical and logical inconsistencies.

After the opening passage on the Earthly Paradise, the rest of the major themes are dealt with one by one, with little integration into a unified structure of homiletic discourse. Nor does the homilist show much refinement and sophistication in recounting the themes and the several motifs that they contain, though he does rise to rhetorical writing in the passage on the Earthly Paradise (see above) and the conventional end of the homily based on the Doxology (lines 166–80). This may be seen clearly in purely narrative sections. Thus, the Evils of the Sixth Day and Sunday List sections are framed into a list of events which is accumulative and heavily paratactic, of the form: "On this day X happened. And on this day Y happened. And . . ." The lists are interspersed with extended accounts of particular motifs or events which the homilist chooses to dwell upon. But even these accounts are heavily paratactic, with *and* repeated to pile up the sentences that constitute them, as in the passage in the Evils of the Sixth Day section (lines 20–8), which shows a rapid succession of seven *on þam sixtan dæge* . . . statements, and in John's vision of the Apocalypse (lines 48–65), where the Biblical account is adapted into a central motif in the Sunday List in the same way.

After the Harrowing of Hell comes the section on "the wonders of the Eucharist" as Schaefer calls it (Schaefer 1972: 168), again with no bridging explanation for this transition; the section begins simply with the phrase *eac swilce*. It is in this manner that the homilist now turns to Ælfric's homily for an extract for some thirty lines after a brief intro- duction and a Biblical quotation from John 6:57 (lines 94–9). The extract, beginning with a quotation from Matthew 26:26–7, is taken from the *Catholic Homilies*, Second Series, item XV (*Sermo de Sacrificio in Die Pascae*), with considerable alteration. The homilist's method is seen at its most typical where he rewrites Ælfric's explanation of the mystery of the Eucharist through an elaborate analogy with baptism in:

> Hæðen cild bið gefullod. ac hit ne bret na his hiw wiðutan. ðeah ðe hit beo
> wiðinnan awend; Hit bið gebroht synfull þurh adames forgægednysse
> to ðam fantfæte. ac hit bið aðwogen fram eallum synnum wiðinnan. þeah
> ðe hit wiðutan his hiw ne awende; (*ÆCHom* ii. 15.107)

Central to Ælfric's elaboration is the contrast between unchanged out- ward appearance and inward conversion, which he repeats through two sentences which are syntactically parallel (". . . , ac . . . , þeah ðe . . .") but are balanced chiastically, so to speak, in terms of the "changed" and "unchanged" (*Hæðen cild* "changed", *ac* "unchanged", *þeah ðe* "changed", but *Hit* "unchanged", *ac* "changed", *þeah ðe* "unchanged"). This chiastic arrangement has inevitably brought with it a reversed distribution of *wiþutan* and *wiþinnan*, but syntactically again the two words remain parallel in that they both occur finally in the *ac*-clause but medially in the *þeah ðe*-clause, indicating Ælfric's conscious hand running through the passage. All this is apparently not appreciated by our homilist, who destroys Ælfric's rhetoric and prose rhythm by simplifying the extended analogy into one sentence, and the complex structure of three clauses ("..., ac ..., þeah ðe ...") into ordinary coordinate clauses ("..., ac ..."):

> Hæðen cild þe man fullað ne bryt hyt na his hiw wiðutan, ac hit bið swa
> ðeah wiðinnan awend and aþwogen on þam fante fram eallum synnum.
> (*HomS* 27.113)

With Ælfric's two sentences collapsed into one, the homilist's *ac*-clause has two past participles coordinated, drawn together from the original two sentences. It may be noted that the *ac*-clause has acquired the adverb *swa ðeah*. But the phrase does not make up for the lost *þeah ðe*-clause so much as reinforce the contrast between the "changed" and "unchanged" as the homilist reformulates it in simplified terms. The author has simplified the Ælfric homily at the cost of losing its "sophisticated and carefully modulated discussion" of the subject (Lees 1986: 139).

The homilist's insensitivity to Ælfric's careful treatment of the subject is also seen when he rewrites another analogy with the water of the baptismal font which Ælfric introduces immediately following the one just examined (lines 115–18). Ælfric writes:

> Eac swilce þæt halige fantwæter þe is gehaten lifes wylspring. is gelic on
> hiwe oðrum wæterum. and is underþeod brosnunge. ac þæs halgan gastes
> miht genealæhð þam brosniendlicum wætere. ðurh sacerda bletsunge. and
> hit mæg siððan lichaman and sawle aðwean fram eallum synnum. ðurh
> gastlicere mihte; (*ÆCHom* ii. 15.111)

The homilist omits from the opening portion of this the relative clause (*þe is ... wylspring*) and the *and*-clause (*and ... brosnunge*), both of which are obviously essential for Ælfric's explanation of the nature of baptism. Reference to the physical corruptibility of water is again omitted from the following *ac*-clause (rewritten by the homilist as *ac þurh þæs sacerdes bletsunge genealæcð þæs Halgan Gastes miht*) and from a passage which the homilist subsequently entirely omits (see below). Even the small word *mæg* (*mæg ... aðwean*) in the last clause might well be an example of Ælfric's deliberate etymologizing repetition in association with the word *miht* used both before and after it (on Ælfric's use of this rhetorical

device, see Pope 1967: 109–10; Hill 1988). But the homilist has casually
(so one would think) abandoned it in favour of the simple verb form
aþwyhþ.

Not only does our homilist simplify Ælfric's sentences but he also edits
out a long stretch of sentences which Ælfric devotes to theological argument. He does this twice, skipping over, after his line 108, sixteen lines
(in Godden's edition) on the nature of bread and wine signifying the true
nature of Christ and, after line 118, forty-two lines on the physical and
spiritual natures of the housel. Moreover, when he resumes, he goes back
on both occasions directly to Ælfric's text, continuing from where he has
left off without any bridging phrase; but he substitutes, after the first
omission, *heora* for Ælfric's *sacerda* (*se hlaf and þæt win ðe beoð ðurh sacerda
mæssan gehalgode* – *ÆCHom* ii. 15.102), probably referring to *ealle bisceopas
and sacerdas* (line 107), only to bring in a considerable degree of repetition
in what are now consecutive sentences. On the other hand, the homilist
adds the phrase *Eac we rædað þæt* (line 127) to begin the second exemplum
on the mystery of the Eucharist (where Ælfric uses the introductory phrase
only for the first exemplum) and also inserts the words *þa* (line 124) and
sona (line 125), while replacing Ælfric's *ða* by *sona* (line 132) in narrating
the exempla. But in the narrative he again omits (line 122) a relative
clause from the source sentence (. . . *on ðam weofode þe se mæssepreost æt
mæssode* – *ÆCHom* ii. 15.162), despite the power of the mass which Ælfric
seems to emphasize through it. These personal touches show our homilist's
emphasis very clearly; he uses the Ælfric text for the clear story and
dramatic narrative content it contains rather than for its elaborate treatment of theological issues (see Swan 1993: 104; Schaefer 1972: 171).

I have referred earlier to the casualness with which our homilist rewrites
extracts from the Ælfric homily. It is a quality which may, on one hand,
have much in common with "the grammatical and logical inconsistencies"
which were seen to characterize the prose of the opening passage. On
the other hand, it seems to make itself felt as clearly in the treatment of
the Biblical material on which he often draws in developing each of the
five major themes. He gives quotations from the Scriptures which are on
the whole much freer than is usually the case in Old English anonymous
homilies. Thus, in

Þam mannum on þam lande eardigendum under þæs deaðes sceade micel
leoht nu todæg him wæs upcumen. And þæt folc þe þa on helle on þystrum
sæt micel leoht hi þa gesawon [rendering Isaiah 9:2 populus qui ambulabat

in tenebris vidit lucem magnam habitantibus in regione umbrae mortis lux
orta est eis] (*HomS* 27.77)

the details are closely rendered, including the "recapitulatory" personal
pronoun (*Þam mannum . . . him*). But the order of the pair of sentences is
reversed from the arrangement in the Biblical Latin. Similarly, *HomS*
27.140 based on Matthew 25:41 is combined with a *þær*-clause (line 142)
derived from Matthew 25:30, which in turn combines two phrases taken
from distinct sentences of the verse: *þær is toða gristbitung and þa singalan
þystru* (. . . *eicite in tenebras exteriores illic erit fletus et stridor dentium* –
Matthew 25:30). These examples suggest that the homilist is sometimes
working from memory, as Lees (1986: 125) believes (see also Schaefer
1972: 171).

The author's method of treating Biblical material is perhaps seen at its
clearest in an extended passage in the Last Judgement section. In what
immediately follows the Lord's first speech in *HomS* 27.140–3 (see above),
the homilist goes on to quote the exchange of words between the Lord
and the unrighteous in Matthew 25:41–5, but even more casually than
before. He abridges their speech twice, saying only *and ic wæs nacod þa ne
wruge ge me mid eowrum hræglum* (line 145) for verse 43 (*hospes eram et non
collexistis me nudus et non operuistis me infirmus et in carcere et non visitastis
me*), and *swa þearfiendne* (line 148) to refer collectively to the various
occasions of Christ being in need in verse 44 (*esurientem aut sitientem aut
hospitem aut nudum aut infirmum vel in carcere*); expands the wording of
the Bible (e.g. lines 147 *þa unrihtwisan men* (25:44 *ipsi*) and 148 *minum þam
earmestum þe ic eow to sende* (25:45 *uni de minoribus his*)); and finally adds
the concluding sentence *Soð ic eow secge, ne can ic eow* (line 150), drawn,
perhaps by memory, from Matthew 25:12. The homilist gives all this
account of the damned before he deals with the saved, thereby reversing
the treatment in the Bible.

The freedom that the homilist shows with Biblical quotation obviously
comes, in part at least, from the fact that he does not usually quote the
Biblical Latin before he translates it, as in all the examples above. Where
he does – just for once – in *HomS* 27.168, his Latin text (*Uenite benedicti
Patris mei percipite regnum quod uobis paratum est ab origine mundi*) differs
from the Vulgate (Matthew 25:34 *venite benedicti Patris mei possidete paratum
vobis regnum a constitutione mundi*). Nor does his translation of the sentence
agree with the accepted one, reading *Cumað ge gebletsode and onfoð mines
Fæder rice . . .* and not *Cumað ge gebletsode mines Fæder and . . .* as in the

West-Saxon Gospels. Our homilist's treatment might not have been entirely an inaccuracy, since there is evidence to suggest that it is based on a Latin text current in his days beside the Vulgate (see Godden 1979: 353). One feels inclined all the same to ask if the homilist understood Latin rather indifferently – an impression which one also gets from *HomS* 27.154: *swa hit on þam godspelle awriten is, "Drihten cymð swa se þeof cymð þonne he stelan wile"*, where, quite apart from the *þonne*-clause, which is the homilist's addition, "[t]here is some confusion in the text of the Biblical translation" (Schaefer 1972: 190). Lees detects a similar confusion on the homilist's part of two verses from the Apocalypse as he deals with John's vision in the Sunday List section (Lees 1986: 131). All this evidence of free rendering would reinforce what we have seen earlier of possible colloquialism in some details of the homilist's language, and the generally casual writing which is seen in his work.

De Descensu Christi Ad Inferos

If *In Die Sancto Pasce* is a homily which "lacks a consistent narrative or a consistent exegetical commentary" (Lees 1986: 125), our second anonymous Easter homily *De Descensu Christi ad Inferos* (*HomS* 28) differs sharply from it in having both. It is a dramatic account of the Harrowing of Hell in which the homiletic design is sustained by consistent exegetical remarks which it introduces as it goes on, including a passage which is taken from a different Ælfric homily. This basic contrast between narrative and exegesis is reinforced by several distinctive features the homily shows in language and style, though their origin remains partly a problem. In the Harrowing scene of the middle section (lines 79–160), to which Blickling Homily VII provides a related version, those features are often likely, as we shall see, to be derived from a Latin work which both our homilist and the Blickling homilist might have used as source material. For the rest of the homily (apart from the excerpt from Ælfric), no related text is known to exist, and one may safely assume with Swan (1997: 6–7) that it was written by the homilist himself.

The homily is a consistent narrative of the Harrowing of Hell. It is entirely devoted to the account of how Christ descended into hell and bound the devil and led all the elect out of there, with a detailed account of the roles played by the devil and Christ in man's history leading to the Harrowing (lines 5–78) and the Ascension at the end (lines 196–202).

More importantly, it shows the unity of a single homily, with its parts welded into and echoing each other both in wording and narrative structure – "a coherent structure which never loses sight of his [the homilist's] primary theme", as Campbell (1982: 141) says, illustrating it with the motif of the fall of Adam used in it.

We can also see how the homilist moves from one section into another to achieve a continuous narrative, by looking at the exegetical remark made about the Crucifixion in the opening "background" section. After the devil's first speech in hell, in which he boasts of the plot against Christ, the homilist adds that Christ was then crucified but the devil was misled into thinking himself victorious because he could not see Christ's divinity (lines 36–8). But, the homilist continues, the devil was soon conquered, not so much by force as with right (lines 43–8). With these remarks the homilist makes a central point to which he comes back later in appealing to the simile of the devil as fish swallowing the bait but not seeing the hook, and the idea of the devil forfeiting his right over mankind, both developed in a passage from Ælfric's *Dominica Palmarum* (*Catholic Homilies*, First Series, item XIV), which he uses virtually verbatim. Swan, with a slightly different emphasis, sees this "devil-as-fish" simile of the Ælfrician passage as linked rather with the first section through its "devil/lion and devil/dragon similes" (Swan 1997: 7). Whichever of the two is the more important link, they put it beyond any reasonable doubt that use is not made of the Ælfrician passage indiscriminately, but as a result of careful thought by the homilist about the structure and wording of his homily. It should also be noted that in the second exegetical remark above the homilist refers to the devil as *mid ecum bendum gebunden and mid ecum geniðerungum geniðerad* (with alliteration and etymological repetition). The phrase is distinctly the homilist's own (as opposed, for example, to *gebunden mid isenum racenteagum* in *In Die Sancto Pasce*, line 85), and is repeated in varied forms at lines 69, 85 and 202, providing a case of coherence achieved at the hands of one homilist through the details of the language of the homily.

The extract from the Ælfric homily has been the primary focus of interest for most of the scholars who have discussed the anonymous *De Descensu* homily. But they have paid little attention to the extract in relation to the other parts of the homily which called it forth, as described above. Nor has its use been analysed closely enough. Two things demand notice here. First, Schaefer says that "our passage is identical to the text in Thorpe's edition [of the *Catholic Homilies*]" (Schaefer 1972: 165), but this identity is not quite exact. The homilist in one place (line 168) changes word order – from Ælfric's *wurdon we* to *we wurdon*, missing a possible fine flourish of rhetoric in the source; Ælfric might have meant the VS order preceded by *þurh his . . . deaðe* as a chiasmus to SV followed by *to cristes cweale* in the previous sentence (*He hit forwyrhte þa ða he tihte þ folc to cristes cweale þæs ælmihtigan godes; Ᵹ þa þurh his unsceððian deaðe wurdon we alysede ꞉ fram þam ecan deaðe – ÆCHom* i. 14.169). On the other hand, the homilist follows the source perhaps too closely when he opens the passage, just as Ælfric does, saying *We habbað oft gesæd and gyt secgað*, for here Ælfric was, as Godden shows, "possibly . . . referring to his own preaching rather than written texts" (Godden 2000: 117). Whether or not our homilist was conscious of this implication but ignored it, one cannot say. But the faithful use here, as generally elsewhere in the extract, emphasizes the homilist's attitude to his Ælfrician source, which is distinct from that of the *In Die Sancto Pasce* homily. The use of the particular passage from the *Dominica Palmarum*, as against the two exempla in the latter, itself emphasizes exegesis as a central feature of the homily, which makes it unique among the anonymous homilies of the period, when there seems to be no other "composite homily which could be described as explanatory or exegetical" (Godden 1975: 65, where he says he does not know of any such homily).

In addition to the extract from the Ælfric homily just discussed, there are half a dozen Biblical references on which exegetical remarks are based, interspersed throughout the account of the Harrowing of Hell. The homilist's method of exegesis is generally elaborate and effective. For example, in a passage (lines 182–7) explaining how Christ did not lead out all the people he met in hell, based on *O mors, ero mors tua, morsus tuus ero, inferne* (Hosea 13:14), he exploits the word *helle bite* as gloss for *morsus*, developing it into the phrase *dæl genam and . . . dæl forlet* and finally explaining that phrase with: *Ðæt wæs þonne þæt he þær geleafulra manna sawla onfeng and sinfulle þær forlet*.

Another indication of the homilist's method is given by a passage where he explains the Crucifixion as instigated by the devil, just before he turns to the central account of the Harrowing. He begins: *and þa wæron ealle þing underþeod urum Drihtne Hælende Criste, se ðe be him sylfum mycele ær sang and þus cwæð: Si exaltatus fuero a terram omnia traham ad me ipsum* (*HomS* 28.53) and then, "inject[ing] a bit of exegesis" (Schaefer 1972: 158), translates the Latin as: *Gif þæt gelimpð þæt ic beo on rode up ahafen, þonne teo ic ealle þing to me*, with an addition of two words (*on rode*) which makes his subsequent explanation the more pointed: *Ealle þing he to him teah, ða þa he on rode gefæstnod wæs, and he his gast to God Fæder asende. Þa him wæron ealle gesceafta underþeod*. The addition does not mean that the homilist, unlike the *In Die Sancto Pasce* homilist, is casual in his Biblical references. On the contrary, he is a translator careful enough to begin the *gif*-clause with *þæt gelimpð*, to render the Latin future perfect *fuero*. He is also careful to cite the Biblical Latin here as elsewhere, which he translates reasonably and clearly, if not always perfectly (see Campbell 1982: 139; Schaefer 1972: 158–9).

In the passages discussed above our homilist follows the method of traditional exegesis. What is more characteristic of him is theological exposition couched in dramatic direct speech, which I would argue is a different kind of exegetical commentary in the homily. This appears first in the devil's speech to his companions in hell, referring to John the Baptist through a gospel passage (Matthew 11:11 and Luke 7:28):

> Ða cwæð he to his geferan: "Geseoð nu, þis is þæs sawle, be ðam wæs cweden þæt betweox were and wife ne arise nan mærra wer, þonne Iohannes wære se Fulluhtere." (*HomS* 28.20)

Schaefer says: "Placing this speech in the mouth of the devil is a fanciful treatment of Christ's words" (Schaefer 1972: 156). I would rather say a *characteristic* treatment. The homilist starts speaking as the devil but soon switches, perhaps without realizing that he does, into the persona of homilist commenting on the devil; his voices as narrator and commentator are fused into one in this portion of the speech. One might think, alternatively, that in the boast against John the devil is made to assume a sarcastic tone which reference to Christ's words as above would enhance. Sarcasm, however, hardly makes sense in the light of the devil's subsequent words (lines 30–2), where he refers to himself as intending to instigate the Jews to 'charge falsely' (*onleogan*) and 'to calumniate maliciously' (*forwregan niðfullice*) Christ. These words, which the devil would never have used himself to his own dishonour, obviously indicate the homilist's faith in Christian theology, turning the whole sentence in which they occur into an interpretive commentary in disguise. Placed beside this, Christ's quoted words, too, may be seen more definitely as explanation or exegesis – "dramatic exegesis", so to speak, since it is exegesis given through the devil's dramatic voice, echoing the homilist's own earlier use, in a narrative sentence, of Christ's speech about John (lines 16–17).

Use of dramatic direct speech continues into the central section dealing with the Harrowing of Hell, and so does "dramatic exegesis" in the sense just explained. This time it is through the speech of the devil's companions in hell that the homilist gives his commentary. Frightened at the great light, they are apprehensive of what has gone contrary to their expectations (lines 86–93), and then go on to accuse their leader of failure to bring about what he has promised:

> Gehyr nu, ure ealdor: þa ðu þine welan ðe þu on þam ærestan men begeate ðurh forhogodnysse Godes beboda, nu ðu þæt forlure þurh rode treow. Geseoh nu þæt eall ðin blis þe losade mid þam ðe þu Crist on rode ahenge; ac ne mihtest ðu næfre geseon, ne ðe gifeðe næs, þa forwyrde þines rices. Ðu hine on deað gelæddest butan ælcere scylde, and þu ðær gylt beheolde þar þu næfre nænne ne fundest. For hwon dorstest þu him æfre æthrinan? (*HomS* 28.93)

Throughout this passage *þu* is the grammatical subject, sharpening the focus on the devil as the accused, even more so than in the Blickling version. Yet the passage does not voice the personal resentment of the lost souls so much as the homilist's own denunciation of the devil – as is perhaps implied in the preceding use of *ðe* as indirect object of *foregehete* ('you promised to yourself', line 91), which indicates our homilist's point of view against the devil, rather than his companions', which is emphasized in both the Blickling (*þu us . . . gehete* – *BlHom* 85.19) and Latin (*nobis . . . promittebas*) versions. His point of view is more clearly seen in the above passage from the use of 'exegetical' words such as *butan ælcere scylde* ('[led to death] without any sin') and, most importantly, from the last sentence (*For hwon . . . . æthrinan?*), which again echoes Christ's words as used by the homilist himself in an earlier exegetical passage on the devil's fate: *Næs he na swa mid mægne ofercumen, swa swa he mid rihte gehyned wæs . . . Swa se Hælend sylf be þam cwæð: 'Hwæt gemettest þu yfeles on me? For hwon hrine ðu on me?'* (*HomS* 28.47). These are all our homilist's own innovations, with no equivalents in the Latin homily (as represented by pseudo-Augustine 160) from which he is making "an abridgement" at this point (Schaefer 1972: 160). The Blickling version of the passage (*BlHom* 85.29–87.2) has reference to Christ being crucified without any sin but lacks the other exegetical elements. The Blickling version then has a sentence describing the breaking of the gates of Hell. This our homilist omits, moving directly to the speech of the good souls which ensues. His exegetical tone seems to linger on in this speech, where the souls say to Christ: *Alys nu forðferede and þa ðe on helle gehæfte synd* (*HomS* 28.105). The plea sounds more homiletic and universal than the one in the Blickling version, with its contextually bound *us* (*Ales us nu of deofles onwalde & of helle hæftnede* – *BlHom* 87.13).

As can be seen in this discussion, the Harrowing of Hell section provides us with an unusual opportunity to examine the language and style of the homily, in comparison with the Blickling version of the Harrowing and with the Latin text which seems to underlie both Old English versions, though the textual relationship seems to be far from a simple one of immediate dependence of one on another. It is generally accepted that the two Old English versions are independent translations of a Latin text (now lost) which is very close to that of pseudo-Augustine 160 (for lines 79–99 of our homily) and the fragmentary Oratio of the *Book of Cerne* (for lines 100–52 – Schaefer 1972: 130–3, 159–64; Campbell 1982: 138–41). One cannot think in terms of changes made to one of the two Old English texts to arrive at the other. But one can make comparisons, and one can also consider the results of the comparison in terms of the source material which is now represented closely, if not exactly, in the two Latin texts just mentioned. We are concerned here with differences between the two Old English versions and whatever they may tell of our homilist's use of language, rather than the textual history of the Old English Harrowing of Hell literature.

It has been pointed out that our homilist often "translates more closely than Blickling VII" (Schaefer 1972: 164). Perhaps the best illustration is the prayer of the good souls in hell to Christ (lines 103–21) and the subsequent prayers of Adam and Eve (lines 124–35 and 136–57), in which direct appeal to Christ to be merciful and forget their sins is the central motif, uniting the whole scene closely, with insistent use of the words *mildheortnys* (lines 109, 112, 124 and 141) and *gemiltsian/milts* (lines 124 and 125). Our homilist takes over verbatim all this insistence from the Latin text (as represented by the *Book of Cerne*), translating its *misericordia* and *miserere/miseratio* directly as above. He might well have continued to do so, even after the *Book of Cerne* text breaks off, in the rest of Eve's speech made in the same vein and in Abraham's words, which conclude the scene with yet another reference to Christ's *mildheortnys* (line 159). The Blickling homilist, on the other hand, has no relevant sentences in the speech of the good souls nor any reference to Christ's mercy in Abraham's words; in this latter he emphasizes Christ as conqueror of death instead: *We ondettaþ þe, Drihten, & þe hergeaþ; forþon þe þu us alesdest from deaþes fruman* (*BlHom* 89.30). With the same slant, the Blickling text (*BlHom* 87.22–5) reads at one place in the speech of the good souls entirely differently from our homily (lines 119–21), which again translates the Latin directly. The different emphases which thus distinguish the two Old English versions might be suggestive, as Campbell (1982: 138–41) thinks, of different source texts of a Latin homily rather than different degrees of dependence on a Latin text. But the question is of secondary importance for our concern here. What is important for us is to notice that our homilist was probably conscious of the *misericordia* theme running through the Latin text he follows closely, for he reinforces it by the word *milde*, which he introduces independently of his Latin text, first, prior to the appearance of the Latin *misericordia*, in . . . *þæt ðu þinne ðone mildan ansyne us fram ne acyrre* (*HomS* 28.107) and then in line 132 (see below), where the Blickling homilist's *arfæst* translates the Latin *propitius* more closely. Our homilist is no mere slavish translator.

The homilist also often follows closely the discourse structure of the Latin text, which tends to be rhetorical. Thus, he keeps the rhetorical balance of the Latin in *Nu ðu to us come, middaneardes Alysend, and nu þu to us come, þone we . . . , and nu ðu to us come, þu ðe . . . sealdest* (*HomS* 28.103 – Latin *Aduenisti redemptor mundi. Aduenisti quem . . . Aduenisti donans . . .*), *Bletsie, min sawl, Drihten . . . Se is milde . . . , se gehælde . . . , se alysde . . . , se gefylde . . .* (*HomS* 28.132 – Latin *Benedic anima mea dominum . . . Qui . . . qui . . . Qui . . . qui . . .* , rendered with consistent *þu* by the Blickling homilist), and *Ac ne gemun ðu, min Drihten, þa gyltas mines geogeðhades and minre dysinysse, and ne acyr ðu . . . , and ne ahyld þu . . .* (*HomS* 28.139 – Latin *Sed tu domine delicta iuuentutis et insipientiae meae ne memineris. Ne auertas . . . et ne declines . . .*). Even in details of syntax, the homilist sometimes uses "Latinisms", as in *nelle þu* (line 107, for Latin *noli*) and *wæs geðuht* (line 89, for Latin *visus est* – see *OES*: §§917 and 1049–51).

Yet direct translation is not entirely the characteristic of our homilist's language in the Harrowing of Hell section. It was seen above that he can be independent of his Latin text in his choice of adjectives. This he is in a certain group of sentences from the speeches of Adam and Eve, as in line 139 (see above), where he, unlike the Blickling homilist, follows the negative pattern but otherwise arranges the words in the order VSO in accordance with the usual Old English pattern. Similarly, he prefers in the rest of the group not to follow the Latin word order, putting the subject at the clause-initial position: *forðon ic þe anum gesyngade and ic yfele dyde beforan ðe* (*HomS* 28.125 – Latin *quia tibi soli peccaui et malum coram te feci*, rendered literally as *forþon þe anum ic gesyngade, & mycel yfel beforan þe ic gedyde* (*BlHom* 87.29)) and *Drihten, þu eart rihtwis and þin dom is riht* (*HomS* 28.136 – Latin *IUstus es domine et rectum iudicium tuum*, rendered as *Soþfæst eart þu, Drihten, & rihte syndon þine domas* – *BlHom* 89.6); it is again the Blickling homilist who imitates the Latin word order. Another group of sentences shows our homilist preferring sentence-initial position for the adverb *þa*, whether with following VS or SV (lines 123, 131, 153 and 158), and *þa gyt* (lines 122 and 136), in clear contrast to the Blickling homilist, who never fails to place these words immediately after the subject which comes initially in the corresponding sentences (*BlHom* 87.26, 35, 89.24, 28; and 87.25, 89.5). In these cases, our homilist often agrees with the Latin (with initial *tunc* and *adhuc*), but the evidence of the Latin text is not complete. His word order here is at any rate as idiomatic Old English as that of the Blickling homilist.

If our homilist's word order points to independence from the Latin text in favour of natural and idiomatic Old English prose, some other details of his style confirm this direction. Particularly noteworthy are expressions that illustrate our homilist's tendency to be concise and suc-cinct, using *ec ofer þæt* (line 85) instead of *nis no þæt an þæt . . .* (*BlHom* 85.15) and avoiding repetition and redundancy (e.g. lines 122–4, beside *BlHom* 87.25-7) – a tendency which is best seen in *Drihten, þu wast þæt ic eom gedrorenlic dust* (*HomS* 28.143) as compared with *Drihten, þu wast mine geheowunga, þæt ic eom dust & axe* (*BlHom* 89.15) and *HomS* 28.83–6 as compared with *BlHom* 85.11–14 (so clumsily written as to lead Förster to propose an emendation; Förster 1892: 183). It may also be the same tendency that accounts for the difference between our homilist (with one verb phrase less) and the Blickling homilist in rendering the Latin *lacrimabili uoce et obsecratione saluatorem deposcunt dicentes . . . : wependre stemne and mid micele halsunge þone Hælend bædon and þus cwædon* (*HomS* 28.102) and *. . . to þæm Hælende onluton, & mid wependre halsunga hine bædon, & þus cwædon* (*BlHom* 87.7). It is remarkable that our homilist in his turn uses the *onlutan/alutan*-phrase (though in slightly different forms) at three places, including two (lines 117 and 154) where the Blickling text has no equivalent, to describe the actions of the good souls and Eve after their respective prayers, thereby making the wording in Eve's case closely parallel to the description of Adam (line 132). Moreover, he adds the intensive *geornlice* together with the *onlutan* phrase on both these occa-sions; his use of the verb phrase may be rhetorical as well as descriptive.

This last point takes us back to rhetorical aspects of our homilist's language. It was shown earlier that he often moulds his paragraphs upon the rhetoric of the Latin text. Just as this "Latinate rhetoric" is translated into what proves, in details of wording, to be natural, idiomatic Old English prose, so it is reinforced by the homilist's own stock of rhetorical devices, of which the use of *onlutan/alutan* and *geornlice* mentioned above may be examples. Details of this stock are given by Fadda (1972: 995–6), who describes it in terms of nine "verbal figures", including word pairs, alliteration, etymological association and parallelism with variation. With the single exception of this last, Fadda's examples are all taken from the sections of the homily other than the Latin-based narrative of the Harrowing, emphasizing the importance of these rhetorical figures for the homilist's own prose. But he does employ many of them in the Harrowing of Hell section, the most important being word pairs, which are almost as frequent here as in the other sections and are sometimes derived only partly from the Latin. One feature not noted by Fadda may be included here. It is the grammatical recapitulation (see *OES*: §§1447–8), by which the homilist seems to reinforce the organization of his sense and paragraph, both in the Harrowing of Hell section (lines 108–10 and 119–20), and later in an exegetical passage:

> Ne wene nu æfre ænig mann þæt Drihten Crist ealle þa of helle gelædde þe he ðær gemette; ac þa ane ða þe heora lif her on worulde rihtlice leofedan, þa he ðanon gelædde. And he þær forlet morðwyrhtan and dyrne forligras and rihtes geleafan wiþersacan and þeofas and gitseras; and þa ðe heora yfeldæda betan nellað, þa he næfre þanon alyseð (*HomS* 28.177)

Just as it focuses, in the first two passages, on the contrast between glory in heaven and mercy on earth (*Ðu ðe þines wuldres tacen . . . , . . . þin mildheortnys . . .*) and between Christ and the saved (*þu ðe . . . , þe we . . .*), so recapitulation emphasizes the distinction between the chosen good and the bad in the last example (*þa ane . . . , þa . . . ; and þa . . . , þa . . .*). Schaefer's reading for this last (his lines 185–90), with a period instead of comma between the last *þa* and *nellað*, destroys the logical plan the homilist presents in it, which depends partly on the paired verbs (*leofedan . . . gelædde*, and *nellað . . . alyseð*) in the preterite and present tenses.

Our homilist's own rhetorical figures are thus no mere stylistic embellishments, but are geared to the contents and contexts of the sentences which have called them forth. Altogether, these features, many of them common to the sections supposedly written by the homilist himself and the Latin-based section, suggest a conscious style in which he has made a consistent homily out of different sources. And it is this individual style which carefully moulds narrative and exegesis and dramatic direct speech and narrative statements, welding the various sources they come from into a unity characteristic of its user.

Conclusions

Despite the shared feature of being an Easter homily with an Ælfrician passage incorporated into it, *In Die Sancto Pasce* and *De Descensu Christi ad Inferos* differ from each other substantially in a number of ways. The former is built around several themes that are associated loosely with Easter Sunday, with little effective linking between them; the other is a homily devoted to a consistent narrative of the Harrowing of Hell interspersed with consistent exegetical commentaries. The difference is accompanied by predictable variation in language and style. The narrative of the Harrowing of Hell is executed in a style which welds different sources and different modes of discourse into a unity and is at times almost literary. The homilist owes some of this literary merit to the Latin text which he generally follows closely, but he has added his own innovations, thereby enhancing the rhetorical language which he seems to value in the Latin. The *In Die Sancto Pasce* homilist, on the other hand, is unpretentious and can be even casual in thought and wording. This distinction also makes itself felt clearly in the ways the two homilists make Biblical references. Here again, the *De Descensu* homilist shows on the whole a better treatment.

The different natures of the two homilies also called forth dissimilar passages for incorporation, excerpted from different items of Ælfric's *Catholic Homilies* – one consisting mainly of exempla on the mystery of the Eucharist and the other an exegetical commentary using the "devil-as-fish" simile. The excerpts are accordingly given different treatments. On the whole, the *In Die Sancto Pasce* homilist seems to be less appreciative of Ælfric's careful writing and subtleties of thought and expression. The two homilists are good illustrations of the varied methods of combining Ælfric's homilies and non-Ælfrician material into composite homilies which are seen in the period (Swan 1993: 331).

Yet the two homilies agree in one respect. By making an excerpt from the original context of the Ælfric homily, they are both against the original author's instructions (stated in the final prayer of the Second Series) for the careful preservation and transmission of his own homilies. And they are not alone in this breach. Observations have been made of "a consistently free use of C[atholic]H[omilies] excerpts from the late tenth to the second half of the twelfth century", as Swan (1993: 325) says, and Swan concludes her study of this process with these words:

> the clearest point to emerge from my study of the use of the CH in Ælfric/
> anonymous texts is the tension between Ælfric's self-image and representa-
> tion of the Reform as expressed in his work, and what can be deduced of
> the real reactions, interpretations and practical needs of the wider Anglo-
> Saxon church. (Swan 1993: 333)

This tension continues well into the twelfth century, as Swan has shown in detail in another study (Swan 2000). The two composite homilies examined in this study, both preserved in eleventh-century manuscripts, are products of the period which saw all this development and are important witnesses to the changing attitudes with which homiletic literature continued to be produced in late Old English to early Middle English.

Note

This is an abridged version of my unpublished study "*In Die Sancto Pasce* and *De Descensu Christi ad Inferos*: two Easter homilies using Ælfrician material". Old English homilies are cited from the following: Lees (1986) (*HomS* 27), Fadda (1972) (*HomS* 28, with a few corrections), Morris (1874–80) (*Blickling Homilies*), and Clemoes (1997) and Godden (1979) (*Catholic Homilies*). For Latin texts, I use Weber's edition of the Vulgate and Schaefer's text (1972: 160–4) of the Latin source for *HomS* 28.

References and Further Reading

Campbell, J. J. (1982). To hell and back: Latin tradition and literary use of the 'Descensus ad Inferos' in Old English. *Viator*, 13, 107–58.

Cross, J. E. (1972). The literate Anglo-Saxon – on sources and disseminations. *Proceedings of the British Academy*, 58, 67–100.

Dalbey, M. A. (1973). Patterns of preaching in the Blickling Easter Homily. *The American Benedictine Review*, 24, 478–92.

Ericson, E. E. (1932). *The Use of Swa in Old English*. Göttingen: Vandenhoeck & Ruprecht.

Förster, M. (1892). Zu den Blickling Homilies. *Archiv*, 91, 179–206.

Godden, M. R. (1975). Old English composite homilies from Winchester. *ASE*, 4, 57–65.

Hill, J. (1988). Ælfric's use of etymologies. *ASE*, 17, 35–44.

Hill, J. (1993). Reform and resistance: preaching styles in late Anglo-Saxon England. In J. Hamesse & X. Hermand (eds), *De l'Homélie au Sermon: Histoire de la Prédication Médiévale* (pp. 15–46). Louvain-la-Neuve: Université Catholique de Louvain.

Scragg, D. G. (1979). The corpus of vernacular homilies and prose saints' lives before Ælfric. *ASE*, 8, 223–77.

Swan, M. (1993). Ælfric as source: the exploitation of Ælfric's Catholic Homilies from the late tenth to twelfth centuries. PhD diss., University of Leeds.

Swan, M. (1997). Old English made new: one Catholic Homily and its reuses. *LSE*, 28, 1–18.

Swan, M. (1998). Memorialised readings: manuscript evidence for Old English homily composition. In P. Pulsiano & E. M. Treharne (eds), *Anglo-Saxon Manuscripts and their Heritage* (pp. 205–17). Aldershot: Ashgate.

Swan, M. (2000). Ælfric's Catholic Homilies in the twelfth century. In M. Swan & E. M. Treharne (eds), *Rewriting Old English in the Twelfth Century* (pp. 62–82). Cambridge: Cambridge University Press.

Chapter 11

Latin Influence on an Old English Idiom: "To Wit"

Matti Rissanen

One of the most fascinating topics in the study of Old English is the gradual development of written language alongside the spoken level of expression. Written Old English, which by the end of the period was even standardized to some degree, was quite naturally influenced by Latin, as most of the religious and scientific writings were either translations or adaptations of Latin originals. In this process King Alfred's educational programme, which involved the translation of a number of religious, philosophical and historical Latin texts, was certainly of great importance. Another major influence in the development of written Old English was of course Bible translation, which took the form of both interlinear glossing and continuous translations of various Old Testament books and the four gospels of the New Testament.

The Latin influence concerns both Old English vocabulary and syntax. In the field of vocabulary, abstract concepts in particular needed new lexical means of expression; words were borrowed from Latin, or they were created from native resources, often using Latin words as models. But these methods of increasing the expressive capacity of the Old English language were not restricted to single words. Even Latin pragmatic expressions, important for the discourse although containing relatively little meaning, were imitated. One of these so-called discourse markers was the combination of the verb "to be" and the inflected infinitive form *to witenne*, which lies behind the present-day English idiom *to wit*. Tracing the development of this expression, which translates the Latin phrase *sciendum est* or *notandum est*, concerns both lexis and syntax: the change and weakening of meaning of an important basic verb meaning 'to know' on the one hand, and a special use of a non-finite verb form rapidly disappearing from the language on the other.

A detailed study of the development of the vocabulary and syntax of the earliest stages of English, from the first appearance of Old English continuous writing, dating from the eighth century, to the end of the Middle English period, around 1500, must be based on a careful analysis of the available written evidence. In the last decade or two, computerized corpora have decisively improved our possibilities for finding examples of the occurrences of words and constructions rapidly and reliably. The time spent on collecting material has been reduced from months or years to days or weeks. It is good to keep in mind, however, that such gigantic works as Bruce Mitchell's *Old English Syntax* and Tauno F. Mustanoja's *Middle English Syntax* were written before the time of corpora or even microfiche concordances. The mastery of language, the richness of evidence and the accuracy and reliability of the conclusions to be found in these major treatises of Medieval English are most admirable, and they can be regarded as cornerstones for all future studies of the structure of Old and Middle English even in the era of computers and the Internet.

In the present paper I will give a survey of the origin and early development of the phrase *to wit*, based on the material which can be found in the computerized corpora covering practically all extant Old English texts and a large number of Middle English writings. I hope to show how these electronic resources facilitate the collecting, organizing and analysis of available textual evidence in our attempt to clarify the earliest semantic and syntactic development of a discourse marker based on a foreign model.

Old and Middle English Corpora

There are two major corpora containing Old English texts available at the moment. The more impressive and complete is the *Old English Corpus* (OEC) connected with the *Dictionary of Old English* Project at the Centre for Medieval Studies at the University of Toronto. This corpus, available through the Internet, consists of practically all extant Old English texts, all in all c. 3.5 million words (see http://www.doe.utoronto.ca). The dictionary itself is in preparation; the letters A–F have been available on CD-ROM since 2003.

The other useful corpus for the study of Medieval English is the *Helsinki Corpus of English Texts*, which has been available for scholarly use since the early 1990s. This corpus covers the period from the eighth century to the beginning of the eighteenth century, and its Old English part consists of c. 413,000 words. Thus the size of this part is only one-seventh of the *Dictionary of Old English Corpus*, and samples of longer texts between 2,000 and 20,000 words are included. This corpus has the advantage of being systematically structured, and each text has been coded according to the author (when known), date, dialect, type of text, foreign original if any, etc. (see Kytö 1996; http://khnt.hit.uib.no/icame/manuals/HC/INDEX.HTM).

Middle English texts can be studied through the c. 600,000-word Middle English part of the *Helsinki Corpus*. Another important resource is the *Middle English Compendium* (see http://ets.umdl.umich.edu/m/mec), which consists of the *Corpus of Middle English Prose and Verse* and a database of all the examples included in the recently completed multi-volume *Middle English Dictionary*. The corpus part of the *Compendium* consists of complete texts, with a bias towards the fifteenth century. The *Dictionary* database is an excellent, although somewhat less organized, treasury of examples of the occurrences of all the words found in Middle English texts.

There are also corpora including grammatical coding, based on the Old and Middle English parts of the Helsinki Corpus but with a wider range of texts. These versions are the results of international projects directed from the University of York in the UK and the University of Pennsylvania in the United States (see http://www-users.york.ac.uk/~sp20/corpus.html; http://www.ling.upenn.edu/mideng).

Late Middle English can also be studied through special corpora, many of which were produced or are being compiled at the Research Unit for Variation and Change in English, at the University of Helsinki (see http://www.eng.helsinki.fi/varieng). These include the *Corpus of Early English Correspondence*, the *Helsinki Corpus of Older Scots* and the *Corpus of Early English Medical Writing*. The CD-ROM version of Chaucer's *Canterbury Tales*, produced by the Canterbury Tales Project at De Montfort University, Leicester is also worth a special mention (see http://www.cta.dmu.ac.uk/projects/ctp).

Computerized corpora have decisively enhanced the variationist approach to the study of language, which aims at explaining linguistic change as the result of synchronic variation and the competition between roughly synonymous forms. Change involves the loss of certain words and structures and the emergence of others, or, perhaps more often, the increasing use of some expressions and decreasing use of others. Studies based on variation pay special attention both to language-internal processes of change, such as grammaticalization, and to language-external factors affecting the choice of variant forms. The main groups of the external factors are (a) sociolinguistic variation, including social class, education, gender, etc.; (b) dialectal or more generally regional (American English, Australian English, etc.) variation, including language contact; and (c) text- or genre-based variation, including medium (speech or writing), the purpose of the text, the audience or readership, etc. Large amounts of textual evidence, with easy quantification provided by corpora, are essential for the variationist.

It is good to keep in mind, however, that despite their obvious advantages, corpora do not give any ready-made answers to the questions and problems concerning the earliest stages of English. They can never replace the brain-work necessary for the analysis and synthesis based on the evidence. Furthermore, even the best corpus only represents a small part or slice of the reality of language; the reliability of the generalizations to be drawn from the evidence depends on the scholar's insightfulness, and, above all, his or her mastery of the language form studied.

In the present paper, all Old English examples are taken from the OEC. The reference number used in the corpus to identify the text is given (e.g. B1.9.1 for Ælfric's *Grammar*). Some of the texts, e.g. the *Bodley Homilies*, date from the twelfth century and could also be regarded as specimens of the earliest Middle English although they no doubt go back to Old English originals.

The Middle English examples are taken from the *Helsinki Corpus* (HC) and the *Corpus of Middle English Prose and Verse* (CME). The list of the capitalized abbreviated titles (e.g. MPPSALT for the *Earliest Complete English Prose Psalter*) can be found in the Manual to the *Helsinki Corpus*. A list of the CME texts can be found at the Internet address given above.

The Old English Construction *is to witenne > to wit*

Witan, which goes back to the Indo-European root meaning 'to see' (cf. Latin *videre*), was by far the most common verb indicating knowing in Old English. Other verbs with roughly the same meaning were *cnawan* (> *know*), which mainly occurs in prefixed forms *be-, on-, to-, gecnawan* and *cunnan*, which is the same verb as present-day English *can* and fairly rare in the meaning 'know'. In Early Middle English, the verb *ken* appears as a borrowing from Old Norse. For the senses and uses of these verbs in Old and Middle English, see the entries in the *Anglo-Saxon Dictionary* and its *Supplement*, s.v. *cnawan, cunnan, witan*, and the *Middle English Dictionary*, s.v. *connen, kennen, knouen, witen* (v.1).

It is an interesting and intriguing question why the verb *wit* has disappeared almost totally from English, being replaced by *know*, so that it can now only be found in the idiomatic phrase *to wit*, a grammatical element connecting two proposals in apposition, with little semantic content. As a result, English has lost the simple lexical means of distinguishing between two types of "knowing" indicated by *kennen* and *wissen* in German, *känna* and *veta* in Swedish, *connaître* and *savoir* in French and *tuntea* and *tietää* in Finnish. The details of this development and loss of *wit* in Middle and Modern English have been discussed by Gutch (1979), Rissanen (1993) and Koivisto-Alanko and Rissanen (2002).

The essential element of the Old English idiom under discussion is the inflected infinitive formed by the preposition *to* and the ending *-enne* (*-anne, -onne, -ene, -ane*). Mitchell's description and analysis of the uses of this verb form, frequent in Old English but disappearing in Middle English, gives an excellent starting-point for our discussion (*OES*: 386–409, §§920–971). Reference should also be made to Callaway's (1913) thorough treatise on the Old English infinitives. Mitchell classifies the uses of the infinitive according to the part of speech with which the infinitive is linked: noun or pronoun, adjective, or verb. The use of the inflected infinitive with the verb "to be" (Old English *beon* or *wesan*) is divided into two groups, according to the meaning of the construction: (a) expressing necessity or obligation, and (b) expressing futurity. *Is to witenne* most obviously belongs to the first group, although the indication of obligation is very weak, owing to the idiomatic character of the phrase. Mitchell points out that, in this group, "those on whom the obligation or necessity falls" may be expressed by a noun or pronoun in the dative or be implied. In many instances the pronoun *hit* or *þæt* occurs as the grammatical subject of the verb "to be" (*OES*: 394–5, §936). These types occur also with the idomatic *is to witenne*, as can be seen in examples (1)–(6):

(1)   SCIENDVM EST, QVOD NEVTRA VERBA DEFICIVNT IN SOPINO
      is to witenne, þæt ða word, ðe synd NEVTRA gehatene, ateoriað on
      ðus geradum SOPINVM. (Ælfric *Grammar* [1001 153.15] B1.9.1)

(2) **To witanne is** þæt ðæt nis þæt an <þæt> an wordum he lærde þa
     wæccan, ac eac swylce mid his agenre bysene he getrymede, (*Vercelli
     Hom.* [0043 80] B3.2.11.5)

(3) **Hit is to witenne,** þæt ðas naman habbað mislic andgyt, be ðam ðe
     hi gesette beoð. (Ælfric *Grammar* [0728 113.13] B1.9.1)

(4) **Us is to witenne** þæt on ðreo wisan bið geðyld æteowod. oðre ðing
     sind þe we fram gode ðoliað. oþre . . . (Ælfric *Cath. Hom* II, 42 [0091
     315.155] B1.2.46)

(5) **Þæm lareowe is to wietanne** ðæt he huru nanum men mare ne
     beode ðonne he acuman mæge, (Alfred *Past. Care* [2494 63.459.6]
     B9.1.3)

(6) For mine saule alisendnesse gean cristes chirican inne Ghantwareberi
     landas on mine gerihte, **þæt is to wittenne** Sandwich & Æstre.
     (Charter 1636 Dugdale [0002 2] B15.7.3)

The evidence given by the OEC clearly indicates that the most common
usage of the inflected infinitive form of *witan* was the idiomatic use seen
in examples (1)–(6). In no fewer than 84 out of the total number of 146
instances *to witenne* can be regarded as a discourse marker or pragmatic
phrase corresponding to, and often translating, the Latin *sciendum est* and
meaning, roughly, 'let it be known (to x) that . . .' or 'it is to be noted that'
or, simply, 'that is to say', 'in other words'. The phrase almost always
begins a sentence and introduces a subordinate noun clause, most often
beginning with *þæt*. This subordinate clause consists of the proposition
to which particular attention is called by the discourse marker.

There are 62 instances of the non-idiomatic uses of *to witenne*. In most
of these, the infinitive occurs with verbs other than "to be" (7)–(9). If the
verb is "to be", the subject of the phrase is in most cases a noun or a
pronoun other than *hit* or *þæt* (10)–(12); the infinitive is often appended
to an adjective (13)–(15). The order of the elements in these types can, of
course, vary:

(7) Ac we witon ðonne eall þæt we nu **wilniað to witanne,** ge æac
     þæt þæt we nu na ne wilniað to witanne. (*Soliloquies* [0030 67.29]
     B9.4.4)

(8) sweotollice **us gedyde nu to witanne** Alexander hwelce þa hæðnan godas sindon to weorþianne, (Orosius [0196 9.69.28] B9.2.4)

(9) Heræfter **gebyraþ to witanne** hwanon þa concurrentes cumað þe mid þissum regulares irnan sceolon. (Byrhtferth *Enchiridion* 3.1 [0018 18] B20.3.1)

(10) Ðæs forman monðes angin **ys to witanne** fram VIII idus Martii oð nonas Aprelis, (Byrhtferth *Manual* [0867 3.1.42] B20.20.1)

(11) Her is **mucel andgit eow monnum to witenne**, and we nimæð herto to ðissere trahtnunge Augustinum ðone wisæ, ðe we wæl truwiæð (*Bodley Hom.* [0014 48] B1.5.7)

(12) Nis na **eow to gewitenne** þa tid. oððe þa handhwile þe min fæder gesette þurh his mihte. (Ælfric *Cath. Hom.* [0007 345.12] B1.1.23)

(13) Depplicu is seo acsung and **winsumu to witanne** þam þe hyt witan mæg; (*Soliloquies* [0471 53.1] B9.4.2)

(14) Ac forðæmðe hit swa **earfoðe** is ænegum menn **to witanne** hwonne he geclænsod sie, he mæg ðy orsorglicor forbugan ða ðegnunga; (Alfred *Past. Care* [0167 7.51.4] B9.1.3)

(15) And scandlic is to specenne þæt geworden is to wide & **egeslic is to witanne** þæt oft doð to manege . . . (Wulfstan *Hom.* [0027 85] B2.4.2.)

Examples (1)–(6) give the main types of the idiomatic, discourse marker use of *is to witenne*. Example (1) represents the basic pattern: it is a direct translation of a Latin phrase, with no elements added. The addition of the formal subject *hit*, as in (3), is only to be expected. The dative plural of the noun or pronoun appears in (4) and (5). Example (6) shows an interesting development: *þæt is to witenne* is used as an appositive link, indicating, roughly, 'that is to say', 'in other words' (cf. Latin *scilicet*, *videlicet*). This usage is most obviously the earliest form of present-day English *to wit*.

We can say that these idiomatic types represent the first step in the process of grammaticalization of the verb meaning 'know' which results in the present-day fully grammaticalized appositive link *to wit*. By

grammaticalization we mean the change in which semantically meaningful words or phrases become structural or grammatical elements of the
language: in typical cases, nouns, adjectives and verbs become adverbs,
prepositions or conjunctions. Good examples of grammaticalization in
English are such connective words as *because (of)* (conj., prep.), from the
noun *cause*; *notwithstanding* (adv., prep.), from the verb *withstand*; or *while*
(conj.) from the noun with the same form (see e.g. Hopper & Traugott
1993).

That the usage was not completely idiomatized or frozen in Old English can be seen from the variant expressions in which elements are added
to the phrase. In fact, instances of the "plain" types exemplified in (1)–(6)
are in the minority in the *Old English Corpus*. These elements are most
often connective adverbs (16)–(20) or intensifiers (21)–(26):

(16) **Eac is to wietanne** ðætte hwilum bið god wærlice to miðanne his
      hieremonna scylda & to licettanne suelce he hit nyte; (Alfred *Past.
      Care* [0702 21.151.8] B9.1.3)
      Sciendum quoque est quod aliquando subjectorum vitia prudenter
      dissimulanda sunt (*Patrologia Latina* 77: 44)

(17) **Us is nu to witane**, men þa leofestan, þæt for þan Cristes aldoras
      þy feowertigan dæge hine brohton to þam Godes temple for þan
      þe ðæt wæs þeaw & Godes bebod. (*Vercelli Hom.* [0011 28] B3.3.19)

(18) ** Þonne is manna gehwilcum to witanne**, þæt ælc ðæra manna, ðe
      ðæne deofollican unðeaw hæfð, þæt he wile . . . (*Hom. Assmann* 12
      [0006 21] B3.2.16)

(19) **Hit is þeah to witanne**, hwy þeos feorðe boc sy uncapitulod, nu þa
      ærran bec synt gecapitulod, (*Penitentials* [0197 (4.0)] B11.3.1.1)

(20) **Ac forþon us is to witanne**, þæt þam deadum mannum seo halige
      onsægdnes gehelpeþ & wel nyt byþ (Wærferth *Dial. Greg.* [0914
      59.348.4] B9.5.6)
      Sed sciendum est quia illis sacræ victimæ mortuis prosint
      (*Patrologia Latina* 77: 425)

(21) **Eornostlice is to witenne** þet þæt is soð dædbot þe mon mid mycele
      stiðnesse deþ, (*Hom.* Belfour [0022 44] B3.2.15)

Table 11.1 The types of the idiomatized *is to witenne* in the *Old English Corpus*

	Plain	With conn.	With intens. (+ conn.)	Total
Is to witenne	2	28	9	39
With dat.	7	20	3	30
Hit is to witenne	3	2	1	6
Þæt is to witenne	5	2	2	9
Total	**17**	**52**	**15**	**84**

Plain = no additional elements in the phrase; Conn. = connective; Intens. = intensifying adverb.

(22) **To witanne is weotodlice** þæt þæt fæsten mid godum worcum is Gode swiðe andfenge. (*Vercelli Hom.* [0065 122] B3.2.11.5)

(23) **Is nu swyðe to witenne** þæt nis næfre nan synn to ðam swiðe micel þæt man ne mæg gebetan her on ðisum life, (Ælfric *Hom.* [0060 213] B1.4.6)

(24) **Cuðlice hit is to wytene,** þæt æighwylc man swylce forgyfonysse onfohð æt Gode, swylce he her his þan nexten, þe wið hine agyllteð sylleð. (Alcuin *De virtutibus* [0084 185] B9.7.4)

(25) **Us ys georne to witenne & to gehlystenne** for hwylcum þingum we ðas gangdagas healdað (*Vercelli Hom.* [0023 58] B3.2.34)

(26) **Eow is soðlice to gewitenne** þæt furðon nan asolcen man nis orsorh. be onfangennysse godes feos; (Ælfric *Cath. Hom* II, 43 [0066 323.162] B1.2.47)

Table 11.1 shows the distribution of the main types. In the table the term "conn[ective]" refers to such adverbs as *eac* 'also', *nu* 'now', *þonne* 'then', *þeah* 'however', *forþon* 'therefore', etc. When a connective and an intensifier occur in the same context, as in example (23), the instance is included in the "Intensifier" column.

The variability of the phrase in discourse marker use can be clearly seen in the figures of Table 11.1, as well as in examples (16)–(26).

The Latin basis of the idiomatic use of *is to witenne* becomes obvious if the readings of the Latin original of two close Old English translations, King Alfred's version of Gregory's *Pastoral Care* and Bishop Wærferth's translation of Gregory's *Dialogues*, are compared with the Old English renderings. *Is to witanne* occurs eight times in both *Pastoral Care* and in the *Dialogues*. In thirteen instances out of these sixteen, the Old English idiom translates the Latin *sciendum . . . est*, see (16) and (20) above and (27) below, and in two *notandum (est)* (28).

(27)   Gregorius him andswarode: <eac> **us is to witanne**, þæt fulloft þa sawla, þe þonne gyt wuniað in heora lichaman, geseoð hwæthugu witelices be þam gastlicum wisum (Wærferth *Dial. Greg.* [0628 40.323.25] B9.5.6)
       GREGORIUS: Sciendum quoque est quia nonnunquam animæ adhuc in suis corporibus positæ poenale aliquid de spiritibus vident (*Patrologia Latina* 77: 389)

(28)   **Eac is to wietanne** ðæt æresð bið se wah ðurhðyrelod, & siððan mon wyrcð duru to. (Alfred *Past. Care* [0738 21.157.14] B9.1.3)
       Notandum itaque est quia prius foramen in pariete, ac deinde ostium cernitur (*Patrologia Latina* 77: 45)

The type *þæt is to witenne*, which occurs nine times in the OEC, deserves a special mention as the idiom has the same kind of connective function as the Present-Day English *to wit*. This function is obvious in (6) above, and in (29), (30) and most probably in (31), below:

(29)   Augustinus cwæð þæt þa halgan festen beoð swyþe stronge flan ongean deofles costungæ, & heom mon swiðe raþe ofercymæð mid þare forhæfdnesse.
       Þæt is to witænne, þæt ða festenu mid oðre godum dedum beoð swiðe anfencge; (*Bodley Hom.* [0052 123] B3.2.15)

(30)   Men, us is swiðe þearle to efstanne, þæt we ure lif and ure þeawas gebeterian and þæt we bewepan, þæt we ær to yfele gedydon, and ofer þis ðære syngunge geswican, forðan ðe god ne besceawað na, hwilce we ær wæron, ac he besceawað, hwilce we beon, þonne we dælan sceolon sawle and lichaman.

Þæt is to witanne, þæt god ne secð na þæs godan weorces angin, ac he secð þæne ænde, forðan ðe ælc man sceal beon demed be ðam geearnungum, þe he hæfð, þonne he of ðisum life hwyrfan sceal. (*Hom.* Assmann [0042 140] B3.2.16)

(31) Do gehwa georne on godes est, be þam þe hine fyrmest onhagie. And **þæt is to witanne**, þeah þe seo ælmesse on ælcne sæl god beo gedon, huru þinga man sceal on þissum dagum hy dælan swa forð, swa mannes mihta fyrmeste beoð. (*Hom.* Assmann [0034 85] B3.2.16)

In the following instances, the use of the phrase corresponds to the non-appositive *Hit is to witanne*:

(32) Hwæt þu þæt seolfa leornadest in bebode þære aldan cyðnesse, þætte fore wæpnedbearne heo sceolde heo ahabban from Godes huses ingonge þreo & þritig daga, fore wiifcilde syx & syxtig daga.
      Þæt is hwæðre to weotanne, þætte þæt is on gastlicum geryne ongyten. (Bede [0332 16.76.9] B9.6.3)

(33) Gyf hyt byð embolismaris oððe embolismus, þæt ys eall an, þænne beoð þy geare þreohund daga & fif & hundeahtatig daga.
      Þæt ys wislice to witanne, þæt bissextus, þe we ymbe synd sprecende, þæt he gebyrað ægðer ge to þære sunnan ryne ge to þæs monan. (Byrhtferth's *Manual* [0477 2.1.131] B20.20.1)

Cf. also Byrhtferth's *Manual* [0131 1.2.27], [0466 2.1.100] and *Blickling Homilies* ([0084 248] B3.2.46).

The development from the discourse marker to an appositive connective is not surprising; it only needs the change of the cataphoric (forward pointing) reference of the pronoun *þæt* to an anaphoric (backward pointing) reference. The pronoun *þæt* was more clearly demonstrative and less common as a formal subject than *hit*, and was thus the appropriate form to be used in appositive contexts.

Of the other verbs having roughly the same meaning as *witan*, the uses of *ongitan* 'to perceive, understand, know' and *understandan* are of some interest (*-cnawan* does not occur in idioms of this kind). The inflected infinitive forms of these verbs occur in similar kinds of phrases as *to witenne*:

(34)   Nu ðonne, nu ða lichomlican læcas ðus scyldige gerehte sint, nu **is to ongietanne** æt hu micelre scylde ða beoð befangene (Alfred *Past. Care* [1861 49.377.21] B9.1.3)

(35)   Eac **us is to ongytene** þæt hie cwædon, Hæl us on eorþan (*Blickl. Hom.* [0100 275] B3.2.21)

(36)   Forþon **hit is to ongytene** þæt seo <ylce> fylnes & se mist, þe þær gesewen wæs, us þæt getacnað, þæt . . . (Waerferth *Dial. Greg.* [0622 38.323.7] B9.5.6)

(37)   **Is eac to understandenne** þæt þæt egyptisce folc wearð mid tyn witum geslagen. (Ælfric *Cath. Hom.* II [0146 119.334] B1.2.13)

(38)   **Us is to understandenne** ðas endebyrdnyssa. (Ælfric *Lives of Saints* [0065 258] B1.3.17)

(39)   **Be ðisum is to understandenne.** þæt se ðe for oðrum gebit fremað him sylfum micclum. (Ælfric *Cath. Hom.* II [0113 266.199] B1.2.37)

Of special interest is the use in which the phrase *is to understandenne* is an appositive link, in the same way as *is to witenne* in examples (29)–(31) above.

(40)   Sarai wæs his wif gehaten. þæt is gereht min ealdor: ac god hi het syðþan sarra þæt is ealdor: þæt heo nære synderlice hire hiredes ealdor geciged: ac forðrihte ealdor: **þæt is to understandenne.** ealra gelyfedra wifa moder. (Ælfric *Cath. Hom.* [0019 225.36] B1.1.7)

(41)   God cwæð eft nu to þe: Ic forgife nu ærest þe, forgif þu hure syððan, and gif ðu swa ne dest on eornost, ic wulle habban eft æt þe þæt þæt ic ðe ær forgeaf; **ðis is to understandenne**, mid inneweardre heortan. (*Bodley Hom.* [0054 185] B1.5.7)

Note the use of *ðis* in (41).

    These uses of *to ongitenne/understandenne* are, however, less frequent than *is to witenne*; the occurrences of the inflected infinitive of the two verbs in other contexts clearly outnumber the types quoted in (34)–(41) above.

Later Developments

In the course of the Middle English period, the verb *wite(n)* gradually gives way to *knowe(n)*, although it is fairly common throughout the period (see Rissanen 1993). Both the types *it is to wite(n)* (42)–(44) and *that is to wite(n)* (45)–(49) occur in Middle English, although the former type seems to be rapidly disappearing by the end of the period and is mainly restricted to translations from Latin, such as the medical text *A Latin Technical Phlebotomy and its Middle English Translation* (43). The connective use with *þæt* gains ground; it is common in Dan Michel's *Ayenbite of Inwyt*, which is a close translation of a French original and dates from the first half of the fourteenth century (45), and in documentary texts dating from the late fourteenth and fifteenth centuries (47)–(48). By the side of the simple infinitive marker *to* the combination *for to*, which originally indicated purpose, appears (48).

(42)   22. Ʒyf we forʒate þe name of our Lord, and putten forþe our hondes to a strange God,
      23. **It is to witen**, Ʒif God shal nouʒt asken þes þynges; for he knewe þe hidynges of þe hert. (c. 1350 *Prose Psalter* MPPSALT 54 HC)

(43)   **It is to wete** þat in flebotomie 4 þyngis are principalli attendid: *sc.*, custome, tyme, age, & vertue. (c. 1400–1425 *Phlebotomie* PHLEB 39 HC)

(44)   **It is to wetyn** þat xxvii dayes *ben* beforn euery prime tyl the chaungyng of the mone. (1470–1500 *Commonpl. Book of Robert Reynes* REYNES 158 HC)

(45)   Þe sixte article is / of his arizinge. **þet is to wytene**. þet þanne þridde day / efter his dyaþe. uor to uoluelle þe writinges: he aros uram dyaþe. (1340 *Ayenbite of Inwyt* 13 CME)

(46)   he beleued þe fals mannys talys & wryynge, & sent yn-to Irland four Messagers, **that ys to wytten**, Robert the power, Osbern of herford, Wyllyam Berynger, & Adam of yarnemouth (15th c. *English Conquest of Ireland* Ch. 41 102 CME)

Table 11.2   Occurrences of *it/that is to wite(n)* in the Corpus of Middle English Prose and Verse

	It is to w.	That is to w.	That is for to w.
Ayenbite of Inwyt (c. 1340)	–	12	–
Documents			
English Guilds (late 14th–early 15th c.)	–	6	7
London Indenture (1384)	–	1	–
Secreta Secretorum (late 15th c.)	10	–	–
Arderne, Fistula in Ano (c. 1425)	14	–	–
English Conquest of Ireland (15th c.)	–	3	–
Ratis Raving (late 15th c.)	1	–	–
Total	**25**	**22**	**7**

(47)   And who-so entres in to yis ffraternite, he schal pay ye fees of yis hous: **yat is to weten**, to ye Alderman, ij.d.; ye clerk, a peny; ye dene, a peny . . . (15th c. Guild of St. John Baptist, *Lenne Petri* Ch. 38 101 CME)

(48)   And what man so entre in to þis fraternite, sone he is comen in, he shal . . . paien his fees, **þat is for to wyten**, ij.d. to þe aldirman . . . (15th c. Guild of St. George the Martyr, *Lenne* Ch. 29 76 CME)

(49)   vnresonable mysdedes that reynart the foxe hath don to me and to my wyf **that is to wete** he is comen in to my hows ayenst the wylle of my wyf (1481 *Reynard the Fox* REYNARD 7 HC)

Tables 11.2 and 11.3 give the frequencies of the two types in the texts of the *Corpus of Middle English Prose and Verse* (CME) and in the text samples of the Middle English part of the *Helsinki Corpus of English Texts*. The smaller but chronologically and textually more structured *Helsinki Corpus* adds instances from a few texts not included in the CME. It is remarkable that in both corpora all the occurrences of *that is (for) to wite(n)* are of the appositive type while all the instances of *it is to wite(n)* are of the discourse marker type.

Table 11.3 Occurrences of *it/that is to wite(n)* in the Middle English part of the Helsinki Corpus of English Texts

	It is to wite(n)	*That is (for) to wite(n)*
Prose Psalter (MPPSALT c. 1350)	1	–
Documents (RET, PET late 14th or 15th c.)	–	4
Phlebotomy (PHLEB c. 1400–1425)	9	–
REYNES (1470–1500)	2	1
Chauliac (CHAUL early 15th c.)	–	2
Caxton (1477–1484)	–	2
REYNARD (1481)	–	1
Total	**12**	**10**

It is worth noting that, besides *þet is to wytene* (45), the phrase *þet is to zigge* 'that is to say' is very common in the *Ayenbite of Inwyt*: there are altogether more than 80 instances of this phrase used as an appositive connective:

(50) þanne huanne we ziggeþ / *sanctificetur nomen tuum*: **þet is to zigge**. "sire / þis is oure heȝe wyl / þis we bezechiþ toppe alle þing / þet þin holy name . . . by y-confermed ine ous." (1340 *Ayenbite of Inwyt* AYENB I, 106, HC)

Conclusions

Tables 11.2 and 11.3 sum up the early history of (*it/that is*) *to wit*: the uses of the two types become clearly defined, *it is to wit* being used as the discourse marker and *that is to wit* as the appositive connective. The influence of Latin is obvious in the emergence of the Old English idiom. In the Modern English period, the verb *wit(e)* gradually disappears, surviving only in the completely grammaticalized connective phrase *to wit*. This development has been described and analysed in detail in Koivisto-Alanko & Rissanen (2002).

I hope that this brief survey also gives some idea of how the corpora comprising practically all extant Old English texts and several million words of Middle English writing can ease the toil and trouble of finding evidence of the rise and early development of an idiom which in the course of centuries becomes a grammatical element in the language, to wit, an appositive connective.

References and Further Reading

Gutch, U. (1979). Altenglisch – cnawan, cunnan, witan – Neuenglisch know. Diss., Berlin.

Hopper, P. J. & Traugott, E. C. (1993). *Grammaticalization*. Cambridge: Cambridge University Press (2nd edn 2003).

Koivisto-Alanko, P. & Rissanen, M. (2002). *We give you to wit*: Semantics and grammaticalisation of the verb *wit* in the history of English. In H. Raumolin-Brunberg, M. Nevala, A. Nurmi & M. Rissanen (eds), *Variation Past and Present: VARIENG studies on English for Terttu Nevalainen* (pp. 13–32). Helsinki: Société Néophilologique de Helsinki.

Rissanen, M. (1993). The loss of wit 'know': evidence from the Helsinki Corpus. In I. Koskenniemi & R. Hiltunen (eds), *English Far and Wide: a Festschrift for Inna Koskenniemi* (pp. 195–206). Turku: University of Turku.

Appendix: Translations of the Examples

Where available, the translations have been copied, with small changes, from the editions of the texts.

(1)   SCIENDVM EST, QVOD NEVTRA VERBA DEFICIVNT IN SOPINO
It is to be noted that the words that are called neuters lack this kind of supine.

(2)   It is to be noted that he did not only teach vigil with words but also with his own example.

(3)   It is to be noted that these nouns have a different meaning depending on their context.

(4)   We are to know that patience is manifested in three ways; there are some things that we suffer from God, others . . .

(5)   The teacher is to know that he is by no means to impose on any man more than he can bear,

(6) For the redemption of my soul I grant to Christ's church in Canterbury the lands that are my right, that is to say, Sandwich and Estre.

(7) But we shall know then all that we now wish to know, and also what we now do not wish to know.

(8) Clearly Alexander now made us to know which heathen gods are to be worshipped,

(9) Hereafter it is appropriate that we know wherefrom the epacts come that must run with these regulars.

(10) The beginning of the first month must be looked for from 8 March until 5 April,

(11) Here is much meaning for you people to know, and we make use of the exposition of the wise Augustine, in whom we have great confidence

(12) It is not for you to know the time or the moment which my Father has appointed through his might.

(13) It is a profound question and good to know for whoever wants to know it;

(14) But since it is so difficult for any man to know when he is purified, he can with so much the less hesitation decline the ministry;

(15) And it is disgraceful to speak of what has happened too widely and it is horrible to know what too many people often do . . .

(16) It is also to be known that it is sometimes good to conceal the sins of his subjects, and pretend not to know it;

(17) We should now know, dearest men, that Christ's parents brought him on the fortieth day to God's temple because it was the custom and God's command.

(18) Then everybody should know that each man that has the devilish vice, that he wishes . . .

(19) It is to be noted why this fourth book is without chapter headings, while the earlier books have headings,

(20) But therefore we should know that the holy sacrifice is helpful and useful for dead men

(21) Truly it is to be noted that that is true repentance that is done with great rigour,

(22) It is truly to be noted that abstinence from food joined to good deeds is very agreeable to God.

(23) It is to be truly noted that no sin is so great that it could not be amended in this life,

(24) Truly it is to be noted that God will give everybody such pardon as he gives here to his neighbour who has sinned against him.

(25) We should willingly know and hear why we observe these Rogation days

(26) You should truly note that no slothful man is secure with regard to receiving God's treasure;

(27) Gregory answered him: we should also note that very often the souls which still live in their bodies see something burdensome concerning spiritual things

(28) It is also to be noted that the wall is first pierced, and then a door is added.

(29) Augustine said that holy fasts are very strong arrows against the Devil's temptations and that these temptations are very quickly overcome with abstinence. That is to say that fasts with other good deeds are most acceptable;

(30) Men, we must be in a hurry to improve our lives and habits and to weep for all the evil we have done and to give up committing sin, because God does not consider what we were earlier but he considers what we will be when our soul leaves our body. That is to say that God does not look for the good deed's beginning, but he looks for the end, because everybody shall be deemed by his desert, when he leaves this life.

(31) Let everybody eagerly please God as best he can. And that is to say, although giving alms is always good, one must especially these days give them to the best of one's ability.

(32) You have yourself learnt in the ordinances of the Old Testament that for a man-child she should abstain thirty-three days from entering God's house, for a woman-child sixty-six days. It must be noted, however, that this is understood as a spiritual mystery.

(33) If the year is *embolismaris* or *embolismus* (it is all the same), then there are 385 days in the year. It ought truly to be known that the leap year, which we are speaking about, pertains both to the sun's course and to the moon's.

(34) If, then, the physicians of the body are thus held guilty, we must consider
      how greatly they sin

(35) Also we should understand that they said, "Save us on earth"

(36) Therefore it should be understood that the same foulness and the mist that
      was seen there signifies to us that . . .

(37) It is also to be understood that the Egyptian people were stricken with ten
      plagues,

(38) We should understand these rules.

(39) By this is to be understood that he who prays for others profits himself
      greatly,

(40) His wife was called Sarai, which is interpreted, *My chief*; but God called her
      afterwards Sarah, that is *Chief*; that she might not be exclusively called her
      family's chief, but absolutely chief; which is to be understood, mother of all
      believing women.

(41) God said again now to you: I shall forgive you now first, forgive you verily
      then, and if you will not do that in earnest, I shall withdraw my forgive-
      ness again from you (for) that which I forgave you before, that is to be
      understood, with sincere heart.

(42) 22. If we forget the name of our Lord, and stretch out our hands to a
      strange God.
      23. It should be known whether God will not ask these things; for he
      knows the secrets of the heart.

(43) It is to be noted that in phlebotomy four things are principally attended: i.e.
      custom, time, age and virtue.

(44) It is to be noted that the change of the moon takes twenty-seven days

(45) The sixth article is of his arising, that is to say that on the third day after his
      death, to fulfil the scriptures, he arose from the dead.

(46) he believed the false man's tales and writing and sent into Ireland four
      messengers, that is to say, Robert . . .

(47)   And whoever enters into this fraternity, he shall pay the fees of this house: that is to say, the Alderman 2d, the clerk, a penny, the dean, a penny . . .

(48)   And whoever enters into this fraternity, as soon as he has come in, he shall . . . pay his fees, that is to say, 2d to the alderman . . .

(49)   unreasonable misdeeds that Reynard the Fox has done to me and to my wife, that is to say, he came into my house against the will of my wife.

(50)   when we say *sanctificetur nomen tuum*: that is to say, "Lord, this is our great wish / this we beseech more than anything else / that your holy name . . . be confirmed in us."

Chapter 12

Germanic *uargaz (OE wearh) and the Finnish Evidence

Fred C. Robinson

With great skill and considerable success philological scholars have re-constructed the hypothetical Germanic parent language from which Old English (OE) and the other documented early Germanic languages (Old High German, Old Norse, Old Saxon, Old Frisian and Gothic) descended. Obscurities in the attested languages such as Old English and Old Norse can often be clarified by reference to Germanic, for the grammar, semantics and phonology (i.e. the sounds) of this reconstructed speech usually give us the starting-point for the grammar, semantics and phonology of the languages which developed from it. Occasionally, however, our hypo-thetical Germanic language lacks details which we need when seeking solutions to puzzles encountered in the attested daughter languages. Being a reconstructed, hypothetical language for which there are no surviving records, Germanic cannot supply the kind of details that we have at our disposal in the case of actual languages which were used by people known to history and recorded by them in written form. There are no actual Germanic words for us to consult and compare with words from Old English, Old Norse, etc. Or so we have been disposed to think. In this essay I shall suggest by the example of the Germanic construct *uargaz that sometimes we do have surviving Germanic words – or at least something very close to such words – which we can use in solving problems encountered in the attested languages.

Germanic *uargaz survives in most of the documented Germanic languages: OE wearh, ON vargr, OHG warg, OS uuarag and the second element of the Gothic compound launawargs. The earliest attestation is in the Latinized form vargus preserved in the Lex Ribuaria 85,2. In its documented forms the word appears to have two basic meanings. On the one hand it can mean 'wolf'; on the other it can mean 'outlaw, criminal, thief'. The immediate purpose of the present essay is to determine, if possible, which of these two meanings is the primary sense: was a word meaning 'wolf' applied by extension to criminals because criminals behave wolfishly, or was a word meaning 'criminal' applied to the animal because wolves prey on livestock and domestic animals in a way analogous to that of criminal predators?

Let us begin by examining the entry for *vargr* in the Cleasby and Vigfusson Old Icelandic dictionary:

> **VARGR,** m. [A.S. *wearg*; Hel. *warag* . . .]: – *a wolf*; berr björn, bítr vargr, N.G.L. 1, 341; ríða á vargi, Hkv. Hjörv.; trolkona sat á vargi [These quotations mean, respectively, 'bear smites, wolf bites', 'to ride on a wolf' and 'a troll-woman sat on a wolf'.]
>
> II. a law phrase, metaph., *an outlaw*, who is to be hunted down as a wolf, esp. used of one who commits a crime in a holy place, and is thereon declared accursed; hann hafði vegit í véum ok var hann vargr orðinn, Eg. 259; vargr í véum, *a wolf in the sanctuary*, Fms. Xi, 40 (goð-vargr): also of *a trucebreaker,* . . . [The first quotation means 'He had fought in a sanctuary and was declared a *vargr*'.]

Cleasby and Vigfusson leave no doubt as to the direction of the semantic development: the basic meaning of the word is 'wolf' and it is metaphorically extended to criminals. The modern Scandinavian languages would seem to confirm this interpretation of the evidence. Modern Swedish and Norwegian *varg* means 'wolf', and Modern Icelandic *vargur* means 'fox'. (This shifting of such a term from one animal to another is not unprecedented linguistically: cf. Latin *vulpus* 'fox', which is cognate with English *wolf*.) In the forty-fifth stanza of the Old Norse *Voluspa* appears the compound *varg-old*, which Cleasby-Vigfusson renders 'an age of wolves', and subsequent translators of the poem agree. E.g.,

> Brothers will die,   slain by their brothers,
> incest will break   kinship's bonds;
> woe to the world then,   wedded to whoredom,
> battle-axe and sword-rule,   split shields asunder,
> storm-cleft *age of wolves*   unless the world goes down,
> only hatred   in the hearts of men.
>
> (Terry 1969: 9)

John R. Clark Hall's *Concise Anglo-Saxon Dictionary* seems to be in agreement with Cleasby and Vigfusson's interpretation of the semantic development of the word:

Wearg (e) I. m. (*wolf*), *accursed one, outlaw, felon, criminal, Rood, WW; Æ*[lfric].

The parenthesis gives the basic meaning of the word, and then the derived senses follow. In his translation of *Beowulf* Frances B. Gummere stays faithful to the primary sense indicated by Clark Hall when he translates OE *heorowearh* in line 1267 as 'war-wolf':

> There woke from him
> such fate-sent ghosts as Grendel, who,
> *war-wolf* horrid, at Heorot found
> a warrior watching and waiting the fray . . .
> (Gummere 1909: 79)

One of the many OE compounds containing *wearg* is *weargtrèow* meaning 'gallows, cross'. One might suppose that the likeliest interpretation of this word would be 'criminal tree' since gallows (and in Roman times crosses) are what criminals are hanged on; but another term for 'gallows, cross' in OE is *wulfheafodtrèow*, literally 'wolf-head tree', and this might lead one to assume that there was some fancied association between gallows and wolves.

With so much evidence pointing the same way, one might conclude that there is no reason to doubt that Germanic **uargaz* meant 'wolf' and that 'criminal, thief' is a metaphorical extension of this meaning.

But there are other data that might give us pause. When we have recourse to the *Microfiche Concordance of Old English* (Healey & Venezky 1980), we discover that in all the many attestations of *wearg* and its numerous compounds it never (with the possible exceptions of *heorowearh* and *wulfheafodtrèow*) means anything but 'criminal, outlaw, thief'. Moreover, when we return to the word *wulfheafodtrèow* for a second look, we discover that the OE word *wulfheafod* is documented only with the meaning 'outlaw'. To be sure, the compound is based upon a metaphorical extension of the literal meaning 'wolf', but the compound itself occurs only with the meaning 'outlaw' and so provides analogical support for the interpretation of *weargtrèow* as 'criminal-tree' rather than 'wolf-tree'. Evidently Clark Hall's '(wolf)' in his definition of *wearg* was based on nothing more than Cleasby and Vigfusson's inference. Another point to consider is that in the earliest attestation of a word descended from *uargaz, that in the *Lex Ribuari*, the meaning is 'outlaw', and when we turn to the documentations of the cognates of *uargaz in OHG and OS texts, we discover that there the word means only 'outlaw, thief', not 'wolf'.

warg, *st. m.* G. I, 979; (tyrannus): *Übeltäter.* (Starck-Wells 697)

> lietun sia qualm tholon
> an them *uuarag*treuue

they let them [the two thieves next to Christ] suffer pain on the criminal-tree [i.e. the cross].

(*Heliand* 5562–3)

> *uuaragas* tholodun
> lêîas lòngeld

the criminals suffered retribution for evil.

(Vatican *Genesis* 319–20)

Since the Gothic adjective *launawargs* 'ungrateful' has no conceivable relation with the meaning 'wolf', it would appear that only in the Scandinavian languages is a sense 'wolf' demonstrable.

At this point we may be tempted to despair of resolving this question. Only by interrogating a native speaker of Germanic and asking her what *uargaz meant to her could we discover the direction of semantic change in *uargaz and its descendant forms, and we obviously have no way of gaining access to the thoughts of a native Germanic speaker.

But perhaps we do after all – if we consult the Finnish evidence. During the Primitive Germanic period (roughly the centuries immediately before the beginning of the Christian era) the wandering Germanic tribes came into contact with Finns, a non-Indo-European people who had settled in northern Europe before the arrival of the Germanic people. During this period hundreds of Germanic words were borrowed into Finnish, and the Finnish language over the years has preserved these words in forms remarkably close to those they had when they were borrowed. Finnish, it appears, has not undergone the radical phonological changes that other languages (notably English) have experienced, and the meanings of the

Germanic words seem to have remained equally stable over the centuries. For example, the Germanic word from which OE *cyning*, OS *kuning*, ON *konungr*, Swedish *konung*, Danish *konge*, Dutch *koning* and Modern German *könig* all derive has been confidently reconstructed as **kuningaz*. The ancient Finns borrowed this word from Germanic, and today it remains in the Finnish language with the form *kuningas* and the meaning 'king'. The Germanic word from which OE *sàr* (noun) 'sickness' and *sàr* (adj.) 'sore, painful' derive was **sairaz*. This too was borrowed into ancient Finnish and is preserved today in the Finnish word *sairas* 'sick'. Germanic **habuka* 'hawk' yields modern Finnish *havukka*. And so on.

Now if the ancient Finns borrowed the Germanic word **uargaz*, then we should have the answer to the question entertained throughout this article. They did, and we do. The modern Finnish word *varas* (gen. *varkaan*) is the modern reflex of Germanic **uargaz*, and its meaning is 'thief'. Evidently the original sense of **uargaz* was 'thief, outlaw, criminal', and Scandinavian speakers used the word sometimes to refer to the wolf – probably a euphemistic denomination of a feared animal that one did not want to summon by pronouncing its actual name (cf. the famous example of Russian *medved* 'honey-eater' used to replace the original word for 'bear').

This happy solution to the problem of the semantics of **uargaz* has several implications for Old English and Old Germanic philology. First, we are able to correct some errors of interpretation made by scholars in the past, who laboured under the misapprehension that the basic meaning of *wearh*, *vargr*, etc. was 'wolf'. Thus Gummere's rendering of *heorowearh* in *Beowulf* 1267 as 'war-wolf' is unwarranted. The word means 'fierce outlaw', which is exactly what Grendel was. (He was not a wolf.) OE *weargtrèow*, OS *uuaragtreuue* mean 'criminal-tree', not 'wolf-tree'. Cleasby and Vigfusson's (and subsequent translators') rendering of ON *vargold* as 'age of wolves' should be reconsidered. In stanza 45 from the *Voluspa* the age being described is one of criminality – fratricide, violence, whoredom and incest; it is not described as an age of wolves. Careful scrutiny of interpretations of other occurrences of *wearg*, *vargr* and their compounds will probably reveal other instances of skewed renderings which can now be corrected.

In a broader view, the Finnish solution to the philological puzzle of **uargaz* should alert us to the potential for further philological enlightenment from the remarkable museum of Germanic fossils that the Finnish language offers us. Phonological as well as semantic problems can be solved using Finnish evidence. There has been uncertainty, for example as to the vowel of the Germanic antecedent of the words for "ring" in surviving Germanic languages – OE, OHG *hring*, ON *hringr*, etc. The original Germanic form could have been *hringaz or *hrengaz. We do not know which form to postulate since *e* before nasal consonants became in all the Germanic languages *i*. The Umbrian word *krenkatrum* 'shoulder girdle', if it is cognate with the Germanic word, would lead us to suspect that the vowel was *e*, but the presumed connection between the two words is tenuous. A Finnish word, however, removes all doubt: Germanic *hrengaz was borrowed into ancient Finnish, and the word remains in Finnish today with the form *rengas*. If the Germanic word had been *hringaz, then the modern Finnish word would be *ringas. Phonological uncertainties as well as problems of semantic development in the Germanic languages may well find resolution by reference to the evidence preserved in modern Finnish.

References and Further Reading

Clark Hall, J. R. (1960). *A Concise Anglo-Saxon Dictionary*, 4th edn with a supplement by Herbert D. Meritt. Cambridge: Cambridge University Press.

Cleasby, R. & Vigfusson, G. (eds) (1957). *An Icelandic–English Dictionary*, 2nd edn with a supplement by Sir William A. Craigie. Oxford: Clarendon Press (1st edn 1874).

Gummere, F. B. (1909). *The Oldest English Epic: 'Beowulf,' 'Finnsburg,' 'Waldere,' 'Deor,' 'Widsith,' and the German 'Hildebrand.' Translated in the original metres.* New York: Holt.

Starck, T. & Wells, J. C. (1971–1990). *Althochdeutsches Glossenwoerterbuch.* Heidelberg: Carl Winter.

Terry, P. (trans.) (1969). *Poems of the Vikings: the Elder Edda.* Indianapolis: Bobbs-Merrill.

Chapter 13

How the Leopard Got His Spots: English Grammatical Categories, Latin Terms

John Walmsley

The language we speak, and the choices it offers – or forces us to make – through the way it is structured, are central to the way in which we codify our experience of the world we live in. Language is at the same time an important part of this world. But unlike any other phenomenon in the natural world, language functions both as the object and the medium of description: it is at the same time a thing-talked-about, and the instrument of codification – object-language and "metalanguage". This metalinguistic function comprises the entire discourse which we employ when we use language to talk about itself, and thus includes linguistic terminology and grammatical nomenclature. And just as language sets up for us the categories by means of which we structure our external and interior worlds, the particular linguistic metalanguage we choose for our descriptions fixes the categories in terms of which we formulate this description. The very power of this instrument – language – means that linguists need to think carefully about its nature, structure and use: "the fact that natural languages contain, or appear to contain, their own metalanguages is absolutely central to the theory and practice of linguistic description . . . It is high time that the practitioners of such a logically peculiar discipline began to ask themselves . . . just what they think they are up to when they employ language to talk about language" (Lyons 1980: 292–3).

That the linguist should pay careful attention to his tools is not simply a pious duty to which one pays lip-service before turning to the business in hand: it is only by studying the history and structure of the metalanguage which has come down to us that we can begin to view it objectively

– from the outside, as it were – to understand its weaknesses and limitations, as opposed to being its insouciant victims.

Down to the twentieth century the metalanguage used for linguistic description was derived from so-called Traditional Grammar (TG). But, generally speaking, Traditional Grammar has not had a good press. Levin wrote in 1960 of "the fallacy represented by discussing the grammar of English on the basis of preconceptions derived from the grammar of another language (say Latin)" (Levin 1960: 262). According to Crystal, a decade later, earlier approaches were "all too often wrong" (Crystal 1971: 70). "Often a grammarian would take over and work within a traditional frame of reference, assuming that it was satisfactory for his purposes . . . a more conscious awareness of linguistic principles would have shown that it was not . . . [and] . . . the best example . . . [of this is] . . . the attempt to describe modern languages as if they were variants of Latin" (Crystal 1971: 69). And Dinneen criticized linguists for "obscuring the grammatical requirements of English by discussing facts of English form in the vocabulary designed to codify Greek and Latin" (Dinneen 1967: 170).

Earlier English grammarians do indeed seem to have fallen into the trap of formulating their descriptions in terms of a framework devised for the description of some other language. And this practice has, like the writing of grammars of Latin and Greek, a long tradition. Old English on the other hand, despite earlier grammatical forays into the language, has no such history of continuous study to draw upon (*OES*: I. lix). In this respect, writing a descriptive syntax of Old English is more akin to writing the grammar of a newly discovered language than it is to producing yet another description of Greek or Latin. The problem is, how does one do justice to the individuality of the language while describing it in commonly understood terms and categories? At one extreme the structuralists would have us describe the language exclusively on it own terms, using a non-Latinate nomenclature. At the other, the universalists would postulate – as Roger Bacon did, or Jespersen – a deeper unity underlying all natural languages, which would then differ only in their surface representations.

The solution to the problem lies in an approach which postulates both an underlying universal structure and (potentially) universal surface structure categories which may be realized in different ways, or not at all, in individual languages. Mitchell chose the terminology recommended by the Joint Committee explicitly because the categories postulated there facilitate comparison across the boundaries of individual languages: if not universal, the categories appear to work at least for Indo-European languages (Anon. 1911). Chomsky went further, and placed TG firmly in the history of universal grammar: "The goal of traditional 'universal grammar' was, of course, to give a substantive general account of these categories, thus fixing a universal 'vocabulary' for the generative grammars of all languages" (Chomsky, 1964: 941, fn. 28). The question, then, is this: did the earliest grammarians to apply a Latin-based terminology to English do so out of ignorance and incompetence? Or were they, as Chomsky suggests, postulating a set of universal categories to serve as a basis for the description of all languages?

The most obvious place to look for answers to these questions would seem to be at the point when Latin categories were first applied to English. By common consent, William Bullokar's *Pamphlet for Grammar* (1586) was the first vernacular grammar of English (Turner 1980). This grammar assigned to English almost all the fundamental categories to be found in Latin. But Bullokar was writing at a time when the teaching of Latin was undergoing something of a revolution. At the turn of the sixteenth century, Colet and Lily had produced grammars of Latin which were ultimately integrated, and designated by royal proclamation as the only grammar to be used for teaching Latin in English schools – *A Shorte Introduction of Grammar*. In the second half of the century this grammar was available in both Latin and English. When he sat down to write his *Pamphlet for Grammar*, Bullokar thus had an English terminology ready to hand. What could be more natural than for him to take over the Latin system and fit the grammar of English into this Procrustean bed? And indeed, this is just what his commentators have accused him of:

> Bullokar's major, though understandable, error . . . lies in his attribution to the vernacular of Latin categories which it does not formally mark. In pursuit of this mistaken aim, he ascribes to English the five cases nominative, accusative, dative . . . , genitive . . . , and vocative. With a single exception none of these cases is morphologically marked in the vernacular. (Padley 1985–1988: II, 236)

There are, however, difficulties with this line of thought. The first is that although Bullokar may have been the first to write a grammar of English in English, he was not the first to use a Latinate grammatical terminology in English. In fact, Bullokar lived towards the end of a two-hundred-year period in which a vernacular terminology – English, though based on

Latin – had been introduced, refined and extensively applied to English. To find the real beginnings of the application of Latinate terminology to English, then, we must look back further still.

A second difficulty in presenting Bullokar as unthinkingly taking over an unsuitable terminology is that it leaves out of account the time and the prevailing intellectual climate in which Bullokar lived. Bullokar wrote during a period of strong national sentiment, when uncertainty about the worth of the vernacular was giving way to an ebullient self-confidence. Robins has shown how, far from being the naive propagator of an un-suitable system, Bullokar set out to demonstrate that English could act as a rival to Latin. In a world which divided "rule-governed" languages from languages which could not be subjected to rules (and were hence "unruly"), what better way for Bullokar to demonstrate this than to show that English could be made to fit the rules of grammar almost as well as Latin? "To dismiss this grammar book as 'little more than a translation into English of the system used in William Lily's grammar' (of Latin) as is done by Turner (1980: ii), Funke (1941: 25, 78), Vorlat (1975: 22), and Padley (1988: 230–1), is to miss the point" (Robins 1994: 21). In other words, the more closely Bullokar could make the grammar of English resemble that of Latin, the closer he got to achieving his aim.

To understand how and why the description of English was forced into a Latin mould, then, we need to look to the point at which a con-tinuous tradition of vernacular grammar-writing began. English possesses the earliest vernacular grammatical terminology of any west-European language. As Mitchell pointed out, Ælfric, in the tenth century, wrote a grammar in Old English for his own pupils (*OES*: I, lxi; Porter 2002). For a long time it was believed that Ælfric's grammar was not so much a grammar of English as a grammar of Latin, written in English. Menzer has recently argued however, very plausibly, that Ælfric did indeed intend his work to be both a vernacular introduction to Latin grammar and an illustration of "how grammatical concepts work in English, showing his readers that English has grammar" (Menzer 2004: 114). However, the upheavals in the language ecology which followed the Norman Con-quest made a smooth development from Ælfric's initiative impossible. It was to be another four hundred years before a generation of grammarians grew up writing their grammars in English.

The first manuscripts to be written in a continuous tradition of grammar-writing in England were thus grammars of Latin, written in English. The standard narrative has it that in England Latin grammar was taught in

French until the mid-fourteenth century. At that time, linguistic functions in the community were shared by three languages – French, Latin and English. To some degree the same had been true before the Conquest, but the roles assigned to each of the three languages then had been different. The social, religious and political changes set in train by the Conquest triggered a concomitant shift in the language ecology. By the fourteenth century forces were gathering to cause a general swing away from using French and Latin for purposes of record, in administration, the church and the law, back to English. These changes slowly made themselves felt in all areas of social activity, including teaching.

The swing is vividly captured by Trevisa in his translation of Higden's *Polychronicon*:

> Þys manere [teaching Latin in French] was moche i-vsed to fore firste deth, and is siþthe sumdel i-chaunged. For Iohn Cornwaile, a maister of grammer, chaunged þe lore in gramer scole and construccioun of Frensche in to Englische; and Richard Pencriche lerned þe manere techynge of hym, and . . . oþere men of Pencrich; so þat now, þe ȝere of oure Lorde a þousand þre hundred and foure score and fyue, of þe secounde kyng Richard after þe conquest nyne, in alle þe gramere scoles of Engelond, children leueþ Frensche, and construeþ and lerneþ an Englische . . . (Babington & Lumby 1869: II, 159–61)

While observing the general trend towards an increasing use of the vernacular, it is worth asking why and how this trend spread into teaching. Here we must distinguish between "the vernacular" and – specifically – English. Normally for this period the distinction is drawn between the vernacular and Latin. However, if Trevisa is to be believed, the transition which took place was not one from teaching grammar in Latin to teaching it in "the vernacular", but from teaching Latin in one vernacular (French) to teaching it in a different vernacular (English). So why the switch?

There is a close relation between social groupings and the structure of disciplines. When a subject is opened up to new social groups, the discipline itself is prone to change. "English" at school and university is not the same on mainland Europe as it is for native speakers in the USA or Britain and Ireland. If this observation is correct, then it ought to be possible to reverse the equation and, when we note a significant change in the way a subject or discipline is treated, ask whether the change is not related to a change in the population. In the case under consideration it seems plausible to suppose that the change in the medium of instruction correlated with a change in the range of pupils. It seems as though the supply of candidates for employment coming from households where French was the language of communication was no longer sufficient, so that an increasing number of pupils were sent to school whose first language was English.

Pressure for change may have resulted from the inroads made into the population by the Black Death in the fourteenth century. It seems not unlikely that John Brian himself fell a victim to the plague: nothing more is recorded of him after he made his will in 1349 (Bland 1991: 90). Thirty years later, New College was founded on a piece of land adjacent to St Edmund Hall, Bruce Mitchell's college, expressly to counter the fewness of the clergy, arising from pestilence, wars and other miseries, and to convert poor and indigent scholars into men of learning fruitful to the church, the King and the realm (Sherwood & Pevsner 1974: 166).

The picture we have before us, then, is that John Brian of Cornwall first began to teach his pupils Latin in English around the mid-fourteenth century. This innovation spread through the influence of his students and, probably in the last decade of the century, the first texts of a new genre began to appear – of Latin grammars written in English. These texts mark the real beginning of a continuous tradition of vernacular grammar-writing in England. This, then, would seem to be the most plausible point at which to start looking for the imposition of Latin grammatical categories onto English.

Latin-teaching in England

To understand how the transfer took place, we need to look at the conditions under which the grammarians were working, and what they were trying to do.

Since at this time Latin was the language of higher education in England, the grammar master had to lay a foundation which would enable the pupil ultimately to understand, write and speak Latin. That it was unavoidable in the course of this process to speak *about* the language being taught (in other words, about the object-language – Latin), was taken for granted. In this situation, two options are in principle available – one can teach the new language by means of the language being taught (i.e. teach Latin grammar in Latin), or one can teach it through some other language (in this case, English). The roles assigned to Latin and English, as object-language and metalanguage respectively, in turn determine the choice of grammatical terminology: in the first case the terminology would be Latin, whereas in the latter a new vernacular terminology would be required.

The assumptions underlying this teaching in turn constrained the procedures. Central pillars of the method were parsing and analysis – analysis providing the necessary foundation for translation. In parsing a word, the pupil would be expected to state its primary syntactic category (PSC, or "part-of-speech" in the Middle Ages – cf. Lyons 1968: 274), its attributes or secondary grammatical categories (SGCs – case, number, tense etc.) and the values for these attributes (e.g. nominative, singular, preterite), together with the word's function. For instance, the pupil would be expected to parse "I" as: "a pronoun, first person, singular number, subject of the verb . . .". And to be able to translate into English, the pupil needed to understand the Latin original properly, which meant being able to analyse a sentence correctly. To help him to do this, various algorithms were available, such as "find the main verb . . ."; "look for the subject . . ."

The grammarian's task, then, was to teach Latin grammar; and the language used in teaching it was English. We would expect the grammatical categories – the parts-of-speech and the secondary grammatical categories – to be presented in such a way as to enable the pupil to identify them as unambiguously as possible, either by their form or by listing them, the lesson to be reinforced where necessary by Latin examples. And this is indeed what we find: "How do you know a noun substantive?" the master asks. The standard answer is that it can take one, or two, Latin articles: "For he may stonde by hymmself without þe helpe of a nodyr worde and is declyned in Laten with oon artikyll . . . or with ij at most as *hic et hec sacerdos*:" (F:16–19 – letters refer to the sigla in Thomson's *Edition*, 1984). This corresponds to the standard assignment of the roles of object-language and metalanguage, and the more-or-less standard procedure. But one does not have to read far into these texts before strange things begin to happen. To help the pupils, the master draws attention to comparable forms in English, as with the so-called present participles: "How knos þu a partycypull of þe presentens? By my Englysch and by my Latyn. How by þi Englysch and how by þi Latyn? Wen my Englysch endys with '-yng' and my Latyn endys in *-ens* or in *-ans* . . . as *amans*: 'louyng'" (A:249–53). In another step, the master asks the pupil to identify a particular "part of reason" (part-of-speech) – but this time the part-of-speech is no longer Latin, but English: "Qwat parte of reson is þis noun 'qweche' ['which']?" (W:19).

Similar patterns are evident when it comes to the secondary grammatical categories. The comparative of adjectives or adverbs (positive, comparative, superlative) is explained in Text A, for instance, by giving an English example (only!) for the positive: "How knos þu þe positiue degre? For he setys þe grownd of all oþer degres of comparisons and ys formyt of non, as 'whyt', 'blak', 'rede' . . ." (A:28–30); the comparative is explained by giving the Latin form (*magis*) and its English equivalent, but with only *English* examples: "he passys hys posytiue degre with þis aduerbe *magis*, and hys Englysch endys in '-vr' as 'whyttur', 'blakyr' . . ." (A:31–3). The superlative is treated similarly, Latin *maxime* being equated with English *-est*: "as 'wyttyst : most wyt', 'blakyst : most blak' . . ." (A:37).

In Text C, the process is carried further still, in that Latin is now no longer referred to, only English: "How knowyst þe posityf degre of aduerbe? For he endyth in Englysch most comunly in '-ly' as 'fayrly', 'goodly', 'swetely' and soche oþer" (C:485–7).

This curious situation, in which the roles of Latin and English seem to be becoming confused, is epitomized by the grammarians' treatment of case, the exposition of which is in some texts carried through exclusively with reference to English: "Whareby knawis þow þi case? By þaire takyns. Whylk er þay? Þe nominatif 'þe mayster', genitif 'of þe mayster', datif 'to þe mayster' . . ." (GG:3–5). These examples illustrate a process observable across a wide range of texts. At first, the forms or items discussed are exclusively Latin, and the examples are Latin. The next stage sees direct comparison being made between Latin categories and corresponding categories in English. In some texts this order then comes to be reversed, so that the pupil is first introduced to the categories in English, and these are then related to their Latin equivalents. In a fourth step, the categories are exemplified only on English, with no reference at all made to Latin, and no Latin examples. So much for parsing.

To translate, the pupil needed first to identify the principal verb in a sentence and then find its subject (its "nominative case"). Texts are extant, however, in which the author sails straight into the analysis of an *English* sentence, presumably as a preliminary to translating from English into Latin: " 'The church is a place which Cristen men ben much holden to luff.' Which is thi principall verbe in this reson ['sentence']?" (Y:1–2).

The pupils are thus being encouraged to speak – and think – of the two languages as if the grammatical categories were identical for both. What we witness, in other words, is a subtle change in the roles of Latin and English in successive steps. Latin – the object-language in step 1 – has been replaced by step 4, by English. This process gives rise to examples which border on the grotesque, in which the procedure the pupil is invited to perform is not logically possible, as in the definition of the impersonal verb: "Qwerby knowes þu a verbe impersonill? For he hase nouther nowmbur ni person ny nominatyf case, and is declinet in þe voyce of the thridde person, and comes in Englissh with one of these sygnes 'hit' or 'me', as 'Hit behose me to lorne,' *Oportet me adiscere*" (W:191–5). Here we are told that a significant class of Latin verbs takes no overt subject ("nominative case") and is conjugated in the third person. We are then told that the impersonal verb appears "in English" with one of the signs *it* or *me*. The example of an impersonal verb is, "It behoves me to learn", with the Latin equivalent *oportet me adiscere*. Note that the features listed apply – where they apply at all – to Latin: the English "It behoves me to learn" *has* an overt subject. Why does the author say, "and comes in English with . . ."? How can a Latin impersonal verb such as *oportet* "come in English" with anything? Clearly, what the author is trying to do is to get the pupil to fix the English equivalent of the Latin construction in his mind.

This is one of several instances where although a literal reading may fail to make much sense, one can see what the author is getting at. To understand it, the pupil has to juggle with equivalents in two languages; he has to mentally read into the text, where necessary, ideas such as "the equivalent in the other language". The grammatical categories of the two languages have to be fused in the mind of the pupil, and the pupil in his interpretation has to flit from the words of one language to the words of the other to make sense of it all.

A comparable example appears in the sentence used for analysis: "'A chirche is a place the wheche Crystyn menne bem [*sic* = 'are'] mecull [be]holdon to loue.' Wheche ys thy pryncypall uerbe in þis reson? 'Is.' When þis uerbe *sum, es, fui* is thy pryncypall uerbe, how schall þu knoo wheche ys thy nominatyue case? By þis Englyche worde 'Whoo or what?,' as 'Whoo or what ys? The chirche is' . . ." (U:33–8). How can a pupil identify the principal verb in an English sentence by looking for *sum, es* or *fui*? Again, although the writing may not be literally clear, one can see how the pupils were supposed to put it all together in a procedure not very different, perhaps, from some used today.

There are other examples in these texts in which the pupils are required to keep signals in the two languages apart in their minds before joining them together to make sense of an otherwise illogical text: " 'to' before a verbe ys syne of infynytyf mode, as *Iohannes amat audire doctrinam magistri...*" (B:197–8). How can *to* be a sign of the infinitive in a Latin sentence? How can *in* + *to* be a mark of the accusative in: "*Currit in campum Iohannes in quo pueri ludent.* This word *campum* is the accusatif case, for 'yn' with 'to' is sine of þe accusatif case" (BB:297–9). Latin sentences containing English *to* must have a probability of occurrence of around zero. Yet if both languages are held in suspension in the mind, as it were, and the appropriate equivalences set up: English 'into + field' corresponding to Latin *in campum* [Acc.], then the message becomes clear.

The Metalanguage

The way in which English almost imperceptibly slips into the role of object-language in these texts is not their only curious feature. In a sort of crossover movement, it seems at times as if Latin, too, were beginning to switch roles – to take over from English the role of metalanguage. Since Latin is the object of description it is of course natural that – in the form of examples and model sentences – it should be embedded in the English discourse. And since the English grammarians were drawing on a centuries-old tradition of Latin teaching, it is equally understandable that quotations from Latin sources such as Donatus should appear in Latin in the texts, and even that Latin hexameters should be given to the pupils to help them memorize rules and exceptions. The pupils would – even in lessons taught in English – frequently be given an illustrative example followed by an explanatory rule. This would be summarized in a Latin hexameter to be committed to memory:

Ihoannes et Robartus qui bene adiscunt diligentur a magistro. This relatiue *qui* ys the plurell number, for ij anticedens singuler w[ith] an *et* coniuncion copulatiue cum betwene will haue a relatiue plurell.

Post duo nomina singula des plurale relatum
(A:51–7)

It is also understandable that the teacher should accidentally use – or perhaps deliberately slip in – the occasional word or phrase in the language the pupils were learning, to help them get used to hearing it. Indeed, most of the texts contain examples of this kind. (It must be said at once that these texts can in no sense be taken as transcripts of classroom discourse – no one seems to have worked out the precise relation between the texts we have before us and the teaching. Nevertheless they do give some indication of the intention, if not a record, of how the teaching might have been done.) From this point of view, the texts offer a wide spectrum of usage – from texts which contain no Latin words whatsoever, via texts in which forms, examples and model sentences are in Latin, through texts with a liberal sprinkling of Latin words and phrases, to texts at the other end of the spectrum in which the discourse starts out in English but finishes entirely in Latin.

First to be introduced are the Latin words and phrases which it would be natural to slip in between Latin examples: such words as *vt*, *vel*, *exemplum*, *scilicet*. One can easily understand how if one were giving Latin examples it would be simpler to remain in the Latin mode than to switch back and forth for such short English words. Some phrases are the kind of thing we throw into our English conversation today – "i.e." (*id est*); "*et cetera*". From here, it would be a relatively simple step for the grammar master to fall back on other Latin terms, particularly when a vernacular terminology still remained to be fixed: such words as *nominativo*, *genitivo*, *dativo* etc. – and these again were sometimes embedded in larger teaching structures: "Quot modis regitur nominativus casus? Octo modis. Quibus?" – only for the discourse to continue in English once the question has been answered (Bland 1991: 171). Or, to make the comparative: ". . . as *albus*, *-ba*, *-bum*, genitiuo *albi*, addita *-or*, fit *albior* . . ." ('as *albus*, *-ba*, *-bum*, genitive *albi*, [with] *-or* added makes *albior*' – D:41–2). Such patterns may be varied by exceptions – "sed *iuuenis* facit *iunior*" ('but *iuuenis* makes *iunior*' – D:45–6) and may even alternate with parallel English structures: ". . . *facilis* do awey the *-s* and sette ther-to *-imus* and that makyth *facilimus*" ('*facilis* – take away the *-s* and add *-imus*, and that makes *facilimus*' – D:70–1 and cf. D:370–3 *et passim*).

Other texts are more highly saturated with Latin words, phrases and formulae. In some, the degree of saturation reaches a point at which the discourse has effectively switched into Latin. About two thirds of the way through Text EE, for instance, where the author explains how the verb *sum*, in *ego sum homo* governs both its subject and complement, he continues "*Homo* regitur in the same manere of *sum* . . ." ('*Homo* is governed in the same way by *sum*'). From this point on, the author increasingly slips into Latin until there are hardly any English words left in the text: "The accusatyf case is gouerned of the verbe in twey maners. O[ne] manere ex vi transicionis, vt *Video te*: *te* regitur de *video* ex vi transicionis. Quare? Quia verbum transitiuum est et regere potest accusatiuum casum, et cetera. Secundo modo . . ." ('The accusative is governed by the verb in two ways. One way [is] by "the power of transition" – Why? Because the verb is transitive and . . .' etc. – EE: 318–22).

The extreme of this role-reversal between object-language and metalanguage is reached in the verses which the authors lay down as an aid to memory. Although the discourse is essentially English it is, as we have seen, not unusual for rules already cast in Latin hexameters to be set for learning by heart. But what happens when – as we have also seen – reference is made to the grammar of English as opposed to Latin? There are instances in these texts in which the information encoded in the Latin hexameters for the pupils to commit to memory refers unambiguously to English. (In this extract, *quartum* means the fourth case, i.e. the accusative, whereas *sextum* is the sixth, the ablative):

> "Into" vult quartum, sine "to" vult ponere sextum.
> *In campo curro* si sis, bene dicis, in illo;
> Si sis exterius *in campum* sit tibi cursus
>
> (BB:300–2)

"Into" requires the fourth [case – i.e. acc. J.W.], without "to" use the sixth [ablative].
"I run in the field" – (if you are in it) – you say, correctly;
Should you be outside [it], your course will be "into the field" . . .

At this point, the reversal of the roles of English and Latin is more or less complete: English has become the object-language, Latin the metalanguage.

Forces for Change

In the light of the above, applying to English some of the grammatical categories originally devised for Latin can be seen as a natural consequence of an interplay between the task of the grammar master in a concrete situation and his assumptions as to how Latin was best learned and taught. Since reading, writing and speaking Latin were the long-term goals, and translation part of the chosen route, it was useful for pupils to view English structures through Latin spectacles – they needed to perceive equivalences between small chunks of the two languages from an early stage. The grammar masters tried to achieve this by juxtaposing those categories and equating them as closely as possible. Thus, though the Middle English of the texts displays scarcely more evidence of case than present day English, which has none (cf. Hudson 1995), since Latin had six cases which had to be translated into English, English equivalents had to be found for them.

Procedures of this kind provided the driving-force for the change of role we observed above. Far from being the result of ignorance or a clumsy oversight, it was in the masters' interests to encourage pupils to map the categories of Latin onto the structures of English, and to identify "English" categories in Latin texts. Though such an identification is not literally possible, it is psychologically possible, if one can see how the pupil is being required to juggle with the two languages, and mentally substitute the structures of one for the structures of the other.

In the same way as these procedures help to explain the apparent shift in the object-language from Latin to English, the long-term objectives help to explain the increasing use of Latin in these discourses. The occasional use of Latin words and phrases may be seen as slips, as momentary deviations in an otherwise monolingual discourse on the part of the teacher. They can also be seen, though, as a natural procedure for someone whose ultimate aim was to get his pupils to converse in Latin. By constantly hearing such words such as *vel*, *vt*, *exemplum* used in the classroom, and phrases such as *id est*, *et declinatur sic* ('and is declined thus'), or *vt per versus patet* ('as is known by the verses'), pupils could be encouraged to try a few Latin words and phrases themselves. That this was not a purely unconscious strategy is attested in texts HH and CC, in which the pupil, after identifying the case of a given NP in a Latin model sentence, is given the explanation in English, but is then called upon to re-phrase the explanation or rule in Latin: "What case ys *creatoris mei* in the Latyne byfore? The ienetyfe case, for casualle wordys [words having grammatical case – Thompson 1984: 282) þat perteyneth to oon thyng schall be set in leke case. Say thys in Latyn. *Casualea ad idem pertinencia in simili casu sunt ponenda*" (HH: 35–8 and cf. HH: 5ff.; 14ff. *et passim*).

Latin Terms

Although the task of the grammar masters and the conditions under which they carried out their task go some way to explaining how grammatical structures of English came to be analysed in terms of conceptual categories derived from Latin, it does little to explain the terms themselves. The view has been put forward that English at certain periods was somehow deficient in its capacity to convey scientific ideas. According to Schäfer, "Around 1500 English was incapable of providing a linguistic medium for traditional scholarship and for the rapidly developing scientific disciplines since it lacked the necessary terminologies" (Schäfer 1989: II, 1). This assumption runs counter to accepted linguistic doctrine. Linguistic orthodoxy has it that in principle every language has at its disposal the resources necessary to encode the concepts it requires, including the metalinguistic functions (Lyons 1980: 293). These resources include the capacity to invent new words (neologisms); derivation; compounding; borrowing; calquing; extending the meaning of a word – perhaps by metaphorical use; and periphrasis. English has deployed many of these resources, with different preferences at different times.

To create new words Old English made free use of both native and borrowed material. In applying the rules of derivational morphology, for instance, it was possible in Old English to attach native affixes to non-native roots. In *un-declin-igen-lic* ('indeclinable') the native affixes *un-* and *-igen-* have been attached to the Latin root of *declinare – declin-*. At first glance, this would seem to suggest that Old English had no native equivalent for *declinare*. However, Old English had – as German has – a verb which could be used as an alternative – *gebigan* based on the root 'bend'. Two possibilities for rendering the Latin *declinatio* (declension) were thus available in Old English: *declin + ung* and *ge-biged-nys*.

Old English also offered a range of possibilities for creating compounds. Latin *adverbium* was rendered as *wordes-gefera* ('word's-companion'). Where grammatical terms are concerned, however, by far the greater number was introduced by means of translation equivalents for Latin originals, i.e. calques. Thus we have Old English *word* as the equivalent of Latin *verbum*; or *gebigednys* (also) for Latin *casus* ('case') alongside the borrowed Old English *casus*. Particularly striking are those calques in which an element-for-element translation seems to have been adopted:

betwux-â-weorpen-nys for Latin *inter-ject-io* ('interjection') or *fore-set-nys* for Latin *prae-posit-io* ('preposition').

The Middle English terminology which begins to emerge towards the end of the fourteenth century draws more strongly on the Latin-Romance tradition. For instance, Middle English had *figure* (of speech) for Latin *figura* where Old English had *hîw*; it had *tense* for Latin *tempus* where Old English had *tîd* or *tîma*; it had *person* for Latin *persona* where Old English had *hâd*, and *degree* for Latin *gradvs* where Old English had *stæpe*. Where concepts were necessary for which no terms seemed to be readily available, the Middle English grammarians resorted to different strategies. Functional terms such as "subject" and "object" were not in common use, so "nominative case (to the verb)" and "accusative case (to the verb)" were used to denote subjects and objects, respectively. Nor were there current, commonly accepted terms for thematic relations such as "agent" or "patient".

Here the grammarians adopted one of three strategies not unlike those pursued in the same area of the grammar today. The first strategy is to postulate a small, finite set of core terms, such as "agent". The second assumes that the constellation of arguments determined by the valency of each individual verb is unique, and labels the thematic relations with names derived from the verb. And between these two extremes, in the Middle Ages there nestled a third, semi-abstract view which rendered the concept by means of a paraphrase.

Grammarians pursuing the first strategy used the terms *doer* and *sufferer* to denote "agent" and "patient". To identify the subject of a verb, the learner was instructed to see "whedyr hit betokyn 'to do' or 'to suffer', and 3yf hit betokyn 'to do' þe doer shall be nominatyf case and þe sufferar shall be suche case as þe verbe will haue after hym" (V:23–5). Grammarians pursuing the second denoted the agent by means of a derivative. In the case of "to lack" for instance, "*Desum, -es*, Englyshede 'to lacke' or 'want', is construed with a datyue case of þe lackar" (KK:21–2). The third expressed the relations periphrastically. For this group the agent became "þe þyng þat doþe þe dede of þe verbe" (Z:272–3) and the patient "the person þat the dede of the verbe passyth ynto" (HH:412–13).

If the terminological differences between Old English and Middle English cannot plausibly be ascribed to lack of resources in the language, how are they to be explained? In approaching this question it may be useful to divest ourselves of some of the knowledge we have accumulated over the past six hundred years. We think we know what the terminology of Middle English grammar was like because we can relate it to today's terminology. Furthermore, we know which of the words of this terminology came from French, from Latin or from Old or Middle English. We have to accept, however, that the grammarians of the period may have seen things differently. In making the choice between *time, tense* and *tempus,* or between *name* and *noun* they may have been as little interested in the origins of these words as the modern native-speaker is in the fact that *door, window* and *chair* are of Germanic, Old Norse and Romance origin respectively. Far from striving for a blanket application of an unsuitable Latinate terminology to English, the medieval grammar-master may be imagined as having a pool of terms at his disposal from which those we use today have emerged as the most appropriate by a sort of natural selection. Those who favour a "native" non-Latin terminology will be interested to learn that a number of pairs – or even triples – of words occur in the medieval grammatical texts, from which one or more of the candidates has gradually been removed. Thus, *kind* has given way as a possible rival to *gender; time* and *tempus* have disappeared in favour of *tense; name* in favour of *noun,* and so on.

There are good general and local reasons why this should have happened, and even why it should have happened in the way it did. Words closer to the native stock lead to potential confusion between our descriptions of the world and our descriptions of language. *Time* calls up in the mind an experiential concept, whereas *tense* fixes the mind on the object-of-description "language", which is not the same thing. Treating the categories of our construction of the world and our categories of grammar under the single term *time* does nothing to dispel the erroneous notion that because English divides our experience of time into three (past, present and future), the language must also have three tenses instead of two (past and non-past).

A further reason for preferring a Romance terminology to a Germanic one is its greater morphological flexibility. From "grammar" we can make "grammatical", "ungrammatical", "grammatically", "(un)grammaticality" etc. If we had stuck to the Old English *stæf-cræft* ('grammar'), would we want to be talking today about "staff-craft-y," "un-staff-crafty" and "un-staff-craft-ily"? And what would "(un)grammaticality" be? A further criterion which may have helped to eliminate some terms in preference to others may have been convenience in speech. If, every time we wanted to say *pluperfect,* we had to say *forþgewiten mare þonne fulfremed* instead ('past tense more than completed') we might (perhaps with the benefit of hindsight) conclude that *pluperfect* is simpler and more compact.

Apart from these more general considerations there were factors in the immediate context which help to explain the processes of selection further. First and foremost was the purpose to which the terminology was put. A Romance-based terminology was being used to teach pupils Latin grammar via the medium of a Germanic vernacular. It made sense to use words related to the words which the pupils would read in their Latin grammatical texts anyway, and words which were already being used in the Latin hexameters to commit rules and lists of exceptions to memory. Further, the fact that much of the terminology was ultimately taken from Latin via French is understandable at a time when a transition was being made from a tradition of teaching grammar in French to teaching it in English.

How the Leopard Got its Spots

The apparent switch in roles between object-language and metalanguage was the first step towards providing English with a new, comprehensive grammatical terminology. In the course of this role reversal, extensive areas of English syntax were brought within the scope of the new terminology. The significance of this step cannot be overestimated. It is doubtful whether we would describe many of the categories of English in the way we do if the terms and their concepts had not been delivered to us in advance by our metalanguage. Conversely, we find it difficult to identify categories for which we have not inherited terms, and very difficult to coin acceptable terms for any new category we may isolate. In other words, writers of grammars do indeed tend to discover in English the categories for which Latin has provided words, and overlook those for which Latin made no provision. Among the PSCs, for instance, "it is doubtful whether any general theory of syntax would bring together as members of the same syntactic class all the forms that are traditionally described as 'adverbs'" (Lyons 1968: 326). And among the secondary grammatical categories case, future (tense), passive (voice) and gender are at least problematic. Despite what is frequently retailed by popular books on English, there is no sound reason for postulating a category "case" in present-day English and, as far as the so-called passive is concerned, "if we were now starting for the first time to construct a grammar of modern English, without knowledge of or reference to the classics, it might never occur to us to postulate a passive voice at all" (McKerrow 1922: 163).

Against this, English has taken over terms for some modal structures such as *I will leave* . . . or *I would advise* . . . but not for others, such as *I must wait* . . . or *I can swim* . . . Why? ". . . the treatment of this subject has been needlessly complicated by those writers who speak of combinations with auxiliary verbs, e.g. *may he come* | *he may come* | *if he should come* | *he would come,* as if they were subjunctives of the verb *come* . . . Scholars would hardly have used these expressions if they had had only the English language to deal with . . . it is merely the fact that such combinations in some cases serve to translate simple subjunctives in German or Latin that suggests the use of such terms" (Jespersen 1924: 315).

These observations leave unresolved such important questions as how much of modern English grammatical description is still carried out along lines laid down in the Middle Ages, or what a grammatical description of English would look like if we could somehow magically remove the spectacles provided for us by the Latin terminology and start again from the raw data. Equally unclear are the changes which have taken place inside the systems – conceptual and terminological – on the long journey from their inception to today: which terms have been lost from the system? Which have been added, and why? Which terms have been retained in connection with a more or less unchanged concept (e.g. *person*) and which retained, but with a modified concept (e.g. *default*)?

To return to our introductory theses: if this sketch of how the grammatical categories of Latin came to be applied to English is – in its broad outlines – correct, then it goes some way towards explaining why the grammarians who stood at the beginning of this new development went about their task as they did. English grammar got its Latin categories not by accident, nor through incompetence, nor even (strictly speaking) as part of a programme to fix a universal vocabulary for the generative grammars of all languages, as Chomsky thought. The transfer of categories was rather the natural outcome of grappling with the task of teaching English students enough Latin to enable them to read, write, understand and converse in it. The identification of categories and their fusion in the two languages were something the methods and terminology were calculated to reinforce.

But this narrative has another moral. Structuralist linguists criticised earlier grammarians for describing other languages as if they were variants of Latin: if only the earlier grammarians had been more conscious of linguistic principles, it was argued, and had cast off their Latin-based preconceptions, they would not have fallen into error. This looks remarkably like P. Menard's hermeneutic programme in reverse – something along the lines of: "Get my training in linguistics; acquire my conscious awareness; know what I know; become *me*." If we want to understand the history of linguistics, then looking back from a vantage point in the present and evaluating the past in the light of what we know now is not a productive way of going about it. As Nettleship remarked in another context (and this is something which the history of linguistics shares with philology), "we must . . . fling modern analogies to the winds" (Nettleship 1887: 11).

References and Further Reading

Anon. (1911). *On the Terminology of Grammar. Being the Final Report of the Joint Committee on Grammatical Terminology*. London: John Murray.

Chomsky, N. (1964). The logical basis of linguistic theory. In: H. G. Lunt (ed.), *Proceedings of the Ninth International Congress of Linguists*, Cambridge, MA, 27–31 August 1962 (pp. 914–78). Den Haag: Mouton.

[Colet, J. & W. Lily] (1549). *A Shorte Introdvction of Grammar: Generally to be used in the Kynges Maiesties Dominions* . . . London: Wolfe.

Crystal, D. (1971). *Linguistics*. Harmondsworth: Penguin.

Dinneen, F. P. (1967). *An Introduction to General Linguistics*. New York: Holt, Rinehart & Winston.

Funke, O. (1941). *Die Frühzeit der englischen Grammatik*. Bern: Lang.

Hudson, R. A. (1995). Does English really have case? *Journal of Linguistics*, 31, 375–92.

Jespersen, O. (1924). *The Philosophy of Grammar*. London: George Allen & Unwin.

Levin, S. R. (1960). Comparing traditional and structural grammar. *College English*, 21, 260–5.

Lyons, J. (1968). *Introduction to Theoretical Linguistics*. Cambridge: Cambridge University Press.

Lyons, J. (1980). Rev. of Rey-Debove: *Le Métalangage: Étude linguistique du discours sur le langage*. Paris: Le Robert, 1978. *Journal of Linguistics*, 16, 292–300.

McKerrow, R. B. (1922). English grammar and English grammars. *Essays and Studies*, VIII, 148–67.

Menzer, M. J. (2004). Ælfric's English *Grammar*. *JEGP*, 103, 106–24.

Nettleship, H. (1887). *The Study of Modern European Languages and Literatures in the University of Oxford*. Oxford: Parker.

Padley, G. A. (1985–1988). *Grammatical Theory in Western Europe: trends in vernacular grammar*, 2 vols. Cambridge: Cambridge University Press.

Robins, R. H. (1994). William Bullokar's *Bref Grammar for English*: text and context. In: G. Blaicher & B. Gläser (eds), *Anglistentag 1993 Eichstätt: proceedings* (pp. 19–31). Tübingen: Niemeyer.

Schäfer, J. (1989). *Early Modern English Lexicography*, 2 vols. Oxford: Clarendon Press.

Sherwood, J. & Pevsner, N. (1974). *Oxfordshire.* (The Buildings of England). Harmondsworth: Penguin.

Vorlat, E. (1975). *The Development of English Grammatical Theory 1586–1737.* Leuven: Leuven University Press.

Walmsley, J. (1998). English grammatical terminology from the 16th century to the present. In L. Hoffmann, H. Kalverkämper & H. E. Wiegand (eds), *Fachsprachen. Languages for Special Purposes: an international handbook of special-language and terminology research*, vol. 2 (pp. 2494–502). Berlin: Walter de Gruyter.

A Bibliography of
Writings by Bruce Mitchell
1956–2004

1956

Review: *The Concessive Relation in Old English Poetry* by Randolph Quirk. Yale Studies in English 124 (1954). xiv + 150 pp. 32s. 6d. *MÆvum*, XXV, 36–40.

1958

Review: *The Peterborough Chronicle 1070–1154*, ed. Cecily Clark (Oxford: 1958). *The Oxford Magazine*, 77, 48.

1959

Subordinate clauses in Old English poetry, Oxford University DPhil dissertation.

1960

Review: *Syntax und Semantik der modalen Hilfsverben im Altenglischen: "magan," "motan," "sculan," "willan"*. Von Ewald Standop (Beiträge zur englischen Philologie, 38. Heft). H. Pöppinghaus, Bochum-Langendreer, 1957; pp. 178. *N&Q*, CCV, 273–4.

1962

Review: *The Use of English* by Randolph Quirk (London, 1962). *The Oxford Magazine*, 3, 124.

Review: *The Published Writings of Eilert Ekwall*: a bibliography by Olof von Feilitzen. CWK Gleerup, Lund, and Ejnar Munksgaard, Copenhagen, 1961. 52 pp. No price given. *MÆvum*, XXXI, 228.

1963

The '*Use of English*' paper. *The Oxford Magazine*, 3, 180–3.
'Until the dragon comes . . .' Some thoughts on *Beowulf*. *Neophilologus*, 47, 126–38.
Old English syntactical notes. *N&Q*, CCVIII, 326–8.
The couplet system in *Havelok the Dane*. *N&Q*, CCVIII, 405–6.
Adjective clauses in Old English poetry. *Anglia*, 81, 298–322.

1964

A Guide to Old English. Oxford: Basil Blackwell.
Pearl, lines 609–610. *N&Q*, CCIX, 47.
Pronouns in Old English poetry: some syntactical notes. *RES*, n.s. XV, No. 58, 129–41.
Syntax and word-order in the *Peterborough Chronicle* 1122–1154. *NM*, LXV, 113–44.
The faery world of *Sir Orfeo*. *Neophilologus*, 48, 155–9.
Review: *An Introduction to the Pronunciation of English*. By A. C. Gimson. Pp. xvi + 294. London: Arnold, 1962. 30s. net. *RES*, n.s. XV, 113–15.
Review: *Twelve* Beowulf *Papers 1940–1960. With additional comments*. By Adrien Bonjour. Pp. 194. Neuchâtel: Faculté des Lettres; Genève: Librairie E. Droz, 1962. *RES*, n.s. XV, 306–7.
Review: *An Anthology of* Beowulf *Criticism*. Edited by Lewis E. Nicholson. Pp. xii + 386. Notre Dame: University of Notre Dame Press, 1963. $2.50. *RES*, n.s. XV, 414–15.

1965

The Battle of Maldon and Other Old English Poems. Trans. K. Crossley-Holland, introduced and edited by Bruce Mitchell. London: Macmillan. Repr. 1966, 1974, and in Papermac edition 1967.
Some problems of mood and tense in Old English. *Neophilologus*, 49, 44–57.
Bede's *habere* – Old English *magan*? *NM*, LXVI, 107–11.
The status of *hwonne* in Old English. *Neophilologus*, 49, 157–60.
Review: *La Structure de la Phrase Verbale à l'Époque Alfrédienne* by Paul Bacquet. (Publications de la Faculté des Lettres de l'Université de Strasbourg 145), Paris, 1962. 775 pp. *MÆvum*, XXXIV, 244–5.

1966

Review: Paul Bacquet, *La Structure de la Phrase Verbale à l'Époque Alfrédienne* (Publications de la Faculté des Lettres de l'Université de Strasbourg, 145), Paris, 1962. 775 pp. *NM*, LXVII, 86–97.

Review: *The Structure of Beowulf*. By Kenneth Sisam. Pp. vi + 88. Oxford: Clarendon Press, 1965. 18s net. *RES*, n.s. XVII, 190–1.

1967

An Old English syntactical reverie. '*The Wanderer*', lines 22 and 34–36. *NM*, LXVIII, 139–49.

Swa in Caedmon's Hymn, line 3. *N&Q*, CCXII, 203–4.

Vale atque ave (Address before the Graduate School Convocation at the 199th Annual Commencement of Brown University, Providence, Rhode Island, 5 June 1967). *Brown Alumni Monthly*, 67(9), 27–9.

Old English prose and the computer. *Modern Language Association of America Old English Newsletter*, 1(2), 4–5.

Review: *Chicken Inspector no. 23*, by S. J. Perelman. New York, 1966. *Brown Alumni Monthly*, 67(4), 26.

Short Notice: *The Wanderer*. Edited by R. F. Leslie. Pp. x + 100 (Old and Middle English Texts). Manchester: University Press, 1966. 12s. 6d. net. *RES*, n.s. XVIII, 104.

1968

A Guide to Old English, 2nd edn. Oxford: Basil Blackwell. Repr. 1971, 1975, 1978, 1981.

Beowulf. Trans. K. Crossley-Holland, introduced by Bruce Mitchell. London: Macmillan, and in Noonday paperbacks. Repr. 1970, 1972.

More musings on Old English syntax. *NM*, LXIX, 53–63.

Some syntactical problems in *The Wanderer*. *NM*, LXIX, 172–98.

Two syntactical notes on *Beowulf*. *Neophilologus*, 52, 292–9.

Review: *Sweet's Anglo-Saxon Reader in Prose and Verse* (Fifteenth Edition). Revised throughout by Dorothy Whitelock. Pp. xiv + 404. Oxford: Clarendon Press, 1967. 25s. net. *RES*, n.s. XIX, 415–16.

1969

Five notes on Old English syntax. *NM*, LXX, 70–84.

Postscript on Bede's *mihi cantare habes*. *NM*, LXX, 369–80.

Review: *A Reading of* Beowulf. By Edward B. Irving, Jr. Pp. x + 256. New Haven and London: Yale University Press, 1968. 54s. net. *RES*, n.s. XX, 202–4.

1970

Introduction to *Beowulf*, in a translation by K. Crossley-Holland. Argo Record Company ZPL 1057.

Introduction to the *Battle of Maldon* and other Old English Poems, in a translation by K. Crossley-Holland. Argo Record Company ZPL 1058.

[Contribution]. In A. Cameron, R. Frank & J. Leyerle (eds), *Computers and Old English Concordances* (pp. 83–7). Toronto: University of Toronto in association with the Centre for Medieval Studies, University of Toronto.

The subject–noun object–verb pattern in the *Peterborough Chronicle*. A reply. *NM*, LXXI, 611–14.

Review: *Old English Poetry: fifteen essays*. Edited by R. P. Creed. Pp. xii + 332. Providence: Brown University Press, 1967. $10.00. *RES*, n.s. XXI, 185–6.

Review: *A Descriptive Syntax of the* Ormulum by Robert A. Palmatier. The Hague and Paris, 1969. *MÆvum*, XXXIX, 370–3.

1971

Review: *A Descriptive Syntax of Old English Charters* by Charles Carlton. Mouton, The Hague and Paris, 1970. 200pp. Dutch guilders 48. *MÆvum*, XL, 181–4.

1972

The narrator of *The Wife's Lament*. Some syntactical problems reconsidered. *NM*, LXXIII, 222–34.

Review: *An Analysis of Syntactic Patterns of Old English*. By Faith F. Gardner. Pp. 88 (Janua Linguarum Studia Memoriae Nicolai van Wijk dedicata Series Practica, 140). The Hague: Mouton, 1971. D. fl. 24.00. *RES*, n.s. XXIII, 461–3.

1973

Review: *The Guest-Hall of Eden: four essays on the design of Old English poetry*. By Alvin A. Lee. Pp. x + 244. New Haven and London: Yale University Press, 1972. £3.95 net. *RES*, XXIV, 195–6.

Review: *The Interpretation of Old English Poems*. By Stanley B. Greenfield. Pp. x + 188. Boston and London: Routledge & Kegan Paul, 1972. £2.50 net. *RES*, XXIV, 319–21.

1974

The *'fuglas scyne'* of *The Phoenix*, line 591. In R. B. Burlin & E. B. Irving, Jr. (eds), *Old English Studies in Honour of John C. Pope* (pp. 255–61). Toronto: University of Toronto Press.

Bede's account of the poet Caedmon: two notes. In G. Turville-Petre & J. S. Martin (eds), *Iceland and the Mediaeval World: studies in honour of Ian Maxwell* (pp. 126–31). Melbourne.

Review: *Imperative Constructions in Old English*. By Celia M. Millward. (Janua Linguarum, Series Practica, 124). The Hague: Mouton. 1971. 75pp. Price D. fl. 15. *ES*, 55, 387–9.

Review: *The Language of the Parker Chronicle*, Volume II: *Word-Formation and Syntax*. By C. Sprockel. Pp. xiv + 284. The Hague: Martinus Nijhoff, 1973. Fl. 45.00. *RES*, n.s. XXV, 452–4.

1975

Linguistic facts and the interpretation of Old English poetry. *ASE*, 4, 11–28.

Short titles of Old English texts (with C. Ball & A. Cameron). *ASE*, 4, 207–21.

1976

No 'house is building' in Old English. *ES*, 57, 385–9.

The expression of extent and degree in Old English. *NM*, LXXVII, 25–31.

Some problems involving Old English periphrases with *beon/wesan* and the present participle. *NM*, LXXVII, 478–91.

1977

Old English *ac* as an interrogative particle. *NM*, LXXVIII, 98–100.

Short Notice: *English–Old English, Old English–English Dictionary*. Edited by Gregory K. Jember with John C. Carrell, Robert P. Lundquist, Barbara M. Olds, Raymond P. Tripp, Jr. Pp. xxxiv + 178. Boulder, Col.: Westview Press, 1975. *RES*, n.s. XXVIII, 248.

1978

Prepositions, adverbs, prepositional adverbs, postpositions, separable prefixes, or inseparable prefixes, in Old English? *NM*, LXXIX, 240–57.

Old English *oð þæt* adverb? *N&Q*, CCXXIII, 390–4.

1979

Old English *self*. Four syntactical notes. *NM*, LXXX, 39–45.

F. Th. Visser, *An Historical Syntax of the English Language*: some caveats concerning Old English. *ES*, 60, 537–42.

Short titles of Old English texts: addenda and corrigenda (with C. Ball & A. Cameron). *ASE*, 8, 331–3.

The language of Shakespeare. *Spicilegio Moderno. Letteratura Lingue Idee*, 12, 3–17.

Review: The Long Crendon Resurrection Plays from the York Cycle, 1979 performance. *The Crendon Crier*, 6–7 May.

Review: *A Concordance to the Anglo-Saxon Poetic Records*, edited by J. B. Bessinger, Jr.; programmed by Philip H. Smith, Jr.; with an index of compounds compiled by Michael W. Twomey. Ithaca and London: Cornell University Press, 1978; pp. xxxviii, 1510; £31.50. *N&Q*, CCXXIV, 347–9.

Review: *Les Propositions Relatives en Vieil-Anglais* by Georges Bourcier. Editions Honoré Champion, Paris, 1977. iv + 626 pp. 120 FF. *MÆvum*, XLVIII, 121–2.

Short Notice. *AT versus ON, IN, BY: on the early history of spatial AT and certain primary ideas distinguishing AT from ON, IN, BY.* By Karl-Gunnar Lindkvist. Pp. 90. (Acta Universitatis Stockholmiensis, Stockholm Studies in English XLVIIII). Stockholm: Almqvist & Wiksell International, 1978. *RES*, n.s. XXX, 244.

1980

The dangers of disguise: Old English texts in modern punctuation. *RES*, n.s. XXXI, 385–413.

Prepositions, adverbs, prepositional adverbs, postpositions, separable prefixes, or inseparable prefixes in Old English? A supplementary bibliography (with A. Kingsmill). *NM*, LXXXI, 313–17.

Review: Genesis A. *A New Edition.* Edited by A. N. Doane. Pp. xiv + 416. Madison and London: The University of Wisconsin Press, 1978. £24.50 net. *Waldere.* Edited by Arne Zettersten. Pp. viii + 40. Manchester: University Press, 1979. £4.50 net. *RES*, n.s. XXXI, 198–200.

1982

A Guide to Old English Revised with Texts and Glossary (with Fred C. Robinson), 3rd edn. Oxford: Basil Blackwell. Repr. 1983, 1984.

Beowulf, lines 3074–3075: The damnation of Beowulf? *Poetica* (Tokyo), 13, 15–26.

Old English *man* 'one': two notes. In: J. M. Anderson (ed.), *Language Form and Linguistic Variation: papers dedicated to Angus McIntosh* (pp. 277–84). (Amsterdam Studies in the Theory and History of Linguistic Science, IV. Current Issues in Linguistic Theory, 15). Amsterdam: John Benjamins.

1983

Bruce Mitchell, *Old English Syntax* (OUP): a preview. *Medieval English Studies Newsletter* (Tokyo), 8, 3–7.

A preview of *Old English Syntax. Revista Canaria de estudios ingleses*, 7, 155–8 (reprint of previous item).

A note on negative sentences in *Beowulf*. *Poetica* (Tokyo), 9–12, 15–16.

Review: *Anglo-Saxon Oral Poetry: a study of the traditions.* By Jeff Opland. Pp. xii + 290. New Haven and London: Yale University Press, 1980. £12.60 net. *RES*, n.s. XXXIV, 200–1.

Review: *A Bibliography of Publications on Old English Literature to the End of 1972.* By Stanley B. Greenfield and Fred C. Robinson using the collections of E. E. Ericson. Pp. xxii + 438. Toronto and Buffalo: University of Toronto Press, 1980. Published in Great Britain by Manchester University Press, 1980. £35. *RES*, n.s. XXXIV, 320–1.

1984

The origin of Old English conjunctions: some problems. In J. Fisiak (ed.), *Historical Syntax* (Trends in Linguistic Studies and Monographs 23) (pp. 271–99). Berlin: Mouton.

Review: *Old English Syntax: a handbook.* By John McLaughlin. Pp. xii + 106 (Sprachstrukturen, Reihe A: Historische Sprachstrukturen 4). Tübingen: Max Niemeyer Verlag, 1983. DM 28. *RES*, n.s. XXXV, 217–18.

1985

Old English Syntax, 2 vols. Oxford: Clarendon Press. Repr. 1985, 1987, 1997–8.

Approaches to life. An address at Jiju-Gakuen School, Tokyo, 20 November 1984. *Gakuen Shinbun* (*Papers of the Jiju Gakuen*), 356, 4 and 357, 4.

Caedmon's Hymn, line 1: what is the subject of *scylun* or its variants? *Sources and Relations: studies in honour of J. E. Cross. LSE*, 16, 190–7.

Some lexicographical problems posed by Old English grammar words (with S. Butler). In A. Bammesberger (ed.), *Problems of Old English Lexicography. Studies in memory of Angus Cameron* (Eichstätter Beiträge Abteilung Sprache und Literatur Band 15) (pp. 79–89). Regensburg: Friedrich Pustet.

The syntax of *The Seafarer*, lines 50–52. *RES*, XXXVI, 535–7.

1986

A Guide to Old English. Revised with prose and verse texts and glossary (with Fred C. Robinson), 4th edn. Oxford: Basil Blackwell. Repr. 1987, 1988, 1990, 1991.

Short Notice: *Learning and Literature in Anglo-Saxon England: studies presented to Peter Clemoes on the occasion of his sixty-fifth birthday.* Edited by Michael Lapidge and Helmut Gneuss. Pp. xiv + 460. Cambridge: Cambridge University Press, 1985. £45 net. *RES*, n.s. XXXVII, 550–1.

Short Notice: *The Old English Catalogue Poems.* By Nicholas Howe. Pp. 208. (Anglistica XXIII). Copenhagen: Rosenkilde & Bagger, 1985. Da. kr. 290. *RES*, n.s. XXXVII, 624.

1987

Old English Syntax: happy second birthday? *Old English Newsletter*, 20, 2, A30–1.

Short Notice: *Studies in Earlier Old English Prose: sixteen original contributions.* Edited by Paul E. Szarmach. Pp. vi + 420. Albany, N.Y.: State University of New York Press, 1986. Cloth, $49.50; paper, $19.50. *RES*, n.s. XXXVIII, 291.

1988

On Old English. Selected papers. Oxford: Basil Blackwell.

Relative and personal pronouns in *Beowulf*: eight notes. In K. Oshitari, Y. Ikegami, E. Suzuki, S. Sato, T. Kubouchi, Y. Yano & S. Karakida (eds), *Philologia Anglica: essays presented to Professor Yoshio Terasawa on the occasion of his sixtieth birthday* (pp. 3–12). Tokyo: Kenkyusha.

Beowulf, line 1020b: *brand* or *bearn*? In M. A. D'Aronco, A. M. Luiselli Fadda & M. V. Molinari (eds), *Studi sulla Cultura Germanica dei Secoli IV–XII in onore di Giulia Mazzuoli Porru* (Romano Barbarica, 10) (pp. 283–92). Rome: Herder.

1989

Beowulf: six notes, mainly syntactical. In G. Barnes, S. Jensen, L. Jobling & D. Lawton (eds), *Studies in Honour of H. L. Rogers*, LSE, n.s. XX, 311–18.

Preview of Bruce Mitchell, *Old English Syntax: a critical bibliography of publications to the end of 1984* (Oxford: Basil Blackwell, forthcoming). *Medieval English Studies Newsletter* (Tokyo), 20, 13–14.

Review: Daniel Donoghue, *Style in Old English Poetry: the test of the auxiliary* (Yale Studies in English, 196). New Haven and London: Yale University Press, 1987. Pp. xiii, 234; numerous tables. $30. *Speculum*, 64, 407–9.

1990

A Critical Bibliography of Old English Syntax to the End of 1984 including Addenda and Corrigenda to Old English Syntax. Oxford: Basil Blackwell.

Extracts from lectures given in Japan April 1989. *Medieval English Studies Newsletter* (Tokyo), 21, 33–5.

Shigeru Ono: an appreciation. In Koichi Jin *et al.* (eds), *Studies in English Philology in Honour of Shigeru Ono* (pp. 11–13). Tokyo: Nan'un-do.

Old English Syntax: a review of the reviews. *NM*, XCI, 273–93.

Review: *The B Text of the Old English Bede: a linguistic commentary*, by Raymond J. S. Grant, Costerus NS 73 (Amsterdam: Rodopi, 1989). *MÆvum*, XLI, 380–1.

1991

Ælfric's *Catholic Homilies* ii. 440.20: an example of *habban* with the accusative and infinitive? *N&Q*, CCXXXVI, 17–18.

Prefatory note to The function and development of prefixes and particles in three early English texts. In Y. Niwa (ed.), *The Beginning of the Phrasal Verb Volume I* (p. i). Tokyo: Kinseido.

1992

H. M. Chadwick, *The Study of Anglo-Saxon: fifty years on* (H. M. Chadwick Memorial Lectures, 2). Cambridge: University of Cambridge Department of Anglo-Saxon, Norse and Celtic.

A Guide to Old English with Prose and Verse Texts and Glossary (with Fred C. Robinson), 5th edn. Oxford: Basil Blackwell. Repr. 1992 (twice), 1994, 1995, 1996 (twice), 1997 (twice), 1998, 1999, 2000.

A Critical Bibliography of Old English Syntax: supplement 1985–1988 (with S. Irvine). *NM*, XCIII, 1–56.

Literary lapses: six notes on *Beowulf* and its critics. *RES*, n.s. XLIII, 1–17.

Parataxis and hypotaxis. A review of some terms used for Old English syntax (with Daniel Donoghue). *NM*, XCIII, 163–83.

How to study Old English syntax? In M. Rissanen, O. Ihalainen, T. Nevalainen & I. Taavitsainen (eds), *History of English: new methods and interpretations in historical linguistics* (Topics in English Linguistics 10) (pp. 92–100). Berlin: Mouton de Gruyter.

Consolidated index of authors and reviewers to *A Critical Bibliography of Old English Syntax and 'Supplement 1985–1988.'* *NM*, XCIII.1 (1992). Privately printed (with S. Irvine).

1993

Five notes on Old English syntax. In R. Hiltunen, M. Gustafsson, K. Battarbee & L. Dahl (eds), *English Far and Wide: a festschrift for Inna Koskenniemi* (Annales Universitatis Turkuensis B: 197) (pp. 143–52). Turku: Turun Yliopisto.

Bruce Mitchell, *An Invitation to Old English and Anglo-Saxon England*: a preview. *Medieval English Studies Newsletter* Tokyo, 29, 20–4.

1994

The Englishness of Old English. In M. Godden, D. Gray & T. Hoad (eds), *From Anglo-Saxon to Early Middle English: studies presented to E. G. Stanley* (pp. 163–81). Oxford: Clarendon Press.

1995

Bruce Mitchell, *An Invitation to Old English and Anglo-Saxon England* (Oxford: Basil Blackwell, 1995). *Teachers of Old English in Britain and Ireland Newsletters*, 1, 2.

An Invitation to Old English and Anglo-Saxon England. Oxford: Basil Blackwell. Repr. 1996 (twice), 1997 (twice), 1998, 2000.

Interview: on Old English studies today. A. Bravo Garcia & Bruce Mitchell, *Journal of the Spanish Society for Mediaeval English Language and Literature*, 4, 133–9.

'Fredesleod' [a poem in honour of Fred C. Robinson]. *Medieval English Studies Newsletter* (Tokyo), 33, 38–9.

J. R. R. Tolkien and Old English studies: an appreciation. In P. Reynolds & G. Goodknight (eds), *Proceedings of the Conference held at Keble College, Oxford, England, 17th–24th August 1992 to celebrate the centenary of the birth of Professor J. R. R. Tolkien* (pp. 206–12). Milton Keynes and Altadena: The Tolkien Society & The Mythopoeic Press.

1996

A Critical Bibliography of Old English Syntax: supplement 1989–1992 (with S. Irvine). *NM*, XCVII, Part I: 1–28; Part II: 121–61; Part III: 255–78.

1997

A preview of *Beowulf: an edition with relevant shorter texts. Bruce Mitchell and Fred C. Robinson, including 'Archaeology and Beowulf' by Leslie Webster* (Oxford: Basil Blackwell) (with Fred C. Robinson). *Medieval English Studies Newsletter* (Tokyo), 36, 19–22.

Unexpressed principal clauses in Old English? In T. Nevalainen & L. Kahlas-Tarkka (eds), *To Explain the Present: studies in the changing English language in honour of Matti Rissanen* (Mémoires de la Société Néophilologique de Helsinki Tome LII) (pp. 125–34). Helsinki: Société Néophilologique.

The sign 7 in the annal for 871 in the Parker Chronicle, MS Cambridge, Corpus Christi College 173. In J. Roberts & J. L. Nelson with M. Godden (eds), *Alfred the Wise: studies in honour of Janet Bately on the occasion of her sixty-fifth birthday* (pp. 127–33). Cambridge: D. S. Brewer.

1998

The *Dream of the Rood* repunctuated. In: P. S. Baker & N. Howe (eds), *Words and Works: studies in medieval English language and literature in honour of Fred C. Robinson* (pp. 143–57). Toronto: University of Toronto Press.

Beowulf: an edition with relevant shorter texts, including 'Archaeology and Beowulf' by Leslie Webster (with Fred C. Robinson). Oxford: Blackwell. Repr. 2000.

1999

APO KOINOU in Old English poetry? *NM*, C, 477–97.

2000

Beowulf *Repunctuated* (with S. Irvine) (*Old English Newsletter* Subsidia 29). The Medieval Institute, Western Michigan University and its Richard Rawlinson Center for Anglo-Saxon Studies.

Graham. St Edmund Hall Oxford, 1941–1999 (with R. Alton). London: Farrand Press.

2001

A Guide to Old English Revised with Prose and Verse Texts and Glossary (with Fred Robinson), 6th edn. Oxford: Basil Blackwell.

2002

A Critical Bibliography of Old English Syntax: supplement 1993–1996 (with S. Irvine). *NM*, CIII, Part I: 3–32; Part II: 179–204; Part III: 275–304.

Phoenix 71–84 and 424–42: two syntactical cruces involving punctuation, *American Notes and Queries*, 15, 38–45.

2003

Some differences between the syntax of Old English prose and of Old English poetry. Extracts from a lecture given at the University of St Petersburg on 26 April 2002. Supplement to *Yazyk i rechevaya deyatel' nost'* (*Language and Language Behaviour*), 5. *The Linguistic Society of St Petersburg Lecture Series*, 38–51.

2004

Old English *befeallen* in Beowulf, line 1126a. *NM*, CV, 187–9.

In Press

A Many-Coloured Life. School Teacher: Army Officer: Businessman: Oxford Don and Old English Syntactician. An Autobiography of Bruce Mitchell.

The relation between Old English alliterative verse and Ælfric's alliterative prose.

Some reflections on the punctuation of Old English prose.

In Preparation

A Critical Bibliography of Old English Syntax: supplement 1997–2000 (with S. Irvine).

Select Bibliography

Baker, P. S. & Howe, N. (eds) (1998). *Words and Works: studies in medieval English language and literature in honour of Fred C. Robinson*. Toronto: University of Toronto Press.

Bessinger, J. B. & Kahrl, S. J. (eds) (1968). *Essential Articles for the Study of Old English Poetry*. Hamden, CT: Archon Books.

Bessinger, J. B. & Smith, P. H. (1978). *A Concordance to The Anglo-Saxon Poetic Records*. Ithaca, NY: Cornell University Press.

Blockley, M. E. (2001). *Aspects of Old English Poetic Syntax: where clauses begin*. Urbana, IL: University of Illinois Press.

Bosworth, J. & Toller, T. N. (eds) (1882–98). *An Anglo-Saxon Dictionary*. London: Oxford University Press.

Callaway Jr, M. (1913). *The Infinitive in Anglo-Saxon*. Washington, DC: Carnegie Institution.

†Cameron, A., †Amos, A. C. & Healey, A. diP. (eds) (2003). *The Dictionary of Old English: A to F*. Toronto: Pontifical Institute of Mediaeval Studies for the Dictionary of Old English Project.

Campbell, A. (1959). *Old English Grammar*. Oxford: Clarendon Press.

Campbell, A. (1972). *Anglo-Saxon Dictionary*. See under Toller, J.

Clemoes, P. & Hughes, K. (eds) (1971). *England before the Conquest: studies in primary sources presented to Dorothy Whitelock*. Cambridge: Cambridge University Press.

Frantzen, A. J. (ed.) (1991). *Speaking Two Languages: traditional disciplines and contemporary theory in medieval studies*. Albany, NY: State University of New York Press.

Gneuss, H. (2001). *Handlist of Anglo-Saxon Manuscripts: a list of manuscripts and manuscript fragments written or owned in England up to 1,100* (Medieval and Renaissance Texts and Studies, 241). Tempe, AZ: Arizona Center for Medieval and Renaissance Studies.

Godden, M., Gray, D. & Hoad, T. (eds) (1994). *From Anglo-Saxon to Early Middle English: studies presented to E. G. Stanley*. Oxford: Clarendon Press.

Greenfield, S. B. & Robinson, F. C. (eds) (1980). *A Bibliography of Publications on Old English to the end of 1972. Using the collection of E. E. Ericson.* Toronto: Toronto University Press.

Healey, A. diP. & Venezky, R. L. (1980). *A Microfiche Concordance to Old English.* Toronto: The Dictionary of Old English Project, Centre for Mediaeval Studies.

Holthausen, F. (1934). *Altenglisches etymologisches Wörterbuch.* Heidelberg: Carl Winter.

Kemble, J. M. (1837). *A Translation of the Anglo-Saxon Poem* Beowulf *with a Copious Glossary, Preface and Philological Notes.* London: William Pickering.

Ker, N. R. (1957). *Catalogue of Manuscripts Containing Anglo-Saxon.* Oxford: Clarendon Press.

Kuhn, H. (1933). Zur Wortstellung und -betonung im Altgermanischen. *BGDSL,* 57, 1–109.

Kytö, M. (1996). *Manual to the Diachronic Part of the Helsinki Corpus of English Texts: coding conventions and lists of source text,* 3rd edn. Helsinki: University of Helsinki, Department of English.

Lapidge, M. & Gneuss, H. (eds) (1985). *Learning and Literature in Anglo-Saxon England: studies presented to Peter Clemoes on the occasion of his sixty-fifth birthday.* Cambridge: Cambridge University Press.

Liuzza, R. M. (2000). *Beowulf: A New Verse Translation.* Peterborough, Ontario: Broadview Press.

Mitchell, B. (1968). Some syntactical problems in *The Wanderer. NM,* LXIX, 172–98. Repr. in B. Mitchell (1988) *On Old English* (pp. 99–117).

Mitchell, B. (1980). The dangers of disguise: Old English texts in modern punctuation. *RES,* XXXI, 385–413. Repr. in B. Mitchell (1988) *On Old English* (pp. 172–202).

Mitchell, B. (1985). *Old English Syntax,* 2 vols. Oxford: Clarendon Press.

Mitchell, B. (1988). *On Old English: selected papers.* Oxford: Basil Blackwell.

Mitchell, B. (1994). The Englishness of Old English. In M. Godden, D. Gray & T. Hoad (eds) (pp. 163–79).

Mitchell, B. (1995). *An Invitation to Old English and Anglo-Saxon England.* Oxford: Blackwell.

Mitchell, B., Ball, C. & Cameron, A. (1975). Short titles of Old English texts. *ASE,* 4, 207–21.

Mitchell, B., Ball, C. & Cameron, A. (1979). Short titles of Old English texts: addenda and corrigenda. *ASE,* 8, 207–21.

Mitchell, B. & Robinson, F. C. (2001). *Guide to Old English,* 6th edn. Oxford: Blackwell.

Momma, H. (1997). *The Composition of Old English Poetry* (CSASE, 20). Cambridge: Cambridge University Press.

Mugglestone, L. (ed.) (2000). *Lexicography and the OED: pioneers in the untrodden forest.* Oxford: Oxford University Press.

Mustanoja, T. F. (1960). *A Middle English Syntax*. Pt. I. *Parts of Speech* (Mémoires de la Société Néophilologique de Helsinki, XXIII). Helsinki: Société Néophilologique.

Nicholson, L. E. & Frese, D. W. (eds) (1975). *Anglo-Saxon Poetry: essays in appreciation for John C. McGalliard*. Notre Dame: University of Notre Dame Press.

O'Brien O'Keeffe, K. (1990). *Visible Song: transitional literacy in Old English verse* (CSASE, 4). Cambridge: Cambridge University Press.

Rosier, J. L. (ed.) (1970). *Philological Essays: studies in Old and Middle English language and literature in honour of Herbert Dean Meritt* (Janua Linguarum, Series Maior, 37). The Hague: Mouton.

Sievers, E. (1882). *Angelsächsische Grammatik*. Halle: M. Niemeyer (3rd edn 1898; rev. edn, Brunner, K. & Sievers, E. (1942) *Altenglische Grammatik: nach der Anglesächsischen Grammatik von Eduard Sievers*).

Sievers, E. (1893). *Altgermanische Metrik*. Halle: M. Niemeyer.

Stanley, E. G. (ed.) (1966). *Continuations and Beginnings: studies in Old English literature*. London: Thomas Nelson & Sons.

Stanley, E. G. (1994). *In the Foreground: Beowulf*. Rochester, NY: D. S. Brewer.

Szarmach, P. E. & Rosenthal, J. T. (eds) (1997). *The Preservation and Transmission of Anglo-Saxon Culture: selected papers from the 1991 meeting of the International Society of Anglo-Saxonists* (Studies in Medieval Culture, XL). Kalamazoo, MI: Medieval Institute Publications.

Toller, T. N. (ed.) (1972). *Supplement to An Anglo-Saxon Dictionary. With revised and enlarged addenda* by A. Campbell. Oxford: Clarendon Press (repr. of 1st edn, 1921).

Treharne, E. & Rosser, S. (eds) (2002). *Early Medieval English Texts and Interpretations: studies presented to Donald G. Scragg*. Tempe, AZ: Center for Medieval and Renaissance Studies.

Venezky, R. L. & Butler, S. (comps.) (1985). *A Microfiche Concordance to Old English: the high-frequency words*. Toronto: Pontifical Institute of Mediaeval Studies.

Internet references (URLs)

The Old English database: University of Toronto, Pontifical Institute of Mediaeval Studies, Dictionary of Old English Project <http://www.chass.utoronto.ca>

The Helsinki Corpus of English Texts: University of Helsinki, Department of English, Middle English Compendium <http://ets.umdl.umich.edu/m/mec/>

List of Editions Used

References in this volume to Old English poetry are to the Anglo-Saxon Poetic Records (ASPR) unless otherwise stated. Quotations from Old English prose texts are, unless otherwise specified, from the Dictionary of Old English (*DOE*) database.

Anderson, J. E. (ed.) (1986). *Two Literary Riddles in the Exeter Book: Riddle 1 and the Easter Riddle*. Norman, OK: University of Oklahoma Press.

Babington, C. & Lumby, J. R. (eds) (1865–86). *Polychronicon Ranulphi Higden, Monachi Cestrensis: together with the English translations of John Trevisa and of an unknown writer of the fifteenth century* (Rolls Series, 41), 9 vols. London: Longman, Green, Longman, Roberts & Green.

Bately, J. (ed.) (1980). *The Old English Orosius* (EETS, s.s. 6). Oxford: Oxford University Press.

Bethurum, D. (ed.) (1957). *The Homilies of Wulfstan*. Oxford: Clarendon Press.

Blake, N. F. (ed.) (1964). *The Phoenix* (Old and Middle English Texts, 4). Manchester: Manchester University Press.

Bland, C. R. (ed.) (1991). *The Teaching of Grammar in Late Medieval England. An edition, with commentary, of Oxford, Lincoln College MS LAT 130*. East Lansing, MI: Colleagues Press.

Brooks, K. R. (ed.) (1961). *Andreas and the Fates of the Apostles*. Oxford: Clarendon Press.

Chambers, R. W., Förster, M. & Flower, R. (eds) (1933). *The Exeter Book of Old English Poetry*. London: Percy Lund, Humphries & Co.

Clark, C. (ed.) (1958). *The Peterborough Chronicle: 1070–1154*, 2nd edn. Oxford: Clarendon Press (2nd edn 1970).

Clemoes, P. (ed.) (1997). *Ælfric's Catholic Homilies: the first series text* (EETS, s.s. 17). Oxford: Oxford University Press.

Crawford, S. J. (ed.) (1929). *Byrhtferth's Manual (A.D. 1011)* (EETS, o.s. 177). London: Oxford University Press.

Doane, A. N. (ed.) (1978). *Genesis A: a new edition*. Madison, WI: University of Wisconsin Press.

Doane, A. N. (ed.) (1991). *The Saxon Genesis: an edition of the West Saxon Genesis B and the Old Saxon Vatican Genesis*. Madison, WI: University of Wisconsin Press.

Dobbie, E. V. K. (ed.) (1953). *Beowulf and Judith* (ASPR, IV). New York and London: Columbia University Press and Routledge & Kegan Paul.

Dunning, T. P. & Bliss, A. J. (eds) (1969). *The Wanderer*. London: Methuen.

Earle, J. & Plummer, C. (eds) (1892). *Two of the Saxon Chronicles Parallel*, 2 vols. Oxford: Clarendon Press.

Fadda, A. M. L. (1972). 'De Descensu Christi ad Inferos': una inedita omelia anglosassone. *Studi Medievali*, 13, 989–1011.

Farrell, R. T. (ed.) (1974). *Daniel and Azarias*. London: Methuen.

Fehr, B. (ed.) (1914). *Die Hirtenbriefe Ælfrics: in altenglischer und lateinischer Fassung* (rev. edn P. Clemoes 1966). Darmstadt: Wissenschaftliche Buchgesellschaft.

Finnegan, R. E. (ed.) (1977). *Christ and Satan: a critical edition*. Waterloo, Ontario: Wilfrid Laurier University Press.

Garmonsway, G. N. (ed.) (1939). *Ælfric's Colloquy*. London: Methuen & Co (2nd edn 1947; rev. edn, 1991, Exeter: University of Exeter Press).

Godden, M. (ed.) (1979). *Ælfric's Catholic Homilies. The second series text* (EETS, s.s. 5). London: Oxford University Press.

Gollancz, Sir I. (ed.) (1927). *The Caedmon Manuscript of Anglo-Saxon Biblical Poetry Junius XI in the Bodleian Library*. Oxford: Oxford University Press, for the British Academy.

Gradon, P. O. E. (ed.) (1958). *Cynewulf's 'Elene'*. London: Methuen.

Griffith, M. (ed.) (1997). *Judith*. Exeter: Exeter University Press.

Jack, G. (ed.) (1994). *Beowulf. A student edition*. Oxford: Clarendon Press.

Jost, K. (ed.) (1959). *Die "Institutes of Polity, Civil and Ecclesiastical." Ein Werk Erzbischof Wulfstans von York* (Schweizer anglistische Arbeiten, 47). Bern: Francke.

Judic, B. (ed.) (1992). *Grégoire le Grand: Règle pastorale* (Sources chrétiennes, 381 and 382), 2 vols. Paris: du Cerf.

Kellner, L. (ed.) (1890). *Caxton's Blanchardyn and Eglantine. c. 1489* (EETS, e.s. 58). London: Oxford University Press.

Kemble, J. M. (ed.) (1833). *The Anglo-Saxon Poems of Beowulf, the Traveller's Song and the Battle of Finnes-Burgh*. London: Pickering.

Kemble, J. M. (ed.) (1845–8). *The Dialogue of Salomon and Saturn, with an Historical Introduction*. London: Ælfric Society.

Kiernan, K. S. (ed.) (1993). *Electronic Beowulf*, 2 CD-ROMs. London: The British Library and The University of Michigan Press.

Klaeber, F. (ed.) (1950). *Beowulf and The Fight at Finnsburg*, 3rd edn. Boston, MA: Heath (1st edn 1922).

Klinck, A. L. (ed.) (1992). *The Old English Elegies: a critical edition and genre study*. Montreal: McGill-Queen's University Press.

Krapp, G. P. (ed.) (1931). *The Junius Manuscript* (ASPR, I). New York and London: Columbia University Press and Routledge & Kegan Paul.

Krapp, G. P. (ed.) (1932). *The Vercelli Book* (ASPR, II). New York and London: Columbia University Press and Routledge & Kegan Paul.

Krapp, G. P. & Dobbie, E. V. K. (eds) (1936). *The Exeter Book* (ASPR, III). New York and London: Columbia University Press and Routledge & Kegan Paul.

Lees, C. A. (1986). Theme and echo in an anonymous Old English homily for Easter. *Traditio*, XLII, 115–42.

Leslie, R. F. (ed.) (1966). *The Wanderer* (rev. edn. 1985, Exeter: University of Exeter).

Liebermann, F. (ed.) (1903–16). *Die Gesetze der Angelsachsen*. Halle: Niemeyer.

Lucas, P. J. (ed.) (1977). *Exodus*. London: Methuen (rev. edn 1994, Exeter: University of Exeter Press).

Malone, K. (ed.) (1963). *The Nowell Codex: British Museum Cotton Vitellius A. xv. Second MS* (EEMF, 12). Copenhagen: Rosenkilde & Bagger.

Menner, R. J. (ed.) (1941). *The Poetical Dialogues of Solomon and Saturn* (Modern Language Association of America, 13). New York: Modern Language Association of Amercia.

Mitchell, B. & Irvine, S. (eds) (2000). *Beowulf Repunctuated. Old English Newsletter* (Subsidia, 29). [Kalamazoo, MI]: Published for the Old English Division of the Modern Language Association of America by the Medieval Institute Western Michigan University and its Richard Rawlinson Center for Anglo-Saxon Studies.

Mitchell, B. & Robinson, F. C. (eds) (1998). *Beowulf: an edition with relevant shorter texts*. Oxford: Blackwell.

Moffat, D. (ed.) (1990). *The Old English 'Soul and Body'*. Wolfeboro, NH: D. S. Brewer.

Morris, R. (ed.) (1874–80). *The Blickling Homilies*, 3 vols (EETS o.s. 58, 63 and 73). London: Oxford University Press (repr. as 1 vol., 1967).

Muir, B. J. (ed.) (2000). *The Exeter Anthology of Old English Poetry*, 2nd edn, 2 vols. Exeter: University of Exeter Press.

Muir, B. J. (ed.) (2004). *A Digital Facsimile of Oxford, Bodleian Library MS Junius 1*. (Bodleian Digital Texts, I). Oxford: Bodleian Library.

Muir, B. J. (ed.) (2005). *The Electronic Exeter Anthology of Old English Poetry*, 2 CD-ROMs. Exeter: University of Exeter Press.

Nickel, G. (ed.) (1976). *Beowulf und die kleineren Denkmäler der altenglischen Heldensage Waldere und Finnsburg. In drei Teilen*. Heidelberg: Winter.

Nordal, S. J. (ed.) (1978). *Voluspá* (Durham and St Andrews Medieval Texts, 1). Durham.

Pope, J. C. (ed.) (1967–8). *Homilies of Ælfric: a supplementary collection* (EETS, o.s. 259 and 260). London: Oxford University Press.

Porter, D. W. (ed.) (2002). *Excerptiones de Prisciano: the source for Ælfric's Latin–Old English Grammar* (Anglo-Saxon Texts, 4). Woodbridge: D. S. Brewer.

Roberts, J. (ed.) (1979). *The Guthlac Poems of the Exeter Book*. Oxford: Clarendon Press.

Rosier, J. L. (1964). 'Instructions for Christians.' A poem in Old English. *Anglia*, 82, 4–22.

Schaefer, K. G. (ed.) (1972). An edition of five Old English homilies for Palm Sunday, Holy Saturday, and Easter Sunday. PhD diss., Columbia University, OH.

Scragg, D. G. (ed.) (1981). *The Battle of Maldon*. Manchester: Manchester University Press.

Scragg, D. G. (ed.) (1992). *The Vercelli Homilies and Related Texts* (EETS, o.s. 300). Oxford: Oxford University Press.

Sisam, C. (ed.) (1976). *The Vercelli Book* (EEMF, 19). Copenhagen: Rosenkilde & Bagger.

Swanton, M. (ed.) (1970). *The Dream of the Rood*. Manchester: Manchester University Press.

Swanton, M. (ed.) (1978). *Beowulf, Edited with an Introduction, Notes and New Prose Translation*. Manchester: Manchester University Press.

Sweet, H. (ed.) (1871). *King Alfred's West-Saxon Version of Gregory's Pastoral Care* (EETS, o.s. 45). London: Oxford University Press.

Thomson, D. (ed.) (1984). *An Edition of the Middle English Grammatical Texts* (Garland Medieval Texts, 8). New York: Garland.

Turner, J. R. (ed.) (1980). *The Works of William Bullokar II* (Leeds Texts and Monographs, n.s. 1). Leeds: University of Leeds School of English.

Weber, R. (ed.) (1983). *Biblia Sacra Iuxta Vulgatam Versionem*, 3rd edn, 2 vols. Stuttgart: Deutsche Bibelgesellschaft.

Williamson, C. (ed.) (1977). *The Old English Riddles of the Exeter Book*. Chapel Hill, NC: University of North Carolina Press.

Woolf, R. (ed.) (1955). *Juliana*. London: Methuen (1966, New York: Appleton-Century-Crofts).

Wrenn, C. L. (ed.) (1973). *Beowulf with the Finnesburg Fragment*. London: Harrap.

Wyatt, A. J. (ed.) (1968). *Beowulf with the Finnsburg Fragment. New edition revised with introduction and notes by R. W. Chambers*. Cambridge: Cambridge University Press.

Zupitza, J. (ed.) (1880). *Aelfrics Grammatik und Glossar. Text und Varianten*. 2nd edn H. Gneuss. Berlin: Weidmann (repr. 2003, Hildesheim: Weidmann).

Zupitza, J. (ed.) (1882). *Beowulf* (EETS, o.s. 77). Oxford: Oxford University Press (2nd edn, N. Davis (EETS, 245). Oxford, 1967).

Internet References

Rosselli Del Turco, R. (ed.). *Digital Vercelli Book*, 2003 <http://islp.di.unipi.it/bifrost/vbd/dvb.html>

The Old English database: University of Toronto, Pontifical Institute of Mediaeval Studies, <http://www.chass.utoronto.ca>

Index of Names

Index of Old English
Words and Phrases

Index of Subjects